RESEARCH METHODS
IN THE SOCIAL SCIENCES

RESEARCH METHODS
IN THE SOCIAL SCIENCES

AN **A-Z** OF KEY CONCEPTS

JEAN-FRÉDÉRIC **MORIN**

CHRISTIAN **OLSSON**

ECE ÖZLEM **ATIKCAN**

OXFORD
UNIVERSITY PRESS

Great Clarendon Street, Oxford, OX2 6DP,
United Kingdom

Oxford University Press is a department of the University of Oxford.
It furthers the University's objective of excellence in research, scholarship,
and education by publishing worldwide. Oxford is a registered trade mark of
Oxford University Press in the UK and in certain other countries

Published in the United States of America by Oxford University Press
198 Madison Avenue, New York, NY 10016, United States of America

British Library Cataloguing in Publication Data
Data available

Library of Congress Control Number: 2020948799

ISBN 978–0–19–885029–8

Printed in Great Britain by
Bell & Bain Ltd., Glasgow

ACKNOWLEDGEMENTS

The editors would like to thank Alessandra Bonci and Simon Paquet for their assistance. Editing this book was a pleasure thanks to your careful and meticulous work.

This publication has received funding from the European Union's Horizon 2020 research and innovation programme under the Marie Skłodowska-Curie Grant Agreement No. 722826.

This publication has also received funding from Université Laval's Center for Interdisciplinary Studies in International Trade and Investment.

Centre for Interdisciplinary Studies in
International Trade and Investment

CONTENTS

LIST OF FIGURES AND TABLES

Figures

Tables

LIST OF CONTRIBUTORS

Ece Özlem Atikcan, University of Warwick

Elena Avramovska, Université libre de Bruxelles

Kevin Barnes-Ceeney, University of New Haven

Leeann Bass, Princeton University

Nina Baur, Technische Universität Berlin

Guillaume Beaumier, University of Warwick and Université Laval

Pierre-Olivier Bédard, Université Laval

Louis Bélanger, Université Laval

Andrew Bell, University of Sheffield

Kenneth Bertrams, Université libre de Bruxelles

Philippe Blanchard, University of Warwick

Damien Bol, King's College London

Alessandra Bonci, Université Laval

Virginia Braun, The University of Auckland

Chloé Brière, Université libre de Bruxelles

Sabine Caillaud, Université Lumière Lyon 2

Mauro Caprioli, University of Louvain

Roberto Carrillo, Université libre de Bruxelles

Caterina Carta, Université Laval

Adam William Chalmers, King's College London

Victoria Clarke, The University of the West of England

Céline C. Cocq, Université libre de Bruxelles & Université de Genève

Thomas Collas, Université de Strasbourg

Ramona Coman, Université libre de Bruxelles

Pierre-Marc Daigneault, Université Laval

Mark Daku, World Food Programme

Stephan Davidshofer, University of Geneva (Global Studies Institute) and Geneva Center for Security Studies

Brittany I. Davidson, University of Bristol

Francois Dépelteau, Laurentian University Center for Security Studies

Andreas Dimmelmeier, University of Warwick and Copenhagen Business School

Lucas Dolan, American University

Sheila Dow, University of Stirling

Érick Duchesne, Université Laval

Arnaud Dufays, Université Laval & Université de Namur

Yannick Dufresne, Université Laval

Claire Dupuy, University of Louvain

Brian D. Earp, Yale University

Eric Fabri, Université libre de Bruxelles and University of Oxford

Uwe Flick, Freie Universität of Berlin

Mathilde Gauquelin, Laval University and Ghent University

Laura Gelhaus, University of Warwick & Université de Genève

Suzan Gibril, Université libre de Bruxelles

Lior Gideon, John Jay College of Criminal Justice

Dominik Giese, Universität Hamburg and University of Warwick

Jessica Luciano Gomes, University of Hamburg & Université libre de Bruxelles

Seda Gürkan, Université libre de Bruxelles

Nicholas Haagensen, Copenhagen Business School and Université libre de Bruxelles

Juraj Halas, Comenius University in Bratislava

Jasmin Hasić, Sarajevo School of Science and Technology

Jacob A. Hasselbalch, Copenhagen Business School

Nicky Hayes, Canterbury Christ Church University

Lasse Folke Henriksen, Copenhagen Business School

Jannis Hergesell, Technische Universität Berlin

Olga Herzog, University of Hamburg

Louis M. Imbeau, Université Laval

Patrick Thaddeus Jackson, American University

Jonathan Joseph, University of Bristol

Kevin Kalomeni, LUISS Guido Carli di Roma and Université Laval

Aysel Küçüksu, University of Copenhagen

Noémie Laurens, Université Laval

Dirk Leuffen, University of Konstanz

Ulf Liebe, University of Warwick

Anne-Laure Mahé, Institut de Recherche Stratégique de l'École Militaire

Chowra Makaremi, École des hautes études en sciences sociales (EHESS)

Yasmina Malki, National School of Public Administration

Kamil Marcinkiewicz, University of Hamburg

Laurence Marquis, LUISS Guido Carli di Roma and Université Laval

Matrakova Marta, Université libre de Bruxelles and LUISS Guido Carli di Roma

Theodore McLauchlin, Université de Montréal

Jean-Frédéric Morin, Université Laval

Elisa Narminio, Université libre de Bruxelles & Waseda University

Kimberly A. Neuendorf, Cleveland State University

Lidia Núñez, Université libre de Bruxelles

Christian Olsson, Université libre de Bruxelles

Mathieu Ouimet, Université Laval

Yannis Panagis, University of Copenhagen

Piergiuseppe Parisi, University of York

Andrew Parker, Ridley Hall Theological College, Cambridge

Heikki Patomäki, University of Helsinki

Gianfranco Pellegrino, LUISS Guido Carli di Roma

Vicki L. Plano Clark, University of Cincinnati

Julien Pomarède, Université libre de Bruxelles

Frederik Ponjaert, Université libre de Bruxelles

Jochem Rietveld, LUISS Guido Carli di Roma and University of Warwick

Mélanie Samson, Université Laval

Miriam Gomes Saraiva, Rio de Janeiro State University

Shunsuke Sato, Kokugakuin University

Stefan Schmidt, University of Freiburg

Kai-Uwe Schnapp, Universität Hamburg

Leonard Seabrooke, Copenhagen Business School

Holli A. Semetko, Emory University

Stephanie Anne Shelton, University of Alabama

Vivien Sierens, Université libre de Bruxelles

Arthur Silve, Université Laval

Ora Szekely, Clark University

Amal Tawfik, University of Lausanne and School of Health Sciences HESAV, HES-SO University of Applied Sciences and Arts Western Switzerland

Olesya Tkacheva, Vesalius College, VUB

Sule Tomkinson, Université Laval

Jonathan Tritter, Aston University

Manfredi Valeriani, University of Hamburg and LUISS Guido Carli di Roma

Onna Malou van den Broek, King's College London

Emilie van Haute, Université libre de Bruxelles

Virginie Van Ingelgom, FRS-FNRS and University of Louvain

Alban Versailles, FRS-FNRS and University of Louvain

Claudius Wagemann, University of Frankfurt

Didier Wernli, University of Geneva

Anne Weyembergh, Université libre de Bruxelles

Irene Wieczorek, University of Durham

Auke Willems, London School of Economics

Johann Wolfschwenger, Université libre de Bruxelles and Université de Genève

Kevin L. Young, University of Massachusetts Amherst

INTRODUCTION

AN INTRODUCTION TO RESEARCH METHODS IN THE SOCIAL SCIENCES

Ece Özlem Atikcan, University of Warwick
Jean-Frédéric Morin, Université Laval
Christian Olsson, Université libre de Bruxelles

Introducing research methods in the social sciences is not an easy task given how complex the subject matter is. Social sciences, like all sciences, can be divided into categories (disciplines). Disciplines are frequently defined according to what they study (their empirical object) and how they study it (their particular problematization of the object). They are, however, by no means unitary entities. Within each discipline, multiple theories typically contend over the ability to tell provisional truths about the world. They do so by building on specific visions of the nature of the world (see the contribution on ONTOLOGY), reflections on how to generate scientific truth (see the contribution on EPISTEMOLOGY), systematic ways of collecting and analysing data (methods) and of justifying these methods as part of a coherent research design (methodologies).

Theories connect these various elements—ontological, epistemological, and methodological propositions—in the interpretation of specific scientific problems. Importantly, theories follow certain patterns and do not create these connections in an entirely haphazard way. However, such connections are never automatic or self-evident. One does not necessarily need to carry out discourse analysis if adopting a post-positivist stance. Theoretical considerations are not unimportant but they do not have to entirely determine our methodological choices. Our approach to research methods in the social sciences is based on this core idea: method(ologie)s are partially autonomous. They are important to consider in and for themselves rather than merely as part of pre-existing ontologies or epistemologies. We approach disciplines, theories, epistemologies, and ontologies primarily through methodological framings and questions.

While this is only one approach to teaching and learning social sciences among many, it has a number of advantages. First, methods offer a coherent entry point into social sciences, allowing for a step-by-step and bottom-up pedagogical approach to theories and theoretical concepts. Second, since you are immediately exposed to methodological debates in carrying out your own research, this approach offers a hands-on and concrete way of helping you in this endeavour. Third, our approach also allows you to explore the great variety of possibilities in social scientific research in a theoretically agnostic way, rather than treating methods as a necessary implication of your theoretical choices (which are often not yet consolidated at this stage of your learning). It is neither necessary nor desirable to always start with the main 'theories', 'schools of thought', or 'paradigms' as if everything else flowed naturally and inevitably from there.

This is why we offer an interdisciplinary and theoretically agnostic research toolkit that focuses primarily on research method(ologies) in the social sciences. Our contributors come from different disciplines, different theoretical backgrounds, and from a range of different countries.

AN INTERDISCIPLINARY LOOK AT THE SOCIAL SCIENCES

This book favours an interdisciplinary approach to research methods in the social sciences (see the contribution on INTERDISCIPLINARITY). It does not include any contributions that would be relevant for only one discipline. Instead, all the contributions speak to several disciplines of social sciences. Yet, our approach does not overlook the distinctiveness of individual disciplines, let alone their existence. It favours an interdisciplinary rather than a transdisciplinary approach because we acknowledge that disciplines heavily structure the conduct of scientific inquiry. The days of Leonardo da Vinci, who could blend arts, philosophy, technical engineering, and the study of biological anatomy, or of René Descartes, who was a philosopher as much as a mathematician, are long gone. From the nineteenth century, we inherited a division of scientific knowledge into distinct disciplines. Although these disciplines are social constructs, we as social scientists are well positioned to recognize that even social constructs have real-world effects.

The existence of disciplines has the advantage of reducing complexity and helping the communication of research results. It facilitates the creation of consensus on what research is and should be. Which questions are important? What empirical domains should one focus on? Which debates could one contribute to and how can existing theories be improved? Every discipline also imposes a set of rules defining the appropriate behaviour for members of a scientific community. It is no accident that the word 'discipline' can refer either to a branch of knowledge or to a system of sanctions to induce certain behaviours (e.g. 'this child needs discipline'). Each discipline has its own rules for dealing, for example, with research funding, peer reviewing, data management, research collaboration, writing style, and career strategies. Institutions, such as university departments, professional organizations, research councils, and scientific journals, enforce these rules and sanction deviant behaviours. Despite multiple efforts to break up research silos and favour interdisciplinary research, disciplines remain surprisingly resilient. Conducting interdisciplinary research can even be risky, especially for early career scholars, who are more vulnerable to 'disciplinary' sanctions. Several of the contributions in this book acknowledge differences across disciplines and contrast their different practices. The contribution on BEHAVIOURISM, for example, discusses the different influences that B. F. Skinner had on psychology and political science. Likewise, the contribution on HERMENEUTICS compares the practice of interpretation in law and history.

This book nevertheless goes well beyond the mere juxtaposition or comparison of different disciplines. Its interdisciplinary approach relies on the assumption that social science disciplines have more similarities than differences. Three main reasons explain these similarities. First, social sciences share largely the same intellectual foundations. Plato, Locke, and Foucault, for example, influenced disciplines as diverse as law, sociology, geography, and psychology. Second, all social sciences study complex phenomena, for which it is particularly difficult to establish causal relations. The social world is much less stable and predictable than the physical world due to a multiplicity of ever-evolving and interconnected variables. Third, social scientists are themselves part of the world they study, creating an ambiguous relationship between the object and the subject of scientific inquiry. This situation raises methodological challenges that natural and physical scientists do not have to face most of the time (quantum physics is an exception in this regard), while also opening up opportunities for reflexive and critical approaches.

For these reasons, similar intellectual trends and methodological debates have emerged across social science disciplines. Positivism, Marxism, and constructivism, for example, have influenced all social sciences, although to different degrees. Similarly, new empirical questions have emerged more or less at the same time in different disciplines. Gender issues, as well as the relation between humans and their natural environment, became prominent questions in all the social sciences in a way that would have been difficult to imagine fifty years ago.

Not only has the social world influenced social sciences in similar ways, but also social science disciplines have influenced one another. Having cultivated expertise in a particular method, some disciplines have pollinated others with their expertise. Today, rigorous archival research is not limited to history, advanced statistical analysis is used beyond economics, social network analysis software is extensively used outside sociology, and participatory observation is taken seriously in disciplines other than ethnography. Debates that have emerged in one discipline have also diffused to other disciplines. Issues related to ethics with human participants, data availability, replication, and publication bias that appeared first in psychology, for example, have since informed debates in several other disciplines.

This cross-fertilization is a productive process. The most innovative ideas often arise by connecting previously disconnected literature streams. Cutting-edge research in the social sciences often develops at the crossroads of different disciplines. Behavioural economics, for example, emerged at the intersection of psychology and economics. Tellingly, Daniel Kahneman, who received the Prize in Economic Sciences in Memory of Alfred Nobel in 2002 for his research in behavioural economics, is a trained psychologist, and not an economist. Likewise, the hybridization between economics and other disciplines has given rise to many vibrant fields of study, including political economy, law and economics, ecological economics, and economic sociology. If social science disciplines are discrete islands, they are nonetheless part of the same archipelago; they are connected by various bridges, and some of the most creative of their inhabitants frequently travel across them.

On the one hand, by reminding you of the disciplinary anchorage of scientific debates, this book bears testimony to the fact that scientific knowledge is always limited and the product of disciplinary histories. On the other, by putting the focus on interdisciplinarity, it prompts you to keep in mind the socially constructed nature of disciplines and hence the possibility of questioning their borders. With this perspective in mind, contributors to this volume come from various disciplines, including political science, law, economics, sociology, philosophy, psychology, criminology, history, and anthropology. Several contributions were even co-authored by researchers from different disciplines. Moreover, all the contributions cover different disciplines, sometimes comparing their methodological approaches, and at other times discussing how one discipline has learned from another.

A THEORETICALLY AGNOSTIC YET THEORETICALLY INFORMED RESEARCH MANUAL

In the same way as the entries of this book are committed to interdisciplinarity, they all try to avoid focusing on a single theoretical perspective. Except for a few dealing with particular theoretical-epistemological orientations (see the contributions on SCIENTIFIC REALISM, CRITICAL REALISM, and POSITIVISM, POST-POSITIVISM, AND SOCIAL SCIENCE), the entries in this volume primarily focus on particular methods or concepts viewed through the lenses of their methodological implications.

That being said, methods and methodologies are never disconnected from wider theoretical considerations. Theoretical debates and questions cannot be avoided altogether. This book aims to strike a balance between foregrounding methodology and recognizing that methodological choices and debates are always rooted in ontological, epistemological, and theoretical choices and assumptions. However, our main point is that the rooted nature of methodological choices does not mean that they have to be determined by these roots.

This is why authors and co-authors have been chosen in order to favour theoretical pluralism. All the authors try to consider method(ologie)s independently from their own theoretical preferences in order to achieve this goal. They all recognize, to varying degrees and within limits, that researchers with different theoretical interests can draw on similar methods. Methods and methodologies can and do travel across disciplinary and theoretical (including epistemological and ontological) divides: methods like social network analysis or ethnographic fieldwork can span the divide between holistic and individualist ontologies, or between positivist and post-positivist epistemologies. Similarly, all the authors recognize that researchers with similar theoretical preferences can, for a multiplicity of reasons, opt for dissimilar research methods. Rational choice theorists can opt for quantitative, qualitative, or mixed methods depending on their research object, research question, data availability, or their epistemological choices (e.g. instrumentalist empiricism or scientific realism). Some authors even engage in what is referred to as 'methodological eclecticism', which builds on the idea that the researcher can use several (even seemingly incompatible) methods when exploring a research object in order to triangulate the results or to see how the results from various methods compare. However, methodological eclecticism is not a necessary consequence of the type of methodological pluralism we advocate.

One of the reasons for the (however limited) portability of methods across disciplinary and theoretical divides is that their concrete epistemological implications depend on what a researcher does with them—how they are put to work in the context of a concrete research project. Methods are tools that always have to be adapted and reflexively tailored to the purposes of a specific piece of research. It is also worth noting here that because different methods are more or less used, and more or less developed, depending on different academic contexts, we have consciously strived for geographical diversity among the contributors (UK, Canada, Germany, US, Belgium, Switzerland, Denmark, France, Italy, Finland, Slovakia . . .).

HOW TO USE THIS BOOK?

This book offers a systematic, state-of-the-art index on research methods, and is organized as an easily accessible encyclopedia, with seventy-one entries presented in alphabetical order. The idea of this textbook originated from our hands-on experience in leading methodology seminars in the social and political sciences. We strongly felt that there was a pedagogical need for a student-centred, comprehensive yet compact, systematic, and conceptual index in teaching research methods.

Because it is student-centred, it provides much-needed practical information about a wide range of research methods including the most recent trends such as big data, all interconnected with cross-references, with concrete, real-world examples and 'how-to' advice built into the discussion of each concept. Because it is comprehensive, it is aimed at those of you following courses in any of the social sciences, which share the same methodological framework of reference, at least at the introductory level. All the contributions provide references and examples from different social science disciplines.

The selection of entries was an important part of preparing this book. We sought to make it comprehensive but compact, and this led to a few key decisions. We opted to focus on methodological concepts as opposed to more theoretical ones, although the line between the two is sometimes difficult to draw. We started the process by designing the book index, which covered many potential entries and identified the cross-cutting themes among them (such as 'validity'). We decided to offer a discussion of these cross-cutting themes in several entries. We thus selected only the most important concepts and ensured a broad coverage for each of them. This meant that, while maintaining an important degree of consistency across different entries, we gave our contributors the necessary space and flexibility to offer you a diversity of disciplinary and methodological standpoints.

This book targets students enrolled in both undergraduate and postgraduate programmes in the social sciences. Each entry is organized to work at two levels. On the one hand, each methodological concept is explained in detail, in a way that does not assume prior specialist knowledge, and with examples that provide an accessible introduction to the topic. On the other hand, each entry also provides more advanced tips and advice that will be extremely helpful for those of you in postgraduate programmes who are starting to conduct your own research projects.

The entries include not only the classical and well-established concepts of the field but also emerging and innovative ideas such as big data, network analysis, automated text analysis, and prosopography. Each entry provides a definition of the given methodological concept, discusses its underlying assumptions, presents its historical evolution, embeds it within the relevant methodological and theoretical debates, illustrates its practical and concrete use, identifies its strengths and weaknesses, pinpoints its current status in academic practices, and presents the recent controversies relating to its use. Moreover, each entry presents real-world examples to demonstrate how that methodological concept applies to the social sciences and is also accompanied by carefully selected references for further reading. While contributions expose you to various viewpoints and identify the relevant criticisms directed at the concepts, they deliberately avoid any normative judgement or policy recommendations, and remain open to the epistemological pluralism in the social sciences.

Importantly, this book is designed to have a flexible format. As an encyclopedia, it consists of a collection of short stand-alone entries, instead of presenting each topic in a linear manner, as a lecturer would do orally in class. This allows instructors to assign various contributions for different weeks without following a linear logic. You can read each contribution independently from the others. Similarly, it enables you to easily browse any concept whenever you need to. Each entry is connected to other entries by a cross-referencing system, using bold, grey capital letters. These cross-references, as demonstrated in our network diagram in Figure 1, will help you to link related concepts together and build a comprehensive understanding of research methods.

We believe this format, which is at the heart of our student-centred approach, best suits your needs, habits, and interests. At times, you can use the table of contents or the index to rapidly find the specific information you are looking for. At other times, you can navigate through the book following your mood and explore its content by jumping from one entry to another with the help of the cross-referencing system. This flexibility favours a learning process in which you progressively connect the dots and expand your knowledge according to your interests, starting with what you already know. In other words, while the book brings together the methodological concepts shared by social scientists, its format enables a highly individualized reading. You may choose to stay in your comfort zone to consolidate your prior knowledge or, alternatively, to discover new concepts and methods that may be of interest for your research.

In sum, this is a student-focused, comprehensive, and compact volume that offers practical information on research in the social sciences from a wide variety of disciplines and theoretical viewpoints. We hope that you will navigate through the book in creative ways and gain practical advice on how you could conduct your own research.

FIGURE 1 Network of contributions linked by cross-references

ARCHIVAL RESEARCH

Chloé Brière, Université libre de Bruxelles

INTRODUCTION

Throughout history, humans have stored information by means that reflect the evolution of technologies (papyrus, argyle tablets, parchment, etc.). Archives have evolved accordingly. The notion of archives covers a variety of repositories, gathering both published and unpublished materials, in any format. Examples include manuscripts, letters, photographs, moving images and sound materials, artwork, books, diaries, artefacts, and so on. Archived materials can sometimes be unique, specialized, or rare objects.

The storage and conservation of these materials is inextricably linked to a certain subjectivity, as the entity collecting, storing, and conserving materials does so with specific objectives, which determine the criteria for selecting the documents included in the archive. Archives are not a value-neutral repository of objective knowledge, and researchers must be aware of this element and factor it into their analysis of the materials in the archive (see **BIAS**). Depending on the archive, the objectives pursued and criteria used for selecting documents may be openly disclosed, or may be difficult to determine. Corporations may create comprehensive archives to better analyse market developments and customer behaviour. Private individuals may create their own personal archives without clearly disclosing how they choose the documents included. States' archives are also representative of the inherent subjectivity of archives, since archives constituted by public authorities are in themselves a tool of power, used for instance to collect private information on individuals. These archives represent key resources for researchers, either as a study on their own, or as sources of information and data to be analysed.

The digitization of materials offers further opportunities to constitute new archives and/or enrich existing ones, allowing for their storage and collection on large servers. A phenomenon of massive archiving is also noticeable in a few countries, and notably concerns audiovisual contents, easily accessible and open to all, such as contents posted on YouTube or social networks (see **BIG DATA**). In this context, the purpose and nature of an archive may also undergo significant changes. No longer restrained to 'sanctioned' collections, or physical resources, researchers are able to create new knowledge out of materials and sources they collected themselves, thus creating their own very personal and specialized archive.

All these various types of archives constitute a precious resource for researchers, and in many disciplines, such as sociology, political sciences, law, or history, archival research occupies a central place. Depending on the field of research, analysis may be limited to a single archive (such as the archives of a legislative body for determining the considerations of the legislator when a particular norm was enacted) or require a comprehensive COMPARATIVE ANALYSIS of various archives, taking into account their diverse nature and purposes (such as a comparison of public, clerical, and private archives to analyse the relationship between state authority, religious institutions, and civil society in a particular time period). Archival research has, for instance, been relied on by scholars analysing the evolution of US foreign policy since World War II (Sewel and Ryan 2017) or reconsidering the Warsaw Pact in the light of international relations in Eastern Europe (Crump 2015).

THE IMPORTANCE OF METHODOLOGY FOR ARCHIVAL RESEARCH

Archival research can be defined as finding, using, and correlating information within primary and secondary sources (for instance in history see Torou et al 2010). *Primary sources* are sources created by persons directly involved in the event, reflecting their point of view, such as personal diaries or letters. In contrast, *secondary sources* are sources not based on a direct observation of an event, or on evidence directly associated with the subject (see SOURCE CRITICISM), and they rely on pre-existing primary sources. The distinction between primary and secondary sources is not immutable, and it depends on the way the researcher frames the research object. For example, a researcher analysing the work of a political scientist will use the works published by that person as primary sources, even though these publications themselves build on research into different primary sources, such as state archives, and therefore constitute secondary sources with regard to their object of research.

MAIN STEPS

Archival research refers to the process through which researchers employ their scientific knowledge, experience, and intuition to formulate queries (e.g. for a historian, who was involved in an event, when did an event occur, etc.) and subsequently try to locate the pertinent information from their sources (Torou et al 2010). This process includes discovery research to identify available sources and research plans defining how to deal with the 'documentary universe' (Barnickel 2002). Secondary sources are often

A

essential for locating primary sources, and a LITERATURE REVIEW can often point to archives, databases, and other sources that can be used.

The difficulty of locating sources depends on the research topic and the types of archives where these are stored. Some sources may only be stored in state archives, which remain secret for a certain period of time due to national security concerns. Thus, certain events may only be comprehensively researched after several decades, when the respective archives are made accessible. By way of example, access to declassified Soviet archives—composed of scholarly works, political pronouncements, novels, plays, etc.—was used to research the mechanisms of the institutionalization of official historical memory in the Ukrainian Soviet Socialist Republic (Yekelchyk 2004). Even when access is granted, it may not cover the entirety of the archive, depending on the sensitivity of the documents stored there, or it may exclude personal data that cannot be disclosed to protect the privacy of its holder.

Once the relevant materials have been located, the researcher must secure access to them. As the materials stored in archival collections are sometimes unique, or in a fragile condition, access may be strictly regulated and/or limited. Although digitization of materials has facilitated greater access to materials, accessing them may still require travelling to the physical place where the materials are located to consult digitized versions stored in a local server.

These preliminary steps are necessary to identify the relevant sources and allow the researcher to proceed to the analysis of the materials. Such analysis will typically follow a methodology that evolves throughout the exploration of the archive and is influenced by the materials available (see CONTENT ANALYSIS). This process of analysis often remains undisclosed, as the researcher may only present the results of the archival research.

METHODOLOGY

Various methodological discussions intervene in the field of archival research, sometimes addressing the process of archiving itself, or the use of archives by scholars of various disciplines.

A common element lies in the importance of treating sources transparently, associating the external critique (focusing on its production, its author, the context of its elaboration, its nature and function) with the internal critique (focusing on its content). Transparency also requires researchers to discuss the factors that may impact their 'systematic method of gathering evidence' and their interpretation of this evidence. This would for instance imply the disclosure and discussion of what they considered as archival materials, how and under what circumstances and conditions they obtained access to those materials, potential personal connections with the subject, etc. (L'Eplattenier 2009).

Such discussions also extend to work based on digital archival research, as this creates new opportunities, challenges, and limitations (Solberg 2012). These limitations include the difficulty in assessing the extent of archives, the impossibility of accessing

A

materials not updated to the new technological formats, or the limited access to marginalia. More pragmatically, researchers may find themselves facing large volumes of heterogeneous data, not always directly relevant for their research question(s) (see RESEARCH QUESTION), and an essential step of the research is then to clean, recode, and sort out the data and make it ready for use.

Further transparency on archival research methods is thus encouraged, particularly to assist researchers in designing their own methodology (Fisher 2004). Beyond the mere description of the materials contained in a given archive, methodological discussions also raise awareness of gaps and fissures in archival research, in turn allowing future researchers to identify potential new methods and areas of research. Such disclosures are also necessary to improve trust in the analysis and interpretation proposed, by disclosing the construction process behind it (L'Eplattenier 2009).

NEW CHALLENGES IN ARCHIVAL RESEARCH

The development of online archives, separate from or complementing physical archives, constitutes an advantage for researchers. It makes it easier to locate sources and obtain access, as many entities, including states, have created comprehensive and easily accessible online databases bringing together a diversity of materials.

These online databases allow for new methods of exploring the archived materials, for instance through an automatic search function with keywords (see AUTOMATED TEXT ANALYSIS). Consequently, a key issue stressed in methodological manuals is the importance of identifying the appropriate vocabulary to conduct such an exploratory search. This is true for legal archival research for instance. Legal documents, and especially case law, often use specific forms of syntax, specific words, and a specific style, changing with the period concerned. Very often each type of court (administrative and judicial courts, civil and criminal courts, national and international courts) develops its own 'style', requiring a certain familiarity with it before being able to trace relevant sources (Nissen et al 2014).

Recent methodological discussions also highlight the importance of familiarity with the way materials are archived and the modalities of research available (in summary, full text searches, where indexation is made automatically by algorithms, vs catalogue searches, where the organization/entity managing the catalogue creates an index of the materials). Indeed, lack of familiarity with these elements may lead the researcher to face either too much noise (too many documents not relevant for their research) or silence (insufficient results).

Finally, the evolution of technologies allows each researcher to collect, store, and analyse materials such as academic sources, transcribed interviews, etc., thus potentially constituting his or her own archive. Although the process presents advantages and offers new avenues for research, it also faces limitations. A researcher may for instance create a personal archive gathering sensitive personal information, potentially breaching the privacy of the persons concerned. This leads to new methodological constraints/requirements, such as the need to obtain prior ethical clearance (see **ETHICS IN RESEARCH**).

A good illustrative example of archival research can be found in Vauchez's analysis of the origins and success of the narrative of 'Europeanization-through-case-law' applied to two landmark judgments of the Court of Justice of the European Union (ECJ), namely the cases *Van Gend en Loos* and *Costa v ENEL*, in which the ECJ defined the principle of direct effect of European Union (EU) law and its primacy over national law (Vauchez 2010). The author attempted to trace all references to and quotations of these judgments between 1958 and 1965 in the various European political, academic, and bureaucratic fora, as well as in national settings. The sources were collected in specialized law libraries (Cujas, ECJ, European University Institute) and national public libraries in France and Italy, as well as the Historical Archives of the European Union. In addition, the author looked for individual resources, personal ties, and interlocking networks of lawyers. This enabled him to chart the various social arenas—national as well as European, legal but also bureaucratic, economic, or political, etc.—in which the meaning, scope, and implications of the two judgments have been commented on, progressively polishing and codifying them into one judicial theory of Europeanization. This work can insert itself in the literature exploring legal integration, framing it to speak to the international relations debate about the nature of interactions between law, politics, and society in the EU, notably on the basis of quantitative and qualitative analysis of ECJ case law (see **CONTENT ANALYSIS, QUALITATIVE COMPARATIVE ANALYSIS**) (for an overview of such studies, see Conant 2007).

REFERENCES

Barnickel, Linda. 2002. 'A Firm Foundation: Archival Research and Interpretation at Historic Sites'. *Archival Issues* 27(1): 9–21.

Conant, Lisa. 2007. 'Review Article: The Politics of Legal Integration'. *Journal of Common Market Studies* 45(1): 45–66.

Crump, Laurien. 2015. *The Warsaw Pact Reconsidered: International Relations in Eastern Europe, 1955–1969*. London and New York, Routledge.

Fisher, Stephen (ed.) 2004. *Archival Information: How to Find It, How to Use It*. Westport, CT, Greenwood.

L'Eplattenier, Barbara E. 2009. 'An Argument for Archival Research Methods: Thinking Beyond Methodology'. *College English* 72(1): 67–79.

Nissen, Cécile, Eric Geerkens, Anne-Lise Sibony, and Audrey Zians. 2014. *Méthodologie juridique: Méthodologie de la recherche documentaire juridique*, 5th edition. Brussels, Larcier.

Sewel, Bevan and Maria Ryan. 2017. *Foreign Policy at the Periphery: The Shifting Margins of US International Relations since World War II*. Lexington, University Press of Kentucky.

Solberg, Janine. 2012. 'Googling the Archive: Digital Tools and the Practice of History'. *Advances in the History of Rhetoric* 15(1): 53–76.

Torou, Elena, Akrivi Katifori, Costas Vassilakis, George Lepouras, and Constantin Halatsis. 2010. 'Historical Research in Archives: User Methodology and Supporting Tools'. *International Journal on Digital Libraries* 11(1): 25–36.

Vauchez, Antoine. 2010. 'The Transnational Politics of Judicialization: *Van Gend en Loos* and the Making of EU Polity'. *European Law Journal* 16(1): 1–28.

Yekelchyk, Serhy. 2004. *Stalin's Empire of Memory: Russian-Ukrainian Relations in the Soviet Historical Imagination*. Toronto, University of Toronto Press.

A

AUTOMATED TEXT ANALYSIS

The Application of Automatic Text Processing in the Social Sciences

Yannis Panagis, University of Copenhagen

INTRODUCTION

Automated text analysis (ATA) describes the different methodologies that can be applied in order to perform text analysis with the use of computer software.

ATA is a computer-assisted method for analysing text (see CONTENT ANALYSIS and DISCOURSE ANALYSIS), whenever the analysis would be prohibitively labour-intensive due to the volume of texts to be analysed. ATA methods have become more popular due to current interest in BIG DATA, taking into account the volume of textual content that is made easily accessible by the digitization of human activity.

Key to ATA is the notion of *corpus*. A corpus is a collection of texts. A necessary step before starting any analysis is to collect together the necessary documents and construct the corpora (plural of corpus) that will be used. Which texts need to be included in this step is dictated by the RESEARCH QUESTION. After text collection, some processing steps need to be taken before the analysis starts, for example tokenization and part-of-speech tagging. Tokenization is the process of splitting a text into its constituent words, also called *tokens*, whereas part-of-speech tagging assigns each word a label that indicates the respective part of speech. For the word 'write', the corresponding part of speech is *verb*.

CORPUS-BASED ANALYSIS

Corpus-based analysis focuses on using corpora to observe textual patterns that in turn support some research HYPOTHESIS. In the simplest form of corpus-based analysis, one chooses keywords describing a concept, searches the corpus with those keywords, and retrieves all keyword contexts, or *concordances*. The study of concordances can be a first step to drive DISCOURSE ANALYSIS. An advantage of this technique is that it allows all possible uses of a keyword to be discovered; these uses can then be manually classified, for example into semantic categories. However, as Baker et al. (2008: 285) observe, it is very labour-intensive to conduct those analyses when the corpus size is large, and therefore *down-sampling*—keeping only a fraction of the initial corpus—is frequently an option. Often, down-sampling is carried out, by maintaining the same proportions for the various text categories to be studied. Baker et al. (2008: 285) down-sample newspaper articles, to the articles one week before certain incidents that they are studying.

More complicated analysis methods are based on statistics. Unlike DISCOURSE ANALYSIS, statistical methods obtain greater validity as the size of the data set grows.

The downside is that they are prone to missing relatively rare language patterns. The *raw frequency* of the words appearing in the corpus is a common statistic, and usually one examines word lists ordered by word frequency. However, terms with the highest frequency are either stop words, for example articles such as 'the' or 'a', pronouns, or boilerplate terms: expressions that commonly appear in specific document categories, like scientific papers. Some examples of boilerplate terms in the case of papers are the terms 'abstract', 'conclusion', and 'bibliography'. The presence of stop words and boiler-plate terms renders the analysis by word frequency detrimental. Another caveat is that when comparing term occurrence across different corpora, raw frequency comparison is unreliable if the corpora are unequal in terms of number of words. Hence, *frequency per million words* should be used.

Another popular technique is *collocations*. Collocation is a lexical relation between two words in the corpus. As Baker et al. (2008: 278) note, collocation is more discern-ible in a large amount of data, and is therefore less accessible to manual analysis. Collocation analysis employs different statistical metrics to measure collocation strength. Although several collocation metrics are used, the metrics allowing the discovery of interesting collocations are MI-score (Mutual Information score), log-likelihood, Dice, and logDice. Definitions of the statistics can be found in Dunning (1993) and Lexical Computing (2015). Log-likelihood can be also computed online (Rayson 2020). MI-score is subject to overestimating collocation significance when the word counts are small (Dunning 1993: 62) and its results should therefore be cross-checked with one of the other scores.

Baker et al. (2008) use frequency-based collocations of words related to immigra-tion from a relevant British newspaper corpus. Subsequently, they employ Critical Discourse Analysis to manually classify the collocates into predefined categories and interpret unusual findings on how immigration is discussed.

A comprehensive study of how corpus-based analysis can be applied to international courts is given by Potts and Kjær (2016). The authors build a corpus of the judgments of the International Criminal Tribunal for the former Yugoslavia, and demonstrate a diachronic shift in the language used by the court, as well as linguistic patterns corrob-orating what the court considers its achievements.

Corpus-based analysis ranging from creating a corpus, to computing statistics can nowadays be achieved by the means of certain software tools, like AntConc (Anthony 2019), which is freely available, and SketchEngine (2020).

DICTIONARY APPROACHES

The dictionary approach entails maintaining one or more dictionaries of word cate-gories, scanning the texts with the help of software, and assigning each word to the dictionary category in which it belongs. The related software will tally all the words falling into the dictionary categories, thereby producing summary statistics, which can further be used as indicators of certain text characteristics such as text complexity, au-thor personality, and sentiment.

A

A potential problem of the dictionary approach is the consideration of words in isolation. For example, court judgments will probably include the term 'no violation', which has rather positive meaning. A dictionary considering just the word 'violation' will assume, though, that the word has negative connotations.

MACHINE LEARNING

Machine learning has recently gained great popularity in the social sciences. One of the reasons is a technique called *topic modelling*, in which the computer generates topics describing the entire corpus. The topics, in turn, comprise words that are estimated to be semantically similar, thus allowing researchers to represent each text as a range of topics. A recent topic modelling variant is *structural topic modelling* (Roberts et al. 2014), where the method covaries each topic with text metadata VARIABLES, such as author and political affiliation, and hence allows associations of certain topics with the VARIABLES to be observed.

Roberts et al. (2014) apply the above technique to open-ended survey responses (see SURVEY RESEARCH), inter alia on public views of immigration and the most important problems in the US 2008 election, while also collecting data about gender and political affiliation. They thus show differences in the answer-topics depending on the responder's affiliation.

Topic modelling has been empirically proven to produce meaningful results on many occasions. It requires, though, the user to provide the number of topics in advance. However, sometimes the generated topics contain boilerplate or irrelevant terms. This phenomenon is more pronounced in corpora with long texts spanning several topics.

REFERENCES

Anthony, Lawrence. 2019. *Software: AntConc (Version 3.5.8)* [computer software]. Tokyo, Waseda University. Available at https://www.laurenceanthony.net/software (Accessed 19 February 2020).

Baker, Paul, Costas Gabrielatos, Majib Khoshravinik, Michal Krzyżanowski, Tony McEnery, and Ruth Wodak. 2008. 'A Useful Methodology Synergy? Combining Critical Discourse Analysis and Corpus Linguistics to Examine Discourses of Refugees and Asylum seekers in the UK Press'. *Discourse & Society* 19(3): 273–306.

Dunning, Ted. 1993. 'Accurate Methods for the Statistics of Surprise and Coincidence'. *Computational Linguistics* 19(1): 61–74.

Lexical Computing Ltd. 2015. *Statistics used in the SketchEngine*. Available at https://www.sketchengine.eu/wp-content/uploads/ske-statistics.pdf (Accessed 19 February 2020).

Potts, Amanda and Anne Lise Kjær. 2016. 'Constructing Achievement in the International Criminal Tribunal for the former Yugoslavia (ICTY): A Corpus-based Critical Discourse Analysis'. *International Journal for the Semiotics of Law* 29(3): 525–555.

Rayson, Paul. 2020. *Log-likelihood and Effect Size Calculator*. Available at http://ucrel.lancs.ac.uk/llwizard.html (Accessed 19 February 2020).

Roberts, Margaret E., Brandon M. Stewart, Dustin Tingley, Christopher Lucas, Jetson Leder-Luis, Kushner Shana Gadarian, Bethany Albertson, and David G. Rand. 2014. 'Structural Topic Models for Open-ended Survey Responses'. *American Journal of Political Science* 58(4): 1064–1082.

SketchEngine. 2020. *Sketch Engine* [language corpus management and query system]. Available at https://www.sketchengine.eu/ (Accessed 22 July 2020).

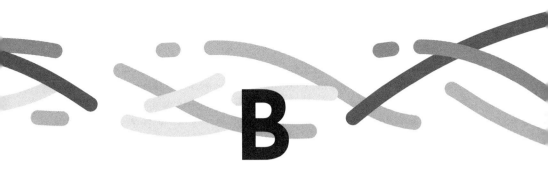

B

BAYESIAN INFERENCE

Arnaud Dufays, Université Laval & Université de Namur

Bayesian inference refers to the Bayesian statistical method for estimating the parameters of a model and for testing a **HYPOTHESIS**. It relies on subjective statistics and extensively uses Bayes's theorem.

BAYES'S THEOREM

Before stating the theorem, let us assume that your teenage son is finishing his secondary schooling and you discover that he is involved in a romance. You are concerned and decide to calculate the probability of him passing his exams. Bayes's theorem gives a consistent rule for computing this probability. Bayes's theorem is mathematically stated as

$$P(H|E) = \frac{P(E|H)P(H)}{P(E)}$$

Each term of the theorem should read as follows:

- P(H|E) is called the 'posterior probability' and denotes the probability of a **HYPOTHESIS** that is conditional on the observation of the evidence E. This is the probability that the son passes his exam (Hypothesis) given that he is involved in a relationship (Evidence).

- P(E|H) denotes the probability of evidence E occurring, which is conditional on the fact that the hypothesis is true. In our illustration, this is the probability of being in a romantic relationship if the teenager has passed his exam.

- P(H) is called the 'prior probability' and stands for the probability of the hypothesis being true regardless of the evidence E. In our example, it denotes the probability of the teenager passing his exam before you learned he was in a relationship.

- P(E) is the probability of event E occurring regardless of the hypothesis H, that is the probability of being in a relationship when finishing secondary school.

The theorem shows that you need additional information to figure out the posterior probability. First, you look at the school records and learn that one hundred students took the exams last year and seventy of them were in a relationship. Of the eighty successful students, fifty-two of them were engaged in a romance. Now, by combining these figures, Bayes's theorem tells us that the probability of success is 74.3 per cent (i.e. $P(H) = 80/100$, $P(E) = 70/100$, and $P(E|H) = 52/80$). Of course, many other factors affect the student's performance. They can be taken into account by applying Bayes's theorem successively. This technique is called Bayesian learning and is often used in TIME SERIES contexts.

BAYESIAN INFERENCE

Bayesian inference consists of inferring any abstract quantities using Bayes's theorem. It extends the scope of Bayes's theorem to any non-random value. In this framework, the HYPOTHESIS H can relate to any discrete or continuous parameters. For instance, a Bayesian statistician will use Bayes's rule to assess the fairness of a dice, the existence of a monotheist God, or to quantify the COVARIANCE between US inflation and the US unemployment rate.

Let us further illustrate the Bayesian paradigm with a financial example. An investor wants to invest in stocks that exhibit a high expected return (i.e. the parameter). Using past returns and assuming some future stability, he can rely on Bayes's theorem to calculate the posterior probability of the expected return. To make a parallel with the above equation, the HYPOTHESIS H relates to the expected return and is a continuous random VARIABLE. The event E denotes the historical performance of the company.

It is worth mentioning that Bayesian inference is an alternative to classical inference (see REGRESSION ANALYSIS) and classical statisticians find Bayesian statistics controversial for two reasons. First, they assume that an unknown but non-random true value exists, which means the expected return should be a constant. For Bayesian statisticians, the randomness of the parameter indicates that the available data do not provide all the information required in terms of the inferred quantity. Consequently, the classical viewpoint is arguably compatible because the posterior probability over the parameter quantifies the data's uncertainty over the true value.

Second, Bayes's formula can be applied to infer the probability over a parameter value if the prior probability of the parameter is known (i.e. $P(H)$). This corresponds to the statistician's state of knowledge about the parameter before the data are observed. In the financial example, it implies making subjective statements about the likely values of the expected return. Therefore, an optimistic investor may choose different prior odds to a pessimistic investor. This probability constitutes a weakness due to its subjectivity. In fact, every prior probability produces a different posterior probability. However, the state of knowledge about a parameter value or a HYPOTHESIS can be automatically included in the prior probability.

The main drawback of the Bayesian approach lies in the computation of the posterior probability. The analytical computation of the posterior probability is a complex problem for any application, and this has limited Bayesian statistics for years. In the early 1990s, Bayesian statistics boomed with the emergence of SAMPLING TECHNIQUES. These new tools rely on the computational power to sample from (rather than evaluate) the posterior probability. Basically, sampling from the posterior probability can be understood as generating the most likely values of the distribution (e.g. simulating the success or failure of students who are in a relationship). The prominent simulation method is called Markov Chain Monte Carlo (MCMC). Other very powerful techniques now exist, such as the Sequential Monte Carlo approach and the Approximate Bayesian Computation algorithm. These methods can benefit from parallel computing, which means they have an advantage over MCMC algorithms and could even replace the latter in future.

Bayesian principles are discussed in Stone (2013), where the Bayes rule is explained using simple calculations and graphics. Deeper mathematical derivations with advanced Bayesian economics modelling can be found in Koop (2003). For advanced statisticians, Geweke's (2005) publication provides mathematical demonstrations for state-of-the-art models, as well as for standard SAMPLING TECHNIQUES.

REFERENCES

Geweke, John. 2005. *Contemporary Bayesian Econometrics and Statistics*. Hoboken, NJ, John Wiley and Sons Ltd.

Koop, Gary. 2003. *Bayesian Econometrics*. Hoboken, NJ, John Wiley and Sons Ltd.

Stone, James V. 2013. *Bayes' Rule: A Tutorial Introduction to Bayesian Analysis*. Sheffield, Sebtel Press.

BEHAVIOURISM

Olga Herzog, University of Hamburg

Behaviourism is a methodological approach that involves the observable measurement of individual behaviour. Therefore, it is closely related to the EPISTEMOLOGY of POSITIVISM and empiricism, which emphasize the observation and verifiability of individual or social phenomena to generate knowledge. Hence, behaviourists focus on the study of perceptible reactions of humans or animals to different situations. This differs from the introspective or interpretive methods applied in HERMENEUTIC approaches. Behaviour is understood as reflexive or conscious reactions to different stimuli and does not presume an underlying rationality. Traditional behaviourists study the actions of humans or animals exclusively in a controlled environment, such as a laboratory. Thus, behaviourism follows the logic of the natural sciences, by relying on objective, observable information based on sensory experiences.

THE ORIGINS OF BEHAVIOURISM

The term behaviourism was first coined by the psychologist John B. Watson in the early twentieth century. In 'Psychology as the Behaviorist Views It' (1913), Watson distanced himself from an introspective approach in psychology and proposed that behavioural observation should be the focal point of research:

> Psychology, as the behaviorist views it, is a purely objective, experimental branch of natural science which needs introspection as little as do the sciences of chemistry and physics. It is granted that the behaviour of animals can be investigated without appeal to consciousness. (Watson 1913: 176)

Initially, behaviourists did not consider inner motivations for actions. However, Edward G. Tolman argued that in order to understand behaviour, inner processes should be taken into consideration, such as intentions or how actions are organized. By studying the way rats search for food in mazes, he concluded that the animals' persistence demonstrated the purpose of their actions (Tolman 1925). According to Tolman, behavioural observations can reveal imperceptible purposes and strategies that can be traced in behaviour.

In the 1940s, Burrhus F. Skinner revived the strict approach, calling it 'radical behaviourism'. He rejected inner determinants of behaviour and limited his research to the observable effects of particular stimuli. In this context, Skinner developed the concept of 'operant conditioning'. An 'operant' represents a class of responses connected with certain consequences; 'conditioning' these responses means reinforcing certain behaviour with a stimulus (Skinner 1953: 62–67). According to Skinner, behavioural research should concentrate on the systematic modification of behaviour through carefully chosen stimuli: 'The most important feature of the laboratory method is the deliberate manipulation of VARIABLES: the importance of a given condition is determined by changing it in a controlled fashion and observing the result' (Skinner 1953: 37).

In accordance with Skinner, all behaviourists agree that behaviour is best examined in controlled experimental environments, where the researcher determines the dependent and independent variables (Moore 1999). Throughout an experiment, the researcher triggers a stimulus (the independent variable) and observes the response of the study object (the dependent variable). The goal of such a controlled setting is to examine the actual causes of behaviour, while excluding alternative explanations. For examples, see the entry on EXPERIMENTS.

Thus, the behaviourist approach is directly connected to experimentation. This approach is not limited to psychology, but is also applied to other disciplines, including economics, sociology, communication studies, and political science in the twentieth century. This development is part of the so-called 'behaviourist revolution', which involved the shift of social inquiry to the study of individuals' observable behaviour, modelled on the methodology used in the natural sciences (Moore 1999). Previously, in most disciplines of the social sciences, analysis concentrated on the understanding and interpretation of texts following HERMENEUTIC approaches. Behaviourists analyse individual behaviour in controlled settings and demand that sensory experiences determine the results and conclusions of research, which is central to POSITIVIST and empirical approaches. In this regard, the behaviourist revolution separated history, law, and philosophy from the field of social sciences.

B

BEHAVIOURISM ACROSS DISCIPLINES

In some disciplines, the behaviourist principles adopted did not take the stringent form of Skinner's radical behaviourism. Instead, they were adjusted to include inner processes and motivations as observable behaviour in individuals. In political science, this led to the specific term 'behaviouralism'. Behavioural studies in politics share the empirical approach of behaviourism and its focus on individual behaviour. However, they explicitly include norms, ideas, and attitudes of individuals as explanatory VARIABLES and consider the environment in which the individual is embedded (Easton 1962). Behaviouralism remains the dominant approach applied to electoral studies and related research areas.

In many social sciences, behaviourist researchers do not just use experiments, but rely on field observations and surveys to measure individuals' behaviour. Some research topics, however, are not suitable for experimental methods or are ethically questionable. Disciplines like sociology or political science are often concerned with real-life events that are embedded in particular contexts and cannot be fully recreated in laboratories. Furthermore, experiments on violent behaviour may be dangerous for the subjects under study, which raises ethical questions. Since the so-called Milgram experiment, where participants were urged to punish the other participants with fake electric shocks if they gave wrong answers (for details see Milgram 1964), a debate on ETHICS IN RESEARCH led to the establishment of ethical standards to protect research subjects.

Psychological behaviourism was seriously criticized during the cognitive revolution in the 1950s. Cognitive researchers, such as Noam Chomsky, criticized the fact that mental states and inner processes were excluded from behaviourist studies, which limits research to the description of actions and fails to offer a profound explanation of their causes. Another critique involves the assumed objectivity of observations, which ignores the researchers' role and theoretical assumptions. The researchers' objectivity—even in laboratory conditions—is questionable since they design the setting, select a stimulus, and interpret the observed facts in their reports.

Despite this criticism, behaviourism remains an important methodological approach in psychology, as well as in other disciplines that focus on individual behaviour (though not usually in its radical form). Experimental research has been extended to include neuroscience techniques to observe inner processes that concern behaviour. Since 1974, the Association for Behaviour Analysis International (ABAI)[1]

---

[1] Further information is available at https://www.abainternational.org.

has connected researchers from different disciplines. It promotes the behaviourist approach and its methodology through regular meetings and publications.

REFERENCES

Easton, David. 1962. 'Introduction: The Current Meaning of "Behavioralism" in Political Science', in *The Limits of Behavioralism in Political Science*, ed. James C. Charlesworth, 1-25. Philadelphia, The American Academy of Political and Social Science.

Milgram, Stanley. 1964. 'Group Pressure and Action Against a Person'. *Journal of Abnormal and Social Psychology* 69(2): 137-143.

Moore, Jay. 1999. 'The Basic Principles of Behaviorism', in *The Philosophical Legacy of Behaviorism: Studies in Cognitive Systems*, Volume 22, ed. Bruce A. Thyer. Dordrecht, Springer.

Skinner, B. Frederic. 1953. *Science and Human Behavior*. New York, Simon and Schuster.

Tolman, G. Edward. 1925. 'Behaviorisms and Purpose'. *The Journal of Philosophy* 22(2): 36-41.

Watson, John B. 1913. 'Psychology as the Behaviorist Views It'. *Psychological Review* 20(2): 158-177.

BIAS

Unavoidable Subjectivity?

Aysel Küçüksu, University of Copenhagen
Stephanie Anne Shelton, University of Alabama

The term 'bias' refers to an uninvited, but inevitable aspect of conducting research. It is usually equated with subjectivity, the distortion and manipulation of data, or a lack of objectivity, which undermines the credibility of the research.

DIFFERENT EPISTEMOLOGICAL VIEWS ON BIAS

The long-standing POSITIVIST interpretation of bias considers that it is an inherently problematic 'ethical issue' (Roulston and Shelton 2015). Yet, contemporary research has called for a 'reconceptualization' of this perception of bias in order to encourage a more nuanced view. It has attempted to draw attention to the epistemological and theoretical assumptions in which bias is perceived as a problem. As Roulston and Shelton (2015: 5) rightly observe, 'bias conceptualized as a problem is inextricably entwined with epistemological questions concerning how knowledge about the social world is produced, what counts as research, and how the quality of research is assessed'.

The foundationalist EPISTEMOLOGY is one relevant example. It assumes that humans (or more specifically 'men') can achieve pure objectivity by employing reason to discover the absolute 'truth' that already exists out there, waiting to be found. It therefore seeks to eliminate bias because of the underlying assumption that 'there is indeed a reality out there that the mind can discover, describe, and know' (St Pierre 2000: 494). Presumably, if a rational researcher could eradicate their own bias, they could uncover truth. Bias is perceived as a threat, and its presence, in any shape or form, is an 'indication of poor quality study' (Roulston and Shelton 2015: 1). Therefore, eradicating bias constitutes the primary goal. In contrast, post-foundationalist approaches such as post-modernism and post-structuralism, among others, suggest that the idea of eliminating bias is untenable and linked to outdated beliefs in absolute objectivity.[1] The post-foundationalist epistemological approach rejects the idea that a single exclusive form of reality can be discovered through reason. It adopts the stance that truth is interpreted and contingent on the ways that humans experience and see the world—in short, based on our biases. It also refuses to view researchers as objective neutral agents. Instead, researchers are considered to be 'co-constructors of knowledge' (Lincoln, Lynham, and Guba 2011: 110). As a result, bias is transformed into a useful, enriching phenomenon because it encourages reflexivity, an important means of addressing bias by reflecting on the assumptions that we might otherwise take for granted.

In the social sciences, bias is a manifestation of how cultural and political standing affects our approach to science. Bias is inevitable in research. Although findings may be subjective as a result of bias, the aim is not to avoid bias completely. Instead, bias should be acknowledged early on to ensure that both researchers and readers have the critical tools necessary to recognize it and evaluate its influences. This approach originated in anthropology and is known as 'positionality'. It suggests that position influences discourse (see also DISCOURSE ANALYSIS). Thus, the resulting bias is not rejected, but accepted as inevitable because reality is necessarily perceived from a specific point of view. Bias comes in many forms. This entry discusses the two that are the most common in the literature: gender bias and confirmation bias.

GENDER BIAS

Gender bias is the unfounded and unequal treatment of women and men (see also ETHICS IN RESEARCH). It occurs in research when an aspect or stage of the research process erroneously demonstrates favouritism towards one particular gender (Rothchild 2007). For example, it may arise when researchers conduct surveys

---

[1] For an excellent summary of certain post-foundationalist approaches to bias and how they construe the researcher's role, see the following article: Kathryn Roulston and Stephanie Anne Shelton, 'Reconceptualizing Bias in Teaching Qualitative Research Methods'. *Qualitative Inquiry* (2015) 21(4): 332–342.

and opinion polls that involve significantly more males than females, despite the fact that females are of equal importance as a target group (see also **SAMPLING TECH-NIQUES**) or when more women are recruited for clinical trials in cancer research, although men are equally affected (Gilpin 2001). Substantial research has revealed gender bias in a wide range of disciplines. It provides an explanation for the real-life implications of gender bias and how it distorts research.

Gender bias can occur in both qualitative and quantitative research. For example, in statistical work such as a public opinion survey, a researcher often has to resort to so-called 'weighting techniques'. In other words, the researcher has to decide how to 'rank' various categories, such as age, height, education, and other demographics, in order to arrive at a statistical finding. However, rather than being 'objective', the subsequent ranking reflects the researcher's biases and assumptions. An example scenario could arise if a particular study asks respondents to designate their gender and 52 per cent of respondents select 'female', 46 per cent choose 'male', and 2 per cent pick 'other' or do not respond. The researcher who runs those numbers for a statistical analysis might split the difference of the 2 per cent between 'female' and 'male', then adjust the other responses with a 'weight' of 53 per cent female and 47 per cent male, effectively erasing respondents who either did not fall into or did not wish to answer based on the gender binary. Alternatively, the researcher might deem the 2 per cent as an 'anomaly' and not incorporate it into the findings at all. In this latter scenario, the researcher just 'weights' the results based on 98 per cent of the responses and treats the other 2 per cent as 'invalid'. This would be an example of gender bias in statistical research.

CONFIRMATION BIAS

Confirmation bias is a subset of selection bias. It occurs when research findings are skewed by 'the seeking or interpreting of evidence in ways that are partial to existing beliefs, expectations or a **HYPOTHESIS** in mind' (Nickerson 1998: 175). The highly distortive effect of this bias is easy to perceive by comparing two approaches to research: in the first, evidence is assessed impartially, whereas in the second, a case is constructed to validate a conclusion drawn beforehand. The latter involves 'selectively gather[ing], or giv[ing] undue weight to, evidence that supports one's position while neglecting to gather, or discounting, evidence that would tell against it' (Nickerson 1998: 175). This definition implies intent—for example, a prosecution lawyer may consciously gather evidence—but confirmation bias in research methodology is usually unintentional. Research results may reveal confirmation bias even if there is no deliberate attempt to confirm the initial **HYPOTHESIS**. Confirmation bias can be either subconscious or deliberate. Yet, in both cases, it has a highly distortive effect on research outcomes since it 'perpetuate[s] beliefs independently of their factuality' (Nickerson 1998: 208).

Interview-based qualitative research is often criticized for involving bias. Open-ended questions characterize discovery-oriented rather than confirmatory research.

This involves personal interactions between the interviewer and the interviewee and presents a set of challenges in terms of 'instrumentation rigor and bias management' (Chenail 2011: 256). An important example is when the interviewer belongs to the population under study, which makes them an 'insider'. To address the various types of bias that a researcher may encounter in qualitative interviewing, Chenail proposes a bracketing interview or an approach that involves 'interviewing the investigator'. By analysing the data generated in the process, the investigator can develop a more reflexive attitude.

In general, if a researcher focuses exclusively on their own particular theory and outcomes, they tend to generate considerable research bias. To avoid this, researchers should try to provide alternative explanations and interpretations (not simply their own), even if they undermine their own theory or refute their findings in the process.

It is important for researchers and scholars alike to recognize bias as an inevitable part of conducting research. Instead of perceiving bias as a 'threat' or 'risk', acknowledging it in research design or results can enhance methodological insight and may generate more responsible and credible research. In addition, understanding research bias sharpens our critical approach to the literature.

Acknowledging the epistemological and theoretical assumptions about knowledge and thought production is essential when it comes to understanding the perception of bias and how it is addressed. Indeed, 'unpacking the conceptualizations of bias that students bring to their work gets at the heart of how knowledge about the social world is produced and how assessments of quality are made in relation to the design and conduct of research' (Roulston and Shelton 2015: 9).

REFERENCES

Alexander, Lorraine K., Brettania Lopes, Kristen Richetti-Masterson, and Karin B. Yeatts. 2015. 'Selection Bias: Epidemiologic Research and Information Center (ERIC)'. Notebook Periodical 2(1).

Chenail, Ronald J. 2011. 'Interviewing the Investigator: Strategies for Addressing Instrumentation and Researcher Bias Concerns in Qualitative Research'. The Qualitative Report 16(1): 255-262.

Gilpin, Adele K. 2001. Study Estimates Gender Bias in US Clinical Trials, Finds Men—not Women—Underrepresented in Most Research. Johns Hopkins Bloomberg School of Public Health website. Available at https://www.jhsph.edu/news/news-releases/2001/gender-bias-trials.html (Accessed 22 July 2020).

Lincoln, Yvonna S., Susan A. Lynham, and Egon G. Guba. 2011. 'Paradigmatic Controversies, Contradictions, and Emerging Confluences, Revisited', in The SAGE Handbook of Qualitative Research, 4th edition, ed. Norman K. Denzin and Yvonna S. Lincoln, 97-128. Los Angeles, CA, SAGE Publications.

Nickerson, Raymond S. 1998. 'Confirmation Bias: A Ubiquitous Phenomenon in Many Guises'. Review of General Psychology 2(2): 175-220.

Rothchild, Jennifer. 2007. 'Gender Bias', in The Blackwell Encyclopedia of Sociology. Hoboken, NJ, Wiley-Blackwell.

Roulston, Kathryn and Stephanie Anne Shelton. 2015. 'Reconceptualizing Bias in Teaching Qualitative Research Methods'. Qualitative Inquiry 21(4): 332-342.

St Pierre, Elizabeth A. 2000. 'Poststructural Feminism in Education: An Overview'. International Journal of Qualitative Studies in Education 13(5): 477-515.

BIG DATA

Yannick Dufresne, Université Laval
Brittany I. Davidson, University of Bristol

Defining big data is not a simple task. The main difficulty arises from '*big data*' being a relatively new concept that is still evolving. This problem is compounded by the term being used across a vast array of disciplines (see **INTERDISCIPLINARY**), which do not necessarily converge towards a common definition. Big data can, and does, often refer to the characteristics of data—for example, size. However, the term also originates from the computational challenges that data generates. Previously, these computational challenges were caused by insufficient data storage capabilities, and an inability to effectively handle and analyse this data. However, more recently, the definition has evolved to refer to the analytical, theoretical, and even social opportunities created by the increasing availability of data. This is further shown by methodological advances, which have allowed for more advanced analyses, as well as making the applications of big data more accessible across both academia and industry (Boyd and Crawford 2012).

Within the social sciences, big data could refer to an emerging field of research that brings together academics from a variety of disciplines using and developing tools to widen perspective, to utilize latent data sets, as well as for the generation of new data (Lazer and Radford 2017). For example, Ellis et al. (2017) studied repeated non-attendance to doctors' appointments in the UK, and found several key factors that increased the likelihood of an individual missing more than one appointment in a year (N = 550 083). These include: being aged between 16 and 30, or over 90 years old, and coming from a low-socio-economic background. This is an interesting and impactful demonstration of utilizing data that was not designed for this purpose. The research provides valuable insights into the NHS, and how millions of pounds could be saved every year by understanding these patterns in behaviour. Further, Ellis and Jenkins (2012) studied 'weekday effects' on attendance at medical appointments in the UK, and found that many factors predicted increased likelihood of missing appointments (study one, N = 4,538,294; study two, N = 10,895). It was found across two studies that the highest 'Did not attend' rate occurred on Mondays, and the lowest was on Fridays, which led to suggestions on how to better allocate appointments in the NHS. Both of these papers demonstrate multiple disciplines of research coming together (specifically, collaborations between computational social science, psychology, biostatistics, and medicine).

CHARACTERISTICS OF DATA

Another way to define big data in the social sciences refers to data corresponding to at least one of the 'Three V's of big data: volume, variety, or velocity (Laney 2001). These characteristics are widely used by researchers attempting to define and distinguish new types of data from conventional ones. First, the *volume* characteristic asks: '*How big is big data?*' Arguably, it is insufficient to define big data solely on the basis of volume: what is considered '*big*' depends almost entirely on the context. For example, if we imagine a data set of 10,000 individuals from the NHS, we would struggle to consider this big data due to the discrepancy between the sample size and the population. However, if we consider the data collected from a wearable device that tracks user location (GPS), heart rate, steps taken, etc. over the space of several months, this generates millions of data points, which would be considered big data, even though it came only from one individual. Hence, again, we can ask what is '*big*'?

The *variety* of data is a fundamental characteristic of big data. Previously, most data sets in the social sciences were in simple rows-and-columns (.csv) formats. However, data is now found in a variety of forms. These new formats reflect changes in content within data. For instance, social media data differs fundamentally from conventional survey data (.csv format). This is due to the data containing not only metadata, but also non-numerical data, e.g. text (see AUTOMATED TEXT ANALYSIS), image, audio, and video, which may or may not be in real time (see TIME SERIES).

Big data can also be distinguished from other data based on its *velocity*—for example, Google search queries, city surveillance videos, or wearable devices (e.g. smart watches). Each of these data sources not only produces data in a variety of formats, but the sheer quantities of data being produced continues to grow. This can be utilized across several disciplines, for example wearable devices informing healthcare interventions (Ellis and Piwek 2017), which will have implications not only for research but also for industry. This is only one example of how effective use of data sets can inform and improve businesses, which could lead to wider governmental improvements in services and society.

Alongside the *volume* and *variety* characteristics of big data, there lies the intrinsic issue of computational challenges. However, newer data analysis techniques such as data mining and machine learning are mitigating these challenges. Machine learning, broadly, is the use or development of methods to automate finding patterns in data, which can be then used for prediction (Murphy 2012). There are a number of machine learning techniques, which fall into three broad categories: supervised, semi-supervised, and unsupervised machine learning. Supervised refers to the algorithms being trained on a data set with *correct* classifications (labelled data) assigned in order to predict specific outcome variables (the labels)—e.g. to which of the predetermined groups does x belong? This then allows researchers to evaluate the performance of the model. In contrast, unsupervised machine learning typically relates to questions needing to find hidden patterns in data, which is unlabelled data. Examples of this would be clustering techniques or topic modelling (Sathya and Abraham 2013). Finally, semi-supervised machine learning combines both labelled and unlabelled data (Zhu and Goldberg 2009).

Researchers now have the ability to reveal patterns in (big) data that would not have been possible using raw manpower alone, via the use of machine learning, deep learning, and neural networks. For example, Davidson et al. (2019) used clustering and classification techniques to detect changes in user behaviour over time, to understand user roles and leadership (at group level) within online ideological communities. These methods also provide opportunities for both academia and industry (e.g. healthcare, finance, marketing). However, with advancements in deep learning, where there is no supervision whatsoever, we have increasing numbers of '*black box*' methods, also known as *unexplainable* AI (artificial intelligence) or machine learning, which in itself creates questions and challenges. For example, how do we explain or understand the decisions being made by various algorithms? What impacts might this have on the individuals and groups that are impacted by these algorithmic decisions?

ETHICAL CHALLENGES

There are a number of ethical and consent issues with big data analytics (see ETHICS IN RESEARCH). For example, many studies across the social sciences utilize big data from the web, from social media, online communities, and the darknet, where there is a question as to whether users provided consent to the reuse of their posts, profiles, or other data shared when they signed up, knowing their profiles and information would be public. However, we must note that these issues are not new: we have the same issues with consent when analysing CCTV footage, where all people captured may not have actively consented to partaking in a study of this retrospective footage. This of course leads to additional questions relating to smart cities, smart homes, and a number of other IoT (internet of things) devices that capture information and data about people without necessarily informed consent, or any ability to opt out. Of course, unfortunately, there are no simple answers or options for these questions; however, researchers must be acutely aware of these challenges and also the inferences being made about the individuals or groups from their analysis (Wachter and Mittelstadt 2019). This has led to a number of issues regarding algorithms making decisions that cannot be explained (e.g. denying loan applications, rejecting a job candidate)

OPPORTUNITIES AND BARRIERS

The Three V's of big data are useful in an attempt to define big data. However, they reveal little about the opportunities and pitfalls that come along with big data (Clark and Golder 2015). Hence, an increasing number of scholars include a fourth 'V' to their definition of big data: *veracity*. While this characteristic is not specific to big data, it shows an increasing concern regarding the quality of data (Jungherr and Theocharis 2017). There are intrinsic issues with attempting to infer insights from unstructured data (Gandomi and Haider 2015), and even more so when we attempt to merge data sets, which is becoming increasingly common in data science and analytics. We must remember big data is often not designed with specific RESEARCH QUESTIONS in mind, which can sometimes lead to selection BIAS in their analysis (see SAMPLING TECHNIQUES).

Further, big data asks the researchers an interesting epistemological question: deductive or inductive approaches (see DEDUCTIVE, INDUCTIVE, AND RETRODUCTIVE

REASONING)? We can be theory-driven (inductive approaches), or conversely, via the use of several machine learning clustering techniques, we fall towards a deductive approach via classification methods (e.g. a simple k-means clustering technique, Markov chain modelling, and deep learning techniques). Here, we can see the variance in applications, from the researchers innately looking for something within the data (often seen in behavioural science, psychology, sociology, etc.), or using techniques in order to find patterns in the data (often seen in computer science, computational social science, mathematics, etc.).

Hence, we must appreciate the opportunities provided by big data, as well as approaching it with caution. When increasing complexity of the data, this innately creates complexity in all stages of data analysis, starting from collection, then cleaning the data, analysis, and providing useful insights.

REFERENCES

Boyd, Danah and Kate Crawford. 2012. 'Critical Questions for Big Data: Provocations for a Cultural, Technological, and Scholarly Phenomenon'. *Information, Communication & Society* 15(5): 662–679.

Clark, W. Robert and Matt Golder. 2015. 'Symposium. Big Data, Causal Inference, and Formal Theory: Contradictory Trends in Political Science?' *Political Science & Politics* 48(1): 65–70.

Davidson, Brittany I., Simon L. Jones, Adam N. Joinson, and Joanne Hinds. 2019. 'The Evolution of Online Ideological Communities'. *PLoS ONE* 14(5): e0216932.

Ellis, David A. and Rob Jenkins. 2012. 'Weekday Affects Attendance Rate for Medical Appointments: Large-scale Data Analysis and Implications'. *PLoS ONE* 7(12): e51365.

Ellis, David A., Ross McQueenie, Alex McConnachie, Philip Wilson, and Andrea E. Williamson. 2017. 'Demographic and Practice Factors Predicting Repeated Non-attendance in Primary Care: A National Retrospective Cohort Analysis'. *The Lancet Public Health* 2(1): e551–e559.

Ellis, David A. and Lukasz Piwek. 2017. 'When Wearable Devices Fail: Towards an Improved Understanding of What Makes a Successful Wearable Intervention'. Paper presented at the 1st GetAMoveOn Annual Symposium, 25 May. https://getamoveon.ac.uk/media/pages/publications/thinkpieces/2760415640-1563382512/ellis-piwek-web-version.pdf

Gandomi, Amir and Murtaza Haider. 2015. 'Beyond the Hype: Big Data Concepts, Methods, and Analytics'. *International Journal of Information Management* 35(2): 137–144.

Jungherr, Andreas and Yannis Theocharis. 2017. 'The Empiricist's Challenge: Asking Meaningful Questions in Political Science in the Age of Big Data'. *Journal of Information Technology & Politics* 14(2): 97–109.

Laney, Doug. 2001. '3D Data Management: Controlling Data Volume, Velocity and Variety'. *META Group Research Note* 6: 70. https://blogs.gartner.com/doug-laney/files/2012/01/ad949-3D-Data-Management-Controlling-Data-Volume-Velocity-and-Variety.pdf

Lazer, David and Jason Radford. 2017. 'Data ex Machina: Introduction to Big Data'. *Annual Review of Sociology* 43(1): 19–39.

Murphy, Kevin P. 2012. *Machine Learning: A Probabilistic Perspective*. Cambridge, MA, MIT Press.

Sathya, R. and Annamma Abraham. 2013. 'Comparison of Supervised and Unsupervised Learning Algorithms for Pattern Classification'. *International Journal of Advanced Research in Artificial Intelligence* 2(2): 34–38.

Wachter, Sandra and Brent Mittelstadt. 2019. 'A Right to Reasonable Inferences: Re-thinking Data Protection Law in the Age of Big Data and AI'. *Columbia Business Law Review* 2019(2): 494–620.

Zhu, Xiaojin and Andrew B. Goldberg. 2009. *Introduction to Semi-supervised Learning*. San Rafael, CA, Morgan & Claypool.

BOOLEAN ALGEBRA

Jasmin Hasić, Sarajevo School of Science and Technology

DEFINITION

In the social sciences, Boolean algebra comes under different labels. It is often used in set-theoretic and QUALITATIVE COMPARATIVE ANALYSIS to assess complex CAUSATION that leads to particular outcomes (i.e. 'dependent variables') involving different combinations of conditions (i.e. 'independent variables'). For example, Boolean algebra can help us determine whether 'losing a war' is necessary or sufficient for 'social revolution' in relation to other conditions and events that occur. In addition, it can help us understand how electoral systems might be organized in different countries by shedding light on the conditions that help determine how proportional representation leads to both multi-party and two-party electoral systems (Caramani 2009). In essence, it examines causal patterns by focusing on set–subset relationships. It helps in explaining the configurations of conditions that can lead to outcomes of major interest and in identifying the combinations of characteristics associated with a particular outcome, by using a logical reduction of various complex, causal, and/or SCOPE CONDITIONS (Fiss 2011: 402).

Boolean algebra is based on Boolean logic. It denotes a system of numerical schemes used to represent logical propositions with binary digits 0 (false) and/or 1 (true), where all elements have only two possible stable states and no unstable states. The basic features of Boolean algebra are the use of binary data, combinatorial logic,[1] and Boolean minimization to reduce the expressions of causal complexity (Greckhamer et al. 2008: 697, 703). By calculating the intersection between the final Boolean equation and the HYPOTHESES formulated in Boolean terms, three subsets of causal combinations emerge: hypothesized and empirically confirmed; hypothesized, but not detected within the empirical evidence; and causal configurations found empirically, but not hypothesized. This approach is both holistic and analytic because it examines cases as a whole and in parts (Ragin 1987: 122).

MINIMIZATION AND FUNCTIONS

The Boolean technique can be used to identify causal regularities that are parsimonious, so they can be expressed with the fewest possible conditions within the whole set of conditions considered in the analysis (Rihoux 2003: 353). The causal configurations can be compared as a code of two columns called the *truth table*. This is a data matrix of binary data listing every causal configuration and the corresponding values for the

---

[1] Always in the context of the presence or absence of other causally relevant conditions.

outcome. Each column is then independently subjected to, and simplified by using, the process of Boolean minimization.

Boolean minimization is used to simplify the formulation of logical expressions, whereby the configurations of **VARIABLE** values—not the individual variables—form the core of the analysis (Goertz and Mahoney 2012: 24). The systematic minimization of a complex configuration involves logical simplification using a bottom-up process, namely a paired comparison of groups of case combinations. Thus, one or several configurations of conditions ('independent variables') can be identified as leading to a particular outcome ('dependent variable'). In this sense, Boolean algebra is used to exclude parts of expressions without changing the logical state of the output.

The two basic operators in Boolean algebra, logical '*AND*' and logical '*OR*', are used to facilitate the analysis of combinations of causal factors.[2] If there are two elements, A and B, then A may be true or false and B may be true or false. The classes that could be formed are as follows:

A true and B false

A true and B true

A false and B true

A false and B false

All statements can be connected by a word 'AND'. Classes can also be formed using the connective word 'OR', which generates a different form of classes. The general rule for calculating case membership with the logical 'OR' is to use the maximum value of a case's membership in the Xs: $Y = \max (X1, X2, X3,$ etc.) (cf. NAVEDTRA 1986). To determine the number of classes or combinations of elements in Boolean algebra, the numerical value of 2^n can be used, where n equals the number of elements.

The logical 'AND' represents the logically possible intersection of sets of the causal attributes involved: it unites the conditions into an overall combination of conditions, denoted with an asterisk (*) or dot (·). The logical 'OR' represents the union of two sets, where either causal condition can lead to the same outcome. It is calculated through the maximum value across the single components and denoted with the plus sign (+)[3] (Schneider and Wagemann 2012: 42). This enables a systematic and replicable comparison between cases because it requires complete transparency in all phases of conceptualization, **OPERATIONALIZATION**, and coding.

Boolean algebra, defined by union, intersection, and complementation operations that are represented by different symbols, can be used to optimize the process of probabilistic risk assessment and safety analysis to obtain combinations that may cause the failure of a system, traditionally calculated by linear and sequential methods. For

---

[2] For the logical 'AND' and the logical 'OR', the *commutativity*, *associativity*, and *distributivity* rules hold (Schneider and Wagemann 2012: 55).

[3] Most languages read the sign '+' as if it was the word 'and'. However, in Boolean algebra, the equivalent for the logical 'AND' in the use of the logic of propositions is the multiplication (*), rather than the addition symbol.

example, 'improper training' for pilots could lead to an event (incident or accident), as one of the possible faults combined with others. For the event ('improper training') to occur, at least one of the other events (like 'improper training simulator' and 'improper criteria') must occur.

$$P(A \text{ or } B) = P(A) + P(B) - P(A \text{ and } B)$$

In Boolean algebra terms, it looks like this:

$$P(A \cup B) = P(A) + P(B) - P(A \cap B)$$

If there are 'n' inputs (for example, another variable like 'improper interface man–machine', or 'lack of pilot's abilities', or 'insufficient training', etc.), the Boolean expression looks like this:

$$Q = A1 + A2 + A3 + \ldots + An$$

In this case, 'improper training' = 'improper training simulator' + 'improper criteria' + 'improper interface man–machine' + 'lack of pilot's abilities' + 'insufficient training' + ... (and so on) (Balan 2015).

REFERENCES

Balan, Casandra Venera. 2015. 'Boolean Algebra Application in Analysis of Flight Accidents'. *INCAS Bulletin* 7(4): 41–49.

Caramani, Daniele. 2009. *Introduction to the Comparative Method with Boolean Algebra*. Thousand Oaks, CA, SAGE Publications.

Fiss, Peer. 2011. 'Building Better Causal Theories: A Fuzzy Set Approach to Typologies in Organization Research'. *Academy of Management Journal* 54(2): 393–420.

Goertz, Gary and James Mahoney. 2012. *A Tale of Two Cultures: Qualitative and Quantitative Research in the Social Sciences*. Princeton, NJ, Princeton University Press.

Greckhamer, Thomas, Vilmos Misangyi, Heather Elms, and Rodney Lacey. 2008. 'Using Qualitative Comparative Analysis in Strategic Management Research: An Examination of Combinations of Industry, Corporate, and Business-unit Effects'. *Organizational Research Methods* 11(4): 695–726.

NAVEDTRA. 1986. *Mathematics, Introduction to Statistics, Number Systems and Boolean Algebra*. Naval Education and Training Professional Development and Technology Centre. Available at http://www.navybmr.com/study%20material/14142.pdf (Accessed 23 July 2020).

Ragin, Charles. 1987. *The Comparative Method: Moving Beyond Qualitative and Quantitative Strategies*. Berkeley, CA, University of California Press.

Rihoux, Benoît. 2003. 'Bridging the Gap between the Qualitative and Quantitative Worlds? A Retrospective and Prospective View on Qualitative Comparative Analysis'. *Field Method* 15(4): 351–365.

Schneider, Carsten and Claudius Wagemann. 2012. *Set-theoretic Methods for the Social Sciences: A Guide to Qualitative Comparative Analysis*. Cambridge, Cambridge University Press.

CASE SELECTION

Laura Gelhaus, University of Warwick & Université de Genève
Dirk Leuffen, University of Konstanz

Case selection is a crucial component of designing social research. Its importance can hardly be overstated because 'the cases you choose affect the answers you get' (Geddes 1990: 131). However, how should researchers select their cases? A careful inspection of the RESEARCH QUESTION, the study's objective, should be the starting point. The RESEARCH QUESTION typically anchors the study in a research area, specifies the universe of cases, and guides its engagement with theory. Ideally, case selection is solely driven by methodology; however, practicality and feasibility considerations frequently make adjustments to the design necessary. Such considerations concern, for instance, the costs of data collection. In sum, the following three questions usually guide case selection:

1. How do the to-be-selected cases relate to all other possible/selectable cases, i.e. the universe of cases?

2. How do these cases relate to the theories used?

3. Can data be obtained for the cases under consideration?

This chapter introduces a few commonly used case selection strategies; more comprehensive typologies, many of which underpin this chapter, are provided, for instance, by Gerring and Cojocaru (2016) and Gerring (2007). In addition, the entry introduces two hotly debated topics in the literature on case selection: selecting on the dependent VARIABLE and random case selection. The overall message of the chapter is simple: case selection should be taken seriously when designing research.

KEY CONCERNS OF CASE SELECTION

In principle, three types of RESEARCH QUESTIONS can be distinguished:

- descriptive questions;
- causal questions; and
- normative questions.

The latter category will be left aside, since case selection primarily concerns empirical and not normative research; if at all, such research draws on illustrative cases to high-light a normative problem. Descriptive questions also do not generally pose major challenges for case selection. They may relate to historically inclined research describing the unfolding of specific events in their temporal and spatial context. In such work, case selection is straightforward: the case of interest is analysed. However, while de-tailed descriptions undoubtedly enhance our understanding of specific events, much social science research investigates more generalizable cause–effect relations. And it is for this kind of objectives that case selection is more challenging.

With respect to questions of causal inference, the literature generally distinguishes research on the 'effects of causes', from research on 'causes of effects'. While the differ-ences between these two approaches may sometimes be overstated (e.g. Gschwend and Schimmelfennig 2007; Goertz and Mahoney 2012), they illustrate different research interests and related case selection challenges. For instance, research investigating whether the introduction of a universal basic income (the cause) enhances the happi-ness of citizens (the effect) follows the 'effect of causes' pattern. One empirical strategy for answering such a question is to conduct a longitudinal analysis of one case, or a num-ber of selected cases (see CROSS-SECTIONAL AND LONGITUDINAL STUDIES) (cf. Gerring and Cojocaru 2016: 401). Hence, a researcher could select a country, a region within a country, a city, or even a specific pilot project that introduced a uni-versal basic income and compare data on happiness—e.g. survey data on reported life satisfaction and/or happiness—before and after the introduction of the treatment (e.g. policy guaranteeing universal basic income). Yet, it is unlikely that findings from one case can be generalized to a broad universe of cases. A cross-sectional alternative with more cases would instead select, for instance, a most-similar systems design for COMPARATIVE ANALYSIS (cf. Przeworski and Teune 1970: 32). This strategy, based on John Stuart Mill's (1986) Method of Difference, selects two or more cases that are similar on all potential third or confounding variables (e.g. culture, political system) but differ with respect to the values of the independent variable (universal basic in-come). If the dependent variable ('happiness') co-varies with the independent vari-able, this suggests the presence of a causal effect. However, the challenge consists in accounting for all third variables in observational, i.e. non-experimental, research—a condition already strongly questioned by Mill himself.

Alternatively, if the aim is to examine the causes of the effects, the values of the de-pendent VARIABLE are often known, while the independent variable is unknown. For example, a researcher may question why countries introduce a universal basic income in the first place. Consequently, they may choose a first instance of such a policy, or index case, and track its genealogy. They may also approach this question by selecting an extreme case with respect to values on the dependent variable (Gerring 2007: 101; Gerring and Cojocaru 2016: 398). Again, both strategies, by selecting a single case, are unlikely to lead to widely generalizable results.

Generally, such concerns should be openly addressed in research and the resulting publications. Arguably, this is facilitated when carefully relating the selected cases to the universe of cases, as well as to the theory used. Finally, issues of practicality should be openly discussed.

First, it is important to examine how a selected case relates to the universe of cases. For example, if the researcher investigates the effects of a universal basic income on happiness, they may want to map all other cases. Hence, if the 2017 universal basic income pilot project in Finland is selected, it is important to consider how this case relates to other examples of universal basic income, for instance projects in Namibia or Brazil. The position of one case in relation to the universe of cases, and relatedly, the number of cases selected, is especially important if researchers want to generalize their findings. A balance between detail of analysis and generalizability needs to be achieved.

Secondly, cases should also be considered in relation to theory, as they can be used to test and/or generate hypotheses. For generating theory and/or hypotheses, a selection of typical cases is usually recommended; however, deviant cases may also serve this purpose (cf. Gerring 2007: 105–108). For example, a researcher starts out with the hypothesis that a universal basic income increases happiness in a country, but then observes a country in which this does not seem to happen. This deviant case presents an opportunity to revisit the original theory, which fails to explain the anomalous outcome.

Crucial cases offer an option for theory testing (Eckstein 1975: 95). If according to a theory a case is *most likely* to produce a certain outcome but fails to do so, the likelihood of the **HYPOTHESIS** being true decreases. For example, if a hypothesis holds that countries with extensive welfare regimes are most likely to introduce a universal basic income, and yet Nordic states fail to do so, this seriously questions the statement. Conversely, if on the theory a case is *least likely* to produce a certain outcome but does so nonetheless, this strongly supports the theory.

Finally, from a practical perspective, it is important to ensure that the analysis is feasible. Even the most rigorous case selection strategy will not help answer the **RESEARCH QUESTION** if the relevant data cannot be accessed, e.g. due to insufficient resources. Crucially, this may introduce error—for instance, if the researcher fails to correctly interpret or critically analyse sources due to restricted knowledge of the case or language barriers (Lieberman 2005: 449). Thus, in practice, case selection is often pragmatic. Here, it is vital that the researcher is transparent about the limitations of the cases selected and points out possible **BIASES**.

SELECTION ON THE DEPENDENT VARIABLE

Selecting cases based on the values of the dependent **VARIABLE** has been a hotly disputed topic in the methodological literature. King, Keohane, and Verba (1994: 129) argued that causal inference is likely to be **BIASED** if cases are selected on the dependent variable (see also Geddes 1990). For example, when testing the effect of a universal basic income on happiness, if only 'happy countries' (e.g. those where the majority of survey respondents report they are 'very happy') are selected, it is difficult to determine whether the outcome is due to the universal basic income (assuming it exists in this country) rather than a third variable. King, Keohane, and Verba (1994: 143) describe this selection as 'cherry picking'. Instead, they suggest that it is important 'to ensure variation in the explanatory variable (and any control variables) without regard to the values of the dependent variable' (King, Keohane, and Verba 1994: 140).

However, there are various exceptions to this view. First, if the research purpose is to identify the causes of effects, research usually starts with knowledge about a specific outcome (cf. Lieberman 2005: 444) and the researcher needs to search for the independent VARIABLES.

Second, both independent and dependent VARIABLES may be known and a co-variation may even be established. Yet, the underlying causal mechanisms may be unclear (see CAUSATION). For example, a researcher may 'know' that a universal basic income makes people happier, without knowing why. In this case, Gerring and Cojocaru (2016: 405) recommend selecting pathway cases that have a strong link between independent and dependent variables. Goertz and Mahoney support this strategy because it avoids indeterminate results and facilitates valuable within-case inferences (Goertz and Mahoney 2012: 184). It is important to note that such strategies have been adopted and promoted by the PROCESS TRACING literature (see Beach and Pedersen 2016).

Third, case selection based on the dependent variable is legitimate when testing necessary conditions (Dion 2003; Goertz and Mahoney 2012: 179). If a researcher sets out to assess whether a universal basic income is a prerequisite for citizens' happiness, they would select cases that score positively on the dependent variable 'happiness'. Consequently, if a case is observed in which citizens are happy, but do not receive a universal basic income, it contradicts the claim that a universal basic income is a necessary condition for happiness.

RANDOM SELECTION OF CASES

Problems of selection BIAS even beyond 'cherry picking' have been emphasized in CASE STUDY research due to the small number of cases investigated. Consequently, researchers may decide to select cases randomly. This brings them closer to the random SAMPLING rationales of large-N studies. For instance, Fearon and Laitin (2010: 757–764) advocate this 'random narrative approach'. In a follow-up to their large-N investigation of the causes of civil war, they randomly select twenty-five countries, stratified by region and civil war experience. They argue that this technique shields against BIAS and facilitates the identification of VARIABLES that have been omitted, which enhances credibility.

However, random selection is claimed to produce unrepresentative results when sample sizes are smaller than five—the typical scale of CASE STUDY research (Gerring 2007: 87). Additionally, random selection may not meet a study's purpose. For example, in the case of rare outcomes, random selection is likely to choose irrelevant cases (Goertz and Mahoney 2012: 183). Hence, while selection bias remains a problem in small-N research, random selection does not necessarily offer a satisfactory alternative. It fails to ensure representativeness in small-N research and risks ignoring informative cases. Therefore, most authors prefer an intentional selection of cases for **CASE STUDY** research.

INCOMPLETE KNOWLEDGE AND TRANSPARENCY

Before concluding this entry, another challenge involved in case selection needs to be highlighted. In practice, researchers often have incomplete knowledge about the universe of cases, confounding **VARIABLES**, or descriptive features of possible cases. Consequently, as the project progresses, a case initially classified as typical may actually turn out to be deviant. Unexpected findings demand revisions and, in fact, contribute to knowledge building. If the initially selected cases prove to be unsuitable for the research purpose, revisions must be enacted. However, when new cases are included in the research, this should be made transparent. Concordantly, it is important to note that different case selection strategies are not mutually exclusive (Gerring 2007: 147); in practice, case selection is often an iterative process. Frequently, a few extensive **CASE STUDIES** can be complemented with several 'mini-case studies', which are comparatively cheap to assemble and enhance the scope of the findings (see Leuffen 2007: 157).

Researchers should be aware that each case selection strategy involves trade-offs. In the end, the quality of case selection depends on whether it helps answer the **RESEARCH QUESTION**. Discarding a seemingly valuable **CASE STUDY** because it does not conform to a specific case selection strategy impedes this goal. Yet, transparency is important in case selection; it is a useful strategy to openly discuss why alternative cases were not selected. Furthermore, if the direction of potential **BIAS** is clearly revealed to readers, it enhances the interpretation of research findings.

Finally, recent developments in mixed methods research and in the rapidly growing literature on causal inference will certainly allow for important advances in the area of case selection in the coming years.

REFERENCES

Beach, Derek and Rasmus B. Pedersen. 2016. 'Selecting Appropriate Cases When Tracing Causal Mechanisms'. *Sociological Methods & Research* 47(4): 837–871.

Dion, Douglas. 2003. 'Evidence and Inference in the Comparative Case Study', in *Necessary Conditions: Theory, Methodology, and Applications*, ed. G. Goertz and H. Starr, 95–112. Lanham, Rowman & Littlefield.

Eckstein, Harry. 1975. 'Case Studies and Theory in Political Science', in *Handbook of Political Science*, vol. 7, ed. Fred I. Greenstein and Nelson W. Polsby, 79–138. Reading, MA, Addison-Wesley.

Fearon, James D. and David D. Laitin. 2010. 'Integrating Qualitative and Quantitative Methods', in *The Oxford Handbook of Political Methodology*, ed. Janet M. Box-Steffensmeier, Henry E. Brady, and David Collier, 756–776. Oxford, Oxford University Press.

Geddes, Barbara. 1990. 'How the Cases You Choose Affect the Answers You Get: Selection Bias in Comparative Politics'. *Political Analysis* 2: 131–150.

Gerring, John. 2007. *Case Study Research: Principles and Practices*. New York, Cambridge University Press.

Gerring, John and Lee Cojocaru. 2016. 'Selecting Cases for Intensive Analysis: A Diversity of Goals and Methods'. *Sociological Methods & Research* 45(3): 392-423.

Goertz, Gary and James Mahoney. 2012. *A Tale of Two Cultures: Qualitative and Quantitative Research in the Social Sciences*. Princeton, NJ, Princeton University Press.

Gschwend, Thomas and Frank Schimmelfennig. 2007. *Research Design in Political Science: How to Practice what they Preach*. Berlin, Springer.

King, Gary, Robert O. Keohane, and Sidney Verba. 1994. *Designing Social Inquiry: Scientific Inference in Qualitative Research*. Princeton, NJ, Princeton University Press.

Leuffen, Dirk. 2007. 'Case Selection and Selection Bias in Small-n Research', in *Research Design in Political Science*, ed. Thomas Gschwend and Frank Schimmelfennig, 145-160. Berlin, Springer.

Lieberman, Evan S. 2005. 'Nested Analysis as a Mixed-Method Strategy for Comparative Research'. *American Political Science Review* 99(3): 435-452.

Mill, John S. 1986. *A System of Logic, Ratioinactive and Inductive: Being a Connected View of the Principles of Evidence and the Methods of Scientific Investigation*, 8th edition. Charlottesville, VA, Ibis.

Przeworski, Adam and Henry J. Teune. 1970. *The Logic of Comparative Social Inquiry*. Hoboken, NJ, Wiley-Interscience.

CASE STUDY

Jessica Luciano Gomes, University of Hamburg & Université libre de Bruxelles

&

Miriam Gomes Saraiva, Rio de Janeiro State University

Case studies are a very common research method in the field of social sciences. Definitions of what constitutes a case generally consist of the 'boundaries around places and time periods' (Ragin 1992: 5) and 'an attempt to understand and interpret a spatially and temporally bounded set of events' (Levy 2008: 2), with the intention to 'shed light on a larger class of cases' (Gerring 2007: 20). With that perspective, Ragin (1992: 2) goes further and argues that 'at a minimum, every study is a case study because it is an analysis of social phenomena and specific to time and space'.

Yet, as stated by Thomas (2011: 14), one should always acknowledge that any event in the world cannot simply be classified as a case study. To that effect, one must examine whether that phenomenon could be categorized as a case *of something*. He uses the example of the Korean War, as merely analysing this tempestuous period of time would not be labelled as a case. Nevertheless, engaging it in an exercise of classification—such as of territorial dispute, for example—would categorize it as a case study, according to Thomas (see **CONCEPT CONSTRUCTION**).

As he puts it, 'the case study is not a method in itself. Rather, it is a focus and the focus is on one thing, looked at in depth and from many angles' (Thomas 2011: 4).

TYPES OF CASE STUDY

Although it might sound simplistic, the research framework for case studies usually has to satisfy a few key points. As claimed by Yin (2009: 9–13), case studies can be divided into separate categories: exploratory, descriptive, and explanatory (see DESCRIPTIVE, EXPLANATORY, AND INTERPRETIVE APPROACHES). They are also directly related to the type of RESEARCH QUESTION being posed from the traditional five types of survey questions: 'who', 'what', 'where', 'how', and 'why'. As Yin argues, a case study would be better analysed using the last two categories, which would also fall into the explanatory classification. This would be justified, according to him, since 'such questions deal with operational links needing to be traced over time, rather than mere frequencies or incidence' (Yin 2009: 9). (See CASE SELECTION.)

Lijphart (1971: 691–692) classifies the possibilities for case studies into six different categories. The first category corresponds to the atheoretical case study, which comprises a singular case study with no intention of creating general HYPOTHESES or formulas; the second category refers to the interpretative case study, which is guided towards an interest in a subject rather than creating generalizations, but paying attention to theories used previously; the third category relates to the hypothesis-generating case studies, that are guided towards the formulation of a strong hypothesis that can be tested among a large population of cases in areas without a pre-existing theory; the fourth and fifth categories cover, respectively, the theory-confirming and theory-infirming case studies, which handle one-case analysis and intend to obtain general statements and test the main proposition related to the VARIABLE; the final category outlined by Lijphart refers to the deviant case analyses, which as the name suggests, deviate from prior general knowledge. When deviating, they can refute the original proposition and create a new one, a valuable tool for qualitative analysis.

For instance, when it comes to theory-confirming and theory-infirming cases, an important example is the article by Allison (1969) on the Cuban missile crisis, which analysed this event according to three models known in the literature—rational policy model, organizational process model, and bureaucratic politics model. The paper is particularly referenced in the area of foreign policy analysis (FPA) because it successfully adopted a single case study in order to test models of concepts.

USING CASE STUDIES

We can often find case studies among both qualitative and quantitative approaches, focusing on a case study per se or on cross-case method. In the realm of QUALITA-TIVE COMPARATIVE ANALYSIS, a case study generally entails the adoption of a larger number of cases. In this way, the difference between a case study and cross-case methods lies in the number of cases involved. A case study typically comprises one case or a low number of cases (small N). When there is a larger number of cases (large N), that normally classifies as a cross-case method. Gerring (2007) uses the analogy of constructing a house as an attempt to learn about construction to differentiate case studies from cross-case methods: the first relates to the construction of a particular house and the second to the construction of many houses. The author also defines case study researchers as analysts who see cases as 'highly individualized phenomena', whereas cross-case analysts 'have a less differentiated vision of the world' in a more homogeneous sense (Gerring 2011: 21). Thus, the case study method looks for a specific element in one or more cases, whereas the comparative method aims to establish differences in the initial point of analysis or in the results.

A good example of a case study is the work by Ipek (2015) exploring how ideas at the domestic level can influence foreign policy changes, as it examines shifts in the behaviour of the Turkish International Cooperation and Development Agency. On the other hand, as stated by Bennett and Elman (2007: 176), an example of the use of cross-case and COMPARATIVE ANALYSIS is the work by Walt (1996) that compares countries before and after revolutions through the analysis of foreign policies. Through this, he explains how some countries that endured revolutions got involved in subsequent wars with their neighbours, while other countries with the same experience did not.

In this way, when it comes to case studies and cross-case studies, the UNIT OF ANALYSIS is an important aspect to consider. As argued by Paterson (2010: 971), the investigation of a single case, taken in its entirety, classifies as a within-case analysis, and it comprises a profound examination of the data. By doing this, the researcher is initially able to analyse the idiosyncrasies of that case alone, and can then proceed to the overall verification of similar patterns across cases. Later on, every single case is used as a contribution to the whole investigation process. Similarly, this method can also be used to perform a cross-case comparison among many individual cases. Furthermore, within-case analysis is a significant component of PROCESS TRACING.

Choosing case studies as a research option is a debatable topic among scholars. As Yin (2009: 14–16) delineates, this is mostly due to its methodological broadness, which makes it difficult to create patterns and to generalize, its research process that usually takes a long time to be concluded, and its challenges in forming causal relations. However, Flyvbjerg (2006) advocates the use of case studies, especially in the social sciences. According to him, among other things, case studies help to provide practical knowledge (what he calls 'context dependent'), since they are based on examples of 'real-life situations' (Flyvbjerg 2006: 223). Case studies are also a good option for FALSIFICATION (Popper 1959), as they can be used to counterpoint a HYPOTHESIS or to dismantle previously conceived notions held by the researcher.

CONCLUSION

It can be said that a case is a selection of a past or current phenomenon in the world, with the aim of explaining its occurrence and outcomes. Choosing appropriate cases is by no means a random activity; it should be guided by suitable questions and be part of a methodological structure. Case studies are important because they provide the examination of samples of a larger atmosphere, therefore enabling researchers with a variety of possibilities: to deepen the analysis of a particular occurrence in the world, to contribute to an existing theoretical framework, and to serve as an instrument of **COMPARATIVE ANALYSIS.**

REFERENCES

Allison, Graham T. 1969. 'Conceptual Models and the Cuban Missile Crisis'. *The American Political Science Review* 63(3): 689-718.

Bennett, Andrew and Colin Elman. 2007. 'Case Study Methods in the International Relations Subfield'. *Comparative Political Studies* 40(2): 170-195.

Flyvbjerg, Bent. 2006. 'Five Misunderstandings about Case-study Research'. *Qualitative Inquiry* 12(2): 219-245.

Gerring, John. 2007. *Case Study Research: Principles and Practices.* Cambridge, Cambridge University Press.

Gerring, John. 2011. 'The Case Study: What it Is and What it Does', in *The Oxford Handbook of Political Science.* ed. R. E. Goodin, 1163-1165. Oxford, Oxford University Press.

Ipek, Pinar. 2015. 'Ideas and Change in Foreign Policy Instruments: Soft Power and the Case of the Turkish International Cooperation and Development Agency'. *Foreign Policy Analysis* 11(2): 173-193.

Levy, Jack S. 2008. 'Case Studies: Types, Designs, and Logic of Inference'. *Conflict Management and Peace Science* 25(1): 1-18.

Lijphart, Arend. 1971. 'Comparative Politics and the Comparative Method'. *American Political Science Review* 65(3): 682-693.

Paterson, Barbara L. 2010. 'Within-case Analysis', in *Encyclopedia of Case Study Research,* ed. Albert J. Mills, Gabrielle Durepos, and Elden Wiebe, 970-973. Thousand Oaks, CA, SAGE Publications.

Popper, Karl. 1959. *The Logic of Scientific Discovery.* New York, Basic Books.

Ragin, Charles C. 1992. 'Introduction: Cases of "What is a case?", in *What is a Case?: Exploring the Foundations of a Social Inquiry,* ed. Charles C. Ragin and Howard S. Becker, 1-17. Cambridge, Cambridge University Press.

Thomas, Garin. 2011. *How to Do Your Case Study.* Thousand Oaks, CA, SAGE Publications.

Walt, Stephen. 1996. *Revolution and War.* Ithaca, NY, Cornell University Press.

Yin, Robert K. 2009. *Case Study Research: Design and Methods,* 4th edition. Thousand Oaks, CA, SAGE Publications.

CAUSATION

Vivien Sierens and Ramona Coman, Université libre de Bruxelles

Causation occupies a central place in the social sciences. In their attempts to understand and explain 'why' social, economic, and political phenomena occur, scholars have dealt with causality in many different ways. For example, in political science, Almond and Verba's (1963) theory of civic culture paved the way for a wide range of studies testing the hypothesis of a causal effect of citizens' attitudes on the establishment and maintenance of democratic regimes (Muller and Seligson 1994). A common conclusion from these studies is that, *ceteris paribus,* countries with high levels of civic culture are more likely to adopt and sustain democracy over time. Yet, while these studies have managed to document a clear correlational pattern between civic culture and democracy, the fundamental question remains: is it really civic culture that accounts for differences in the quality of democracy or is it the other way around? As the correlational relationship between civic culture and democracy does not inform on the directionality of the relationship, civic culture attitudes could also be an effect rather than a cause of democracy (Muller and Seligson 1994). Besides, by focusing on civic attitudes at a country-aggregated level, several intervening and potentially confounding variables, such as gender inequality, may remain overlooked. Gender inequalities in civic culture may affect the average level of political participation as well as being an indicator of the quality of democracy (Coffé and Bolzendahl 2010). As Pippa Norris and Ronald Inglehart (2001: 131) argued, several explanations have been offered to account for the continuing dearth of women in political leadership: 'structural factors, including levels of socioeconomic development and the proportion of women in professional and managerial occupations; the impact of *political institutions*, such as electoral systems based on proportional-representation; and *cultural factors*, like the predominance of traditional attitudes toward gender roles'. Against this backdrop, Norris and Inglehart show that cultural explanations provide a plausible reason why women are more represented in parliaments in the Nordic region than in comparable European societies like Switzerland, Italy, or Belgium. These examples show that identifying a clear causal relationship in the social sciences is not an easy task. Therefore, this contribution discusses the theoretical and methodological challenges that most researches will face when dealing with causation.

Most textbooks on research methods emphasize that 'correlation is not causation'. With this statement, they usually underline that the symmetrical association measured by a correlation coefficient is not a sufficient condition to make a causal claim. This means that a simple association pattern between two phenomena does not inform us on the directionality of this relationship; this could be the result of other intervening factors, also called confounding variables (see MULTI-CAUSALITY AND EQUI-FINALITY). However, little guidance is generally offered to students on how to test for causality in their research.

This lack of guidance is due to the polymorphous nature of causation. The way to define and observe causal relationships has always been at the heart of harsh academic debates in social as well as natural sciences. Drawing on distinctive ontological and epistemological standpoints (see EPISTEMOLOGY and ONTOLOGY), at least four different understandings of causation have emerged in political science. Most authors have adopted a correlational-probabilistic understanding of causation (Brady 2008), but some have preferred a configurational one (Mahoney 2008), while others have adopted a mechanistic or even a counterfactual understanding.

According to the correlational perspective, 'two events are causally related when they are contiguous, one precedes another, and they occur regularly in constant conjunction with one another' (Brady 2008). From a configurational perspective, causation is a complex combination of necessary and/or sufficient conditions for a given outcome (Mahoney 2008). A cause may therefore be an 'insufficient but necessary part of a condition which is itself unnecessary but sufficient for the result' (Mackie 1965: 246).

From a mechanistic perspective, 'two events are causally connected if and only if they are connected by an underlying [. . .] mechanism of the appropriate sort' (Williamson 2011: 421). This perspective shifts the focus from why certain things happen, to how they are produced by these mechanisms. Finally, from the counterfactual perspective, a causal chain is defined as a sequence of counterfactually dependent events. This means that the counterfactual perspective considers the causal nexus as the sequence of events that would have occurred if one initial event had not taken place. These different understandings of causation lead to different research designs.

Over the last few decades, scholars have sought to find a common ground to theorize causation. However, this entry shows that the gap between the quantitative and qualitative research designs is still wide. To illustrate the concrete methodological challenges generated by this theoretical pluralism, this entry discusses how scholars have dealt with causality to explain the impact of European integration on domestic policies and institutions.

TRACING THE DEBATE ON CAUSALITY IN POLITICAL SCIENCE

The lowest common denominator of causality definitions is the idea that causation implies a certain pattern of regularity. This conceptual link between 'causal relationship' and 'regularity' finds its origins in an ontological-epistemological debate. On the one hand, the Humean 'inferential-empiricist' tradition assumes causality to emerge from the existence of an observable constant conjunction between VARIABLES sharing spatial and temporal proximity in a precise sequence. On the other, the 'a priori-rational' tradition considers causality as the result of rational claims on the conditions creating a relationship between causes and effects. While correlational and configurational definitions of causality stem from the 'empiricist' perspective, counterfactual and mechanistic approaches stem from the 'rational' perspective. The first perspective has been privileged in quantitative research designs and focuses on regularity of associations between events. The second perspective has been privileged in qualitative research designs and focuses on the explanatory narratives behind some associations.

To trace the relative weight of the different perspectives on causality in political sciences a bibliometric network analysis of the publications on 'causality', 'causation', or 'causes' has been carried out (see LITERATURE REVIEW and SOCIAL NETWORK ANALYSIS). Figure 2 represents the 500 most frequently cited references dealing with causality in political science journals according to the Web of Science data set. Each circle represents a scientific publication, and the size of that circle is proportional to the reference's number of citations. Larger circles represent the most cited publications in the literature. A link between two circles means that the publications have at least three references in common. When co-citations between related articles are frequent, articles group graphically within a cluster.

As Figure 2 shows, there are at least four different clusters. A first cluster, in the upper left quadrant, represents the qualitative research design. Mechanistic and

FIGURE 2 Bibliometric network graph of the empirical literature dealing with causality in political science

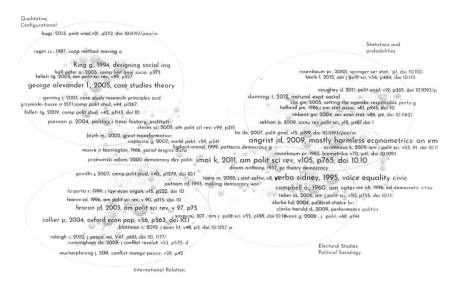

Source: Data set exported from the Web of Science database, including 500 documents matching with 'causality', 'causation', or 'causes' as keywords and their 2005 references. The reference list is available on request.
Note: Representation via VOS viewer.

counterfactual perspectives on causality are well represented in this cluster with publications such as Pierson (2004). Configurational conceptions of causality are also influential within this cluster, with Ragin (1987) (QUALITATIVE COMPARATIVE ANALYSIS) or King, Keohane, and Verba (1994a) and their attempt to develop a unified approach on causality.

A second cluster, in the upper right quadrant, represents the quantitative research design. Correlational and probabilistic definitions of causality are largely dominant in this cluster.

A third cluster, in the lower left quadrant, corresponds to the MIXED METHODS used to measure causality in international relations. Correlational definitions of causality remain largely dominant in this cluster with publications such as Fearon and Laitin (2003).

Finally, a fourth cluster, in the lower right quadrant, forms around causal claims made in electoral studies such as Verba et al. (1995). Correlational and probabilistic definitions of causality are also largely dominant in this cluster.

The structure of these clusters reflects the evolution of the discipline. With the rise of behavioralism in the 1950s the use of correlational and REGRESSION ANALYSIS have become more and more popular. Yet, the methodological debate on causality became more acute in the early 1990s after the publication of the book *Social Inquiry, Scientific Inference in Qualitative Research* (King, Keohane, and Verba 1994b). As Figure 2 shows, dialogue exists within and between these four clusters; however, it remains fairly limited. Quantitative and qualitative conceptions of causality do not cite each other much; there were only a few attempts to bridge the gap between the two research designs (Lijphart 1999). Similar patterns can be observed in the elaboration of research designs on Europeanization.

THE PARADIGMATIC CASE OF EUROPEANIZATION

Since the late 1990s, Europeanization has become a catch-all label for investigating all kinds of transformations allegedly induced by the economic and political unification of the European continent. Scholars from different disciplines have sought to explore the relationship between a cause (located at the EU level) and its effect (located at the domestic level). For instance, anthropologists have looked at the 'everyday experiences in interaction with the EU' and 'the EU interaction with local communities' (Borneman and Fowler 1997). Historians have studied the impact of European integration on the nation state. Sociologists have scrutinized the diffusion of norms and ideas in relation to policymaking in the EU. Political scientists have explored how the integration process reshapes domestic institutions and policies across time and space. Legal scholars have analysed the effects of the European integration through law, while economists have looked at the convergence of macroeconomic policies under the influence of the EU.

Considering that Europeanization is defined as the effect of EU integration, causality has been at the centre of various methodological discussions (Coman, Kostera, and Tomini 2014). To track it down, some scholars have followed correlational/configurational understandings of causality stemming from an 'empiricist' perspective; others have embraced 'rational' approaches. The former seek to show *the extent to which* the EU is relevant and to measure its impact. The latter cast doubt on the EU as the main driver of change and on the strength of its effect, seeking to examine *whether* and *how* it matters and, in so doing, to identify causal mechanisms at work. These different ways to deal with causality in the Europeanization literature are summarized in Table 1 and detailed below.

TABLE 1 Causality in research designs on Europeanization

Type of research question	Methods to trace causality
Does the EU generate change at the domestic level?	Descriptive inference
How much change does the EU generate?	Correlational analysis
Is the EU really the driver of change?	Counterfactual analysis
How does the EU drive change?	Causal mechanisms

At the centre of this literature lies the question of whether national institutions and policies converge as a result of the integration process. Drawing on descriptive inference, scholars have found evidence suggesting that the EU generates change at the domestic level. For example, Daniele Caramani (2015) observed ideological convergences among parties of the same families in Europe. Following a correlational understanding of causality, he concluded that the ideological convergence occurred because of the integration process. In contrast, other scholars have argued that there is little evidence to attest the existence of a causal relationship between European integration and change in party politics. Ladrech (2012: 577), for example, maintains that 'one must be extremely careful in reporting responsibility to an external stimulus—the EU—if the identified causal factor actually has its origins in domestic affairs'.

Aware of the dangers of overestimating the role of the EU, scholars have underlined the complexity of national convergence processes, arguing that more than one cause (see MULTI-CAUSALITY) may be operating at the same time. The impulse for change may find its origins at the EU, domestic, or international level. So how do we avoid miscalculating the EU impact considering that the same outcome can be caused by a combination of different independent VARIABLES (see EQUIFINALITY)? For example, to show the 'net impact' of the EU, Levi-Faur (2004) scrutinized policy change in twenty-eight countries, including EU member states, Latin American countries, and eight well-developed economies in the world (see CASE SELECTION). Comparing EU with non-EU members and integrating control cases, Levi-Faur (2004: 25) found that the major features of the liberalization would have been diffused to most EU member states even if the European Commission and other agents of Europeanization had not existed. Put differently, his study is an illustration of a counterfactual understanding of causality, which allows Europeanization to be distinguished from globalization.

Beyond descriptive, correlational, and counterfactual approaches to causality, in more recent years scholars have questioned *how* this process happens (PROCESS TRACING). In so doing, they have showed that the effects of European integration are shaped by interactions among actors located at different levels. What are the causal mechanisms at work? Is Europeanization produced by socialization or by strategic calculations? Or is it a combination of both? By tracing the process, scholars have tested alternative causal explanations of Europeanization; they showed how the independent VARIABLE produces change and, ultimately, they revealed how to avoid ENDOGENEITY problems, that is situations when the direction of causality is ambiguous.

Research on Europeanization has exposed scholars to a wide range of methodological questions that can shed light on more general debates about causality and inspire researchers from other disciplines beyond EU studies. Overall, this entry shows that different understandings of causality coexist; although they are supported by distinctive sets of methodological assumptions, they complement each other in a comprehensive way.

REFERENCES

Almond, Gabriel and Sidney Verba. 1963. *The Civil Culture*. New York, Sage.

Borneman, John and Nick Fowler. 1997. 'Europeanization'. *Annual Review of Anthropology* 26(1): 487–514.

Brady, Henry E. 2008. 'Causation and Explanation in Social Science', in *The Oxford Handbook of Political Methodology*, ed. Jane M. Box-Steffensmeier, Henry E. Brady, and David Collier, 217–270. Oxford, Oxford University Press.

Caramani, Daniele. 2015. *The Europeanization of Politics: The Formation of a European Electorate and Party System in Historical Perspective*. Cambridge, Cambridge University Press.

Coffé, Hilde and Catherine Bolzendahl. 2010. 'Same Game, Different Rules? Gender Differences in Political Participation'. *Sex Roles* 62(5-6): 318-333.

Coman, Ramona, Thomas Kostera, and Luca Tomini (eds). 2014. *Europeanization and European Integration: From Incremental to Structural Change*. Basingstoke, Palgrave Macmillan.

Fearon, James and David Laitin. 2003 'Ethnicity, insurgency, and civil war.' *American Political Science Review* 97(1): 75-90.

King, Gary, Robert O. Keohane, and Sidney Verba. 1994a. 'Causality and Causal Inference', in *Social Inquiry: Scientific Inference in Qualitative Research*, 75-114. Princeton, NJ, Princeton University Press.

King, Gary, Robert O. Keohane, and Sidney Verba. 1994b. *Designing Social Inquiry: Scientific Inference in Qualitative Research*. Princeton, NJ, Princeton University Press.

Ladrech, Robert. 2012. *Europeanization and National Politics*. Basingstoke, Palgrave Macmillan.

Levi-Faur, David. 2004. 'On the "Net Impact" of Europeanization: The EU's Telecoms and Electricity Regimes between the Global and the National'. *Comparative Political Studies* 37(1): 3-29.

Lijphart, Arend. 1999. *Patterns of Democracy: Government Forms and Performance in Thirty-six Countries*. New Haven, CT, Yale University Press.

Mackie, J. L. 1965. 'Causes and Conditions'. *American Philosophical Quarterly* 2(4): 245-264.

Mahoney, J. 2008. 'Toward a Unified Theory of Causality'. *Comparative Political Studies* 41(4-5): 412-436.

Muller, Edward N. and Mitchell A. Seligson. 1994. 'Civic Culture and Democracy: The Question of Causal Relationships'. *American Political Science Review* 88(3): 635-652. doi:10.2307/2944800.

Norris, Pippa and Robert Inglehart. 2001. 'Women and Democracy: Cultural Obstacles to Equal Representation'. *Journal of Democracy* 12(3): 126-140.

Pierson, Paul. 2004. *Politics in Time: History, Institutions, and Social Analysis*. Princeton, NJ, Princeton University Press.

Ragin, Charles. 1987. *The Comparative Method*. Berkeley: University of California Press.

Verba, Sidney. 1995. *Voice and Equality*. Cambridge, Harvard University Press.

Williamson, Jon. 2011. 'Mechanistic Theories of Causality Part I'. *Philosophy Compass* 6(6): 421-432.

COMPARATIVE ANALYSIS

Céline C. Cocq, Université libre de Bruxelles & Université de Genève

&

Ora Szekely, Clark University

Comparative analysis holds a central place in social science research. It is simply defined as comparing and contrasting two or more phenomena in order to better understand them, or, as Lijphart (1971) describes it, 'a method of discovering empirical relationships among VARIABLES'. As an umbrella term, the 'comparative method' refers to a set of methodologies developed in many disciplines (e.g. sociology, political science, law) and subdisciplines (e.g. sociology of medicine or philosophy of law). Many of these research methods fall under the broader umbrella of comparative analysis, each of which may be more or less appropriate to particular RESEARCH QUESTIONS.

WHY COMPARE?

Comparative analysis can be useful in many different ways. While in the hard sciences it is possible to conduct experiments under controlled laboratory conditions, this is often impossible in social science. Social scientists must therefore find other ways of isolating and testing the impact of VARIABLES and understanding the relationships between them. Accordingly, the goal of comparative analysis is the comparison of phenomena—whether that means comparison within individual cases, among a small group of cases, or the analysis of large amounts of data—to identify key independent variable(s) and establish what link, if any, exists between them and the dependent variable(s).

Comparative analysis can also be useful in establishing the nature of that relationship, assessing whether it is necessary, sufficient, or both. And certain kinds of comparative analysis can be helpful in identifying the causal mechanism linking the variables, to establish a causal relationship and rule out mere correlation.

Furthermore, cross-case comparison allows social scientists to build broad theories that are applicable in different contexts. For instance, by comparing Nazism in Germany and Stalinism in the Soviet Union, Arendt (1973) developed a theory of the origins and nature of totalitarianism. It can also be a useful way of exploring why there are different answers to apparently similar questions, an instrument of harmonization between laws and policies, a way of highlighting the differences between cases, and a means of drawing connections between seemingly unrelated phenomena.

WHAT TO COMPARE: SELECTING CASES

The comparative method is useful at different stages in the research process, beginning with the formulation of the RESEARCH QUESTION, which can be arrived at by observing differences between cases. For instance, comparison of economic data over time might lead a researcher to ask 'why is this country wealthier than its neighbour?' At the next stage of the research process, the comparative method can also be used to generate testable HYPOTHESES, such as 'if a country is democratic for ten years, it will be wealthier than a country which has never been democratic'. And, once the hypotheses are formulated, comparative analysis can be helpful in guiding the research design.

This is particularly true with regard to CASE SELECTION. Unless they are examining the 'universe' of cases of a particular phenomenon (e.g. all voters in a particular election, all students at a particular university, or all countries in the United Nations), researchers will need to select specific cases to compare. J. S. Mill (1843) identified two approaches to doing so: the 'method of difference' and the 'method of agreement', also called 'most similar systems' and 'most different systems' designs. Under the most similar systems approach, selected cases are similar in all respects but one. To explain an outcome (the dependent VARIABLE) in one case, a researcher would select a comparison case similar in all aspects except for the outcome being measured. An example might be two countries which are both democracies, both relatively wealthy, about the same size (e.g. Canada and Australia) but which experience very different electoral results. Comparing cases which are generally similar makes it easier to identify other differences (potential independent variables) responsible for the variation on the dependent VARIABLE. Conversely, the 'most different systems' design involves selecting cases that are different in all ways but one, and seeking to isolate what they might have in common as a means of explaining that outcome. For instance, a sociologist trying to understand why one hundred 15-year-olds from very different economic and geographic backgrounds exhibit similar behaviour on social media might determine that what they have in common—age—is the independent variable responsible.

HOW TO COMPARE: METHODS OF ANALYSIS

The comparative method offers many ways of structuring an analysis. It might involve comparison within a single case (American foreign policy in the 1950s versus the 1980s); the structured, focused comparison of two cases (the law codes of England and France); comparison of a larger number of specific cases (a study of urban poverty in all the EU capital cities); or the analysis of large amounts of data using quantitative, or 'large-N', analysis (the impact of access to early childhood education on poverty) (see REGRESSION ANALYSIS).

Methodologies, and even the terms describing them, can differ substantially among different branches of the social sciences, or even within the same discipline. Comparative research in political science may focus on establishing generalized relationships between VARIABLES, or case-oriented relationships that seek to understand complex units (for further reading, see Dion 1998; George and Bennett 2005; King, Keohane, and Verba 1994). In comparative legal analysis, the methodology (scarcely developed in the literature), nature, and number of cases are mainly determined by the RESEARCH QUESTION. Legal analysis would rarely adopt a 'large-N' approach because this would establish generalization but lack precision. These distinctions can prove challenging in INTERDISCIPLINARY research.

Regardless of disciplinary differences, in general a comparative study analyses the broader principles and dynamics at work in the phenomenon being studied, rather than relying on simple description. For example, when comparing legislation in two countries, the researcher seeks to explain in detail not only that one country has more robust human rights protections than the other, but why this is so. They will need to carefully compare laws in each country, and analyse the mechanisms of enforcement and guarantees.

ADDITIONAL CONSIDERATIONS

1. Stay focused on the research objective

The HYPOTHESIS and RESEARCH QUESTION should drive the case selection and research design. Different kinds of research will require different kinds of comparisons. For instance, while comparative research in law may involve the study of different legal cases, or laws in different countries, comparison in political science may involve comparison of different UNITS OF ANALYSIS, like countries, militant groups, or individual voters.

2. Large-N vs qualitative research?

Quantitative and qualitative research each have their own distinct advantages (Della Porta 2008; Lijphart 1971). Quantitative research allows researchers to examine the full 'universe' of cases of a particular phenomenon (e.g. all of the voters in Great Britain), and provides a wider lens through which a given issue (e.g. changes in public attitudes about the curtailment of civil liberties in the name of fighting terrorism) can be analysed. It is also less vulnerable to selection bias than is qualitative research, and produces arguably more generalizable results. On the other hand, qualitative research is often able to generate more convincing and detailed causal arguments, as it is less vulnerable to charges of relying on correlation rather than CAUSATION. Many researchers combine these two comparative approaches through MIXED METHODS. This can mean using large-N analysis to identify a broad trend and complementing it with a CASE STUDY or interview data to establish the causal mechanism. For instance, to understand the influence of early childhood education on college graduation rates, a researcher might gather data on all the children in a given city over the course of twenty-five years to establish broad patterns. She could then select three different elementary schools to profile as case studies, comparing their curricula and student bodies, and complement this with interviews with teachers and former students.

3. Practical considerations

Practical considerations are also often a factor in the choice of research design. Facility with a language or detailed knowledge of a geographical area is often necessary for qualitative research, particularly in fields like anthropology and sociology. Research can be further complicated by the political or security conditions in the area being studied, access to visas, or other pragmatic barriers (see ETHICS IN RESEARCH). Conversely, quantitative research often requires advanced statistical skills and access to data sets that are not available to all researchers. Constructing these data sets in the first place can also require substantial resources (see REGRESSION ANALYSIS).

In addition, disciplinary factors can impact researchers' choices with regard to the use of the comparative method. For instance, legal doctrine is often nationally and territorially limited, and may determine what kind of argumentation is allowed and which jurisprudential view of legal sources and valid argumentation must be used. Finally, personal factors, including internal BIASES stemming from the researcher's own national background or personal experience, can also shape the use of comparative analysis in unexpected ways.

4. Lost in translation?

When material in different languages is being compared, this may be an important issue. For example, in the EU treaties, the word 'consistency' in English is translated as '*coherence*' in French, although, 'consistency' and 'coherence' in English have different meanings. Creating a multilingual research team can help with these issues.

FINAL THOUGHTS

Comparative analysis plays an important role in both academic and policy-related circles. It is a significant part of legal analysis, having a real impact on institutional and legal frameworks (e.g. evaluation of EU national legislation leading to harmonization), and plays an important role in anthropology, political science, history, psychology, sociology, and other social sciences.

REFERENCES

Arendt, Hannah. 1973. *The Origins of Totalitarianism*. Orlando, Harcourt Books.

Della Porta, Donatella and Michael Keating (eds). 2008. *Approaches and Methodologies in the Social Sciences: A Pluralist Perspective*. Cambridge, Cambridge University Press.

Dion, Douglas. 1998. 'Evidence and Inference in the Comparative Case Study'. *Comparative Politics* 30(2): 127–145.

George, Alexander L. and Andrew Bennett. 2005. *Case Studies and Theory Development in the Social Sciences*. London, MIT Press.

King, Gary, Robert Keohane, and Sidney Verba. 1994. *Designing Social Inquiry: Scientific Inference in Qualitative Research*. Princeton, NJ, Princeton University Press.

Lijphart, Arend. 1971. 'Comparative Politics and the Comparative Method'. *American Political Science Review* 65(3): 682–693.

Mill, John Stuart. 1843. *A System of Logic*.

CONCEPT CONSTRUCTION

Louis Bélanger & Pierre-Marc Daigneault, Université Laval

All social sciences research projects, be they qualitative or quantitative, are dependent on concepts. Research on 'how democracies lose small wars' (Merom 2003) will go nowhere without sound and relevant concepts of *democracy*, *lost war*, and *small war*. In this entry, we first explain what concepts are and why social scientists should be self-conscious in the way they use them. We then describe the methodology of concept construction and present three different ways to structure a concept. Finally, we provide criteria to evaluate the quality of the concepts we have built ourselves or borrowed from others.

WHAT ARE CONCEPTS? WHY DO THEY MATTER?

Although 'concept formation is often regarded as a distraction, a mere prelude to serious research that is given scarce attention' (Schedler 2011: 2), concepts are the essential building blocks of any social science inquiry. First, concepts are central to making valid descriptive inferences. Thus, to determine whether there is a trend towards legalization in international relations, we need a carefully constructed *legalization* concept (Bélanger and Fontaine-Skronski 2012). Second, concept construction is just as important for generating causal inferences (CAUSATION). For instance, to test the following HYPOTHESIS, 'the more cultural difference there is between disputants in an international crisis, the less likely they are to pursue mediation' (Inman et al. 2014: 691), Inman and her colleagues provide us with sophisticated concept constructions for the independent VARIABLE *cultural difference*, the dependent variable *mediation*, and for the UNIT OF ANALYSIS *international crisis*.

Concepts are the most basic units of thinking that we use to make sense of the world (Sartori 2009 [1984]). They are 'symbolic intermediaries between mind (as location of meaning) and the objective world (as location of reference)' (Schedler 2011: 4). Social science scholars inevitably engage in concept construction because the phenomena they study are multidimensional and not immediately observable. For example, we cannot apprehend *democracy*, *workfare*, or *anomie* directly with our senses, but only by connecting some empirical observations to our mental representations of these phenomena. No one has ever seen a *democracy* walking on the street, but scholars can see ballot boxes, read constitutions, count years of party dominance, and connect what they have thereby observed with a definition of what democracy is. Making this operation self-conscious and transparent is an essential requirement for sound scholarship.

There are two polar philosophical positions regarding concepts. For pure nominalists, concepts are definitional tools required to think in general terms and to communicate, but they remain superimposed by the mind on the objective world. For pure realists, concepts reflect properties of phenomena that exist in the objective world, independently of the mind. Most social scientists espouse a softer and more pragmatic version of realism. They build concepts trying to capture the core characteristics of the objects they study—'concepts [. . .] are theories about the fundamental constitutive elements of a phenomenon' (Goertz 2006: 5)—but they are under no illusion that these characteristics can be determined in a totally objective manner. Indeed, scholars will always have different views about what constitutes democracy, individual resilience, or organizational culture.

According to Sartori, inspired by Ogden and Richards, a concept has three components: *term* (the concept's name or label), *meaning* (its connotation/intension), and *referent* (its denotation/extension). The meaning of a concept, usually stated in a conceptual definition, consists of the characteristics (properties, attributes, dimensions, etc.) of this concept. The referent of a concept is the population of empirical objects to which the concept applies, 'the real-world counterparts (if existent) of the world in our head' (Sartori 2009 [1984]: 103). Concepts are 'data containers' that allow scholars to process facts into data and organize those according to conceptual categories (Sartori

1970). By specifying the properties of a concept, scholars can determine whether or not some 'things' meet the requirements to belong to the concept in question. On that matter, ideal-types are a specific type of concept, which represent the 'purest' form of a phenomenon, and do not—or are very unlikely to—correspond to any real-world instance (Goertz 2006: 83–88).

There are various approaches to working with concepts. In this entry, we essentially consider concepts to be analytical instruments that social scientists use to conduct theoretical and empirical investigations within a POSITIVIST or critical realist perspective. Other perspectives on concepts include Schaffer's (2016) interpretivist approach, which seeks to 'elucidate' how social science concepts vary in use in different contexts, how they relate to the meaning and use of concepts in lived practice, and how they are embedded in power relations.

THE METHODOLOGY OF CONCEPT CONSTRUCTION

Concept construction involves two basic operations beyond choosing a term to designate the concept: identifying the fundamental characteristics of the phenomenon of interest, and logically connecting these characteristics. First, selecting the essential attributes should be based on a review of earlier attempts at defining and operationalizing the concept. For instance, Daigneault and Jacob (2009) use as a starting point the dominant conceptualization of *participatory evaluation* and then reconstruct this concept using the tools put forward by Gerring (1999) and Goertz (2006). As Sartori (2009 [1984]) points out, scholars rarely build concepts from scratch, and one should talk of concept *re*construction rather than of concept construction. Indeed, they should avoid creating new concepts when adequate ones exist as this has deleterious consequences for effective communication between scholars and for scientific progress.

Goertz and Mahoney (2012) distinguish between two main approaches to determining which attributes should be included in a concept definition: an indicator-latent VARIABLE approach, and a semantic approach. Quantitative scholars generally use the indicator-latent variable approach as they proceed inductively from already measured variables to concepts. These scholars 'assume an unmeasured or latent variable and then seek to identify good indicators that have a causal relationship with the latent variable' (Goertz and Mahoney 2012: 206). For example, Koremenos uses regressions to construct a concept of *international treaty completeness* from 'variables thought to be related' to this phenomenon, like the complexity of the problem at hand or the length of the treaty (Koremenos 2013: 670). She proceeds in this way because '(a)bsent any strong theories on how to add and weight the various variables that supposedly measure completeness, using factor analysis to identify the latent variable seems preferable to any ad hoc construction' (*Idem*). Qualitative scholars, by contrast, generally use a deductive, semantic approach, which begins by theorizing a concept's fundamental attributes. Their primordial criterion for attributes' selection is ONTOLOGICAL: the properties must be essential for the phenomenon to be what it *is*. A case in point is Levy and Thompson (2010: 5), who first define *war* as 'sustained, coordinated violence between political organizations', and then proceed by theorizing how every single 'component part' of this definition—even the 'apparently innocuous word' *between* (Levy and Thompson 2010: 6)—contributes to make a war a *war*, and to distinguish it from other closely related phenomena.

Although the identification of a concept's fundamental attributes should be primarily guided by ONTOLOGY, Goertz (2006: 3–5) argues that scholars should also pay attention to how these attributes relate to the different causal mechanisms and HYPOTHESES that they or others want to study. For example, one can defend, on ontological grounds, a minimalist concept of democracy centred exclusively on attributes linked to electoral competition (Hollyer, Rosendorff, and Vreeland 2011). Yet, this minimalist concept of democracy could become problematic when used to test some hypotheses derived from democratic peace theory, because it does not include as a core attribute transparency, which is often involved in causal explanations linking democratic regimes to peaceful resolution of international crises. Using a maximalist concept of democracy, like *polyarchy* (Teorell et al. 2019), which includes freedom of expression and the availability of alternative sources of information as core dimensions, would solve this problem.

The next operation in concept construction involves determining a concept's structure, that is, how the attributes are logically connected (Goertz 2006). The 'classical', and often implicit, way to connect the component parts of a concept is the *necessary and sufficient* (NAS) model (Goertz 2006). Under this logic, all the attributes are individually necessary and jointly sufficient to include a specific real-world phenomenon in the category of events covered by the concept. The *war* concept discussed earlier is premised on this logic as all the stated constitutive elements are individually necessary and jointly sufficient conditions; that is, all the component parts must be present for a phenomenon to be classified as a war (Levy and Thompson 2010). Thus, violence must be both sustained *and* coordinated (not sustained *or* coordinated) to qualify as war. A logical implication of the NAS concept structure is that every essential attribute added to a concept's intension reduces its extension because it hardens conditions for membership, and vice versa, moving up and down on Sartori's (2009 [1984]) 'ladder of abstraction'.

An alternative to the NAS model is the *family resemblance* model (FAM) (Goertz 2006). In FAM, none of the constitutive elements of the concept acts as a singular necessary condition for inclusion; inclusion is rather conditioned by subsets of the selected criteria. FAM concept structures have been widely used for the classification of medical syndromes or mental disorders. For example, a concept of *borderline personality disorder* offers eight key diagnostic criteria (attributes). Membership in this concept requires any five of the eight criteria, therefore creating the possibility of ninety-three different subsets of sufficient conditions for reaching a positive diagnosis (Widiger and Frances 1985). Under the FAM logic, contrary to NAS, using more attributes increases the extension of the concept, since adding an attribute multiplies the number of subsets of criteria through which membership can be attained.

Hybrid concept structures that combine NAS and FAM logics are a third possibility. In hybrid structures, one or more of the attributes are considered necessary, but not sufficient conditions; sufficiency is achieved by combining the necessary attributes with a minimal number of non-necessary ones. A case in point is Bélanger and Fontaine-Skronski's (2012) tridimensional concept of *international legalization*: one dimension ('obligation') is necessary before the two others ('precision' and 'delegation') can contribute to the *legalization* of international institutions. Radial concepts follow a hybrid logic. They are characterized by a primary, prototypical concept from which secondary concepts derive their meaning. Primary and secondary concepts share at least one necessary attribute. For instance, we can conceptualize the primary concept of *democracy* as made up of three attributes—'effective political participation', 'limitation of state power', 'egalitarian socioeconomic outcomes'—of which the first is common to the secondary concepts of *participatory*, *liberal*, and *popular democracy*. No other attribute is required for *participatory democracy* but we need to add limitation of state power to have *liberal democracy* and egalitarian outcomes for *popular democracy*, respectively (Collier and Mahon 1993: 848–850).

EVALUATING CONCEPTS

Once we have formed a concept, we need to assess its value. Sartori's (2009 [1984]) two evaluation criteria for concepts are a useful starting point. The first is clarity, which means that there should be a one-to-one correspondence between the term and the meaning of a concept. Second, concepts must be precise and denotative, that is, it must be as straightforward as possible to judge to which real-world objects they apply. Scholars thus need to establish concept boundaries, determine the rules for concept membership, and decide what to do with borderline cases. Beyond (albeit partly overlapping with) these two minimal criteria, Gerring (1999) has proposed eight criteria to help scholars assess the trade-offs involved in concept construction: familiarity (to scholars and lay people), resonance (a term's cognitive appeal), parsimony (the shortness of a term and of its list of attributes), coherence (the logical consistency of the concept structure), differentiation (the distance between related concepts and instances), depth (number of accompanying characteristics of a concept's extension), theoretical utility (a concept's value within a wider field of inferences), and field utility (a concept's value within its semantic field).

Whether implicit or explicit, every conceptual decision that scholars make has significant implications with respect to a concept's intension, extension, and value for social science research. Scholars therefore need to be 'conscious thinkers' (Sartori 1970) with regard to the concepts they use.

REFERENCES

Bélanger, Louis and Kim Fontaine-Skronski. 2012. '"Legalization" in International Relations: A Conceptual Analysis'. *Social Science Information* 51(2): 238–262.

Collier, David and James E. Mahon. 1993. 'Conceptual "Stretching" Revisited: Adapting Categories in Comparative Analysis'. *American Political Science Review* 87(4): 845–855.

Daigneault, Pierre-Marc and Steve Jacob. 2009. 'Toward Accurate Measurement of Participation: Rethinking the Conceptualization and Operationalization of Participatory Evaluation'. *American Journal of Evaluation* 30(3): 330–348.

Gerring, John. 1999. 'What Makes a Concept Good? A Criterial Framework for Understanding Concept Formation in the Social Sciences'. *Polity* 31(3): 357-393.

Goertz, Gary. 2006. *Social Science Concepts: A User's Guide*. Princeton, NJ, Princeton University Press.

Goertz, Gary and James Mahoney. 2012. 'Concepts and Measurement: Ontology and Epistemology'. *Social Science Information* 51(2): 205-216.

Hollyer, James R., B. Peter Rosendorff, and James Raymond Vreeland. 2011. 'Democracy and Transparency'. *The Journal of Politics* 73(4): 1191-1205.

Inman, Molly, Roudabeh Kishi, Jonathan Wilkenfield, Michele Gelfand, and Elizabeth Salmon. 2014. 'Cultural Influences on Mediation in International Crises'. *Journal of Conflict Resolution* 58(4): 685-712.

Koremenos, Barbara. 2013. 'The Continent of International Law'. *Journal of Conflict Resolution* 57(4): 653-681.

Levy, Jack S. and William R. Thompson. 2010. *Causes of War*. Chichester, Wiley-Blackwell.

Merom, Gil. 2003. *How Democracies Lose Small Wars: State, Society, and the Failures of France in Algeria, Israel in Lebanon, and the United States in Vietnam*. Cambridge, Cambridge University Press.

Sartori, Giovanni. 1970. 'Concept Misformation in Comparative Politics'. *American Political Science Review* 64(4): 1033-1053.

Sartori, Giovanni. 2009 [1984]. 'Guidelines for Concept Analysis', in *Concepts and Methods in Social Science: The Tradition of Giovanni Sartori*, ed. David Collier and John Gerring, 97-150. London: Routledge.

Schaffer, Frederic C. 2016. *Elucidating Social Science Concepts: An Interpretivist Guide*. New York, Routledge.

Schedler, Andreas. 2011. 'Concept formation', in *International Encyclopedia of Political Science*, ed. Bertrand Badie, Dirk Berg-Schlosser, and Leonardo A. Morlino, 370-382. Thousand Oaks, CA, SAGE.

Teorell, Jan, Michael Coppedge, Staffan Lindberg, and Svend-Erik Skaaning. 2019. 'Measuring Polyarchy Around the Globe, 1900-2017'. *Studies in Comparative International Development* 54(1): 71-95.

Widiger, Thomas A. and Allen Frances. 1985. 'The DSM-III Personality Disorders: Perspectives from Psychology'. *Archives of General Psychiatry* 42(6): 615-623.

CONTENT ANALYSIS

On the Rise

Leeann Bass, Princeton University
Holli A. Semetko, Emory University

Content analysis is a social science research method that involves the systematic analysis of text, media, communication, or information. Harold Laswell's model of communication—'Who' says 'What' to 'Whom' in 'What Channel' and with 'What Effect?'—can be used to summarize content-based research. The source, the message, the receiver, the medium, and the influence of the message are all topics that have been studied using content analysis and in combination with other methods. Content analysis is often used to address **RESEARCH QUESTIONS** and **HYPOTHESES**. Ole Holsti (1969) described three areas of focus for content analysis—the 'antecedents' of the communication, the 'characteristics' of the communication, and the 'consequences of communication'.

Since Holsti (1969) discussed the uses and value of content analysis for the social sciences, this research method has been applied to projects across a wide array of disciplines. In the fields of public health, nursing, medicine, business, political science, communication science and other social sciences, for instance, content analysis has been used to study a range of topics. In organizational management and business operations, content analysis is often employed to study annual reports, mission statements, proxy statements, internal company documents, open-ended survey questions, trade press, interviews, and more (Duriau, Reger, and Pfarrer 2007).

Content analysis on the visibility or prominence of a topic or actor, along with valence or tone of the content, can be useful in addressing questions about changes in elite and mass opinion. For example, why did Gallup's 2018 global survey in 134 countries find that opinion about the US leadership had dropped 18 percentage points to an approval rate of only 30 per cent in January 2018, down from 48 per cent during the Obama administration (Ray 2018)? Content analysis of elite and mass media coverage of President Trump in 2017, when he pulled the US out of the Paris Accords on climate change, may help to answer this question. Many US companies—such as Apple, Google, Microsoft, Facebook, Target, Timberland, and Campbell's Soup—at least a dozen states and more than 200 city mayors, and over 1,200 leaders in US universities, businesses, state and local politics disagreed with President Trump and promised to uphold the Paris Accords (Domonoske 2017). Content analysis of leading media in various countries can reveal whether Trump and US businesses were equally prominent on this topic, or whether Trump dominated the coverage. It can show whether Trump's decision to pull the US out of the Paris Accords was the most prominent and negative issue in the news in 2017, or whether other issues were more prominent or more negative in various countries.

There are deductive and inductive approaches to content analysis. Two widely cited studies using content analysis take a deductive approach: using predefined categories and variables based on findings and best practices from prior research (Patterson 1994; Semetko and Valkenburg 2000). In *Out of Order*, Thomas Patterson (1994) presents evidence from content analysis of US presidential campaign news spanning three decades and including nine election campaigns from 1960 to 1992. Based on these data, he offers a bold and original critique of the news media's domination of America's political process. Patterson demonstrates: first, that whereas 'in the 1960s candidates received largely favorable news coverage', negative news far exceeded favourable news by 1988 and 1992 (Patterson 1994: 20); second, 'voters' opinions of the candidates' largely followed the news coverage and became more negative (Patterson 1994: 23); third, in the 1960s, election stories were frequently framed in the context of a policy schema but from 1972 onwards they were 'nearly always framed within the context of the game schema'—i.e. the horse race and polls (Patterson 1994: 74); and fourth, the tone of most campaign stories was set by 'words of partisan sources' in the 1960s, mainly the candidate themselves, but from the 1970s onwards it came to be set by the journalist preparing the story (Patterson 1994: 114). These are several of the conclusions from Patterson (1994), who shows the reader that as the space for politicians' statements declined, commentary by journalists came to dominate the focus of election campaign news, leaving little room for 'hard' news about policy while more room was taken by 'soft' news about strategy, the horse race, and opinion polls. In 'Framing European Politics', Semetko and Valkenburg (2000) drew on previous studies of framing to create new measures of five frames most commonly found in the news, then coded over 4,000 news items on a European heads of state meeting. They found that the attribution of responsibility and conflict frames were the most common news frames in reporting on European politics. These two studies provide examples of the steps involved in conducting a study based on content analysis, including: develop a codebook, code the text, test for intercoder reliability.

Studies taking an inductive approach to content analysis, by contrast, have an open view of the content, usually involve a small n sample, and are often based on a qualitative approach (see DEDUCTIVE, INDUCTIVE, AND RETRODUCTIVE REASONING). Such studies can be difficult to replicate, and are not designed for replication. By contrast, a deductive approach to content analysis identifies categories or VARIABLES for analysis and uses human coders or computers to select the sample, address questions about the texts, and score the information for a number of VARIABLES. The deductive approach can be easily replicated, usually involves a large n sample, and draws on pre-tested, valid measures.

Much has been written on methods and approaches to measuring reliability with human coders (Neuendorf 2017; Krippendorff 2013). Traditional content analysis uses human coders, whereas a variety of software has emerged that can be used to download and score or code vast amounts of textual news data, for example from websites, social media, and content search engines such as Factiva or LexisNexis. A dedicated software tool for such analysis is Wordstat, by Provalis Research, for example, which is designed to quickly extract and analyse information from large numbers of documents (https://provalisresearch.com/products/content-analysis-software/), and to create tables, word clouds, and graphics. R, which is open-source software, can also be used design the code needed to extract and mine data for keywords.

TRADITIONAL VERSUS COMPUTATIONAL: THE DEBATE

Zamith and Lewis (2015) identify key benefits and challenges associated with new computational social science tools such as text analysis. While automated methods provide greater transparency, remove data entry error, are faster, allow for easy adjustment to coding protocols, and are reliable, they are not without problems. For example, they are unable to identify irrelevant data automatically, resulting in data quality issues, they are ill-equipped to recognize complexity and nuance, and the measures they produce are commonly considered to be less valid than human-coded data. Despite these issues, Zamith and Lewis (2015) suggest combining computational tools with traditional content analysis to leverage the best features of both. They argue that researchers should use automated methods to gather, organize, and prepare data, as well as to extract simple structural quantities of interest and pre-populate in manual coding tools information which human coders can then use to score more complex quantities of interest—speeding up human coding while reducing data entry error. In this way, content analysis will be faster, more reproducible, transparent, and reliable, but will still be capable of coding complex concepts, resulting in more valid measures than can be achieved through automated methods alone.

Lacy, Watson, Riffe, and Lovejoy (2015) also argue that researchers must do more to establish accepted standards for content analysis research. Lacy et al. (2015) propose that the minimum standard scholars must follow is to provide explicit detail about all methodological decisions made in the course of a study. They highlight a number of challenges facing both traditional and computational content analysis, and suggest standards to ensure the replicability and validity of studies using this method. First, content analysts must disclose the procedure used to assemble their sample of documents, paying careful attention to search terms and databases used, and acknowledging the limitations of the type of sample they use, be it probability, purposive, or convenience. Second, content analysts should be transparent about all aspects of their coding protocol—i.e. the VARIABLES in the codebook and how each is defined, including the number of coders used, how they were trained, how coding disagreements were resolved, and whether variables were dropped due to intercoder reliability issues. Moreover, researchers must measure reliability in multiple ways, checking both intercoder reliability (agreement between two or more coders) and intracoder reliability (the researcher herself recoding the text). Lacy et al. (2015) also argue that studies should report at least two different reliability coefficients.

Taking a more extreme position than other authors, Lacy et al. (2015) argue that traditional content analysis and newer computational approaches are actually two distinct methods. They propose that computer-assisted methods should be termed 'algorithmic text analysis' to recognize that these approaches are not fully automated; the algorithms they deploy require human design. As these methods require unique pre-processing steps, produce data that manual coding could never produce (and cannot replicate many of the measures created using human coding), and do not possess a process for establishing the reliability of coding protocol, the authors suggest that scholars should not regard automated and manual content analysis techniques as different approaches to fulfilling the same research goal; rather they are distinct methods which require their own standards of best practice.

The use of content analysis has greatly expanded over the last decade as political scientists increasingly view text as data (Grimmer and Stewart 2013). However, the rapid rise in the popularity of computational text analysis methods has not yet yielded consensus on best practices. Similar to Zamith and Lewis (2015), Pashakhanlou (2017) proposes that researchers should combine traditional content analysis with automated approaches to perform 'fully integrated content analysis'. Manual or human-scored content analysis focuses on latent, often complex VARIABLES in order to answer 'how' and 'why' questions, providing rich and detailed interpretation, but scholars face challenges of time, costliness, and reliability. Computer-assisted, quantitative content analysis is concerned with manifest variables that answer 'what' questions in a fast, reliable manner that can be applied to massive quantities of data. By using automated methods to identify relevant documents and provide a quantitative overview, then manually reading texts closely to provide interpretation of latent meaning and context, researchers in international relations can harness the increased reliability of computer-assisted methods and the greater validity of manual coding.

Grimmer and Stewart (2013) provide a more optimistic view of the potential for applying AUTOMATED TEXT ANALYSIS methods to RESEARCH QUESTIONS in political science. Instead of relegating these methods to document identification and summary, Grimmer and Stewart (2013) identify two key research objectives that text analysis can address. The first uses classification tasks to partition a set of documents into different categories. Once categories are predetermined, the researcher can use supervised techniques that employ manual content coding to train computer algorithms. Researchers seeking to discover unknown categories can use unsupervised methods which leverage statistical models to partition documents based on rates of word co-occurrence. Second, text analysis can use political texts to place politicians or groups on ideological scales using both supervised and unsupervised methods, a task which is substantively very useful to political scientists.

Grimmer and Stewart (2013) highlight four principles of AUTOMATED TEXT ANALYSIS which they believe address many existing concerns with the use of these methods. First, the authors acknowledge that, similarly to how game theoretic models simplify and formalize theory (see FORMAL MODELLING), all quantitative models of text are wrong. It is impossible to capture the richness and complexity of language in a statistical representation of text; however, some models simplify language in useful and meaningful ways. The authors urge consumers of research employing these methods to determine whether the techniques help perform a social scientific task, rather than perfectly represent the data-generating process of language. Second, the authors caution that automated techniques will never replace close reading of texts; indeed, close reading is essential to create coding schemes and validate different types of automated models. Third, there is not a 'best' method of text analysis. The technique and model used depend heavily on the specific RESEARCH QUESTION at hand; therefore, much of the debate over the merits of certain models over others is misguided. Finally, careful and thorough validation is essential to establish that these tools are being properly applied. While researchers using supervised methods should show that automated coding can replicate manual coding, those employing unsupervised techniques must establish substantively that their output is measuring the intended concept.

Computational methods are useful for analysing massive amounts of data, with machines trained on a set of topic categories provided by the investigator. For example, in historical studies of how parliamentary speeches have changed over the past fifty to a hundred years, or for analysis of topic and sentiment in millions of social media posts, computational methods enable the investigator to tackle a much larger quantity of data. However, students need to obtain training if they aim to be capable of utilizing computational methods for their research.

Overall, content or textual analysis techniques continue to present great promise across the social sciences. Different fields should both draw on methods used in other subjects to move their own research agendas forward, and consider and address methodological concerns raised by other disciplines. Across fields, the paramount challenge facing all researchers using content analysis is to establish best practices, both for automated methods specifically, and for the integration of automated methods with traditional content analysis. Agreeing on and employing best practices may address some of the many concerns researchers raise with projects that rely more heavily on automated methods. The chief priority for those wishing to convince scholars across and within disciplines of the utility of automated methods is to establish commonly understood standards for validating the output of computer-assisted models. Researchers must pay attention to validity concerns and address them in ways that make sense substantively for their specific study. In so doing, social science scholars may begin to move beyond methodological debate and focus on the substantive merits of content analysis research.

With the growing influence and availability of the Internet, including the Internet of Things (IoT), which refers to the billions of machines, household items, and personal devices online, vast amounts of different types of data are continually becoming available from all sorts of sources online. These comprise what is described as **BIG DATA**, which, like visual media data, also present challenges to automated scoring or coding processes. However, problems with automation are likely to be addressed by advances in machine learning in the coming years.

REFERENCES

Domonoske, Camila. 2017. 'Mayors, Companies Vow to Act on Climate, even as US Leaves Paris Accord'. *National Public Radio (NPR)*, 5 June. Available at https://www.npr.org/sections/thetwo-way/2017/06/05/531603731/mayors-companies-vow-to-act-on-climate-even-as-u-s-leaves-paris-accord (Accessed 8 August 2020).

Duriau, Vincent, J. Rhonda, K. Reger, and Michael D. Pfarrer. 2007. 'A Content Analysis of the Content Analysis Literature in Organizational Studies: Research Themes, Data Sources, and Methodological Refinements'. *Organizational Research Methods* 10(1): 5–34.

Grimmer, Justin and Brandon M. Stewart. 2013. 'Text as Data: The Promise and Pitfalls of Automatic Content Analysis Methods for Political Texts'. *Political Analysis* 21(3): 267–297.

Holsti, Ole R. 1969. *Content Analysis for the Social Sciences and Humanities*. Reading, MA, Addison-Wesley.

Krippendorff, Klaus. 2013. *Content Analysis: An Introduction to Its Methodology*. Thousand Oaks, CA, SAGE Publishing.

Lacy, Stephen, Brendan R. Watson, Daniel Riffe, and Jennette Lovejoy. 2015. 'Issues and Best Practices in Content Analysis'. *Journalism and Mass Communication Quarterly* 92(4): 791–811.

Neuendorf, Kimberly A. 2017. *The Content Analysis Guidebook*. Thousand Oaks, CA, SAGE Publishing.

Pashakhanlou, Arash Heydarian. 2017. 'Fully Integrated Content Analysis in International Relations'. *International Relations* 31(4): 447–465.

Patterson, Thomas E. 1994. *Out of Order*. New York, Vintage.

Ray, Julie. 2018. 'World's Approval of US leadership drops to new low'. *Gallup*, 18 January. Available at https://news.gallup.com/poll/225761/world-approval-leadership-drops-new-low.aspx (Accessed 8 August 2020).

Semetko, Holli A. and Patti M. Valkenburg. 2000. 'Framing European Politics: A Content Analysis of Press and Television News'. *Journal of Communication* 50(2): 93–109.

Zamith, Rodrigo and Seth C. Lewis. 2015. 'Content Analysis and the Algorithmic Coder: What Computational Social Science Means for Traditional Modes of Media Analysis'. *Annals of the American Academy of Political and Social Science* 659(1): 307–318.

C

CONTEXTUAL ANALYSIS

Putting Research into Context

Auke Willems, London School of Economics

Contextual analysis examines the environment in which a given phenomenon operates. It is useful for identifying trends and topics within unstructured data (contexts). In a sense, contextual analysis helps create order out of chaos. It builds on the idea that a given act—which can be a simple comment about last night's football match or a complex statement about the current state of the geopolitical world order—has no meaning per se. In other words, these statements do not operate in a vacuum, but in an interconnected world: 'context matters' (Tilly and Goodin 2006). Hence, these statements have meaning when they are related to other events and/or acts (their relevant context). The main aim of contextual analysis is to assess when and how contexts shape a social phenomenon and vice versa. Contexts can be, inter alia, 'historical, institutional, cultural, demographic, technological, psychological, ideological, ontological, and epistemological' (Tilly and Goodin 2006).

However, this does not mean that context (always) matters. Contextual analysis can be contrasted with thinking of a *ceteris paribus* nature ('all other things being equal'). Indeed, 'covering laws', which are laws that apply irrespective of context, disregard the context.

A wide body of scholarship has developed on the topic of contextual analysis. This contribution aims to review the literature briefly and identify clues and themes relevant to the social sciences. For example, the phenomenon or act under examination may occur in the sphere of legal scholarship (Leyland 2012). When applied to legal research, contextual analysis considers the environment in which a legal principle, a law, or a case operates. This can be internal (in relation to the legal system), or external (comparative legal research, a regional or global approach). A further example is the study of groups within sociological literature (Iversen 1991). When studying the impact of a group on individuals that belong to the group, the focus may be on the group as a context for the individuals in that group. However, there are also situations where the group is not the context. A general claim about the impact of groups on the individual can be stated with a specific reference indicating that it may not always apply. These are just a few examples. Contextual analysis is used widely in social sciences, such as history, managerial and leadership studies, organizational theory, business studies, and political sciences.

HOW DO CONTEXTS MATTER?

Stating that contexts matter may appear obvious, given that both the historical and contemporary environments put an event, happening, or other social phenomenon into perspective. However, the relevant question for a researcher is 'how does context matter'? The context matters in different ways. For example, an inquiry into the causal relation (see also CAUSATION) between the context and the subject of study may be required. If a causal mechanism is established—i.e. what process caused a given outcome—we can start to establish the context parameters. These parameters set the relevant scope of the context under examination and filter out unnecessary information. Information not considered to have a causal link with the phenomenon in question is referred to as 'background noise'. Alternatively, there may be multiple layers of contexts with possible correlations. In other words, since contexts are not one-dimensional, a further examination of how factors are 'linked' within a context may be necessary. The question of layers is located within the sphere/scope of the study. In addition, the researcher may have to determine micro-macro factors (see LEVELS OF ANALYSIS). In the example of legal studies, different levels or claims of authority should be considered, such as national, regional (e.g. European Union Law), and international legal systems (e.g. United Nations). The legal scholar must determine which legal orders are relevant to answering the question at stake. If the question is a purely national concern, there is no need to assess the other 'levels'. For example, contextual analysis may be relevant to compare two national legal systems. This does not constitute a 'new' level, but an 'equal' level. Temporal (when) and locational (where) elements (Dahlberg 1983) should also be considered.

Determining the relevant context depends on the pertinence of a macro and/or micro approach. Macro-level factors include economic, demographic, and social factors. While sometimes highly relevant, they may be non-specific. For example, they could distract from the main research aim of a project that requires a specific micro approach. Despite the fact that certain macro factors arguably have universal relevance, a micro approach may be more appropriate if there is a specific research aim.

Tilly and Goodin (2006) sum this up clearly: 'In response to each big question of political science, we reply "It depends." Valid answers depend on the context in which the political processes under study occur.' The relevance of this statement goes beyond the field of political science. When various processes are described and explained systematically, (a variety of) contexts may have to be considered.

THE SELECTION OF CONTEXT FACTORS

Selecting the relevant context factors for a given research aim is complex. The researcher is faced with a large range of potentially relevant factors. As Paul 't Hart aptly stated in reference to leadership studies ('t Hart 2014: 219), researchers will follow their instincts and experience: 'economists will look for economic factors . . .; historical institutionalists will look for policy legacies, path dependencies for collective memory, and historical analogies; and rational choice institutionalists will look at rule-based strategic incentive structures for leaders assumed to be utility-maximizing cue-takers'. Ultimately, the researcher has considerable scope when it comes to determining which context factors should be taken into account. They can use their own experience and knowledge of the subject and the methodology at hand. However, certain comparisons are specious because unspecified contextual factors are too different. For example, comparative studies rarely combine contemporary and medieval cases because 'the contexts are too different'. In this sense, contextual analysis also calls for limitations and avoids broad trans-historical generalizations.

Most literature on contextual analysis is specific and tailored to particular areas of science. However, the main themes and difficulties outlined in this entry are transversal and apply to more specific social science disciplines. A researcher should select the relevant context factors in order to make sense of a specific phenomenon *within* its relevant context.

REFERENCES

Dahlberg, Kenneth. 1983. 'Contextual Analysis: Taking Space, Time, and Place Seriously'. *International Studies Quarterly* 27(3): 257–266.

Iversen, Gudmund. 1991. *Contextual Analysis*. London: SAGE Publications.

Leyland, Peter. 2012. *The Constitution of the United Kingdom: A Contextual Analysis*. Oxford, Hart Publishing.

'T Hart, Paul. 2014. 'Contextual Analysis', in *The Oxford Handbook of Political Leadership*, ed. R. Rhodes and Paul 't Hart, 210–224. Oxford, Oxford University Press.

Tilly, Charles and Robert Goodin. 2006. 'Introduction—It Depends', in *The Oxford Handbook of Contextual Political Analysis*, ed. Robert Goodin and Charles Tilly, 1–31. Oxford: Oxford University Press.

COUNTERFACTUAL ANALYSIS

Shunsuke Sato, Kokugakuin University

COUNTERFACTUALS: DEFINITION AND SIGNIFICANCE

'Cleopatra's nose: had it been shorter, the whole face of the world would have changed' is a typical counterfactual proposition. 'Counterfactual' is defined as a 'subjective conditional in which the antecedent is known or supposed for the purposes of argument to be false' (Tetlock and Belkin 1996: 4), or 'a "contrary to fact" conditional that identifies a "possible" or "alternative" world in which the antecedent did not actually occur' (Levy 2008). Social science scholars are often interested in studying counterfactual propositions, such as 'whether the end of the Cold War would have been significantly delayed without Gorbachev' or 'whether, without railways, the automobile would have been introduced fifty years earlier in nineteenth-century America'.

Counterfactual inference has been a major topic in methodological discussions in many disciplines such as political science, history, psychology, philosophy, and others. When social scientists attempt to assess HYPOTHESES about the causes of phenomena, counterfactual propositions generally play an important role. Particularly in qualitative small-N research designs, counterfactuals are indispensable tools for causal analysis because all causal statements imply some kind of counterfactual. The theoretical statement 'X causes Y' implies that if X's value were different, outcome Y would be different. Essentially, when scholars explain why a particular outcome Y occurred, they need to explain why Y happened, rather than other possible outcomes (Fearon 1991; see also CAUSATION). When scholars make a proposition that includes necessary conditions, they clarify counterfactual implications: a logical format of necessary conditions— 'if not X, then not Y'—directly expresses a counterfactual's consequent. Therefore, most social scientists inevitably use counterfactual analysis for various purposes.

HOW TO RESPOND TO THE 'FUNDAMENTAL PROBLEM OF CAUSAL INFERENCE'

Social scientists conducting causal analysis based on counterfactual methods are initially faced with the fundamental problem of causal inference: we cannot rerun history with a changed value of X. Therefore, we cannot directly observe the changed value of Y (on the same object) as a consequent of X's changed value. So how can we evaluate the validity of counterfactual propositions?

The answer depends on the research method and focus adopted. For Goertz and Mahoney (2012), scholars who adopt quantitative methods solve this problem by using large-N analysis. For instance, to answer the question, 'with some educational intervention, how much would a student's test performance have improved', scholars can use average causal effects of the intervention computed from large-N data (see Holland 2015). However, estimated average effects are thus calculated without the aid of counterfactual analyses of that individual case.

Scholars adopting qualitative, small-N methods, however, address the problem by using existing generalization and detailed knowledge of cases to test the counterfactuals' validity. Since causal statements contain counterfactuals from the outset, the counterfactuals' validity depends on the validity of the original hypothesized causal statements. If we have evidence that the timing of the end of the Cold War would not have changed even if Gorbachev had not become the Soviet Union's leader, this would be counter-evidence to the counterfactual proposition that 'the end of the Cold War would have been significantly delayed without Gorbachev'. Therefore, to test counterfactuals' validity, we assess the causal statement's validity and demonstrate its robustness, drawing on general theories, principles, and laws, as well as empirical evidence and relevant data, knowledge, and historical facts. In practice, however, demonstrating the robustness of counterfactual arguments can be difficult. The following section suggests some criteria for constructing more plausible counterfactuals for use in such small-N qualitative studies.

CRITERIA FOR EVALUATING COUNTERFACTUAL ANALYSIS

To construct more persuasive and legitimate counterfactual arguments, it would be useful to apply the following criteria—(a) Clarity, (b) Plausibility of the Antecedent, and (c) the Conditional Plausibility of the Consequent—proposed by Levy (2008: 633).

(a) The first criterion, 'Clarity', refers to well-specified causal statements, including well-specified antecedents and consequents. Analysts should be particularly aware of the counterfactuals' consequents. To be testable, counterfactuals should be something more than 'the outcome would have been different'. (b) 'Plausibility of the Antecedent' is the second criterion for a valid counterfactual. It is useless to imagine unrealistic antecedents in assessing whether history might have been different. A counterfactual proposition is more robust in an alternative world almost identical to the real world, except for one VARIABLE. However, in a complex world, a change in one variable induces changes in other variables. Those changes could provoke a huge difference as a result of complex causal chains. Therefore, counterfactual analyses should make as little change as possible to the real world—this is termed the 'minimal rewrite of history' rule (Weber 1949; see also SCOPE CONDITIONS). (c) The Conditional Plausibility of the Consequent is also important. If we can specify an antecedent and a consequent, and if the specified antecedent is sufficiently plausible, the following question is raised: is the hypothesized causal linkage plausible or not? When the hypothesized causal mechanisms are supported by well-established theories and consistent with empirical evidence, the counterfactual's plausibility increases.

For instance, the counterfactual proposed by Lebow, 'without the assassination of Archduke Ferdinand, World War I would not have occurred', meets these criteria relatively well: (a) its causal statement is clear, and (b) its specified antecedent meets the rule of minimal rewrite. Although (c) the plausibility of the claimed causal linkage is contested, Lebow's conscious efforts to prove the linkage contributes to our understanding of this historical event (Lebow 2007).

Of course, the plausibility of counterfactuals is not always indispensable. Imaginative, 'miracle' counterfactuals are also sometimes useful for theory development (see Tetlok and Belkin 1996). However, we can never be sure what would have happened in an alternative world. Therefore, counterfactual analysis requires extreme caution, and every effort should be made to enhance its credibility because of its methodological advantages.

REFERENCES

Fearon, James. D. 1991. 'Counterfactuals and Hypothesis Testing in Political Science'. *World Politics* 43(2): 169-195.

Goertz, Gary and James Mahoney. 2012. 'Counterfactuals', in *A Tale of Two Cultures: Qualitative and Quantitative Research in the Social Sciences*, ed. Gary Goertz and James Mahoney, 115-126. Princeton, NJ and Oxford, Princeton University Press.

Holland, Paul W. 2015. 'Causal Counterfactuals in Social Science Research', in *International Encyclopedia of the Social & Behavioral Sciences*, 2nd edition, ed. James D. Wright, 251-254. Amsterdam, Elsevier.

Lebow, Richard N. 2007. 'Contingency, Catalysts and Nonlinear Change: The Origins of World War I', in *Explaining War and Peace: Case Studies and Necessary Condition Counterfactuals*, ed. Gary Goertz and Jack S. Levy, 85-112. New York, Routledge.

Levy, Jack S. 2008. 'Counterfactuals and Case Studies', in *The Oxford Handbook of Political Methodology*, ed. Janet M. Box-Steffensmeier, Henry E. Brady, and David Collier, 627-644. Oxford, Oxford University Press.

Tetlock, Philip and Aaron Belkin (eds). 1996. *Counterfactual Thought Experiments in World Politics: Logical, Methodological, and Psychological Perspectives*. Princeton, NJ, Princeton University Press.

Weber, Max. 1949. *The Methodology of the Social Sciences*. New York, Free Press.

C

COVARIANCE

A First Step in the Analysis of the Relationship between Two Variables

Virginie Van Ingelgom & Alban Versailles,
FRS-FNRS and University of Louvain

In social science research, we are often interested in the relationship between two different variables: inflation and unemployment, or national and European identities, or voter turnout and media coverage, for example. Relationship between variables is labelled as covariation both in qualitative and quantitative approaches.

On the one hand, in qualitative studies, and in particular in CASE STUDY methods, covariation is an analytical approach used alongside causal PROCESS TRACING and congruence analysis (Blatter and Blume 2008). In the co-variational approach, causal inferences are drawn based on observed covariation between causal factors (independent VARIABLES) and causal effects (dependent variables). In small-N studies, the control for other explaining variables that could influence the dependent variable is not done by statistical means, but researchers use a most similar comparative design as a means of control (see COMPARATIVE ANALYSIS). It is thus the thickness of qualitative analysis 'defined as multiple and diverse observations per case plus intensive reflection on the congruence/resemblance between concrete empirical observations and abstract theoretical concepts' (Blatter and Blume 2008: 317–318) that characterizes the study of covariation as a qualitative analytical approach. The relationship between two variables is theory-driven and not tested statistically.

On the other hand, when the type of data allows a quantitative approach, looking at the covariance constitutes a first step in the statistical analysis (Lynch 2013). The covariance is then a measure of linear association between two VARIABLES. If there is covariance, the two variables co-vary or, in other words, they vary together. For example, a strong sense of national identity paves the way to a feeling of European identity (Duchesne and Frognier 2008). The more a person feels national pride, the more she will feel European as well. The covariance in this case would be positive. (Note that there is also a statistical method called 'analysis of covariance' that should not be confused with the measure of covariance presented in this chapter.) It is thus a general linear model to test the effect of one or more categorical dependent variables on a continuous dependent variable, controlling for the effect of other continuous variables (covariates) (Wildt and Ahtola 1978).

The mathematical definition of the covariance of two random variables X and Y sums the product of X deviation from its mean with Y deviation from its mean. The formula is thus a measure of association between two variables.

$$cov(x, y) = \frac{\sum_{i=1}^{n}(x_i - \bar{x})(y_i - \bar{y})}{n - 1}$$

When two **VARIABLES** are perfectly independent, which means they are not related to each other, the covariance equals zero. When the covariance is positive, it means that as the value of one variable (X) increases, the value of the second variable (Y) increases as well. There is a positive relationship between them. When the covariance is negative, there is a negative relationship: an increase in the value of one variable (X) is related to a decrease in the value of the other variable (Y) (see Figure 3).

FIGURE 3 Illustration of relationship between hypothetical variables X and Y

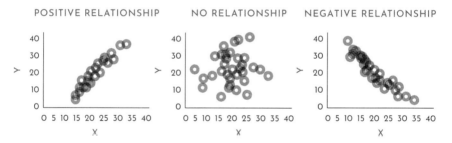

POSITIVE RELATIONSHIP   NO RELATIONSHIP   NEGATIVE RELATIONSHIP

On the methodological level, two important aspects need to be considered when mobilizing the measure of covariance. First, the value of the covariance depends on the scale of the **VARIABLES**. Therefore, there is no comparison possible between different relationships. The method to assess the strength of a relationship is the correlation. The coefficient of correlation (denoted r) is based on covariance but corrects the scale problem by dividing by the standard deviation of each variable.

$$r = \frac{\sum_{i=1}^{n}(x_i - \bar{x})(y_i - \bar{y})/(n - 1)}{sd(x)sd(y)}$$

It is then possible to compare the strength of the relationship as the coefficient evolves between −1, a perfect negative relationship, and +1, a perfect positive relationship. In this regard, it is important to note that any relationship should be assessed for its strength, but also for its **STATISTICAL SIGNIFICANCE**.

Second, as for any other statistical test, the measure of covariance does not imply a causal relationship. Indeed, the observation of covariance—either positive or negative—between two **VARIABLES** does not allow one to argue that X causes Y. For instance, a positive covariation between national and European identities is not enough to argue that a stronger national identification causes a stronger European identification. In the same vein, covariation is not sufficient to rule out the existence of a third variable that is in fact playing a role in the relationship between the two variables at stake. That would then be called a spurious relationship. The well-known example of a spurious correlation can be seen by examining a city's ice cream sales. The sales of ice cream are highest when the rate of drownings in city swimming pools is highest. The two variables are thus correlated positively; they covariate. However, to assert that ice cream sales cause drowning, or vice versa, would be to imply a spurious relationship between the two variables, as in reality a heatwave may have caused both. Finally, it is important to note that no statistical test is sufficient to demonstrate causality, or **CAUSATION**. Such demonstration can only be made based on theory or previous studies.

As a conclusion, the covariance is either a comprehensive qualitative approach or the first step of a quantitative approach to the analysis of the relationship between two **VARIABLES**.

REFERENCES

Blatter, Joachim and Till Blume. 2008. 'In Search of Co-variance, Causal Mechanisms or Congruence? Towards a Plural Understanding of Case Studies'. *Swiss Political Science Review* 14(2): 315–356.

Duchesne, Sophie and André-Paul Frognier. 2008. 'National and European Identifications: A Dual Relationship'. *Comparative European Politics* 6(2): 143–168.

Lynch, Scott M. 2013. *Using Statistics in Social Research: A Concise Approach*. New York, Springer.

Wildt, Albert R. and Olli Ahtola. 1978. *Analysis of Covariance*. London, SAGE Publications.

CRITICAL REALISM

Uncovering the Shades of Grey

Dominik Giese, Universität Hamburg & University of Warwick
Jonathan Joseph, University of Bristol

The term *critical realism* refers to a philosophy of science connected to the broader approach of **SCIENTIFIC REALISM** and initially affiliated to the work of Roy Bhaskar and his book *A Realist Theory of Science* (1975). It must not be confused with political realism, or realist theories of International Relations, such as classical realism or neo-realism. In contrast to other philosophies of science, such as **POSITIVISM AND POST-POSITIVISM**, critical realism presents an alternative view on the questions of what is 'real' (see ONTOLOGY) and how one can generate scientific knowledge of the 'real' (see EPISTEMOLOGY). How you answer these questions has implications for how you study science and society. The critical realist answer starts by prioritizing the ontological question over the epistemological one, by asking: 'What must the world be like for science to be possible?' (Archer et al. 1998: 18).

C

WHAT IS 'REAL' FOR CRITICAL REALISTS?

Critical realism holds the key ONTOLOGICAL belief of SCIENTIFIC REALISM that there is a reality which exists independent of our knowledge and experience of it. This contrasts with interpretivist approaches which insist that we cannot distinguish between a real world and the understandings and interpretations that we have of it, and also the POSITIVIST view which reduces the world to that which can be directly experienced and measured. Critical realists posit that reality is more complex, and made up of more than the directly observable. More specifically, critical realism understands reality as 'stratified' and composed of three ontological domains, (1) the empirical, (2) the actual, and (3) the real: '[1] our experience of events in the world, [2] the events as such (of which we only experience a fraction) and [3] the deep dimension where one finds the generative mechanisms producing the events in the world' (Danermark, Ekström, and Karlsson 2002: 43). Here lies the basis for CAUSATION. This contrasts with the positivist reduction of causality to the constant conjunction of observed events.

For critical realists, scientists should move beyond merely studying sensory data based on experience and consider 'hidden' or 'unobservable' traits of reality, such as social structures. Because these are unobservable, critical realists give a more general definition of these as 'systems of human relationships among social positions' (Porpora 1989: 195). They might be broadly understood as such things as patriarchy, the family, or capitalism; however, more commonly, critical realists distinguish between *structure* as a general set of relationships and those more concrete entities which are *structured* such as actual families, firms, institutions, etc. Underlying structures can be grasped by attempting to uncover various powers, liabilities, and causal (generative) mechanisms. The purpose of scientific inquiry for critical realists is not only to explain the social structures and power relations in society, but also to aim for an emancipatory change of the status quo. Explanation often contains an immanent critique.

HOW DO CRITICAL REALISTS STUDY THE 'REAL'?

The previous discussion leads to an important epistemological conclusion highlighted by critical realism: 'all knowledge claims are socially embedded and dependent on the conceptual and linguistic categories we inherit' (Kurki 2006: 210). Where the natural scientist studies objects that are naturally produced but socially defined (e.g. a mineral such as gold), the social scientist studies objects that are both socially produced and socially defined (e.g. democratization). Social scientists, even more than natural scientists, are 'complicit' subjects to the objects they study, in as much as the objects of their study are subject to the social scientists. Because of this, all knowledge is fallible. The aim of research, therefore, is not to the 'Truth' or to obtain 'objectivity', since this would show naivety about the process of knowledge production, but to find better explanations of how things might be. Alongside ONTOLOGICAL realism about the real world and epistemic relativism about the knowledge we have of it, critical realists advocate judgemental rationalism. In contrast to postmodernism, which gives up on the idea of valid knowledge, critical realists believe that some explanations are better than others in accounting for how the world might be.

This carries over into methodology. Instead of prescribing one acceptable type of method for scientific inquiry, critical realists place importance on revealing causal mechanisms that affect the structures and power relations in society, while advocating for a methodologically pluralist approach. Explanatory adequacy is the basis on which theories and methods are chosen. Methods such as REGRESSION ANALYSIS, qualitative in-depth CASE STUDIES, or DISCOURSE ANALYSIS are all accepted as valid knowledge-producing techniques as long as they help unveil the complex structure underlying objects as well as their relations and processes in (social) reality. In addition, while critical realists study CAUSATION, they do not constrain themselves to explaining *either* how material factors *or* how discursive/ideational factors influence social reality—the former being the common object of research in POSITIVIST studies and the latter in post-positivist studies (Patomäki and Wight 2000). Instead, it is the character of the object of study, the purpose of investigation, as well as the explanatory interests of the researcher that determine which methods will allow for the generation of 'knowledge' about complex 'reality'. It is also worth noting that in reference to modes of inference, a critical realist's research design favours abduction and retroduction over deduction and induction (see DEDUCTIVE, INDUCTIVE, AND RETRODUCTIVE REASONING). This makes conceptual analysis a vital part of scientific explanation. For example, we may empirically examine human practices such as marriage or work practices, but we require conceptual abstraction to understand the underlying structures like capitalism and the nuclear family that these practices reproduce.

For an example of how critical realism is applied, see Bulmer and Joseph's (2016) analysis of European integration. Here they use the structure–agency argument to critique the instrumentalist and functionalist accounts of EU integration, suggesting that integration is the emergent outcome (at the EU level) of competing hegemonic projects located primarily at the domestic level. This provides a more socially stratified account of EU integration, suggesting that EU projects depend on (or indeed often lack) legitimacy among populations in the member states. The analysis also draws a distinction between the more manifest institutional structures of the EU, each with their own historical path dependencies, and the deeper underlying structures—global economy, demographic change, rationalities of governance—that interact with these institutional structures. The authors call their approach 'Critical Integration Theory', while acknowledging that this is underpinned by the ontological and epistemological arguments of critical realism.

For further information: Edwards, O'Mahoney, and Vincent (2014) provide an introductory guide for creating a research design using critical realism. For those interested in how critical realists study discourse, Banta (2012) provides a starting point. Essential readings on critical realism's philosophical underpinnings are summarized in Archer et al. (1998).

REFERENCES

Archer, Margaret, Roy Bhaskar, Andrew Collier, Tony Lawson, and Alan Norrie (eds). 1998. *Critical Realism: Essential Readings*. London, Routledge.

Banta, Benjamin R. 2012. 'Analysing Discourse as a Causal Mechanism'. *European Journal of International Relations* 19(2): 379–402.

Bhaskar, Roy. 1975. *A Realist Theory of Science*. Leeds, Leeds Books.

Bulmer, Simon and Jonathan Joseph. 2016. 'European Integration in Crisis? Of Supranational Integration, Hegemonic Projects and Domestic Politics'. *European Journal of International Relations* 22(4): 725–748.

Danermark, Berth, Mats Ekström, and Jan Ch. Karlsson. 2002. *Explaining Society: Critical Realism in the Social Sciences*. London, Routledge.

Edwards, Paul, Joe O'Mahoney, and Steve Vincent. 2014. *Studying Organizations Using Critical Realism: A Practical Guide*. Oxford, Oxford University Press.

Kurki, Milija. 2006. 'Causes of a Divided Discipline: Rethinking the Concepts of Cause in International Relations Theory'. *Review of International Studies* 32(2): 189–216.

Patomäki, Heikki and Colin Wight. 2000. 'After Post-positivism? The Promises of Critical Realism'. *International Studies Quarterly* 44(2): 213–237.

Porpora, Douglas V. 1989. 'Four Concepts of Social Structure'. *Journal for the Theory of Social Behaviour* 19(2): 195–211.

CROSS-SECTIONAL AND LONGITUDINAL STUDIES

Andrew Bell, University of Sheffield

Cross-sectional studies involve the analysis of usually quantitative data collected at a single snapshot in time. The UNIT OF OBSERVATION might be people or countries, and those are measured only once, all at approximately the same time.

In contrast, longitudinal studies (also referred to as repeated measures studies) involve analysis on multiple occasions over time, where the same individuals (or countries)—the panel—are measured on each occasion (Fitzmaurice, Laird, and Ware 2011). As such, the UNIT OF OBSERVATION is occasions, and there are multiple occasions/measures of each individual. A subcategory of longitudinal studies is *event-history/survival/duration* analysis, where the dependent VARIABLE is binary and the focus is on causes of changes between the two states of the outcome. Note that in comparison, TIME SERIES analysis typically involves fewer individuals (often only one) and a larger number of time points. Longitudinal data can be collected *prospectively*, where the study is designed before the data is collected, or *retrospectively*, where a study uses previously collected data sources.

A third type of study, situated in between longitudinal and cross-sectional studies, is *repeated cross-sectional* analysis, which involves the analysis of multiple cross-sectional data sets over time, and different individuals are measured in each wave of the survey. Here, the UNIT OF OBSERVATION is individuals, and there are multiple individuals measured in each survey wave (see SURVEY RESEARCH).

In both repeated cross-sectional and longitudinal studies, the data structures are inherently multilevel (Snijders and Bosker 2012: 247): occasions (level 1) in individuals (level 2) for longitudinal studies, and individuals (level 1) in survey waves (level 2) for repeated cross-sectional studies. The advantage of longitudinal analysis is that we can assess individual change and not just aggregate change. For example, we can consider the effect of an individual receiving a treatment on their health, rather than the effect of generally increasing the rate of a treatment across a sample or population.

Longitudinal data is, for the most part, more difficult to collect (since it requires multiple surveys and tracking of those being measured). However, there are advantages to longitudinal analysis in comparison to cross-sectional analysis. We can consider the effects of changes over time, and not just differences between groups of people at a static time point, which could have arisen for a myriad of reasons. With cross-sectional analysis, it is particularly difficult to be sure observed correlations are causal, as opposed to simply the result of differences between individuals (see CAUSATION). For instance, if one group of people receives a 'treatment' (whether a medical treatment, a new education policy, a change in legislation, or something else) and another does not, cross-sectional analysis cannot tell us whether differences between those two groups are a result of the treatment, or of some other difference between the two groups. Longitudinal analysis allows us to focus on the *change* experienced with the introduction of a treatment, or a change in another VARIABLE, compared to those that do not receive it.

In this sense, longitudinal analysis is a step towards an experiment (see EXPERIMENTS), in that associations that are the result of a change in a predictor VARIABLE can be differentiated from associations that are the result of individual variation, or reverse CAUSALITY (see ENDOGENEITY). Indeed, a randomized controlled experiment can be thought of as a type of longitudinal study (where individuals are measured at least twice, pre- and post-treatment). However, longitudinal methods are usually not controlled experiments, and do not necessarily control for all unobserved variables, in which case a causal interpretation would not be justified. In this situation, it is more difficult to know if differences seen are a result of changes in another variable.

In the absence of an experimental design, unobserved time-invariant (unchanging) differences can be controlled for in longitudinal studies by using a so-called 'fixed effects' model, or using a 'random effects' model that separates within- and between-individual effects (Bell and Jones 2015). While the former is more commonly used in some disciplines, the latter has several advantages, including being able to extend the model to allow varying relationships (random slopes) across individuals, and the inclusion of time-invariant variables. When analysing countries over time, for instance, one could see how the effects of explanatory variables are different in different countries, or the effect of non-changing country attributes (such as colonial history).

When cross-sectional time-invariant relationships are of interest, these can also be uncovered in longitudinal analyses. The multilevel structure of the data means relationships can be partitioned into longitudinal and cross-sectional components, allowing both to be analysed in a random effects model (Bell and Jones 2015). In contrast, by definition cross-sectional analysis can only consider cross-sectional relationships, and not relationships over time.

However, longitudinal analysis presents certain challenges:

- Most REGRESSION ANALYSIS assumes independent residuals, where each observation is unrelated to other observations once variables in the regression have been accounted for. But when data are longitudinal, it is usual for them to be temporally auto-correlated—sequential observations are more related than temporally distant observations (see TIME SERIES).

- Individuals can change over time as a result of being part of a panel (for example they can 'learn' how to answer questions, or drop out of the study). This can lead to artificial correlations between VARIABLES.

- Another challenge relates to the three ways in which people can change: age (as people get older, things change), period (as time passes people change), and cohorts (individuals of a certain generation are different from other generations). The three are exactly dependent on each other, meaning it is impossible to separate the effects of each without making strong assumptions about at least one (Bell and Jones 2013; Glenn 2005). Despite some claims to the contrary (e.g. Yang and Land 2013), it is now widely accepted that there is no statistical solution to this 'identification problem', and researchers must think carefully about the assumptions they are making in their statistical models (Bell 2021; Fienberg 2013). This is also a problem in repeated cross-sectional studies, and in cross-sectional studies where period is unvarying and age and cohort are exactly correlated.

As an example from my own work, consider a study of mental health in the UK (Bell 2014). I used the British Household Panel Survey, which follows a representative sample of around 10,000 people with yearly measurements of a range of VARIABLES from 1991 to 2008. I was interested, in particular, in how individuals' mental health changed on average over the course of their life. Thanks to the longitudinal nature of the data set, and using a random effects model, we were able to separate the effects of age and birth-cohort effects, which would have been impossible with cross-sectional data. We found that when we did this, on average mental health gets worse up to the age of 30, stabilizes, and then gets worse again into old age. We also found significant variation across the population, by looking at individual people's trajectories over the study period.

REFERENCES

Bell, Andrew. 2014. 'Life-course and Cohort Trajectories of Mental Health in the UK, 1991–2008—a Multilevel Age-period-cohort Analysis'. *Social Science & Medicine* 120: 21–30.

Bell, Andrew (ed). 2021. *Age, Period and Cohort Effects: Statistical Analysis and the Identification Problem*. Abingdon: Routledge.

Bell, Andrew and Kelvyn Jones. 2013. 'The Impossibility of Separating Age, Period and Cohort Effects'. *Social Science and Medicine* 93: 163–165.

Bell, Andrew and Kelvyn Jones. 2015. 'Explaining Fixed Effects: Random Effects Modelling of Time-Series Cross-Sectional and Panel Data'. *Political Science Research and Methods* 3(1): 133–153.

Fienberg, Stephen. 2013. 'Cohort Analysis' Unholy Quest: A Discussion'. *Demography* 50(6): 1981–1984.

Fitzmaurice, Garrette, Nan Laird, and James Ware. 2011. *Applied Longitudinal Analysis*, 2nd edition. Hoboken, NJ, Wiley-Interscience.

Glenn, Norval. 2005. *Cohort Analysis*, 2nd edition. London, SAGE Publications.

Snijders, Tom and Roel Bosker. 2012. *Multilevel Analysis: An Introduction to Basic and Advanced Multilevel Modelling*, 2nd edition. London, SAGE Publications.

Yang, Yang and Kenneth Land. 2013. *Age-Period-Cohort Analysis: New Models, Methods, and Empirical Applications*. Boca Raton, FL, CRC Press.

C

D

DEDUCTIVE, INDUCTIVE, AND RETRODUCTIVE REASONING

Dominik Giese, Universität Hamburg and University of Warwick
Kai-Uwe Schnapp, Universität Hamburg

Deduction, induction, and retroduction are three forms of reasoning that explain observations or develop new explanations from observations, by connecting sentences to a logical structure. Deduction explains individual occurrences of a phenomenon based on general sentences (laws) and respective circumstances. Induction derives general sentences (laws) from repeated observations of similar events. Retroduction, also often referred to as 'abduction',[1] is an educated guess about the likely explanation for an observation, which can then be tested. The purpose of applying these forms of reasoning to observational studies is to make logic an explicit tool that applies extant knowledge, or develops new knowledge. While deduction applies extant knowledge, induction and retroduction develop new knowledge.

THE STRUCTURE OF THE ARGUMENTS

The basic structure of all three forms of reasoning is derived from classical syllogisms (arguments), i.e. a structure in language that combines sentences (premises) to a conclusion. In classical syllogisms, if the argument is sound and the premises are true, the conclusion necessarily follows from the premises. From a rational POSITIVIST view, a premise is considered true if it constitutes a correct statement about reality, i.e. one that is empirically verified. However, of the three forms of reasoning, deduction is the only structurally sound form of argument. Consider the example 'plurality electoral systems lead to two-party systems'. This is the major premise or *praemissa maior* of the deductive argument, also referred to as a general sentence, rule, or law. 'The USA has a

---

[1] For more detail see Peirce (1992: 141).

plurality electoral system'[2] is the minor premise or *praemissa minor*, also known as the singular sentence or description of a situation. What follows from the major and minor premises is the *conclusio* or the conclusion of the argument: 'The USA has a two-party system'.

Given the deductive logical structure, if the two premises are true, the conclusion necessarily follows. As illustrated in our example, deduction does not produce new knowledge, but uses 'theories and **HYPOTHESES** to make empirical predictions, which are then routinely tested against data' (Seawright and Collier 2004: 284). In other words, it is a way of applying prior knowledge to finding an explanation for something that has happened (i.e. a two-party system) or is going to happen (i.e. an election). The deductive structure and its epistemological role have been discussed by Carl G. Hempel (e.g. Hempel 2007).

Induction and retroduction use similar structural elements, albeit in an order that violates the rules of formal logic. Instead of logical soundness, we gain a reasoning structure that helps us develop new knowledge. Using inductive reasoning constitutes observing several similar objects, which react in a similar way to given circumstances. From the reoccurrence of the similar reaction, we induce a general rule or law. Seawright and Collier define it as 'a method that employs data about specific cases to reach more general conclusions' (Seawright and Collier 2004: 291).

Let us now apply inductive reasoning to our example of electoral and party systems. If we observe a great number of countries with plurality electoral systems (minor premise above) that also have two-party systems (conclusion above), we can induce that there must be some general rule at work, which could be formulated as 'plurality electoral systems *regularly* lead to two-party systems' (major premise above). It is important to note that this inductive inference rests on an argument that is not in itself logically sound. The fact that all our observations so far show the same regularity does not and cannot imply that the consequence of a plurality electoral system can never be anything other than a two-party system—hence the emphasis on *regularly*. Nevertheless, we apply this type of reasoning as a way of deriving new general knowledge from repeated individual observations (Chalmers 1999).

Retroductive reasoning is similar to inductive reasoning in that it produces new knowledge or **HYPOTHESES**, which can then be subjected to empirical verification. Its use differs from induction in that we do not systematically collect observations of like objects in like circumstances. Instead, we observe individual occurrences of objects or processes in order to come up with the most probable explanations, which are based on these systematically collected observations, *as well as* on extant knowledge. Both are then used to develop a plausible explanation of some observed phenomenon. The formal structure of retroductive reasoning applied to our example would look like this: we know that plurality electoral systems lead to two-party systems (rule based on extant knowledge). We also know that the USA has a two-party system (observation).

---

[2] A plurality electoral system is one in which a voter may vote only for one candidate in his or her constituency. The candidate with the highest vote share (the plurality) is elected to the respective office, e.g. the parliamentary seat representing the constituency.

TABLE 2 Formal structure of deduction, induction, and retroduction

Deduction	Induction	Retroduction
Plurality electoral systems lead to two-party systems (major premise)	Countries A, B, C etc. have plurality electoral systems (observation)	The USA has a two-party system (observation)
The USA has a plurality electoral system (minor premise)	Countries A, B, C etc. have two-party systems (observation)	Plurality electoral systems lead to two-party systems (rule as extant knowledge)
Therefore: The USA has a two-party system (conclusion)	We observe the regularity that: Plurality electoral systems lead to two-party systems	It is plausible (but not necessary) to assume that: The USA has a plurality electoral system

We therefore conclude that it is plausible that the USA has a plurality electoral system. Again, this is not sound reasoning. There may be other regularities that produce two-party systems. But this is one plausible assumption that can now be tested. Another example to illustrate retroduction is the work of a detective, who identifies the most likely suspect of a crime based on systematically collected evidence (multiple observations), as well as extant knowledge about how things and people usually behave. However, under the rule of law, the detective then has to conjure evidence which indisputably proves that the suspect can be rightly convicted as the perpetrator of the crime. Most of the time the detective will use deductive logic to achieve this, e.g. using extant knowledge to prove that a shot cannot have been fired by Suspect A because the gunshot residue was found only on the coat of Suspect B. The process of finding out who is a worthwhile suspect for closer scrutiny involves a process of retroductive reasoning (see Peirce 1992: 141–142). Table 2 summarizes the above explanations.

EXAMPLES OF SCIENTIFIC WORK THAT APPLIES THE THREE FORMS OF REASONING

Applying any of the three forms of reasoning exclusively is a practical impossibility. The way social scientific research is usually conducted involves a combination of the three in an iterative process. Researchers rarely follow a pure deductive rule-testing approach. As they are interested in some repeatedly observed phenomena (induction), they will already have a hunch about a plausible explanation (retroduction), based on prior knowledge. This guides their rule-testing in a certain direction (and perhaps away from the original rule at hand). In what follows, we offer some examples of academic work that presents an application of deduction, induction, and retroduction in 'ideal-typical' situations.

For an ideal-typical example of deductive work we draw on a study of law-making in parliamentary democracies by Tsebelis (1999). By using 'veto player theory', Tsebelis derives a series of **HYPOTHESES** (premises) to be tested in a **REGRESSION** model on two data sets. First, he suggests that an increase in the number of veto players (e.g. number of parties in government) and in the ideological distance between them reduces the government's and parliament's ability to produce significant laws. Second, and in contrast, the production of significant laws increases with the duration of government and with 'an increase in the ideological difference between current and previous government' (Tsebelis 1999: 591). His empirical analysis verifies the validity of the premises. Tsebelis's work is a succinct example of deduction because he derives a series of premises from extant knowledge (veto player theory) and then rigorously tests them against the empirical record. Failure to shore up evidence in support of the premises would have provided a tentative **FALSIFICATION** of the theory.

Ideal-typical inductive work is only possible in the realm of the natural sciences, when scientists can conduct controlled observations using **EXPERIMENTATION** and repeatedly experience the behaviour of certain phenomena before making general statements about its regularity. Outside of experimental settings—i.e. in the social world—it is almost impossible to control intervening factors and experience a situation exactly as it happened once before. However, as an example, let us consider what came to be known as 'Duverger's Law' (Duverger 1951). Maurice Duverger, in his comparative study of party and electoral systems, observed that a plurality electoral system leads to a two-party system, whereas a proportional representation electoral system leads to a multi-party system (see footnote 2). The reason the former takes effect is derived from two assumptions: fusion and elimination. First, a plurality electoral system marginalizes weaker political parties, leading them to 'fuse' together and create alliances. Second, voters will be inclined to 'eliminate' weak parties by not voting for them because they have little chance of entering parliament. In contrast, a proportional representation system creates sufficient conditions to foster party development because parliamentary seats are allocated (sometimes with a threshold for the vote share received) according to the proportion of votes received by each party. This way, votes for small parties are not lost and there is less reason to fuse or eliminate. By studying multiple cases with repeated observations over time, Duverger inductively derived several general rules about voting and party systems that are still applied in empirical social science research today.

An ideal-typical example of retroduction can be illustrated through criminal trials, where prosecution and defence present the judge (and jury) with competing theories about a crime. Even evidence, such as a 'smoking gun', does not invariably prove that a suspect is guilty of a crime. The prosecution will have to retroduce a series of plausible propositions about the suspect's connection with the gun before it can be admitted as evidence in the trial. Beach and Pedersen (2016: 159) summarize this process succinctly: 'Propositions about evidence need to describe clearly both what observables are expected to be found and why the observables could in theory be evidence of the causal **HYPOTHESIS** being assessed. Actual evidence is then sought for each proposition and evaluated for whether it actually is what we predicted to find and whether we can trust it.' After the presentation of contradictory pieces of evidence by the defence, the judge will have to assess the relative weight in the direction of the supported proposition. However, this process does not usually work without deductive reasoning, i.e.

the application of known laws (of nature) to prove somebody guilty. This takes us back to the beginning of this section, where we emphasized that the exclusive use of one form of reasoning is a practical impossibility. In this last example on retroduction, we can see that this is true most of the time.

REFERENCES

Beach, Derek and Rasmus B. Pedersen. 2016. *Causal Case Study Methods*. Ann Arbor, University of Michigan Press.

Chalmers, Alan F. 1999. *What is That Thing Called Science?*, 3rd edition. New York, Open University Press.

Duverger, Maurice. 1951. *Political Parties: Their Organization and Activity in the Modern State*. New York, Wiley & Sons.

Hempel, Carl G. 2007. 'Laws and their Role in Scientific Explanation', in *Philosophy of Science: An Anthology*, ed. Marc Lange, 305-318. Malden, MA, Blackwell.

Peirce, Charles S. 1992. 'Reasoning and the Logic of Things', in *Reasoning and the Logic of Things: Charles Sanders Peirce*, ed. Kenneth L. Ketner, 103-288. Cambridge, MA, Harvard University Press.

Seawright, Jason and David Collier. 2004. 'Glossary', in *Rethinking Social Inquiry: Diverse Tools, Shared Standards*, ed. Henry E. Brady and David Collier, 273-313. Lanham, MD, Rowman & Littlefield.

Tsebelis, George. 1999. 'Veto Players and Law Production in Parliamentary Democracies: An Empirical Analysis'. *American Political Science Review* 93(3): 591-608.

DESCRIPTIVE, EXPLANATORY, AND INTERPRETIVE APPROACHES

Louis M. Imbeau, Université Laval
Sule Tomkinson, Université Laval
Yasmina Malki, National School of Public Administration

'Description', 'explanation', and 'interpretation' are distinct stages of the research process. Description makes the link between what is to be described and a concept and its empirical referent. It defines a way to understand empirical reality, as variations, significations, or processes. Description refers to the 'what' question, as the first step towards explanation. When it comes to answering the 'why' and 'how' questions, some social scientists differentiate between explanation and interpretation. For them, the aim of social sciences is to 'understand', that is, to uncover the meanings of individuals' or groups' actions through the interpretation of their beliefs and discourses, whereas the aim of natural sciences is to 'explain', that is, to establish CAUSALITY and general laws. We do not subscribe to this view. The approach presented here offers a broader perspective for the social sciences, advocating an explanatory pluralism that allows for a more ecumenical approach.

An explanation involves relating what is to be explained (the *explanandum*) to what explains (the *explanans*), thus making a social phenomenon intelligible. In this perspective, interpretation is just one form of explanation—i.e. it relates the explanandum to the explanans in a specific way. Such an explanatory pluralism engages us to concentrate on the ways an explanandum can be related to an explanans. Our discussion is guided by the work of the French sociologist Jean-Michel Berthelot (1990), whose enlightening book unfortunately has not been translated into English yet.

We may think of the ways an explanandum (**B**) can be related to an explanans (**A**) on two dimensions.

The first dimension refers to the exteriority of **B** vis-à-vis **A**: is **B** conceptually or empirically outside of **A**, or, equivalently, is the observation of **B** independent from the observation of **A**? If so, **B** is assumed to be outside of **A**; otherwise, **B** is assumed to be within **A**. For example, suppose you want to explain the recurrent fiscal deficits in industrialized countries as being due to the competing interests of the members of a government cabinet—what scholars call 'government fragmentation'. Fiscal deficit would be the explanandum (**B**), government fragmentation the explanans (**A**). **A → B**, or government fragmentation explains fiscal deficits. The observation of the two terms of the explanation would be separate, as you would 'observe' fiscal deficits by looking at the difference between public revenues and expenditures (**B**) and competing interests of cabinet members through their party affiliations (**A**). Hence **B** is outside of **A**. But alternatively, you might want to explain fiscal deficits (**B**) as being due to the role played by the state in the system of accumulation of wealth typical of capitalist societies (**A**). Through public spending and fiscal deficits, the state supports the accumulation process while maintaining social harmony. **A → B**, or the system of accumulation and legitimation explains the level of fiscal deficit, which is part of the system. Here, **B** is within **A**.

The second dimension refers to the nature of the relationship between **B** and **A** and to the way empirical reality is described. In line with Berthelot's thinking, we consider that any explanation in social research can be framed in one or a mix of three types: **B** *depends on* **A** (reality is described as variations), or **B** *means* **A** (reality is described as significations), or **B** *is the result of* **A** (reality is described as processes).

These two dimensions help identify six explanatory approaches (Table 3). Let us first look at the approaches assuming that **B** is outside of **A**.

TABLE 3 Explanatory pluralism: typology of approaches

How is reality described	Nature of the relationship between A and B	Exteriority of B vis-à-vis A	
		B is outside of A	B is within A
As variations	Dependence: B depends on A	Causal approaches	Functional approaches
As significations	Meaning: B means A	Hermeneutic approaches	Structural approaches
As processes	Outcome: B is the result of A	Actantial approaches	Dialectic approaches

Source: Adapted from Berthelot 1990.

In *causal approaches*, reality is described as variations between or within cases where **B** depends on **A**. These approaches are based on the classical notion of CAUSALITY where **B** is the effect, or the dependent VARIABLE, and **A** is the cause, or the independent variable, as in quantitative analysis (cf. COVARIANCE) or in QUALITATIVE COMPARATIVE ANALYSIS. A causal approach explains the characteristics of a social phenomenon by showing that they co-vary with the characteristics of another social phenomenon considered to be its cause. Kontopoulos and Perotti (1999), for example, find a significant positive relationship between the size of a government coalition and the level of fiscal deficits in twenty OECD countries over the 1960–1995 period. For them, the deficit level (**B**) is partly explained by government fragmentation (**A**).

We find HERMENEUTIC *approaches* when the **B**–**A** relationship is one of meaning and reality is described as significations. Here, **A** is a symbolic system (a language, an ideology, a vision of the world, etc.) of which **B** is an expression. This is the approach adopted by Maynard-Moody and Musheno (2003) in their analysis of the evaluation that front-line officers (police officers, teachers, and counsellors) make of citizens with whom these public servants come in contact. The authors collected and analysed everyday work stories from police officers, teachers, and social workers in order 'to uncover their judgements as they see them' (2003: 25) (cf. DEDUCTIVE, INDUCTIVE, AND RETRODUCTIVE REASONING). Trying to explain how these front-line workers make decisions concerning the citizens in front of them—who is exempted from a speeding ticket or who gets the extra help in their job search strategies, for example—(their explanandum), Maynard-Moody and Musheno show that these decisions correspond to the way these public servants size up citizens on the basis of their dominant, yet messy societal views of who is worthy or unworthy, which behaviour is good or bad, etc. (their explanans). Public servants' decisions signify a positive or negative judgement about the citizens they assess.

Finally, we have *actantial approaches* where the **B**–**A** relationship is one of outcome and reality is apprehended as process(es). Here, **B** is the result of the actions or choices of a set of actors and **A** is a system of actions—i.e. a set of actors and the consequences of their actions. For example, Velasco (1999) argued that the government budget is a resource that interest groups use to serve their objectives. According to the theory of the 'Tragedy of the commons', interest groups and their supporters in government overexploit this resource, i.e. they overspend, thus creating recurrent deficits. To explain **B** (recurrent deficits), Velasco shows that **B** is the result of a process involving a set of actors and their actions (**A**).

In the second column of Table 3, where **B** is within **A**, we find *functional approaches* when the relationship between **A** and **B** is one of dependence and reality is described as variations in a system. Here, **A** is a system where **B** is included. Typically, **B** is explained when it is shown to contribute to the equilibrium of a system through a feedback mechanism: the system generates **B**, which in turn contributes to modifying the system (cf. SYSTEM ANALYSIS). Aaron Wildavsky, for example, describes the budgetary process in the USA as a complex decision-making system designed to appropriate government spending to various ends. This system is characterized by a division of labour among participants. 'Administrative agencies act as advocates of increased expenditures, and central control organs [. . .] as guardians of the treasury' (Wildavsky 1975: 7). The efforts of the Minister of Health, for example, to increase her budget (**B**) are explained by the function she performs as a spender in the budgetary system (**A**). If she is ever appointed Minister of Finance, she will then try to limit health spending (**B**) so as to protect the integrity of the whole budget, a switch in position that will be explained by her new function as guardian in the system (**A**).

When the **B**–**A** relationship is one of meaning and reality is described as significations, we find *structural approaches*. **A** is a structure, or a network, in which 'the patterned relationships among multiple alters jointly affect network members' behaviour' (**B**) (Wellman 1997: 20) (cf. **SOCIAL NETWORK ANALYSIS**). The seminal work by Barrington Moore (1966) is a good example of this (structural) approach. Moore seeks to explain why some traditional agricultural societies developed into liberal democracies and others into fascism or communism (**B**). Examining the developmental trajectories of eight countries—Great Britain, France, the United States, China, Japan, India, Russia, and Germany—he shows that it is not the direct action or inaction of the bourgeoisie (**A1**) that explains the occurrence of liberal democracy or fascism, but rather the actual interaction between aristocrats, bourgeois, and peasants (**A2**). Moore uncovers the bourgeoisie's interrelationships with aristocrats and peasants which opened three paths to modernization via different revolutionary means.

Finally, we find *dialectic approaches* when the **B**–**A** relationship is one of outcome. **A** is a process in which a phenomenon engenders its opposite, the contradiction resulting in **B**, the outcome. In other words, this approach shows how a phenomenon (**B**) emerges from contradictory tensions and conflicts in a process extending over time (**A**). One finds an example of a dialectic approach in James O'Connor's analysis of what he calls the fiscal crisis of the American state, that is, 'this tendency for government expenditures to outrace revenues' (O'Connor 1973: 2). O'Connor explains the occurrence of budget deficits (**B**) by showing that they are the outcome of a contradictory process (**A**) of accumulation and legitimization. Through social capital expenses (i.e. expenditures required for a profitable private accumulation) the state supports the accumulation of wealth by one class (thesis). In order to prevent resistance from other classes and to create the conditions for social harmony, the state also indulges in social expenses (anti-thesis). Because of its limited revenues, the state accumulates fiscal deficits that further limit its spending capacity through debt service charges, thus creating a fiscal crisis (synthesis). 'The accumulation of social capital and social expenses is a contradictory process which creates tendencies toward economic, social, and political crises' (O'Connor 1973: 9).

These six explanatory approaches cover the field of social sciences in general and of political science in particular. Each attempt at explaining a social phenomenon is based on one, or often several, of these approaches. This is the essence of explanatory pluralism. There is more than one fruitful approach to relating an explanandum to an explanans. Accepting this premise opens the way, within each explanatory approach, to identifying the main threats to the validity or trustworthiness of our inferences and to developing the best procedures to address these threats.

REFERENCES

Berthelot, Jean-Michel. 1990. *L'intelligence du social: le pluralisme explicatif en sociologie.* Paris, Presses universitaires de France.

Kontopoulos, Yianos and Roberto Perotti. 1999. 'Government Fragmentation and Fiscal Policy Outcomes: Evidence from OECD Countries', in *Fiscal Institutions and Fiscal Performance*, ed. James M. Poterba and Jürgen von Hagen, 81–102. Chicago and London, University of Chicago Press.

Maynard-Moody, Steven and Michael Musheno. 2003. *Cops, Teachers, Counselors: Stories from the Front Lines of Public Service.* Ann Arbor, University of Michigan Press.

Moore, Barrington, Jr. 1966. *Social Origins of Dictatorship and Democracy.* New York, Penguin Books.

O'Connor, John. 1973. *The Fiscal Crisis of the State.* New York, St Martin's Press.

Velasco, Andrés. 1999. 'A Model of Endogenous Fiscal Deficits and Delayed Fiscal Reforms', in *Fiscal Institutions and Fiscal Performance*, ed. James. M. Poterba and Jürgen von Hagen, 37–57. Chicago and London, University of Chicago Press.

Wellman, Barry. 1997. 'Structural Analysis: From Method and Metaphor to Theory and Substance'. *Contemporary Studies in Sociology* 15: 19–61.

Wildavsky, Aaron. 1975. *Budgeting: A Comparative Theory of Budgetary Processes.* Boston and Toronto, Little, Brown & Company.

DETERMINISM, PREDICTIONS, AND PROBABILISM

Francois Dépelteau, Laurentian University

Determinism has been the predominant mode of perceiving the universe in modern sciences. The basic assumption is that any event is the effect of an external cause (see **CAUSATION**). Generally speaking, biological determinism focuses on the biological causes of events, whereas social sciences focus on the social causes.

Classical examples of social determinism include the sociological method proposed by E. Durkheim in *The Rules of the Sociological Method* and his study of the social causes of suicide. He proposed that social phenomena could be considered like societies, and social structures, institutions, and social currents as 'social things', which means they act as 'external' and 'constraining' social forces that exert pressure on all the individuals (Durkheim 2013). However, individuals react in different ways depending on their capacity to deal with social pressure. According to E. Durkheim (2013), social determinism can be seen at the social level, where suicide rates will be determined by the degree of social pressure. There are also some forms of economic determinism in several texts by Karl Marx, with claims that society's economic 'infrastructure' (a mode of production) determines politics and the dominant ideologies (Marx 2004; Marx and Engels 2002). This idea was developed later by structuro-Marxists, such as L. Althusser (1971) and N. Poulantzas (1978). T. Parsons (1971) developed another sociological deterministic theory, where social life is determined by the 'functional needs' of the 'social system' and a universal process of structural differentiation. In one way or another, individuals and groups are subject to the 'causal powers' of external social forces and have no 'free will'.

This mode of perceiving the social universe is typically associated with POSITIV-ISM and, more specifically, social naturalism—or the idea that there is no significant difference between social phenomena and natural phenomena (see EPISTEMOL-OGY). In this logic, it is assumed that social scientists can and should discover 'social laws'—or universal relations of CAUSALITY between a social cause and a social effect. For example, Durkheim (2013)claimed to have discovered that some suicides are the effects of social causes, such as the level of individual social integration. All individuals feel this pressure, but only the weakest actually kill themselves as a result. Marx (2004) affirmed that the history of any society is the effect of class struggles between a dominant class and a dominated class. Parsons (1971)wrote that the American society (which he assumed was the most developed) is the future of any society, since all societies are subject to a universal process of social differentiation. In his famous preface to the first German edition of *The Capital* (volume 1), Marx made a similar deterministic statement about the development of societies. He explained that the 'natural laws of capitalism' work 'with iron necessity towards inevitable results'. Therefore, 'the country that is more developed industrially only shows, to the less developed, the image of its own future' (Marx 2004).

Determinists in the social sciences were obviously impressed by the multiple successes of the natural sciences, and particularly by the theories of Isaac Newton in physics and Charles Darwin in biology. They too were looking for scientific laws, and believed that the discovery of social laws would help us make reliable predictions about social events and history. In sum, if we discover a social law or a universal relation of CAUSALITY (for example: 'low levels of social integration cause higher rates of suicide in a community'), we can predict related social events ('everything else being equal, if the level of social integration decreases in the community, the rate of suicide will increase'). Predictions derived from scientific laws are believed to help us control events ('assuming that the theory is valid, and everything else being equal, we know that if we manage to reinforce a low level of social integration in one community, then the rate of suicide will decrease'). This idea was exciting because it suggested that it was possible to improve society, by resolving social, political, and economic problems through applied social sciences. Legions of social scientists have tried to discover universal relations of CAUSALITY between external and constraining social, economic, and political forces and social, political, and economic effects, notably through the use of VARIABLE analysis.

Determinism in the social sciences has been criticized since its very beginning. We can identify five major critiques:

- In determinism, fluid and dynamic social phenomena are reified as if they were solid and rigid objects.
- Determinism is based on inadequate dualisms, as if the society (institution, social structure, culture, etc.) could be 'external' to the individuals that co-produce it.

- Individuals are treated like the dogs in Pavlov's behavioural **EXPERIMENTA-TIONS**, simply reacting to external stimuli as if they had no subjectivity. For example, symbolic interactionists reject this mode of perception, by insisting that human actions (unlike particles, gases, or plants) are linked to certain 'perceptions' of external objects and are not directly determined by the objects themselves (see **BEHAVIOURALISM**).

- Human beings also have a degree of reflexivity and 'agency', which is not the case for typical entities studied by the natural sciences. In other words, they have the capacity to act in different ways in relation to the typical social patterns or institutionalized behaviour found in a society.

- By denying or neglecting human 'agency', deterministic social scientists cannot explain social change.

In response to these critiques, many social scientists have adopted various forms of 'soft' determinism. It is generally accepted that human action is not simply determined by external forces. A distinction is made between correlations ($A \to B$) that always occur and correlations that occur frequently. Only the latter can be found in a human social universe. Therefore, a number of social scientists turn towards probabilistic determinism (one version of soft determinism), which is based on the general formula: 'A probabilistically causes B if A's occurrence increases the probability of B'.

Soft determinism is also present when social scientists seek more flexible and explicative 'social mechanisms', rather than strict 'social laws'; and/or when they study interactions between the 'causal powers' of social structures and people's 'agency', as if they were two interacting forces, like billiard balls. Here, social structures are still seen as determining external forces, but their 'causal powers' can be counteracted by human beings, if and when they use their 'agency' (typically, thanks to critical reflexivity).

There is another type of social theory that avoids any 'layered' social **ONTOLOGY** and focuses primarily or exclusively on interactions between social actors, rather than between social structures and people. This makes any type of social determinism and probabilistic logic irrelevant. Symbolic interactionism and ethnomethodology are classical examples. More recently, approaches of this type have been reformulated under the influence of **HERMENEUTICS** (King 2004), including Gabriel Tarde's sociology and the philosophy of Gilles Deleuze (Tonkonoff 2017) and a form of processual and relational sociology, often inspired by pragmatism (Dépelteau 2018). In these approaches, social predictions are not seen as necessary characteristics of social sciences.

REFERENCES

Althusser, Louis. 1971. 'Ideology and Ideological State Apparatuses', in *Lenin and Philosophy and Other Essays*, 86-98. New York, Monthly Review Press.

Dépelteau, François. 2018. *The Palgrave Handbook of Relational Sociology*. New York, Palgrave Macmillan.

Durkheim, Emile. 2013. *The Rules of the Sociological Method*. New York, Free Press.

King, Anthony. 2004. *The Structure of Social Theory*. London, Routledge.

Marx, Karl. 2004. *Capital: A Critique of Political Economy*. London, Penguin Classics.

Marx, Karl and Friedrich Engels. 2002. *The Communist Manifesto*. London, Penguin Classics.

Parsons, Talcott. 1971. *The System of Modern Societies*. Englewood Cliffs, NJ, Prentice Hall.

Poulantzas, Nicos. 1978. *Classes in Contemporary Capitalism*. New York, Verso.

Tonkonoff, Sergio. 2017. *From Tarde to Deleuze and Foucault: The Infinitesimal Revolution*. New York, Palgrave Macmillan.

DISCOURSE ANALYSIS

Breaking Down Ideational Boundaries in the Social Sciences

Elisa Narminio, Université libre de Bruxelles and Waseda University
Caterina Carta, Université Laval

FACTS DO NOT SPEAK FOR THEMSELVES

In linguistics, discourse is generally defined as a continuous expression of connected written or spoken language that is larger than a sentence. However, as a method in the social sciences, discourse analysis (DA) gave rise to diatribes about where to set the borders of discourse. As language constitutes the very entry point to the world, some discourse analysts argue that all that exists acquires meaning through language. Does this mean that discourse *constitutes* reality? Is there anything outside text and discourse? Or is discourse one among many means of social construction?

Scholars have addressed these questions differently. The intellectual evolution of DA tells the story of such differences. We can identify three main generations: the first stems from de Saussure's study of systems of signification, Edmund Husserl and Ludwig Wittgenstein's research on the role of reference and sense, and the work of structuralist anthropologist Claude Lévi-Strauss, who approached discourse as the study of systems of signification. The second generation finds its roots in Foucault's work and focuses on the relationship between power and knowledge. Foucault added a historicist twist to the study of discourse and dismissed the beliefs of certain variants of structuralism, which thought it was possible to apply some general methodological rules to the analysis of language (Foucault 1980). Finally, the third generation—premised on Derrida's expression 'there is nothing outside of text'—underscores the conflation of material and ideational components of social life within discourse.

The evolution of DA in social science thus unearths an ontological debate between 'realists' and 'nominalists' (see ONTOLOGY), that eventually reverberates in epistemological strategies (see EPISTEMOLOGY). Realists assume that reality has independent existence that is accessed through language, whereas nominalists suggest that history and society are not 'intelligible totalities . . . but contingent discursive fields that are interlaced by a plurality of logics' (Laclau and Mouffe 2001: 3), so much so that no reality can exist outside of language.

Hence, the ontological positioning of discourse analysts is key to understanding their approach to the agent/structure and text/context nexus in discourse. What counts is the link established between material and ideational components in the making of reality. To sum up, 'macro-architectural' perspectives on discourse focus on structural elements while 'micro-interactional' approaches are geared towards the analysis of utterance, enunciation, linguistics, and narration (Holzscheiter 2014). 'Discourse' is indeed an inherently social concept, distinct from narrative, utterance, text, language, architecture, or enunciation, yet encompassing all these concepts. Theoretical and terminological contestation thus characterizes the field.

As a working definition, which necessarily implies a radical simplification of the heterogeneity of the field, we suggest considering DA as the analysis of the broad semantic and symbolic fields within which social beings make sense of and represent the world around them, thus constantly absorbing, refuting, producing, and reproducing socially relevant meanings.

MOVING BEYOND POSITIVISM

If distinctive approaches to DA preclude us from offering clear-cut methodological guidelines, different discourse analysts share a refusal of POSITIVISM. DA was indeed a reaction to realist and neo-positivist orthodoxies and their attempt to approach the social world through the lens of 'scientism'. As with other critical approaches, during the late 1980s, DA emerged as a solid alternative to mainstream methodologies, prescribing a more HERMENEUTICAL role for the social sciences. The nexus between power and knowledge explains why the social sciences cannot be neutral. For instance, in the field of International Relations, the connotation of the international system as 'anarchic' has profoundly contributed to given representations of both interstate relations and the domestic environment—the former are portrayed as inherently chaotic and the latter as orderly, with the state executive holding the grip of the domestic order (Ashley 1988). The academic discourses of 'anarchy' and 'sovereignty' have thus concurred to structure the ways in which policymakers make sense of and react to the international and domestic environments.

DA helps to unveil the deeper truths that are (purposefully) hidden in both academic and social discourses. The power/knowledge nexus present in discourse helps shed light on what is *omitted* from both the semantic and the social field. For example, the passive construction 'a woman has been raped' conceals the agency of that crime: in other terms, the focus is on the victim and the crime, rather than the perpetrator. From the outset, it is therefore essential to define the perimeter of analysis, and be self-reflective on our own conceptual and theoretical standpoints. Below we present a versatile toolkit you can leverage to study discourse in the social sciences.

LANGUAGE AND ITS UNITS OF ANALYSIS

Discourse can be apprehended as a textual unit (see UNIT OF ANALYSIS), and approached through formal linguistic analysis. This requires attention to subject-predicate structures, grammar, semantics, narrative point of view, narrative progression, figures of speech, and the consequences that their use has on the processes of meaning-making. In this context, CONTENT ANALYSIS and AUTOMATED TEXT ANALYSIS serve a similar purpose, by favouring a quantitative, predominantly computer-assisted examination of textual occurrences.

DA leans towards an interpretive and qualitative-based approach, putting emphasis on both the context of enunciation and the performative power of words themselves. Linguistics therefore offers an organized approach to revealing how the social and semantic fields are co-constituted. The attention to textual analysis, tropes, and figures of speech characterizes, for instance, Fairclough and Wodak's critical discourse analysis (CDA) approach (Fairclough 2003; Wodak and Meyer 2009). CDA tries to analyse textual/contextual elements in parallel, as contiguous but separated social facts. From a slightly different perspective, Milliken (1999: 232–233) recalls the value of predicate analysis—i.e. the analysis of the verbs, adverbs, or adjectives that qualify the subject. Through implicit or explicit parallels, contrasts, comparisons, and images, predicate analysis of diplomatic documents reveals the labelling processes converging into material foreign policy relations between states. Predicate analysis shows the ways in which different countries are constructed either as subjects or objects, with varying attributes (rationality, emotivity, (in)dependence . . .), reflecting power relations in the socio-political arena.

Textual selection is key to performing DA and requires the definition of the scope of analysis, in social, historical, political, and linguistic terms. Since 'any utterance is a link in a very complexly organized chain of other utterances' (Bakhtin 1986: 69), it is also important to include a significant number of discourses emanating from different individuals or groups who are presumed to have authoritative voices on a given issue or hold diverging points of view on that same semantic domain. A linguistic analysis of discourse can serve to reveal, in Foucault's words, the 'dividing practices' (quoted in Dreyfus and Rabinow 1983: 208) at play in language, and the mechanisms that objectivize subjects by circumscribing them to a given linguistic-geographical-functional position (the speakers and the listeners, us and them, the good and the bad, the strong and the weak . . .).

THE SOCIAL PRODUCTIVITY AND
PERFORMATIVITY OF DISCOURSE

DA serves to examine the relations between discourse and materiality. Discourses can be interpreted as acting at the framing, performative, generative, or coordinative level. Some scholars emphasize everyday speech acts (Searle)—highlighting consensual social practices—and others focus on 'serious' speech acts of 'authorized' speakers (Foucault)—tapping into social conflicts. There is an overall consensus on the productivity of discourses. DA therefore aims to unveil the processes through which an elite's 'regime of truth' becomes common sense in a society. Tracing the discursive production of authorities, experts, and their networks helps uncover norm-construction through discourse, e.g. the semantic field that legitimizes the political and ethical system of authority and neutralizes possible resistance.

Teun Van Dijk (1991) has notably looked in parallel at discursive and contextual elements in order to uncover the production and reproduction of racism in elite and societal discourses. He suggested systematically analysing both subtle discursive derogation (e.g. from syntactic structures—like the use of active vs passive forms—to nominalization; from pronominal selection—like us vs them—to global (de)topicalization); and the contextual and social fabric in which such discourses are embedded (including the social functions that certain discourses perform and institutionalized forms of dominance).

A focus on argumentation—a systematic process of reasoning which draws on a hierarchical structure of semantic and schematic categories—helps guide empirical research. Thus, in his analysis of British tabloid editorials, Van Dijk examined the argumentation strategy of some episodes of police violence against ethnic minorities. He found that in particular the conservative press tended to minimize, if not ignore, police violence and unfavourable social conditions, and gave prominence to violence perpetrated by ethnic minorities and their problems of social adaptation. He also remarked that an overemphasis on certain characteristics of a perpetrator of a crime (e.g. emphasizing that the perpetrator is an immigrant, rather than a local) crucially contributes to our understanding of social facts.

Thus, retrieving the origins of a given discourse and its propagation is a method of DA, which allows us to uncover the politics of representation and framing deployed in response to dramatic events. Beyond the productivity of discourse, DA focuses on its performativity. Through words we do things in society (Austin 1962). For instance, the speech in which US President George W. Bush declared war on Iraq in 2003 *materialized* the war.

Hence, reality and discourse are co-constitutive. Meaning emerges from either discursive struggles or 'reasoned consensus' between the emitter and receiver of a discourse. Attention to both subject-positioning within discourse and the process through which meaning surfaces can help retrieve how a given understanding of reality emerges, by means of coercion, persuasion, or neutralization.

THE ROLE OF CONTEXT AND HISTORICAL CONTINGENCY

Context can be approached from either a linguistic or a social perspective. Certain perspectives on DA highlight that discourses acquire meaning only in discursive formations, that is, that literal meanings of given signs require attention to the context of elocution. The literal meanings of speech acts cannot be understood in isolation from other signs (see CONTEXT ANALYSIS). This begs attention to the autonomous realm of the statement itself.

Furthermore, discourse is embedded in social practices and comprises both linguistic and non-verbal data, such as body language, spatial disposition, physical appearance, touch, voice, gaze. Even biological states—e.g. being an infant or elder—are associated with attributes, which define their meaning in use beyond their face value.

Analysts interested in the social context of enunciation and reception are therefore attentive to polysemy in language, proceeding from a shared background of understandings. They take stock of the historical conditions that underpin our conceptualizations, be it the social-political environment, contemporary breaking news, or shared cultures. Depending on context, a statement on racial differences can indeed be an ironic joke ridiculing racist discourse by parodying it, or a blatant insult if the element of irony is lacking. A single statement acquires different meanings depending on context. This confronts us with the articulatory nature of social discourse: discourses are intrinsically open and constantly articulated and co-shaped in a dynamic and unstable relationship with other discourses. We study discourse as a meaning-making palimpsest that keeps being written and rewritten according to its historical and socio-political context.

'Discourse' therefore cannot be approached through a single, isolated, figurative or material text, but requires attention to the broader intertextual milieu. According to Kristeva (1986), studying a text is always an enquiry into its structuration, e.g. the process by which its structure came into being. This enquiry requires attention to both the horizontal (e.g. the relationship between the writing subject and the addressee) and vertical (e.g. the relation between one text and a wider corpus of texts or context) dimensions of the uttered word (Kristeva 1986: 36–37). This reflection suggests two further points. First, 'the meaning of a text is ... never fully given by the text itself but is always a product of other readings and interpretations' (Hansen 2006: 55). And second, no discourse exists in static isolation from others. Discourses develop dynamically in a constant intertextual relationship with one another.

Accordingly, two analytical strategies help set texts into context: intertextuality and interdiscursivity. These strategies prescribe respectively finding the relationship and interconnections between different texts and discourses. The analysis of corpora of texts and discourses is in this case triangulated with the analysis of material, non-discursive elements. Empirical analysis can therefore take into account four LEVELS OF ANALYSIS: the level of the text (or 'immediate language'); the intertextual and interdiscursive level (which highlights the relations among different utterances); the extralinguistic (social) level (or the 'context of situation'); and the broader socio-political and historical contexts (Wodak and Meyer 2009: 31).

CONCLUSION: ACCOUNTING FOR CHANGE

Discourse analysis conceives discourse as both an inescapable medium through which we make sense of, reproduce, or challenge reality, and an instrument of action, which social agents use to produce effects in society. Being concerned with questions of meaning, discourse analysis embeds the study of texts, images, and discourses in their living historical reality. Discourse analysis critically questions taken-for-granted assumptions in both the analysis and the making of politics. It has the merit to infer self-reflectivism into the social sciences and to question the neutrality of both scientific and social discourses.

To conclude, although there is of course a real, material world of objects independent of our knowledge, it is only through meaning-making that these objects become real to us. DA has often been perceived as either lacking testable theories and empirical analysis, as being too descriptive, or as having a limited causal explanatory power. However, these weaknesses do not take away from its core strength: the ability to seize the dynamic context of the socio-political realm. DA can indeed be applied in numerous contexts, stemming from different ontologies, either as the primary method or accompanying method of analysis. Long considered as competing with traditional approaches to International Relations, we argue that DA can be seen as a complementary way of studying not just patterns but processes. DA allows us to grapple with the changing nature of both political ideas and polity structures, by shedding light on the connection between structure/agency and material/ideational components of social reality. Like other methodologies, DA is not an exact science, and can only give partial—though crucial—insight into social phenomena.

REFERENCES

Ashley, Richard K. 1988. 'Untying the Sovereign State: A Double Reading of the Anarchy Problematique'. *Millennium: Journal of International Studies* 17(2): 227-262.

Austin, John L. 1962. *How to Do Things with Words: The William James Lectures Delivered at Harvard University in 1955*. Oxford, Clarendon Press.

Bakhtin, Michael M. 1986. *The Problem with Speech Genres: Speech Genres and Other Late Essays*. Austin, University of Texas Press.

Dreyfus, Hubert L. and Paul Rabinow. 1983. *Foucault: Beyond Structuralism and Hermeneutics*. Chicago, University of Chicago Press.

Fairclough, Norman. 2003. *Analysing Discourse: Textual Analysis for Social Research*. London, Routledge.

Foucault, Michel. 1980. *Power/Knowledge: Selected Interviews and Other Writings, 1972-1977*, ed. Colin Gordon. New York, Pantheon Books.

Hansen, Lene. 2006. *Security as Practice: Discourse Analysis and the Bosnian War*. London, Routledge.

Holzscheiter, Anna. 2014. 'Between Communicative Interaction and Structures of Signification: Discourse Theory and Analysis in International Relations'. *International Studies Perspectives* 15(2):142-162.

Kristeva, Julia. 1986. 'Word, Dialogue and Novel', in *The Kristeva Reader*, ed. Toril Moi, 34-61. New York, Columbia University Press.

Laclau, Ernesto and Chantal Mouffe. 2001. *Hegemony and Socialist Strategy*. London, Verso.

Milliken, Jennifer. 1999. 'The Study of Discourse in International Relations: A Critique of Research and Methods'. *European Journal of International Relations* 5(2): 225-254.

van Dijk, Teun A. 1991. *Racism and the Press*. London, Routledge.

Wodak, Ruth and Martin Meyer. 2009. *Methods of Critical Discourse Analysis*. London, SAGE Publications.

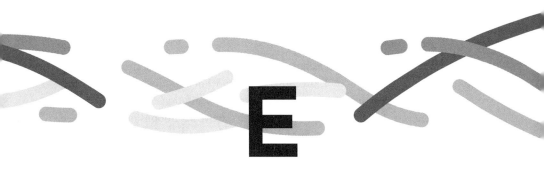

ENDOGENEITY: WHEN THE EFFECT INFLUENCES THE CAUSE

Elena Avramovska, Université libre de Bruxelles

Endogeneity is a problem of multidirectional CAUSALITY. Rather than identifying clear cause and effect relationships, social science research is often challenged by factors that mutually cause each other (Franzese 2007).

Causality patterns in social science research are inherently complex. Three prominent challenges contribute to undermining a simple cause and effect logic. One is multicausality, meaning that the outcomes we try to explain or predict have multiple causes (Franzese 2007; King, Keohane, and Verba 1994). The second is that the effects of an explanatory VARIABLE can depend on the values of one or more other potential factors in the context, commonly referred to as *context-conditionality*. However, the most challenging problem to empirical inference when trying to identify unidirectional, necessary, and sufficient causes is endogeneity. The endogeneity problem describes a problem of direction. Is the outcome we observe truly caused by the factor we claim is responsible, or could it be that the reverse is true? As the following examples show, many scholars have struggled with the direction of their arguments. The causes of such directional problems can sometimes be traced back to the omission of a factor or the lack of sufficient information.

The problem of direction is inherent even to one of the most prominent questions of political science: 'Do strong political institutions foster economic growth?' (Plumper 2011). It seems intuitive that broad and secure property rights and the rule of law foster steady economic development. Countries with weak property rights and rampant corruption have considerably lower economic growth than countries with strong institutions (Menaldo 2011). That seems to suggest that it is possible to establish a correlation between the cause (quality of institutions) and the effect (economic growth). However, what if the direction of CAUSALITY is wrong? The explanatory VARIABLE could be a consequence, rather than a cause of the dependent variable. Higher levels of economic development may in fact foster higher levels of institutional quality.

Overcoming this conundrum means overcoming the problem of endogeneity. It can sometimes be overcome by adding an exogenous instrumental VARIABLE (Menaldo

2011). Acemoglu, Johnson, and Robinson (2002) make an ingenious attempt at doing this and solving the question of direction. Their model defines the quality of institutions by how inclusive they are. They use two types of institutions: inclusive ones that provide citizens with rights and protection, and extractive institutions that are focused purely on the extraction of wealth for the powerful. Comparing the United States and Australia with India and Latin Americas, the authors trace the chicken and egg game between the quality of institutions and economic growth back to the early periods of European colonization. They focus on a factor that had not been considered previously: settler mortality. Hence, they claim that colonizing powers used different strategies for institutional development. Depending on the number of casualties they were facing in a specific geographical location due to diseases or political unrest, the settlers built different institutions on their arrival. According to the authors, the colonizers moved to countries with low settler mortality and built more inclusive institutions, as they saw a long-term perspective for themselves in countries that provided less hostile conditions. Extractive institutions, however, were formed in countries with high settler mortality, as very few colonizers wanted to move to these regions. Only the institutions established in the first case provided incentives conducive to long-term economic growth. The endogeneity problem was thus overcome by the authors. They show that the CAUSATION runs from institutional quality to economic development, and not vice versa.

A similar problem arises in another example. Schlozman, Verba, and Brady (2012) study why African Americans are more politically active than Latin Americans in the United States. One of the key explanatory variables they use is the attendance of religious services. Their theory expects that higher church attendance (independent VARIABLE) causes a higher degree of political participation (dependent VARIABLE). However, their HYPOTHESIS faces an endogeneity problem. It is equally plausible that the more politically active citizens are interested in church attendance in order to train in political skills such as public speaking, or use the church as a platform for political action. Thus, it is not clear if African Americans attend churches because they are already more politically active or if it is church attendance that politicizes them.

The authors approach this problem by splitting their explanatory factor (church attendance) into different traits, and argue that the church as an institution in fact has an impact on political participation in two ways. Firstly, it provides a training ground to attain political skills (e.g. public speaking). Secondly, it exposes attendees to political stimuli (e.g. through political speeches from a politicized clergy). Hence, it is clear that acquiring political skills needs to come before political action (therefore it is exogenous). However, with political stimuli the endogeneity problem remains. One might be more politically active because of political stimulation by a politicized clergy, but it would also be possible that more politically active churchgoers are likely to attend a church where they can hear political speeches.

Thus, by focusing only on the exogenous factor (acquisition of skills) they conclude that the levels of political participation are driven by a factor they did not study before: the organizational structure of the church. While most African Americans belong to Protestant churches—organized on a congregational basis—most Latin

Americans belong to Catholic churches, which are organized in a hierarchical way. Hierarchically organized churches decrease the chance for acquiring participatory civic skills in the first place. Hence, as Catholic Latin Americans have fewer opportunities to develop political skills in church, they end up being less politically active. In sum, the previous two examples show that the problem of endogeneity—or the problem of direction—can be overcome by adding a carefully selected set of new information. This can take place by adding new and exogenous explanatory factors or by reconceptualizing a **VARIABLE**, hence searching for truly exogenous elements.

As long as there is a chance that endogeneity exists, unbiased empirical findings are impossible. As the two examples in this entry have shown, finding solutions might require the researcher to trace processes over long historical periods or to reconsider the conceptualization of the variables in their models.

REFERENCES

Acemoglu, Daron, Simon Johnson, and James A. Robinson. 2002. 'Reversal of Fortune: Geography and Institutions in the Making of the Modern World Income Distribution'. *The Quarterly Journal of Economics* 117(4): 1231-1294.

Franzese, Robert J. 2007. 'Context Matters: The Challenge of Multicausality, Context-conditionality and Endogeneity for Empirical Evaluation of Positive Theory in Comparative Politics', in *The Oxford Handbook of Comparative Politics*, ed. Carles Boix and Susan C. Stokes, 28-72. Oxford, Oxford University Press.

King, Gary, Robert O. Keohane, and Sidney Verba. 1994. *Designing Social Inquiry: Scientific Inference in Qualitative Research*. Princeton, NJ, Princeton University Press.

Menaldo, Victor. 2011. *What is Endogeneity Bias and How Can We Address It?* University of Washington, Political Science. Available at http://faculty.washington.edu/vmenaldo/Stuff%20for%20Students/Endogeneity%20Bias.pdf (Accessed 8 August 2020).

Plumper, Thomas. 2011. 'Model Specification', in *International Encyclopaedia of Political Science*, ed. Bertrand Badie, 1595-1602. Thousand Oaks, CA, SAGE Publications.

Schlozman, Kay L., Sidney Verba, and Henry E. Brady. 2012. *The Unheavenly Chorus: Unequal Political Voice and the Broken Promise of American Democracy*. Princeton, NJ, Princeton University Press.

EPISTEMOLOGY

Gianfranco Pellegrino, LUISS Guido Carli di Roma

Epistemology is the discipline devoted to the study of knowledge and justified belief. Its main questions are: What are the necessary and sufficient conditions of knowledge? What are its sources? What is its structure, and what are its limits? How are we to understand the concept of 'justification'? What makes justified beliefs justified? Is validation internal or external to one's own mind? More broadly, epistemology concerns issues of the creation and dissemination of knowledge in particular fields of inquiry. Assuming that knowledge is distinguished from mere opinion for its being true—

a common assumption in epistemology—truth is also connected to epistemology. In the social sciences, epistemology is a source for methodological criteria employed in research, as well as for guidance on ontological issues—such as the existence of theoretical entities and the relationships between the social and the natural world.

Consider, for instance, a well-known debate in sociology of migration, about the so-called drivers of migration. According to some scholars, migratory decisions may be causally accounted for by socio-economic differences between origin and host countries, assuming that migrants are self-interested, rational agents. According to others, migratory behaviour is not deterministically predictable, as human action has no regularities. Indeed, migratory choices are often driven by ideas and values. This dichotomy refers to a broader divide—the divide between scholars who understand social sciences as positive, objective disciplines, according to the model of natural sciences, and scholars who understand social sciences as less precise, more humanistic disciplines, with a looser standard of objectivity. This divide refers in its turn to an even broader topic, namely the discussion about when and whether objective knowledge can be obtained in the social sciences, and on the very meaning of 'objectivity' and 'knowledge'. This topic belongs to the general field of epistemology.

GENERAL EPISTEMOLOGY

The standard view of the nature of knowledge—derived from Plato—is that knowledge is *justified true belief* (Plato 2004: 201d–210a). Plato thought that belief may be true or false, whereas knowledge is always true. A true belief becomes knowledge when it is justified. The three conditions—truth, belief, and justification—are individually necessary and jointly sufficient.

This view has been challenged by Edmund Gettier (Gettier 1963). Consider this case (found in Goldman 1976 but inspired from Gettier's): Henry drives through a rural area in which what appear to be barns are, with the exception of just one, merely barn facades. From the road Henry is driving on, these facades look exactly like real barns. Henry happens to be looking at the one and only real barn in the area and believes that there is a barn over there. Henry's belief is justified, because he has it in virtue of *evidence*, namely his visual experience (see *evidentialism* later in the chapter). Alternatively, one may say that Henry's belief is justified because it originates from a reliable cognitive process, namely vision (see *reliabilism* later in the chapter). Yet, Henry's belief is true only as a matter of luck. Therefore, it cannot be knowledge. Had Henry noticed one of the barn-facades instead, he would also have believed that there was a barn over there. Henry's belief is merely *accidentally* true. So a further element needs to be added to truth, belief, and justification, to have knowledge. This is the *Gettier problem* (Goldman 1976). Below, two theories about the further element needed to solve the Gettier problem are presented.

According to *evidentialism* or *mentalism* it is the possession of evidence—i.e. of a mental representation of *p* as being true—that gives justification (if the tree in front of you looks green to you, then you have evidence for believing that the tree in front of you is green). According to *reliabilism* a belief is justified if and only if its cognitive origins are reliable—i.e. it derives from processes that tend to produce true beliefs: processes such as perception, introspection, memory, and rational intuition. The emphasis is not on evidence, but on the origins of the mental processes producing it. Consider, for instance, the perceptual effects of external objects. For reliabilists, only sense organs whose capacity for producing true beliefs has been independently tested (for instance by third party testimony) are reliable sources of knowledge. In hallucinating observers, for instance, the organs of sight are unreliable because they produce in the hallucinating subject perceptions not shared by other qualified observers.

For evidentialism, if I am radically deceived on something (for instance, I have the ordinary perceptual experience of having hands, but I am simply a brain in a vat, with no hands, limbs, or torso, kept alive by mad scientists who give me the perceptual experience of having hands through nerve stimulation), I am wrong on what is actually my situation, but not on what I have justification in believing. For reliabilism, by contrast, in such cases I am wrong both on what is actually the case and on what I am justified in believing.

According to *foundationalism*, knowledge and justification are structured like a building, with a foundation and a superstructure. Justification starts from the foundation, which consists of *basic* justified beliefs—i.e. beliefs whose justification does not derive from other beliefs and whose justification is infallible, indubitable, or incorrigible. An example of basic justified beliefs would be perceptive beliefs about the felt appearances (for instance, the seen colours) of objects surrounding us, when our perceptive capacities are functioning well, or logical beliefs such as the non-contradiction principle. For foundationalists, non-basic beliefs get their justification from basic beliefs—i.e. from being derivable from them.

According to *coherentism*, knowledge and justification are like a web. There are no basic beliefs, and beliefs get their justification from their coherence with other beliefs—this coherence being understood as *explanatory* coherence. Explanatory coherence is the idea that a given belief being true better explains the obtaining of this and other beliefs (my belief that your hat is blue is explained by the fact that it actually is blue, and this explains the rest of my perceptual beliefs).

Rationalism is a view of knowledge where mentalism and coherentism are brought together. The main claim of rationalists is that knowledge is a matter of a priori beliefs (i.e. beliefs not originated from the outer world, such as logical or conceptual beliefs) and their internal coherence. Some rationalists believe that certain notions are inborn in humans, whereas others claim that they are constructed out of inborn reasoning capacities.

According to *correspondentism*, knowledge and justification are a matter of correspondence with an external reality. Beliefs are true when they represent accurately an external reality, and justification derives from the representational adherence between their content and external states of affairs. *Empiricism* is a version of correspondentism. The idea is that any knowledge derives from the outside reality impinging on human senses and on the working of the mind on the content it receives from perception of the external world.

According to *sceptics*, there are things we think we know but actually fail to know. Consider again the hypothesis of being a brain in a vat. This is a proposition that cannot be known to be either true or false, by its very definition. If you are a brain in a vat, you would probably believe that you are not, and this experience is indistinguishable from the one you would have if you were *not* a brain in a vat. You cannot establish whether or not you are a brain in a vat (the most you can know is that you are doubting being a brain in a vat or a real person). Sceptics claim that most of our ordinary knowledge is like the knowledge that we are not brains in vats.

E

EPISTEMOLOGY IN THE SOCIAL SCIENCES

Epistemology is directly relevant for the social sciences, in so far as the latter produce knowledge claims about the social world. A radical sceptical attitude—to the effect that any claim on knowable properties of people, societies, or organizations cannot be justified, or shown to be either true or false—would make any scientific social research pointless.

There are a number of specific epistemological issues in the social sciences. First, an issue arises in the general background of the philosophy of natural sciences. As pointed out earlier, for some authors, natural sciences provide the only valid model of objective knowledge, to be exported also within the social sciences. According to Auguste Comte's positivism, society, social groups, and human action, both individual and collective, can be experimentally and systematically studied, like non-human nature and physical matters (Comte 1896). Emile Durkheim partly endorsed Comte's positivism, regarding social facts as objects of empirical enquiry and sources of statistical generalization or systematic modelling (Durkheim 1982). Positivism has been rejected by Wilhelm Dilthey, who sharply distinguished natural sciences from *Geisteswissenschaften*—i.e. sciences of 'spirit' or 'mind', or 'human sciences', including social sciences in the latter category. According to Dilthey, human and social sciences do not yield knowledge, but 'understanding', that is, reflection on human and societal values, ideas, cultural constructs (Dilthey 1989). This view partly influenced Max Weber's claim that objectivity in the social sciences can, but should not, be influenced by evaluative commitments (Weber 1949).

More recently, the empiricist, positivist view has been overcome, and for a while Popper's fallibilism—the idea that there is no clear-cut distinction between data and theory, and that theories can only be disconfirmed, but not confirmed—prevailed (Popper 1959); see FALSIFICATION and POSITIVISM, POST-POSITIVISM, AND SOCIAL SCIENCE. More recently, post-modernist and anti-foundationalist accounts put forward a vision of the natural sciences as a succession of competing paradigms, often derived from power structure and narratives, with no grip with a supposedly objective reality (Kuhn 1962).

This has a direct impact on one's view of society and social entities as objects of knowledge. According to *social constructivism*, social entities are constructed—i.e. they derive from human subjects projecting human concepts and concerns onto their social world. Their constructed reality is a kind of reality, though. However, it is not accountable by natural sciences. According to *reductive realism*, social entities should be reduced to individual actions and natural entities, and whatever cannot be so reduced is to be dismissed as an object of scientific knowledge; see **METHODOLOGICAL INDIVIDUALISM** and **SCIENTIFIC REALISM**. Constructivists generally deny that social sciences can use each and every methodology used in natural sciences, whereas realists often believe that the same methodologies can be used in the two realms. In some forms of constructivism, such as in post-Popperian philosophies of science, social reality is constructed out of power relations (Foucault 1978; Searle 1995). *Reductive realists* or *naturalists* often prefer using quantitative methods—in which social behaviour is described exclusively through statistical generalizations, and only revealed preferences as displayed in explicit behaviour and surveys are admitted—or evolutionary psychology; see **BEHAVIOURISM**. Constructivists, by contrast, add to quantitative methodologies qualitative methods, which allow analyses of languages and discourses or of socially diffused ideas and ideologies.

REFERENCES

Comte, Auguste. 1896. *The Positive Philosophy of Auguste Comte*. London, G. Bell & Sons.
Dilthey, Wilhelm. 1989. *Introduction to the Human Sciences: Selected Works*. Princeton, NJ, Princeton University Press.
Durkheim, Emile. 1982. *Rules of Sociological Method*. New York, Free Press.
Foucault, Michel. 1978. *The History of Sexuality: An Introduction*, Volume I. New York, Pantheon.
Gettier, Edmund L. 1963. 'Is Justified True Belief Knowledge?' *Analysis* 23(6): 121-123.
Goldman, Alvin I. 1976. 'Discrimination and Perceptual Knowledge'. *The Journal of Philosophy* 73(20): 771-791.
Kuhn, Thomas. 1962. *The Structure of Scientific Revolutions*. Chicago, University of Chicago Press.
Plato. 2004. *Plato: Theaetetus*. Newburyport, MA, Focus.
Popper, Raimund. 1959. *The Logic of Scientific Discovery*. London, Hutchinson.
Searle, John. 1995. *The Construction of Social Reality*. New York, Free Press.
Weber, Max. 1949. *The Methodology of the Social Sciences*. Glencoe, Free Press.

ETHICS IN RESEARCH

Laurence Marquis, LUISS Guido Carli di Roma and Université Laval
Mark Daku, World Food Programme

Most research—wittingly or not—carries the risk of causing harm to its participants, and identifying, mitigating, and preventing this harm is integral to the research process. The question of what constitutes an ethical life has been discussed since long before Aristotle and Plato wrestled with it, but as researchers we face different questions: What constitutes ethical research? And what might constitute the ethical researcher?

Ethical research is important for several reasons. Ethics play an important role in scientific inquiry, beyond cases of plagiarism, fraud, and misconduct (Resnick 1996). Importantly, there is a difference between ethical research and ethical researchers. The case of Michael Lacour is instructive. His research on whether preferences for gay marriage were altered by interactions with gay canvassers was not ethically problematic. What was unethical was Michael Lacour himself, who fabricated data, constructed results, and leveraged these to gain a position at Princeton University (later rescinded). In short, we assert that there is a morally correct way to perform research, and that research can be morally acceptable. As such, the application of ethical standards to research circumscribes what we can learn about the world (EPISTEMOLOGY). In other words, what we can ethically investigate is necessarily limited: there are certain things that we cannot know, as to investigate them would be unethical.

Good examples of these limitations include the formal codes of ethical behaviour that emerged from the Nuremberg trials, which exposed horrific experiments on human subjects. Following World War II, military tribunals were tasked with the prosecution of members of the leadership in Nazi Germany. Fundamental to the development of international law (e.g. war crime, crimes against humanity), the Nuremberg trials also conducted the 'doctors' trials' and the judges' trials. In the doctors' trials, twenty doctors were accused of conducting EXPERIMENTATIONS on humans and of mass euthanasia. Of the twenty-three defendants, seven were acquitted, seven condemned to death, and the remainder sentenced to prison. The Nuremburg trials (and other research discussed in this chapter) contributed to the development of guidelines for ethical research. As noted, these guidelines, while necessary, put some areas of knowledge off limits to researchers (EPISTEMOLOGY).

COMMON PRINCIPLES OF ETHICS IN RESEARCH

While principles of ethics in research stem mostly from the biomedical field, they have also been adapted to apply to the social sciences. The application of biomedical protocols to social sciences, however, continues to be criticized. Published in 1979 in the United States by a group of scientists, physicians, ethicists, and philosophers, the Belmont Report established three primary principles for ethics in research: autonomy, beneficence, and justice. The American Association for Psychology, in comparison, structures its code of ethics around beneficence and non-maleficence, fidelity and responsibility, integrity, justice, and respect for people's rights and dignity. These principles are generally addressed through three common principles:

- voluntary participation
- informed consent
- confidentiality.

Voluntary Participation

The essence of this principle is to avoid harm, and as such voluntary participation in research ensures that subjects are not confined or captive. This has not always been the case, and past researchers have relied on captive subjects, often in prisons or universities (see the Stanford prison experiment or the Milgram experiment, discussed later). However, more egregious offences can occur when participants are not aware that they are actually participating in a study. For example, the Tuskegee Syphilis Study, conducted by the United States health service from 1932 to 1972, was designed to study the progression of untreated syphilis in rural African American men in Alabama, and presented as free health care services from the government. While it was discovered in 1947 that penicillin could treat the disease, no participants were treated or even informed they had the disease. In 1972, the experiment was halted and led to the United States enacting regulations to protect participants in clinical studies, requiring informed consent, communication of the diagnosis, and treatment. Another example is that of Facebook in 2014, which had experimented on its users without their consent by manipulating their newsfeeds in order to affect their emotions. While ostensibly more benign than the Tuskegee study, the potential influence that companies such as Facebook has over individuals—and countries—is enormous, and the ethical implications of involuntary corporate EXPERIMENTATION on a large scale are worthy of closer examination (see BIG DATA).

Informed Consent

Closely related to voluntary participation is the principle of informed consent, which ensures that a participant has full information and understanding of the research project and risks involved before, during, and after participation. For informed consent to be recognized, several components must be present, including disclosure, understanding, voluntariness, competence, consent, and exculpatory language (INTERVIEW TECHNIQUES; OBSERVATIONAL METHODS). Generally, researchers should not put human subjects in a situation where they risk harm, be it physical or psychological. Some exceptions to this principle may be allowed when risks are low vis-à-vis the potential gain. For example, in the Milgram experiment, subjects were asked to administer an electrical charge to another individual, who was in fact an actor. Participants were told that they were to obey the researcher at all times, regardless of what they heard. The vast majority of subjects delivered shocks that would have been fatal, despite begging and pleading from the actor supposedly receiving the charge. This experiment, widely used by Milgram to discuss obedience, heavily relied on its controversial ethical approach.

The principle of informed consent also assumes the competence of the participant to be able to consent—that the participant is of legal age, is not impeded by mental status, a disease, or an emergency. Often, informed consent is indicated by a signed document. However, subjects are not always literate, do not necessarily understand what is being consented to, and are not always in a position to consent voluntarily. For example, a farmer in Malawi dependent on support from an international organization cannot refuse consent to take part in a study if they think that it will affect their ability to secure future support. Signed informed consent is often not feasible (see OB-SERVATIONAL METHODS), and can be life-threatening to those involved, as when participants are engaged in illegal or dangerous behaviour. The reliance on signed documents of consent can bias ethics review boards (ERB), increasing the likelihood that research in literate, politically stable, and dominant-language speaking contexts will be approved at the expense of more complicated research. Researchers should be aware of methods to carry out research with marginalized populations ethically, such as getting consent via voice recordings, or marking an 'X' rather than signing one's name. Regardless, great care should be made to ensure that consent is explained in the participant's native language, despite the additional logistical challenge.

Confidentiality

Confidentiality and anonymity are principles designed to protect the privacy of the research subject, and they are fundamental to ensuring that subjects are able to exercise their autonomy and are shielded from potential psychological harm (Sieber 1992). Participants may also be subject to other harms, such as being fired from a job because their employer identifies the person who was making negative remarks about the company. Confidentiality is an integral part of protecting the rights of subjects. If it is to be broken, it must be done with good reason and the informed consent of all involved.

While these general principles provide guidelines by which to assess whether or not research is conducted ethically, no one situation is the same, and the correlation between the principles meant to protect the subjects from harm and the research objectives is never perfect. They are also not exhaustive.

PRINCIPLES FOLLOWED BY SUBJECTS AND RESEARCHERS

Researchers themselves must be wary of a number of other factors that can influence their project and role, such as the supervision of students, or other situations where there is a relationship of authority. Similarly, researchers must be careful not to make misrepresentations to subjects about the project or the related risks, or fail to disclose any conflict of interest. Researchers must take steps to ensure their neutrality so that no preconceptions or personal BIAS can risk influencing the results or subjects.

ETHICS REVIEW BOARDS

Research involving human subjects is rarely as ethically neutral as it may appear. Even simple research can cause unintended psychological, legal, and other harms or risks. In order to ensure that researchers and institutions are conducting ethically responsible research, ERBs are often consulted (Sales and Folkman 2000). As a university-affiliated researcher in North America, ERB approval is almost always necessary from one's university review board for research involving human subjects. Depending on where the research is taking place, there may also be other institutions that a researcher must gain approval from (e.g. both Uganda and Rwanda have country-level ethics boards that researchers must get approval from before conducting their research).

ERBs perform several functions. In addition to ensuring the research is ethically responsible, they also ensure that specific ethical considerations are made for vulnerable populations—like children—before approval is granted. ERBs are also a mechanism by which institutions can shield individuals (and the institutions themselves) from legal issues if something goes awry (Sales and Folkman 2000). This can be a problem in and of itself, as ERBs may tend towards protecting institutional liability and other interests rather than the interests of the researchers or the research itself (Haggerty 2004). It should also be stressed that there is a difference between research being approved by an ERB and the research, or the researcher, being ethical. Researchers may find that following ERB guidance puts respondents at risk and they can easily encounter situations where ERB guidance is not available (Daku 2018).

CONCERNS ABOUT MANAGEMENT OF ETHICAL ISSUES

While the development of key principles to conduct ethical research should be celebrated, perverse effects of this framework should be noted. Delays encountered in obtaining approval, administrative difficulties, and inadequacy of a formal set of guidelines for innovative projects are the main causes of protest against the current ERB system. In the 1990s, for example, researchers and patients protested against the long delays and bureaucracy required to obtain approval for research on cancer and AIDS. In the social sciences, it can be difficult to access data due to confidentiality concerns. For instance, access to granular census data is often on site, in rooms with no Internet connection, where researchers are not allowed to bring data in or out. This limits what research can be done, when, and by whom. Other concerns might be the exclusion of certain groups of subjects, affecting fairness and equity in research participation. This has often been the case for women, due to concerns of potential harm, as in cases regarding pregnancy, oral contraception, or breast-feeding, for example, or for groups which lack the capacity to consent, such as children or individuals with cognitive impairments.

At the extreme end, some have argued that ethics boards hamper critical research, narrow our vision as researchers, and ultimately might encourage unethical behaviour (Haggerty 2004). Others have warned against the legalization of ethics through decisions made and enforced by quasi-judicial institutions, such as ERBs, arguing instead for a profession-determined set of principles (Weinstock 2008). While we believe that ERBs are valuable tools, we should be cognizant of the fact that ethics boards serve not only the researcher, but also their institutions and themselves. Boards may discourage some research or methods because it is ethically or legally problematic, even if ultimately the project is ethically sound.

CONCLUSION: EMERGENT ETHICAL ISSUES

ERBs are not perfect institutions, and need to be flexible to address ethical issues that emerge from changes in context, technology (**BIG DATA**), social norms, or the application of managerial norms of the private sector (quality labels, standardized evaluation, and benchmarking techniques by third parties) to academic research, a culturally and geographically situated phenomenon. A good illustration of this is how the collection and analysis of **BIG DATA** are challenging the concepts of informed consent and anonymity. A recent study (Metcalf and Crawford 2016) used publicly available data to reveal the identity of graffiti artist Banksy. It is notable that an ethics board reviewed, and approved, the study that revealed the identity of someone who wished to remain anonymous, without their consent. Some criteria have been developed to provide for the gathering of electronic information (e.g. asking to ensure that the existence of data banks is known and available, that individuals who have participated can access their data, or that the data collected can only be used for the specific research purpose and may not be shared without the person's consent), as well as the conduct of research through the Internet (Barbour 1993).

A full discussion of critical perspectives on research ethics is beyond the scope of this entry, but the researcher is urged to consider the literature on decolonization of research, feminist research practices, and inclusive and participatory research approaches. Research may not be harmful according to an ERB, but it still may be distressing to participants due to 'inappropriate methods and practices' (Cochran et al. 2008). ERBs—and ethical researchers—will need to continue grappling with these complicated dynamics and changing realities to ensure that the principles and values that we try to uphold as researchers remain firmly in place.

REFERENCES

Barbour, Ian G. 1993. *Ethics in an Age of Technology. The Gifford Lectures 1989-1991.* San Francisco, HarperCollins Publishers Inc.

Cochran, Patricia A. L., Catherine A. Marshall, Carmen Garcia-Downing, Elizabeth Kendall, Doris Cook, Laurie McCubbin, and Reva Mariah S. Gover. 2008. 'Indigenous Ways of Knowing: Implications for Participatory Research and Community'. *American Journal of Public Health* 98(1): 22-27.

Daku, Mark. 2018. 'Ethics Beyond Ethics: The Need for Virtuous Researchers'. *BMC Medical Ethics* 19(Suppl 1): 42.

Haggerty, Kevin D. 2004. 'Ethics Creep: Governing Social Science Research in the Name of Ethics'. *Qualitative Sociology* 27(4): 391-414.

Metcalf, Jacob and Kate Crawford. 2016. 'Where are Human Subjects in Big Data Research? The Emerging Ethics Divide'. *Big Data and Society* 3(1): 1-14.

Resnick, David. 1996. 'Social Epistemology and the Ethics of Research'. *Studies in History and Philosophy of Science* 27(4): 565-586.

Sales, Bruce D. and Susan Folkman. 2000. *Ethics in Research with Human Participants.* Washington, DC, American Psychological Association.

Sieber, Joan E. 1992. *Planning Ethically Responsible Research: A Guide for Students and Internal Review Boards.* Newbury Park, SAGE Publications.

Weinstock, Daniel. 2008. 'Le droit n'est pas l'éthique et l'éthique n'est pas le droit: contre la confusion des genres', in *Le droit à tout faire: exploration des fonctions contemporaines du droit*, 185-204, ed. Pierre Noreau. Montréal, Éditions Themis.

ETHNOGRAPHY

Chowra Makaremi, École des hautes études en sciences sociales (EHESS)

E

Ethnography is a method developed in the practice of ethnology, a subdiscipline of anthropology dedicated to the study of peoples using a micro-analytical and comparative perspective. This empirical method initially focused on cultures and relied on descriptions compiled by travellers who were linked to the colonial enterprise: missionaries, colonial administrators, scientists embedded in excursions. Around World War I, the practice of ethnography witnessed a major shift with the idea that researchers had to build their analyses on their own first-hand observations, and not by relying on second-hand observations (as Marcel Mauss did when he wrote his seminal analysis of gift economy).

This shift rested on a few assumptions that reconfigured ethnography as a field and practice of knowledge. The collection and processing of data were seen as parts of one comprehensive process characterized by two key elements: first, the 'field', that is the site of observation (a multilayered and complex social world, in opposition for instance to laboratories where social and psychological EXPERIMENTS take place); and second, the idea of the inevitable subjectivity of the researcher, who is occupying a place on the field—be it that of a distant observer. Subjective presence and field observation are linked in a phenomenological approach to scientific knowledge (see EPISTEMOLOGY). Ethnographers build relationships, share emotions, and understand beliefs that will introduce them to the psychological realities and the insider points of view on the social world they are observing. They are affected or transformed by their field*work* as a social, emotional, and sensorial experience, and produce knowledge through both intellectual work (conceptualization, erudition) and personal experience.

This approach became the norm through the 'reflexive turn' taken by the discipline in the 1980s (see Clifford and Marcus 1986). Renato Rosaldo took this debate further by turning upside down the assumptions of scientific objectivity and showing how the researcher's emotions could actually foster the production of knowledge through a 'mix of insight and blindness' (Rosaldo 2004). After the accidental death of his wife and colleague Michelle Rosaldo during their fieldwork among the Ilongots in the Philippines, Renato Rosaldo was overcome by anger. The ordeal led him to understand the feeling of rage as an essential component of grief, and subsequently to reconsider from a new angle the practice of headhunting (killing a person and preserving their head) as a ritual of personal and collective mourning, which was the subject of his and Michelle Rosaldo's ethnographic study.

Observations are participant, covert, or non-participant, and can combine these different methods (see OBSERVATIONAL METHODS). For the reasons developed above, participant-observation is favoured, although participation does not necessary imply being active. On the contrary, doing nothing, hanging out, and being bored (as a perceptive experience) are considered important aspects of observation—and ones that may require some competence and learning, since it is not always easy to make one's presence accepted while lazing around. Since the early 2000s, the relationship between observation and participation has sometimes been reversed towards an observant-participation, that is the use of one's embedded position and work (as an employee or volunteer in an NGO for instance) to lead field research. However, this raises many ethical concerns and conflicts of loyalty (see ETHICS IN RESEARCH). A counter-example and limit-experience can be found in the US military programme called the 'human terrain system' that institutionalized ethnographic fieldwork embedded with the US army in occupied Iraq and Afghanistan, and was largely rejected as an illegitimate practice by academic institutions.

Ethnographic INTERVIEWS are traditionally non-directive (or semi-directive) and open (see ORAL HISTORY AND LIFE HISTORY). Within this practice, a specific expertise has developed in the collection of life histories (Crapanzano 1977), which is based on two methodological concepts: first, a shift from the primacy of seeing to the art of listening; and subsequently, the importance of intersubjectivity—a multilevel connection between interviewee and interviewer that goes far beyond the exchange of information, and aims for a co-construction of meaning and knowledge (Fabian 2014). The analytical potentialities of listening and intersubjectivity are illustrated by the 'socio-analyses' produced by Abdelmalek Sayad (2018 [1999]), ethnographer turned sociologist, and the instigator of studies on immigration in France. The name 'socio-analysis' chosen for Sayad's life histories highlights the influence of psychoanalytical knowledge on the forging of ethnographic methods, namely through the emancipatory dimension of the narration for the interviewee, and the aptitude of 'listening' as a main research tool. Besides these generally (very) long-format interviews, ethnographic research relies on informal conversations, serving as covert investigations or for gathering complementary information. These conversations remind us of the decisive, and often understated, role of the 'main informants' who serve as 'fixers', translators, research advisers, and social mentors.

Over the course of several months' everyday (and night) stay on a site, ideally requiring that the ethnographer learns the language of the field, the researcher can get access to a routine, everyday life. Social actors become less self-conscious about their presence, while this presence—and the relationships, sensory worlds, and habits it entails—determines the specific conditions in which data is collected, and the biases of the observation. A critical, reflexive outlook on these biases and involvements is the first step in processing data, which is why researchers are encouraged to keep a research diary alongside their field notes. Objectifying the conditions of production of knowledge through analysing one's relative position, interests, and observation biases is a firmer step towards scientific knowledge than endorsing the fiction of having no subjectivity at all, and considering oneself as a non-existent entity. This reflexive practice has opened a path for highlighting and critiquing social science's open or passive complicity with structures of power, from colonial conquest to post-colonial exploitation and domination. From yesterday to today, this (tacit) complicity has been invisibilized and reframed as a question of getting or preserving access to the field, which sheds a new light on the researcher's ideal of 'neutrality'. The founding symbiosis between ethnography as a field of knowledge and colonialism as a project of power (Asad 1973) has long remained a blind spot in the discipline.

When the question first surfaced, however, it plunged the discipline into a crisis, challenging the premises of its fascination for the exotic and the 'native', and causing many researchers to take their own societies as fields of study—a practice only generalized since the 1990s. Ethnographic methods such as immersion and micro-analysis have influenced qualitative research in sociology since the rise of the Chicago school of sociology, but it is only since the 1970s that anthropologists have started to apply their research methods to their own societies. A founding principle of ethnographic knowledge lies in the notion of alterity and the idea that being an outsider to a culture may bring specific insights and questions about dimensions of social life that are interiorized as 'natural' and obvious by those native to that culture. What opened the path to ethnographizing one's own society was the understanding that this productive and scientific use of alterity was not related to some intrinsic qualities of the researchers or the people they study, but to the ability to develop an estranged gaze, even on one's own social world.

While the interest in faraway peoples and indigenous cultures threatened with extinction is irremediably marked by (post-)colonial power relations, ethnography as a method has ceased to be a trademark of ethnology, becoming a method for in-depth, smaller scale research applied in different fields such as human geography, political science, and international relations (but also business management and marketing). The tradition and history of ethnography is what explains the soft dilution of this scientific knowledge into a set of practices in qualitative studies, but it is also what reminds us that beyond these practices, ethnography implies epistemic and methodological choices: inductive approach, reflexive subjectivity, thinking through experience, emotions, relationships and participation in the field.

REFERENCES

Asad, Thalal (ed.). 1973. *Anthropology and the Colonial Encounter*. London, Ithaca Press.
Clifford, James and George E. Marcus (eds). 1986. *Writing Culture: The Poetics and Politics of Ethnography*. Berkeley, University of California Press.
Crapanzano, Vincent. 1977. *Tuhami: Portrait of a Moroccan*. Chicago, University of Chicago Press.
Fabian, Johannes. 2014. 'Ethnography and Intersubjectivity: Loose Ends'. *HAU: Journal of Ethnographic Theory* 4(1): 199–209.
Rosaldo, Renato. 2004. 'Grief and a Headhunter's Rage', in *Death, Mourning, and Burial: A Cross-Cultural Reader*, ed. Antonius C. G. M. Robben, 167–178. Malden, MA, Blackwell.
Sayad, Abdelmalek. 2018 [1999]. *The Suffering of the Immigrant*. Hoboken, NJ, John Wiley & Sons.

EXPERIMENTS

Damien Bol, King's College London

EXPERIMENTAL AND OBSERVATIONAL METHODS

For decades, social scientists were convinced that experimentations were not for them. Although they generally acknowledged the great merits of the method (see POSITIV-ISM), they thought they could not use it, for practical and ethical reasons. Where it is easy for natural scientists to manipulate non-living elements such as metals, social scientists considered that they could not and should not experiment with their objects of study. Consequently, the use of COMPARATIVE ANALYSIS was recommended as a substitute. The comparison of different-yet-similar people or countries was perceived as the best way to test HYPOTHESES, and in particular those positing a causal relationship between a VARIABLE X and an outcome Y. This idea is at the root of many social sciences methods such as qualitative CASE STUDIES or quantitative REGRESSION ANALYSIS, which I will call 'OBSERVATIONAL METHODS' hereafter.

Yet, since 1990, experiments have become increasingly popular in the social sciences. In experiments, the researcher randomly assigns a VARIABLE X to some of the cases, but not all of them. She can thus observe the value of the outcome Y in the cases that received X and compare it to the other cases that did not. This contrasts with OBSERVATIONAL METHODS, for which the researcher simply observes the variations of X and Y as they occur in reality.

Experiments have two important advantages compared to OBSERVATIONAL METHODS. First, they allow the researcher to clearly identify what the causal VARI-ABLE X is and the outcome Y. This distinction is made by the researcher prior to the analysis, which discards the possibility of reverse causality (see CAUSATION). Second, with OBSERVATIONAL METHODS the precision of the estimates depends on the extent to which the researcher manages to control for the differences between the cases. When she cannot entirely capture these differences, the estimates are likely to be inflated, underestimated, or simply wrong.

EXPERIMENTS AND THE POTENTIAL-OUTCOME FRAMEWORK

Most social sciences researchers aim at testing the causal relationship between X and Y (see CAUSATION). They seek to estimate how much Y increases/decreases when X changes. Here I am considering that X is a binary variable (i.e. an event that either happens or not), and Y is a continuous variable. However, the arguments are also valid for other types of variables.

Traditionally, we approach causal relationships via the 'Neyman-Rubin poten-tial-outcome framework' (Rubin 1979). In this framework, if a researcher wants to estimate the causal effect of X on Y, she needs to observe, for the same case, the value of Y when X happens, and the value of Y when X does not happen. Then, by subtracting one value from the other, she has a precise estimate of how much the value of Y changes when X happens. However, she cannot observe the two outcomes at the same time. In reality, either X happened or not; a given person cannot experience both X and non-X.

Let me give an example: imagine you are interested in testing the causal relationship between going to university (X) and happiness (Y). You observe the level of happiness of a group and know who among them went to university. You might be tempted to estimate the causal effect by comparing the level of happiness of those who went to university to that of those who did not. However, this would not be a meaningful estimate as there are many other **VARIABLES** that influence the level of happiness. Some of these variables directly relate to the probability of going to university, such as whether people grew up in a rich family. Unless you have the capacity to control for all these variables, you do not know whether it is going to university, or any of these other variables, that causes happiness.

What the potential-outcome framework says is that you need to observe, within the group of people who went to university, what would have been their level of happiness if they did not go (and vice versa for those who did not go to university). This is obviously impossible. Yet you can approach the ideal potential-outcome framework by randomizing the **VARIABLE** X (which then becomes 'treatment X'). Typically, this entails randomly splitting the cases into two groups, and deciding that for one of these groups X happens, whereas for the other group, it does not. Then a simple comparison of the average value of Y in the two groups will give the average treatment effect: for all the cases under study, if X happens, Y changes, on average, by the average treatment effect.

Let me come back to the example: imagine you are capable of randomly splitting the group into two and assigning the treatment X 'going to university' to only one of them, making sure that the others do not go. You can then measure the average level of happiness in the two groups and subtract them. This group comparison becomes a meaningful estimate of the causal effect thanks to the random assignment of the treatment X. There are two reasons for that. First, it removes the possibility that other **VARIABLES** that influence X in real life have a disturbing effect (e.g. having rich parents). Second, if the groups are sufficiently large, the differences in Y that are due to variables other than the treatment will cancel each other out (see **STATISTICAL SIGNIFICANCE**).

The way I have presented experiments here is similar to the way they are presented in most textbooks. Yet this is a narrow definition of the method. Sometimes, textbooks present a stretched definition that includes 'natural' and 'quasi-experiments'. The term natural experiments refers to experimental situations that naturally occur in reality. The treatment is randomly assigned by someone other than the researcher. An example of natural experiments is the 1969 draft lottery that was used to determine which young American men would be called to fight in Vietnam. In their paper, Erikson and Stoker (2011) compare the individuals who were randomly selected by the lottery to those who were not (treatment X). They find, among other things, that participation in the Vietnam War caused people to be, years later, more anti-war (outcome Y).

The term quasi-experiments refers to situations in which the treatment X is not completely randomly assigned, but in which this assignment is 'as if' it was random.

An example of quasi-experiments is the study of Hainmueller, Hangartner, and Piet-rantuono (2015), which shows that immigrants tend to be more politically active (out-come Y) when they obtain the nationality of the country in which they live (treatment X). In some cantons in Switzerland, naturalization is decided by popular referendums. The authors compare levels of political activity of immigrants who received Swiss cit-izenship by just a few votes over the majority threshold at these referendums, to those who did not by just a few votes below the threshold. Since only a few votes separate the two, the assignment of the treatment X was as if random (maybe this could have been simply a mistake in counting votes). Natural and quasi-experiments are not ex-periments *stricto sensu*, as it is not the researcher who directly assigns the treatment to individuals.

EXPERIMENTS IN THE FIELD AND IN THE LAB

There are two broad types of experiments: experiments in the field (including sur-vey experiments), and in the lab. In field experiments, the researcher goes out in the field and randomly assigns the treatment X to some individuals as they are living their normal life. Subsequently, she observes their behaviour, and how they respond to the treatment. By contrast, in lab experiments, the researcher recruits some participants and brings them into a lab. It is in this lab that she randomly assigns the treatment X and observes the reaction of the subjects.

Let me give examples of both field and lab experiments. Gerber, Green, and Larimer (2008) conducted a field experiment in Michigan shortly before the 2006 US primary election. They identified about 150,000 people who were registered as voters. Then, they randomly split these potential voters into several groups, and assigned them dif-ferent treatments X, which consisted of various letters encouraging them to vote. Ob-serving the turnout rate in each of the experimental groups (outcome Y), they found that social pressure causes an increase in turnout rate. Turnout is on average 8 percent-age points higher among people who received a letter reminding them that in the US everybody can see who did or did not vote.

In another study, Adida, Laitin, and Valfort (2016) used a lab experiment to test whether religious difference causes prejudice. They recruited French and Senegalese participants and brought them into a lab in Paris. They divided the participants into random groups and asked them whether they were willing to give up to 5 euros to other people in their group, or to keep this money for themselves. They found that French participants donated less money when there were many Senegalese participants in their group, especially if these Senegalese participants had a Muslim first name. The average treatment effect of adding a second Muslim into the group was a decrease in donation of 1.23 euros. They concluded that religious difference in groups causes dis-criminatory behaviours.

Both field and lab experiments have advantages. Field experiments are more realistic in the sense that they build on real social behaviours. Their results thus have more ex-ternal validity compared to lab experiments, in which social interactions are abstracted via lab interactions. For example, Gerber, Green, and Larimer (2008) observed actual turnout rates which are their study topic, whereas Adida, Laitin, and Valfort (2016) studied donation into a lab as a proxy for prejudice against Muslim people. However, in lab experiments, the researcher has more control over her experimental design, and especially the assignment of the treatment. Gerber, Green, and Larimer (2008) did not know whether the participants opened the letter they sent them, whereas Adida, Laitin, and Valfort (2016) showed the names and faces of each participant in the group to make sure that this piece of information was known to all. The choice of field and lab experiments is a trade-off between external validity and the researcher's control.

E

TOWARDS ETHICAL EXPERIMENTS

Experiments are the ideal tools to test causal relationships between a **VARIABLE** X and an outcome Y. However, they also have limits. Experiments cannot be used to study all social sciences topics. There are some **VARIABLES** X that the researcher cannot randomly assign to individuals. Coming back to the example regarding the effect of going to university on happiness, it seems impossible for a researcher to impose that some people go to university and others not. This impossibility is even clearer when it comes to macro phenomena like revolutions, wars, or famine. Yet, this does not mean that the researcher cannot experimentally study these topics. She can, for example, conduct a lab experiment in an area with a recent history of civil war, to evaluate the level of social cohesion among individuals (Gilligan, Pasquale, and Samii 2014).

The question of which topic can be analysed with experiments revolves around the question of **ETHICS IN RESEARCH**. It is crucial that the researcher interested in conducting an experiment thinks through all potential consequences the research could have on the people involved. It is about making sure that it will not create too much harm, anxiety, stress, or embarrassment.

REFERENCES

Adida, Claire L., David D. Laitin, and Marie-Anne Valfort. 2016. 'One Muslim is Enough! Evidence from a Field Experiment in France'. *Annals of Economics and Statistics* 121-122: 121-160.

Erikson, Robert S. and Laura Stoker. 2011. 'Caught in the Draft: The Effects of Vietnam Draft Lottery Status on Political Attitudes'. *American Political Science Review* 105(2): 221-237.

Gerber, Alan S., Donald P. Green, and Christopher W. Larimer. 2008. 'Social Pressure and Voter Turnout: Evidence from a Large-scale Field Experiment'. *American Political Science Review* 102(1): 33-48.

Gilligan, Michael J., Benjamin J. Pasquale, and Cyrus Samii. 2014. 'Civil War and Social Cohesion: Lab-in-the-field Evidence from Nepal'. *American Journal of Political Science* 58(3): 604-619.

Hainmueller, Jens, Dominik Hangartner, and Giuseppe Pietrantuono. 2015. 'Naturalization Fosters the Long-term Political Integration of Immigrants'. *Proceedings of the National Academy of Sciences* 112(41): 12651-12656.

Rubin, Donald B. 1979. 'Using Multivariate Sampling and Regression Adjustment to Control Bias in Observational Studies'. *Journal of the American Statistical Association* 74(366): 318-328.

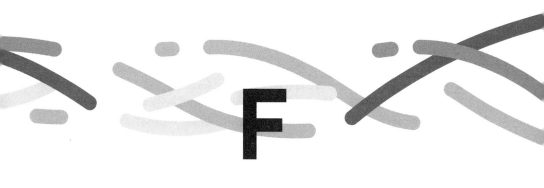

FACTOR ANALYSIS

Uncovering Unobservable Constructs

Ulf Liebe, University of Warwick

Factor analysis is used to test whether a set of observable or manifest **VARIABLES** can measure one or more unobservable or latent constructs that they have in common. Such constructs are called factors. Factor analysis is therefore a data reduction method.

In its foundation period, factor analysis was often applied to the study of general intelligence and mental abilities. For example, Thurstone and Thurstone (1941) studied the primary mental abilities of 1,154 eighth-grade students and identified, based on sixty observable test results per child, several unobservable factors including a verbal-comprehension factor, word-fluency factor, and memory factor. Nowadays factor analysis is a workhorse for quantitative research in the social sciences, humanities, and natural sciences. For example, in political sociology researchers may collect observable variables based on survey questions on immigration, and study whether these variables can be combined to represent respondents' (unobservable) attitudes towards immigration.

There are two types of factor analysis: exploratory factor analysis and confirmatory factor analysis (see **DEDUCTIVE, INDUCTIVE, AND RETRODUCTIVE REASONING**). *Exploratory factor analysis* is used for examining the underlying structures in a set of variables, and it is done in a ' "let's see what happens" spirit' (Child 2006: 6). *Confirmatory factor analysis* is used to test theoretical hypotheses; the researcher assumes that variables are interrelated in a specific way and uses factor analysis to find out whether the assumption is supported by the data—i.e. to what extent the data fits the predefined structure. In this contribution, we will focus on exploratory factor analysis.

THE LANGUAGE AND MECHANICS OF EXPLORATORY FACTOR ANALYSIS

Exploratory factor analysis comes with its own language, including terms such as factor loading and eigenvalue. There are also different approaches to doing factor analysis. Looking at the correlations between variables is a good starting point. If there are remarkable correlations between all or subsets of variables, this provides a hint that the variables have something in common that might form a factor. A *factor* refers to a latent—not directly observable—construct associated with several variables. For example, the attitude towards immigration would be the factor which is related to the variables on immigration included in a survey. A *factor loading* is the correlation between a variable and a factor, for example between each variable on immigration and the factor on immigration. In general, a factor analysis can be based on a correlation matrix or covariance matrix (see **COVARIANCE**). In the following, some of the basic principles regarding the concept of variance are presented (see Child 2006).

In principle, there are as many possible factors as variables (n). Each variable has a *total variance* (TV), of which some *common variance* (CV) is shared with other variables in common factors and some *unique variance* (UV) is uncorrelated with other variables. The sum of common variance of a variable is also called *communality* [i.e. $(CV_1 + CV_2 + CV_3 + \cdots + CV_n)$].

$$Total\ Variance = Common\ Variance + Unique\ Variance$$
$$TV = CV_1 + CV_2 + CV_3 + \cdots + CV_n + UV$$

Constraining the total variance of a variable to a value of 1 results in the following *factor equation* for each variable:

$$\frac{Total\ Variance}{Total\ Variance} = \frac{Common\ Variance}{Total\ Variance} + \frac{Unique\ Variance}{Total\ Variance}$$

$$\frac{TV}{TV} = \frac{CV_1 + CV_2 + CV_3 + \cdots + CV_n}{TV} + \frac{UV}{TV}$$

$$1 = Proportion\ of\ Common\ Variance + Proportion\ of\ Unique\ Variance$$

There are different types of exploratory factor analysis such as principal component, principal factor, and maximum likelihood. For example, *principal component analysis* ignores the unique variance and assumes that all the variance is common variance. It aims to replace the original variables by a lower number of uncorrelated principal components which are linear combinations of the original variables. The principal components are basically the factors. *Principal factor analysis* assumes that variables have both common variance and unique variance. This is often more realistic. Yet, in order to account for unique variance, assumptions about the communality are needed. This information can be obtained using, for example, the squared multiple correlations between each variable and the remaining variables.

Strictly speaking, a principal component analysis is a special case of factor analysis. For some researchers it does not count as a true factor analysis. However, it is frequently employed to reduce the sets of variables, often serves as a starting point in a factor analysis, and in many statistical software packages it is implemented as part of factor analysis. Furthermore, the substantive results of a principal component and principal factor analysis are often quite similar.

The factor loadings can be obtained by taking the square root of the variance values (e.g. $\sqrt{CV_1 / TV}$). A factor loading ranges between -1 and $+1$ and indicates a negative or positive correlation, respectively, between the variable and the factor at hand. The closer the loading to $|1|$, the more 'important' a variable is for a factor. Typically, a factor is based on three or more variables with significant factor loadings. Yet, there is no clear rule as to what significant means, and standards tend to differ across disciplines. While some researchers refer to factor loadings of $|0.30|$ as a bare minimum, others only accept values of $|0.40|$ or $|0.50|$.

The sum of the squared factor loadings for a factor is known as the *eigenvalue* (or *extracted variance* or *sum of squares*). It refers to the extracted variance which can be expressed as a proportion of the maximum possible variance by calculating (Eigenvalue/ Number of Variables) × 100. Following the (Guttman-)Kaiser criterion (Kaiser 1960), researchers should consider factors with eigenvalues greater than 1. The eigenvalues show the relative importance of factors and can be visualized in a scree plot which shows the eigenvalues in descending order of magnitude.

In all types of exploratory factor analysis, *factor rotation* is employed to simplify the analysis by showing more clearly which variables belong together and form a factor. Factor rotation does not alter the common variance but it changes the factor loadings— typically leading to higher loadings for variables strongly correlated with a factor and lower loadings for those weakly correlated with the factor. Various rotation methods can be used, depending on whether it is assumed that factors are independent of each other or correlated. This leads to orthogonal (uncorrelated) or oblique (correlated) factor rotations, respectively.

AN ILLUSTRATIVE EXAMPLE OF EXPLORATORY FACTOR ANALYSIS

In the World Value Survey (Wave 5, 2005–2009), respondents were asked to what extent (on a 10-point response scale from 1 = never justifiable to 10 = always justifiable) they think the following seven actions—claiming government benefits to which you are not entitled, avoiding a fare on public transport, cheating on taxes, acceptance of a bribe, abortion, divorce, homosexuality—can be justified. It is interesting to explore whether the seven variables measure common constructs. The results in Table 4 are based on a principal component factor analysis using the UK data with 862 respondents. The analysis ignores the unique variance—i.e. all communalities are treated as 1. This might not be justified, given the considerable high values of unique variance reported in Table 4. The analysis gives two factors with eigenvalue greater than 1: Factor 1 and Factor 2. The other factors are not shown. All seven variables are highly correlated with unrotated Factor 1, and all factor loadings are greater than 0.40. Yet, the last three variables are also highly correlated with unrotated Factor 2; the corresponding factor loadings are greater than 0.60, i.e. higher than those for unrotated Factor 1. Summing up, the squared values of the factor loadings result in the eigenvalues of 2.49 and 1.99 for unrotated Factor 1 and Factor 2, respectively. Unrotated Factor 1 explains 36 per cent of the total variance $[(2.49/7) \times 100 = 36]$ and unrotated Factor 2 explains 28 per cent of the total variance $[(1.99/7) \times 100 = 28]$.

TABLE 4 A principal component factor analysis

Variables	Factor loadings				Uniqueness
	Factor 1 (unrotated)	Factor 2 (unrotated)	Factor 1 (rotated)	Factor 2 (rotated)	
Claiming govern-ment benefits to which you are not entitled	0.618	−0.410	0.741	−0.042	0.450
Avoiding a fare on public transport	0.726	−0.310	0.783	0.098	0.377
Cheating on taxes if you have a chance	0.725	−0.324	0.790	0.086	0.369
Someone accept-ing a bribe in the course of their duties	0.659	−0.371	0.756	0.012	0.429
Abortion	0.503	0.694	0.084	0.853	0.266
Divorce	0.445	0.737	0.013	0.861	0.259
Homosexuality	0.415	0.677	0.018	0.794	0.370
Eigenvalue/variance	2.49	1.99	2.36	2.12	
Proportion of explained total variance	0.36	0.28	0.34	0.30	

Note: n = 862. Author's analysis.

An orthogonal factor rotation using the varimax method, maximizing the variance of the squared factor loadings within factors, reveals a clearer picture. The four vari-ables claiming government benefits, avoiding a fare on public transport, cheating on taxes, and acceptance of a bribe form the rotated Factor 1 with factor loadings of at least 0.741, while the variables abortion, divorce, and homosexuality form the rotated Factor 2 with loadings of at least 0.794. Now each variable is only loading high on one of the factors.

In this example, a principal factor analysis considering the unique variance and us-ing the squared multiple correlations as estimates of the communality gives a similar picture: rotated factor loadings range between 0.609 (claiming government benefits) and 0.685 (cheating on taxes) for the rotated Factor 1, and between 0.637 (homosexu-ality) and 0.748 (divorce) for the rotated Factor 2.

The interpretation of the results of any factor analysis is rather subjective, and this might be seen as a weakness of the method. The researcher has to make sense out of the factor pattern and typically searches for a label providing a good descrip-tion of a factor. This can be challenging. For the example in Table 4, Factor 1 might be called 'justifiability of corruption', but it is less clear what is the underlying construct of Factor 2.

In subsequent analyses, researchers could use the predicted factor scores for each respondent; depending on the exact method, they are estimated, taking factor loadings of the variables into account. Researchers can also use a naive way of constructing a new variable which represents an additive index, by summing up for each respondent the values of the variables that form a common factor (e.g. an index for corruption). Here, each variable contributes equally to the factor.

Conducting an exploratory factor analysis involves many decisions; it is advisable to compare the results of different methods and to report in publications at least the following (cf. Child 1990: 62/63): the method of factor analysis (e.g. principal component or principal factor analysis); the criterion for numbers of factors (e.g. eigenvalue > 1); the criterion for significant factor loadings (e.g. loadings > 0.40); and the rotation method (e.g. orthogonal or oblique rotation).

REFERENCES

Child, Dennis. 1990. *The Essentials of Factor Analysis*, 2rd edition. London, Cassell.
Child, Dennis. 2006. *The Essentials of Factor Analysis*, 3rd edition. New York, Continuum.
Kaiser, Henry F. 1960. 'The Application of Electronic Computers to Factor Analysis'. *Educational and Psychological Measurement* 20(1): 141–151.
Thurstone, Louis L. and Thelma G. Thurstone. 1941. *Factorial Studies of Intelligence*. Chicago, Chicago University Press.

FALSIFICATION

How does it Relate to Reproducibility?

Brian D. Earp, Yale University

INTRODUCTION

A common way to distinguish science from pseudoscience is that the former puts forward HYPOTHESES that are at least in principle *falsifiable* (Popper 1959). This means that they are capable of being refuted—or falsified—by counter-evidence. To illustrate, astrology is often characterized as a pseudoscience since its predictions are so vague that any number of occurrences could be interpreted as confirmatory. Astronomy, by contrast, is usually seen as scientific in part because it makes extremely precise and hence 'risky' predictions: the predictions could turn out to be false, which would require astronomers to update their theories in light of the evidence.

In reality, matters are rarely so clear. One can always question the validity of the seemingly contrary evidence rather than change one's theory, for example, and this is often justified. Accordingly, contemporary philosophers of science tend to look down on falsifiability as overly simplistic. Nevertheless, among many practising scientists, the notion is still regarded as a useful—if imperfect—heuristic for judging the strength of a HYPOTHESIS in terms of its ability to generate new insights when combined with careful observation (Earp and Trafimow 2015).

Consider the HYPOTHESIS that all swans are white (H1). H1 is falsifiable because a single valid observation of a non-white swan would show H1 to be wrong. This, in turn, would teach us something new about the world (not all swans are white). Now consider the hypothesis that all swans are either white or some other colour (H2). H2, while true, is not falsifiable because it could never be shown wrong no matter how many swans were observed. It renders swan observation uninformative. The lesson for researchers is to try to formulate hypotheses that could turn out to be wrong, and to test those hypotheses in such a way that, if they are wrong, this could be legitimately inferred from the data.

As can be seen with H1, some falsifiable hypotheses can be tested by making simple observations. Others must be tested by experiment, for example the HYPOTHESIS that a given treatment reduces the symptoms of a disease. Based on the principle of falsifiability, designing a convincing experiment requires asking: 'What would count against my hypothesis?' If an experiment is carefully designed to produce such contrary evidence, and yet reliably fails to produce it, the researcher will have good reason to place provisional confidence in the soundness of the hypothesis: it has not yet been refuted. The more such experiments that fail to falsify the hypothesis, the more robust the evidence amassed in its favour (LeBel et al. 2018).

FALSIFICATION AND SELF-CORRECTION

Falsification also relates to *self-correction* in science. Often, erroneous findings make their way into the literature. If subsequent researchers conduct the same experiment as the original and yet it fails to yield the same finding, they are often described as having 'falsified' (that is, shown to be incorrect) the original result. In this way, mistakes, false alarms, and other non-reproducible output is thought to be identifiable and thus able to be corrected.

But this account is far too simple. First, actual attempts at falsification are relatively uncommon. At best, scientists (typically) conduct what are sometimes called 'conceptual' REPLICATIONS: essentially, *variations* on previously published experiments designed to extend existing findings or to generalize across new conditions or methodologies. Such quasi-replication, however, is not sufficient to confirm—or falsify— original results. Put simply, if a conceptual replication 'fails' it could be due to whatever change was made in the materials or methodology, as opposed to any problems with the original experiment or finding (Doyen et al. 2014). Negative results from such experiments are therefore inconclusive. For self-correction of science through falsification, then, what is needed are 'direct' replications.

DIRECT REPLICATION

'Direct' REPLICATIONS are those that (attempt to) follow the original study as closely as possible. Some differences are unavoidable. Ideally, however, the replication is sufficiently similar (SS) to the original along all theoretically relevant dimensions—from design, to method, materials, SAMPLING TECHNIQUE, and so on—that the results from the two experiments can be meaningfully compared.

Sometimes, it is hard to determine if the SS condition has been met. Especially in younger fields such as psychology, it is often the case that certain *auxiliary assumptions* have not yet been exhaustively worked out. An auxiliary assumption is simply a logical or practical assumption needed to link an 'abstract' theory or HYPOTHESIS to something directly observable, such as a response time score or a check mark on a scale. One or more such assumptions may be (inadvertently) violated in a REPLICATION study, even if it is designed to be 'direct'.

Suppose that such a study yields a null finding, whereas the original finding was 'statistically significant' (see STATISTICAL SIGNIFICANCE). This would not entail that the original result (or the HYPOTHESIS that predicted it) had been falsified. Rather, follow-up studies would be needed to narrow down where in the chain of auxiliary assumptions a breakdown or violation may have occurred. In this way, if conducted systematically, REPLICATIONS can be useful for identifying and making explicit unknown or unacknowledged auxiliary assumptions, which can help with hypothesis specification and theory advancement (Cesario 2014).

Such interpretational ambiguities complicate the project of falsification. In fact, REPLICATION results can never definitively prove or disprove (falsify) a reported effect: alternative explanations are always in theory possible. They can, however, be *informative* about its likely existence, magnitude, and theoretical and practical implications. In particular, they can give all-things-considered good reasons to adjust one's confidence in the reliability of the effect upwards or downwards, as a function both of the quality and number of replication attempts (Earp and Trafimow 2015).

THE IMPORTANCE OF AUXILIARY ASSUMPTIONS: AN EXAMPLE

Consider a reported failure to replicate a famous study in which participants exposed to an elderly priming stimulus subsequently walked more slowly down a hallway compared to a control group, as measured by a stopwatch (Bargh, Chen, and Burrows 1996). In the REPLICATION study, an infrared sensor was used instead of a stopwatch, and the slow-walking effect seemed to disappear (Doyen et al. 2012). Since a change was made, one could argue that the replication attempt was only 'conceptual' and therefore not even potentially falsifying. But that would be incorrect. The change was based on a sound auxiliary assumption: namely, that a time measure that is less susceptible to human error would be superior to one that is more susceptible to such error. In other words, the change allowed for a *better* test of the original HYPOTHESIS.

Assuming that there were no other relevant differences between the original and REPLICATION, it would be reasonable to interpret the observed null finding as counting at least somewhat against the validity of the original result. The more the null finding, itself, is replicated in follow-up experiments—so long as they are competently executed and do not violate any further auxiliary assumptions—the more the total body of evidence will support the conclusion that the original result should not be relied on (Earp and Trafimow 2015).

But now consider another change that was made. The priming materials were translated into French. Apparently, the replicating team assumed that the language used for a priming study is irrelevant to the outcome. But *this* auxiliary assumption may be mistaken. Based on a corpus analysis, a different team of researchers showed that the association between priming words and the elderly stereotype was roughly six times stronger for the English words used in the original study than for their translated French equivalents in the REPLICATION study. The lesson here is that potential violations of even seemingly minor auxiliary assumptions can make a big difference for the conclusions it is safe to draw from apparent acts of falsification (see Trafimow and Earp 2016).

CONCLUSION

According to Lakatos (1970: 184), 'given sufficient imagination … any theory can be permanently saved from "refutation" by some suitable adjustment in the background knowledge in which it is embedded'. Similarly, any finding can be indefinitely rescued from falsification if the original scientist is willing to claim that the replicators all made a mistake or violated an important auxiliary assumption (as indeed they may have done). But it is not enough to simply make such claims. Scientists must make explicit all relevant auxiliary assumptions, and clarify the range of conditions under which their purported finding should obtain. If a sufficient number of REPLICATION attempts obey those assumptions and are carried out under those conditions—as judged by an impartial expert—yet still fail to show the originally reported result, it then becomes reasonable for the community of scientists to abandon their confidence in the finding, thus treating it as effectively falsified.

REFERENCES

Bargh, John, Mark Chen, and Lara Burrows. 1996. 'Automaticity of Social Behavior: Direct Effects of Trait Construct and Stereotype Activation on Action'. *Journal of Personality and Social Psychology* 71(2): 230-244.

Cesario, Joseph. 2014. 'Priming, Replication, and the Hardest Science'. *Perspectives on Psychological Science* 9(1): 40-48.

Doyen, Stéphane, Olivier Klein, Cora-Lise Pichon, and Axel Cleeremans. 2012. 'Behavioral Priming: It's All in the Mind, but Whose Mind?' *PLOS ONE*, 7(1): e29081.

Doyen, Stéphane, Olivier Klein, Daniel Simons, and Axel Cleeremans. 2014. 'On the Other Side of the Mirror: Priming in Cognitive and Social Psychology'. *Social Cognition* 32(Spec. issue): 12-32.

Earp, Brian and David Trafimow. 2015. 'Replication, Falsification, and the Crisis of Confidence in Social Psychology'. *Frontiers in Psychology* 6(621): 1-11.

Lakatos, Imre. 1970. 'Falsification and the Methodology of Scientific Research Programmes', in *Criticism and the Growth of Knowledge*, ed. Imre Lakatos and Alan Musgrave, 91-196. Cambridge, MA, Cambridge University Press.

LeBel, Etienne, Randy McCarthy, Brian Earp, Malte Elson, and Wolf Vanpaemel. 2018. 'A Unified Framework to Quantify the Credibility of Scientific Findings'. *Advances in Methods and Practices in Psychological Science* 1(3): 389-402.

Popper, Karl. 1959. *The Logic of Scientific Discovery*. London, Hutchinson & Co.

Trafimow, David and Brian Earp. 2016. 'Badly Specified Theories are not Responsible for the Replication Crisis in Social Psychology: Comment on Klein'. *Theory & Psychology* 26(4): 540-548.

F

FOCUS GROUPS

Trends, Issues, and Debates

Andrew Parker, Ridley Hall Theological College, Cambridge
Jonathan Tritter, Aston University

Focus groups grew out of both a therapeutic and marketing tradition and have been utilized by social scientists for many years. Their format constitutes a type of INTER-VIEW TECHNIQUE where six to twelve people are brought together and encouraged to discuss specific topics for 60–90 minutes in order that underlying issues might be explored (Bloor et al. 2001). Focus groups are often used to investigate areas about which relatively little is known, and they are premised on face-to-face interactions between participants rather than direct responses to questions (Reisner et al. 2017). More recently they have been adapted to online settings, particularly for hard-to-reach populations (DuBois et al. 2015). Participants are asked to engage in focus groups because they have something in common with each other and something which the researcher is interested in—i.e. a lifestyle circumstance or condition, or they share a particular social context. Hence, the 'focus' aspect of the exercise is the basis on which the group takes place and the driving force behind the topic(s) to be addressed.

While semi-structured interviews have long since featured in qualitative and MIXED METHODS research, there is a fundamental difference between 'one-to-one' interviews, 'group' interviews, and 'focus groups' (see Parker and Tritter 2006), the critical point of distinction being the role of the researcher and her/his relationship to the researched (Smithson 2000). For example, in group interviews the researcher adopts an 'investigative' role: asking questions, controlling conversational dynamics, engaging in dialogue with specific participants—a scenario which sees the mechanics of one-to-one interviews replicated on a broader (collective) scale. Focus groups are different. Here, the central role of the researcher is to 'facilitate' discussion *between* participants, thereby allowing the interrelational dynamics of group members to come to the fore (see Barbour and Kitzinger 1998; Johnson 1996). Decisions on when to use focus groups are often guided by the RESEARCH QUESTION(s) under consideration and it is common for them to be organized around a key characteristic or VARIABLE (i.e. gender, age, or occupation). Likewise, the number of groups to be held will largely depend on the scope, remit, and size of the study in question, participant accessibility/availability, and the nature of the data required.

In focus groups facilitation is all about generating in-depth, 'focused' discussion via a logical sequence of open-ended (non-directive) questions or statements that encourage universal participation. Respondent contributions might also be recorded by way of flip charts or post-it notes, which group facilitators may manage. If group dynamics work as they should (and this can take time), what emerges is what practitioners often refer to as a 'synergy' between participants whereby all of those present contribute in some way to the discussion. In turn, a kind of momentum is generated which allows underlying meanings and beliefs to emerge alongside descriptions of individual experience. Thus, a central element of data analysis is an examination not only of the substantive content of discussion but also the interaction *between* respondents themselves (Krueger and Casey 2014). In addition, audio and (increasingly) video recording of focus groups allows both the analysis of discursive content and the tracking of participant interventions. This permits a mapping of the different types of power apparent in the frequency, length, and nature of individual contributions. In terms of the analysis of focus group data, this often follows a grounded theory approach whereby key concepts and ideas are organically developed from participant contributions (see Glaser and Strauss 1967; Charmaz 2014).

Part of the problem of achieving interactional synergy is that, despite their collective interests, participants may not always engage with each other, or alternatively, may know each other so well that interaction is based on pre-existing patterns of social relations that have little to do with the focus group itself. For this reason, participant recruitment is not something that should be carried out simply on an ad hoc or random basis. Rather, issues of sampling and selection are likely to prove crucial in relation to the form and quality of interaction and the kinds of data one gathers. To this end, non-probability or 'snowball' SAMPLING TECHNIQUES with participant peer groups, associates, and friendship networks are not unusual. While such recruitment practices appear relatively straightforward, in many accounts of focus group method these issues are often discussed in relation to the researcher's reliance on a 'local' (i.e. geographic or institutional) contact or key gatekeeper who becomes the pivotal figure in the recruitment process. Of course, another possible approach to recruitment is to use members of pre-existing groups or to convene a focus group as part of an already scheduled meeting (Bloor et al. 2001). Yet neither of these sampling methods provides true informed consent, and both are forms of recruitment that can impact on the quality of the data generated (Krueger and Casey 2014).

Focus groups are valuable because they capture and harness group interaction to prompt fuller and deeper discussion and the triggering of new ideas. But in order for these dynamics to develop, it is vital that people's stories are not already well known to each other. The invisibility of recruitment procedures and the uncritical reliance on the use of either local facilitators or pre-existing groups is problematic and often re-ceives far too little attention in the write-up and presentation of focus group findings. Although focus groups are often 'one-off' encounters, there may well be times when we wish to reconvene the same participants for subsequent meetings; however, recon-vening an identical group on subsequent occasions may prove problematic for a host of reasons (Bloor et al. 2001). A way around this is to include the possibility of sampling a range of prospective groups which may inform the data collection process at a number of different organizational, institutional, or circumstantial levels.

The decision to deploy focus groups as part of a wider research design or strategy may be based on a variety of issues. In their research into the impact of a sporting intervention on youth crime and antisocial behaviour, Parker et al. (2019) used focus groups to explore the personalized experiences of vulnerable and marginalized young people as they engaged with a range of sporting activities. Discussion topics varied, with participants being encouraged to talk about their entry route into the interven-tion, their awareness of its overarching aims and objectives, and 'critical moments' (positive and negative) that defined their experiences. The research team explored testimonies where the intervention had successfully and effectively removed young people from damaging social circumstances associated with crime and antisocial be-haviour, and facilitated their (re)integration in local communities. Focus groups were also carried out with project workers and partner agencies which explored broader perceptions of the young people who engaged with the intervention, the perceived benefits accrued by participants from its various activities, and the extent to which project workers and partners felt that the wider project aims and objectives (around sport for social inclusion, positive youth development, and social change) were being met. As the data collection process progressed, it became clear to the research team that the vulnerability of many of the young people concerned was militating against a sense of openness in one-to-one interviews. Hence focus groups were adopted in order to generate an increased sense of 'safety' and 'collectivity' among the respondents (see also Ahmed Shafi 2018). This resulted in the elicitation of more in-depth data as partic-ipants shared their experiences of the intervention via focus group conversation. Like-wise, focus groups with project workers and partners allowed common experiences to be aired, especially those concerning the kinds of barriers that young people faced in terms of overall engagement.

REFERENCES

Ahmed Shafi, Adeela. 2018. 'Researching Young Offenders: Navigating Methodological Challenges and Reframing Ethical Responsibilities'. *International Journal of Research & Method in Education* 43(1): 1-15.

Barbour, Rosaline S. and Jenny Kitzinger. 1998. *Developing Focus Group Research: Politics, Theory and Practice*. London, SAGE Publications.

Bloor, Michael, Jane Frankland, Michelle Thomas, and Kate Robson. 2001. *Focus Groups in Social Research*. London, SAGE Publications.

Charmaz, Kathy. 2014. *Constructing Grounded Theory*, 2nd edition. London, SAGE Publications.

DuBois, L. Zachary, Kathryn Macapagal, Zenaida Rivera, Tonya Prescott, Michele Ybarra, and Brian Mustanski. 2015. 'To Have Sex or not to Have Sex? An Online Focus Group

Study of Sexual Decision Making Among Sexually Experienced and Inexperienced Gay and Bisexual Adolescent Men'. *Archives of Sexual Behavior* 44(7): 2027-2040.

Glaser, Barney. G. and Anselm L. Strauss. 1967. *The Discovery of Grounded Theory: Strategies for Qualitative Research.* Chicago, Aldine.

Johnson, Alan. 1996. 'It's Good to Talk: The Focus Group and the Sociological Imagination'. *Sociological Review* 44(3): 517-538.

Krueger, Richard A. and Mary Anne Casey. 2014. *Focus Groups: A Practical Guide for Applied Research,* 5th edition. London, SAGE Publications.

Parker, Andrew, Hadyn Morgan, Samaya Farooq, Benjamin Moreland, and Andy Pitchford. 2019. 'Sporting Intervention and Social Change: Football, Marginalised Youth and Citizenship Development'. *Sport, Education and Society* 24(3): 298-310.

Parker, Andrew and Jonathan Q. Tritter. 2006. 'Focus Group Method and Methodology: Reflections on Current Practice and Recent Debate'. *International Journal of Research and Method in Education* 29(1): 23-37.

Reisner, Sari L., Renee K. Randazzo, Jaclyn M. White Hughto, Sarah Peitzmeier, L. Zachary DuBois, Dana J. Pardee, Elliot Marrow, Sarah McLean, and Jennifer Potter. 2017. 'Sensitive Health Topics with Underserved Patient Populations: Methodological Considerations for Online Focus Group Discussions'. *Qualitative Health Research* 28(10): 1658-1673.

Smithson, Janet. 2000. 'Using and Analysing Focus Groups: Limitations and Possibilities'. *International Journal of Social Research Methodology: Theory and Practice* 3(2): 103-119.

FORMAL MODELLING

Érick Duchesne & Arthur Silve, Université Laval

INTRODUCTION

A formal model is the mathematical exposition of reasoning. Its purpose is to formulate consistent and rigorously stated HYPOTHESES, which often shed light on the CAUSATION of a particular social phenomenon. In the words of Gates and Hume (1997: 6), 'formal models can be used to determine inconsistencies in analysis or disjunctures between assumptions and conclusion'.

Every formal model starts with assumptions that are meant to simplify the world. They emphasize certain features of a given phenomenon, and in that sense, rely heavily on Weberian ideal types. For instance, the most recurrent ideal type in the social sciences is the *homo economicus*, a description of human behaviour on which the whole PARADIGM of the *rational choice theory* (RC) is founded. RC relies on METHODOLOGICAL INDIVIDUALISM and on two important working assumptions: individuals *rationally* choose the action to achieve *their preferred* available outcome. In this way, formal models are useful fictions and their purpose is to help formulate FALSIFIABLE HYPOTHESES.

Often, in the social sciences, a formal model is valuable because it can accurately predict behaviour and describe an actual (although unobservable) causal mechanism.

Thus, formal models also allow plenty of space for **DEDUCTIVE REASONING**. According to MacDonald (2003: 554), these are the two alternative epistemological justifications for using formal models: they are useful as fictions or for uncovering actual mechanisms.

Whether they clarify hypotheses or describe a mechanism, the success of formal models remains a matter of debate. Green and Shapiro (1994: 6) suggest that '[t]he case has yet to be made that these models have advanced our understanding of how politics works in the real world'. They criticize RC for its unrealistic assumptions. Individuals are neither rational nor motivated exclusively by self-interest: how, then, can models based on these two assumptions help us understand the world? Green and Shapiro's criticism of RC crystallizes the frustration felt by many scholars with regard to the invasiveness of RC in the social sciences. However, their argument can be readily transposed to Kahneman and Tversky's prospect theory (a theory of decision making under risk that does not assume rationality), agent-based models (a **SYSTEMS ANALYSIS** of the interaction of autonomous agents), evolutionary games, and more.

Rodrik (2015: 45) defends the opposite view: 'Models make economics a science.' Is it that models are useful in economics, but not in political science, as argued by Green and Shapiro? Actually, the usefulness of models is a question that arises across the boundaries between the social sciences.

We propose that formal modelling, in general, is an inevitable feature of research in the social sciences. We present a few examples of useful models and then consider the most frequent criticisms of formal modelling in order to identify a series of good practices for its proper use.

USEFUL MODELS

The supply–demand model epitomizes both the power of a good model and its drawbacks. The supply–demand model yields predictions consistent with our intuition, such as the effect of a shock on the costs of production. It also explains why a tax imposed on producers may actually be paid by consumers, that is, when the price elasticity of demand is high relative to the elasticity of supply. The second result is important, without being intuitive or trivial. Yet, thanks to the model, this result is usually taught in the first half of an introductory course in economics at undergraduate level. The second half of the course provides the occasion to introduce refinements to the model, such as imperfect competition, the role of asymmetric information in markets, or general equilibrium effects. The supply–demand model is not perfect. It fails to capture the non-material motives of human behaviour and a more nuanced description of rationality. These shortcomings are not to be underestimated, especially because, for many students, their first course in economics is also their last (some are discouraged by such simplistic assumptions). This raises the stakes in terms of which model to introduce first or of whether to introduce them to a model at all.

The prisoners' dilemma is another model used to introduce concepts of strategic reasoning in all social science disciplines. It illustrates how the best strategy can still lead to an unsatisfactory outcome when there is no coordination between individuals. It also shows how cooperation can be achieved in the context of an ongoing relationship. These are non-trivial results, which have been used in many disciplines, ranging from anthropology to industrial relations, among others. They are easy to express with the formalism of game theory and with real-life applications, such as the allocation of students to schools or jury selection. Game theory has applications in many fields: even though voting behaviour curricula in political science are more issue-driven than model-driven, formal models now permeate the field. It has also transformed our perception of voting, coalition-building, lobbying, conflict, nuclear deterrence, etc.

F

UNREALISTIC, BUT PARSIMONIOUS ASSUMPTIONS

Many examples fall within the scope of RC. However, behavioural scientists have found limited support either in the laboratory or in real life to demonstrate that individuals always act strategically. Does this mean RC can teach us nothing? Lack of realism is a crucial issue for critical assumptions: if a more realistic assumption can significantly change the results, then the model should probably be reassessed. If the mechanism is immune to deviations from the assumption, then an unrealistic assumption may reduce ambiguity and provide a clear message. In this sense, models are templates for understanding and interpreting the world—useful fictions and even 'fables', according to Rubinstein (2006: 881).

Why aim for simplicity? Why eliminate nuance? Borges (2013: 137) uses the parable of a society of cartographers that aims to produce ever-better maps, until they draw a map at a scale of 1:1. The map is exact, but useless. For maps to be useful, we need to eliminate details and focus on parsimonious assumptions. This is a general feature of models: we need simplified, unrealistic assumptions. Even though RC relies on such assumptions, it has many applications: it accounts for general equilibrium effects, such as the 'Dutch disease', and it sheds light on democratic transitions and so on.

MODELS AS TOOLS, NOT SCENARIOS

Good assumptions are a powerful tool when it comes to clarifying a causal mechanism. Nevertheless, they can be mishandled. It is quite possible that two similar models will yield opposite predictions. What is true of models is true of any tool, even empirical work. Models are most useful when they clarify a mechanism. In real life, several mechanisms often coexist, each associated with the corresponding model, with potentially contradictory empirical predictions. According to Rodrik (2015: 24), 'as with real experiments, the value of models resides in being able to isolate and identify specific causal mechanisms, one at a time'. Different mechanisms may differ in importance, depending on the context, but a toolbox full of mechanisms is what makes theory powerful in social sciences.

Models are least useful when they make unequivocal predictions. Rubinstein (2006: 879) notes that 'presenting the problem formally, as we do in economics, seems to obscure the real-life complexity of the situation'. Without nuance, formal models can be misleading, whether because of an honest mistake or in a deliberate attempt to justify a world view. However, the culprit is not the model, but the unrefined or ill-intentioned researcher.

MATHEMATICS TO CLARIFY, NOT OBFUSCATE

Is mathematics a secret language, designed to keep outsiders out? The feeling that mathematics is used to obfuscate simple ideas and make them appear scientific is widely echoed in fields with a more qualitative tradition. Hence, some people prefer a verbal argument (or analytical model that presents clearly defined interacting elements) to a formal model.

Nonetheless, verbal arguments have a drawback: they make it harder to find a flaw than with a formal model. Verbal arguments—even convincing ones—often collapse under close scrutiny. They may overlook general equilibrium feedback effects, **ENDOGENEITY**, or strategic considerations. According to Rodrik (2015: 32), 'economists use maths not because they're smart, but because they're not smart enough'. Lake and Powell (1999: 5) suggest that 'the strategic-choice approach helps sharpen the logic of our theories'. Mathematics is a language, and those who master it claim that it is an extraordinary source of clarity and consistency. In the end, verbal arguments are more elitist and exclusionary than formal models. Mathematics is not a fancy way to introduce simple ideas. On the contrary, it is a simple way to introduce fancy ideas.

REFERENCES
Borges, Jorge L. 2013. *El Hacedor*. New York, Vintage Español.
Gates, Scott and Brian D. Humes. 1997. *Games, Information, and Politics*. Ann Arbor, University of Michigan Press.
Green, Donald and Ian Shapiro. 1994. *Pathologies of Rational Choice Theory*. New Haven, Yale University Press.
Lake, David A. and Robert Powell. 1999. *Strategic Choice and International Relations*. Princeton, NJ, Princeton University Press.
MacDonald, Paul K. 2003. 'Useful Fiction or Miracle Maker: The Competing Epistemological Foundations of Rational Choice Theory'. *American Political Science Review* 97(4): 551-565.
Rodrik, Dani. 2015. *Economics Rules: The Rights and Wrongs of the Dismal Science*. New York and London, W. W. Norton and Company.
Rubinstein, Ariel. 2006. 'Dilemmas of an Economic Theorist'. *Econometrica* 74(4): 865-883.

G

GRAND THEORY AND MIDDLE-RANGE THEORY

Choosing the Right Tool for Theory Building

Frederik Ponjaert, Université libre de Bruxelles

INTRODUCTION

The study of social phenomena raises the twofold question about the internal and external validity of a HYPOTHESIS. A piece of research is internally valid when it describes the true state of affairs within its own setting. The extent to which its findings can be applied to other settings will determine its relative external validity. External validity is a product of the theoretical aspirations of the research. When grand in scope, theoretical aspirations reject the importance of specific variations and attempt to describe the true state of affairs in all settings. For example, in international relations, despite the clear differences between competing schools of thought, such as Morgenthau and Waltz's realism or Keohane's regime theories, they tend to discount the relevance of variations in state preferences. Conversely, a theory-building exercise with a mid-range scope is bound by a set of conditional statements. Again in international relations, a host of liberal international relations theories illustrate the limitations set by empirically measurable variations, such as state preferences, state–society relations (as a source of state preferences), or rational state behaviours resulting from those preferences.

Different ONTOLOGIES, EPISTEMOLOGIES, and methodologies generate different notions of validity. Therefore, reliable PARADIGMS AND RESEARCH PROGRAMMES should ensure that all three are consistent (with each other) and in line with the stated theoretical aspirations. The purpose can be to apply a given theory simply to test its internal validity or to foster a new theory that frames an externally valid claim. Whereas middle-range theory building is rooted in generalizable empirical propositions, grand theory building is based on internally consistent ontologies. On the one hand, grand theory favours highly abstract theorizing, which is fairly distinct from concrete empirical concerns. On the other hand, middle-range theories reflect more sociologically embedded theorizing, which strives to integrate theory and empirical variations over time and space.

FROM GRANDIOSE TO GRANDEUR? ORIGINS AND DEVELOPMENT OF 'GRAND THEORY'

Grand theory at its most basic is associated with the ambition to develop a way of understanding the world which may hold true over different social, cultural, and historical contexts. Historically, Talcott Parsons's work on structural functionalism is identified as an early modern-day example of such a grand ambition. However, the term 'grand theory', as a CONCEPTUAL CONSTRUCTION, was coined by C. Wright Mills (1959), a staunch critic of such grandiose approaches, which he saw as suffering from conservative BIAS and making unsubstantiated claims to overarching theory. Initially, the term itself was therefore an attempt to denounce structural-functionalists seeking to formulate a single universal functional scheme to understand all social structures. Much criticism of grand theories is fuelled by the fact that its underlying theorizing efforts remain more or less separate from empirical reality. Ontologically, doubts are cast on whether grand theories meet the standards of either FALSIFICATION or REPRODUCIBILITY. Epistemically, the question is whether a single theoretical system is capable of asking all the necessary questions. Methodologically, such theory-building approaches are charged with overlooking the relation between theory and empiricism and, thus, of cultivating BIASED CASE SELECTION. These doubts about the relevance of grand theory to the social world undermined its totalizing claims. Social scientists increasingly accepted that successful theorizing could not simply rely on narrow empiricism consisting entirely of statistical or observational regularities. The growing realization of the need to incorporate insights from a variety of perspectives led to two major evolutions in social science theory building: the rehabilitation of grand theory (by its main proponents); and the development of alternative, middle-range theories.

Grand theorists attempted to preserve the totalizing claims of the earlier structural-functionalists. This involved a shift towards INTERDISCIPLINARITY to integrate various methodological developments from across the social sciences and humanities. There was a series of renewed attempts at CONCEPT (RE-)CONSTRUCTION with the import of concepts from different subdisciplines. As a result, grand theory approaches prompted eclecticism, by encouraging the integration of a variety of epistemologies, such as: critical theory, structuralism, structural Marxism, psychoanalysis, hermeneutics, structuration theory, and even human geography. This ultimately rejuvenated grand theory, as its advocates set out to theorize a given 'social whole'. The validity of their claims was based on the internal ontological consistency of their chosen epistemologies.

In this respect, Skinner's seminal work marked a critical juncture. He contested 'the assumption that natural sciences offer an adequate or even relevant model for the practice of the social disciplines' (Skinner 1985: 6). Recognizing how the growing impact of non-English-speaking knowledge production on the social sciences had eroded core empiricist assumptions while also undermining the positivist ideal of the unification of the sciences, Skinner adopted a range of epistemologies in an attempt to rehabilitate grand theory. While still very different in outlook, the various epistemologies mobilized share a collective scepticism for POSITIVISM as the central philosophy governing the conception of human sciences, as they seek to coin grand theoretical approaches that seek not only to unpack but also to transform the philosophy of social sciences in relation to human sciences. Grand thinkers referenced by Skinner include theorists such as Gadamer, Derrida, Foucault, Kuhn, Habermas, Althusser, Lévi-Strauss, and Braudel. For example, the popularity of Foucault among social scientists across several disciplines is well established. His exploration of the relationship between power and knowledge, and how the former is used to control and define the latter, has become an overarching frame to many a social analysis. The resulting grand 'theory of power' has been mobilized to unpack such varied realities as 'the exercise of authority', 'management practices', 'educational policies', 'medical classifications and protocols', 'gender and sexuality', 'knowledge production and reproduction', 'cultural canons', or the 'legitimation of violence'.

Nonetheless, despite the aforementioned renaissance of grand theories in the social sciences, within the social sciences proper the outcomes have at times proven relatively modest and of limited significance (Brown 2013). While researchers will often seek to anchor their analysis in grand theories by namechecking such authors as Foucault on power and knowledge, Marx on class conflict, Habermas on intersubjectivity, or Weber on ideal types of power and authority, the ensuing analysis rarely engages directly with the referenced theory itself, preferring to use it as a framing device to shorthand certain background elements. Accordingly, often social sciences as varied as international political economy, international relations, education studies, or area studies have been consumers rather than producers of grand theory. Overall, the capacity of interdisciplinary grand theory approaches to theorize about the social world remains an open question, and their conclusions are often more 'world-revealing' than 'action-guiding' (White 1991).

AN EXERCISE IN MUDDLING THROUGH OR ACHIEVABILITY? FOCUS AND LIMITS OF 'MIDDLE-RANGE THEORY'

In response to the criticism of structural functionalism, middle-range theories for their part developed generalizable empirical propositions, rather than a coherent internal ONTOLOGY, to establish their external validity (Merton 1968). Thus, the general statements derived from empirical phenomena were verifiable within the scope of the collectable data. The resulting SCOPE CONDITION S can reconcile contradictory findings, by defining the limited circumstances in which a theory is applicable. Epistemologically, middle-range theories recognize multiple valid and even complementary paths to understanding. Middle-range theories appear restrained. This is the product of their ontological outlook, which considers it 'hopeless and quixotic to try to deter-mine the overarching independent variable that would operate in all social processes' (Boudon 1991: 520).

Middle-range theory building is a by-product of increasing empirical variations. As a result, a growing number of theoretical outlooks can coexist, 'comfortable in the knowledge that [each one] has a power based in the field and debate [occurs] mostly on within-camp issues' (Sylvester 2013: 615). Given this intrinsic pluralism, middle-range theory building must start from a stated and measurable social reality that can be stud-ied as a separate social phenomenon. In political science and international relations, a non-exhaustive list of social phenomena includes: reference groups, social mobil-ity, decision-making or normalization processes, social/policy practices, role conflict/theory, the formation or diffusion of social norms, the emergence and impact of pref-erences, and the relative distribution of resources and interests. This paradigmatic eclecticism has exposed middle-range theories to criticism. Relativists claim there is a lack of political relevance because of insufficient theorizing and contextualizing. Struc-turalists criticize the absence of scientific significance, suggesting that the knowledge produced is poor and fragmented. To counter the risk of Balkanization caused by the-oretical archipelagos, middle-range scholars have called for *ever more self-aware* forms of pluralism (Lake 2013). This includes eclectic mid-level theorizing at the ONTO-LOGICAL level, eclectic HYPOTHESIS testing at the METHODOLOGICAL level, and RESEARCH PROGRAMMES dictated by inductive reasoning at the empirical level (see DEDUCTIVE, INDUCTIVE, AND RETRODUCTIVE REASONING).

Middle-range and pluralist theories have set the social sciences on an ever more empirically driven path. In addition, they have responded to the call for 'critical prob-lem-solving' theories capable of addressing real-world problems. In this respect, the-ories that focus on 'problem solving' should be distinguished from theories geared to 'problem redefinition'. Although both involve middle-range theory building, they are driven by a different understanding of the underlying (empirically separable) socie-tal problem. Problem-solving theories consider that the problems are self-evident and defined by the dominant concerns. On the contrary, problem redefinition necessarily re-characterizes the societal problems themselves. Problem-solving middle-range the-ories vary depending on the target problem. For example, in international relations, the focus could be: problems of coordinating collective action in the case of regime or network theories; the challenges of (European) integration in the case of (neo-)functional, liberal intergovernmental or Europeanization theories. Problem-redefin-ing middle-range theories focus on combating establishment-oriented theories. They adopt a specific critical perspective, which in international relations may include: criti-cal security studies, critical geography, critical international political economy, or crit-ical foreign policy analysis.

Aspirations to develop grand theories have not been abandoned, and grand theo-ries continue to permeate different subdisciplines across the social sciences. Now, the tendency is to reconcile middle-range theories ('action-guiding' research on identi-fiable societal problems) with grand 'world-revealing' theories geared to furthering our understanding of the 'social whole'. For example, a complex and varied social phenomenon such as the 2010 response of the eurozone to the sovereign debt crisis in Greece has proven a fertile stomping ground for both grand and middle-range theorists. Foucauldian grand theory readings, for instance, stress how the EU/IMF-imposed austerity reflects specious knowledge echoing unequal power dynamics geared towards objectivizing the subjects ultimately targeted by the measures. Not contradictorily, but at a different level of analysis, middle-range network theories for their part highlight the measurable networks which underpin the production and circulation of the concepts which came to frame European policymakers' responses. Accordingly, grand and middle-range theory can, but need not, contradict each other as they fulfil different purposes.

In this respect, P. Tetlock (2005) makes a clear distinction between the two, with his analogy of hedgehogs, i.e. *researchers viewing the world through a single lens*, and foxes, i.e. *researchers drawing on a wide variety of experiences*. In other words, middle-range theory building corresponds to the expertise-driven, action-guiding, and problem-solving hedgehog. In contrast, grand theory building based on erudition, world revelations, and forecasts is the fox's preferred approach. It is important for researchers to choose a theory-building tool adapted to their stated objectives.

REFERENCES

Boudon, Raymond. 1991. 'What Middle-range Theories Are'. *Contemporary Sociology* 20(4): 519–522.

Brown, Chris. 2013. 'The Poverty of Grand Theory'. *European Journal of International Relations* 19(3): 483–497.

Lake, David A. 2013. 'Theory is Dead, Long Live Theory: The End of the Great Debates and the Rise of Eclecticism in International Relations'. *European Journal of International Relations* 19(3): 567–587.

Merton, Robert. 1968. *Social Theory and Social Structure*. New York, Free Press.

Mills, C. Wright. 1959. *The Sociological Imagination*. Oxford, Oxford University Press.

Skinner, Quentin (ed.). 1985. *The Return of Grand Theory in the Human Sciences*. Cambridge, Cambridge University Press.

Sylvester, Christine. 2013. 'Experiencing the End and Afterlives of International Relations/Theory'. *European Journal of International Relations* 19(3): 609–626.

Tetlock, Philip E. 2005. *Expert Political Judgement: How Good Is It? How Can We Know?* Princeton, NJ, Princeton University Press.

White, Stephen K. 1991. *Political Theory and Postmodernism*. Cambridge, Cambridge University Press.

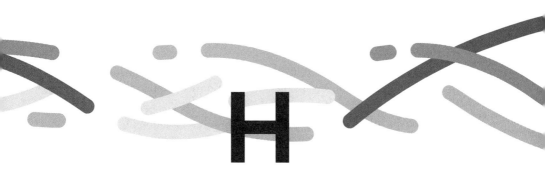

HERMENEUTICS

Theory and Methodology of Interpretation

Mélanie Samson, Université Laval

Hermeneutics can refer to an art, a methodological paradigm, or a philosophical movement. All three aspects of hermeneutics are presented briefly in the first section of this entry. The main focus concerns the relationship between hermeneutics and human sciences. The last section examines hermeneutics as a methodological approach used in legal research and the practice of law.

HERMENEUTICS AND THE SOCIAL SCIENCES

In its primary sense, hermeneutics is the art of interpreting texts correctly. Its origins date back to antiquity. It is one of the disciplines related to the interpretation of sacred or canonical texts, in particular theology, law, and philology. Hermeneutics provides a set of rules for understanding the meaning of texts. Traditional hermeneutics is a doctrine of truth. According to Aristotle, the meaning of a text is an objective reality that exists prior to its interpretation.

In the early nineteenth century, the scope of hermeneutics grew significantly, with the writings of the theologian Friedrich Schleiermacher. He suggested extending the application of hermeneutics to all types of written texts, but also to actions, situations, social symbols, and other phenomena, which require understanding (Schleiermacher 1998). Schleiermacher split the hermeneutic process into two components: objective grammatical interpretation, which examines the linguistic configuration of discourse, and subjective psychological or technical interpretation, which strives to identify the author's thoughts. Knowledge of the language, subject matter, and speaker became indispensable to understanding (see DISCOURSE ANALYSIS). Schleiermacher's work led to the notion of the hermeneutic circle. This metaphor expresses the idea, formulated by Ast in 1808, that each text or analogous element is part of a whole (part–whole relationship), where one cannot be understood without the other. Individual components can only be understood as part of the whole and, conversely, the whole can only be understood through its individual components.

In the second half of the nineteenth century, while attempting to define the human sciences in relation to the natural sciences, Wilhelm Dilthey saw hermeneutics as providing a common methodological basis for all human sciences. He suggested that the natural sciences use a methodology that seeks to provide a causal explanation for phenomena, while the human sciences use methods that provide an understanding of phenomena through interpretation (see DESCRIPTIVE, EXPLANATORY AND INTERPRETIVE APPROACHES). In Dilthey's view, every scientific discipline should satisfy the requirement of universal validity. He suggested that every mental phenomenon has a true meaning, which can only be grasped by placing it within its overall historical context (Dilthey 1988).

Hermeneutics experienced a philosophic shift in the twentieth century, when Martin Heidegger made it into a universal philosophy of understanding. Heidegger's hermeneutics dealt with human existence (Heidegger 1978). In his view, understanding is a practical exercise that precedes interpretation. It is based on an anticipation of meaning. Interpretation clarifies anticipation and expresses what is implicit in understanding.

Hans Georg Gadamer drew from Heidegger's work to revisit the issue of the specificity of human sciences. He suggested that the search for truth cannot be approached in the same way in the human sciences and in the natural sciences. Truth in the human sciences is not the result of a method; it is the outcome of a dialogue between the interpreter and the object being interpreted (Gadamer 1989).

Gadamer saw the claim of objectivity as an illusion and a trap. The interpreter's prejudices cannot be neutralized, nor should they be. They are indispensable for purposes of understanding. Prejudice is a type of pre-judgement, an anticipation of meaning fed by the interpreter's personal experiences and historical tradition. When meaning is based on prejudices, it can subsequently be confirmed, refuted, or clarified through the process of understanding.

Today, hermeneutic method is practised across the human sciences and applied to the study of all types of written texts, actions, and other meaningful material. One of the most articulate contemporary exponents of the hermeneutic perspective is the philosopher and political theorist Charles Taylor. According to Taylor, a human is a 'self-interpreting animal'; the human is not only 'impelled from time to time to interpret himself and his goals, [. . .] he is always already in some interpretation, constituted as human by this fact' (Taylor 1985a: 75). Human conduct always depends on the agent's interpretation of the situation and of himself. Therefore, this interpretation should be taken into account in social scientific explanations. In an influential essay, Taylor (1985b: 28) explains that politics can be the object of hermeneutics. The motives and goals of political behaviour are often unclear. Interpretative methods may be used to make sense of political behaviour.

Interpretative methods are commonly used by researchers in theology, in history, in literature, and in other disciplines in which written texts occupy an important place.

They may be used to discover the meaning of a discourse, a poem, or any other type of text, taking into account in particular the words used by the author and the social, cultural, and historical context.

HERMENEUTICS AND THE LAW

In the field of hermeneutics, the earliest developments occurred in law. Today, interpreting the sources of law is still at the heart of the work performed by legal experts. It is a fundamental aspect of the practice of law and a common methodological approach to academic legal research (Beaulac 2011).

There are two broad notions of legal interpretation. According to the first—the prevailing and most traditional notion—the interpretation of the sources of law is knowledge-based; the interpreter's task is to extract the pre-existing meaning of a legal text, as set out by its author (e.g. legislature, judge, parties to a contract). Like traditional hermeneutics generally, this notion postulates that each text has a single genuine meaning; thus, interpretation can be correct or incorrect. A court applies this notion of legal interpretation when it states that it seeks to determine the intention of the legislature, which is an objective and consistent reality that is empirically identifiable. From this perspective, legal interpretation strictly declares the meaning of an enactment. It is an exercise in understanding the text, which does not require creative input from the interpreter.

According to the second notion of legal interpretation, the activity involves the interpreter's will. The interpreter's task is to attribute meaning to a text, by choosing from several possible meanings. The interpretation is neither true nor false, given that the text does not contain an objectively identifiable meaning. This notion of legal interpretation approaches Gadamer's understanding of hermeneutics. It gives the legal expert considerable power. His role is not merely to identify a rule established by others and apply it almost mechanically to a set of facts. The legal expert called on to interpret the text participates in establishing the rule. Nonetheless, the interpreter must work within several constraints set by the traditions and methods of interpretation in use.

Interpreting both legal and non-legal texts involves several processes associated with five broad methods of interpretation. The *literal or grammatical method* of interpretation looks at the linguistic configuration of the text. This approach presumes that words are used with their common meaning, each word must produce a useful effect, and, in any given text, the same word always refers to the same reality. The *systematic method* of interpretation is designed to maintain consistency between the various parts of a given text, such as the various provisions in a statute or the different clauses in a contract, and between the various sources of law within a given legal system. According to the *teleological method* of interpretation, a text is interpreted in relation to its purpose. Every enactment should be interpreted broadly and liberally to ensure that the general purposes underlying it and the specific objectives of its provisions are achieved. Pursuant to the *historical or psychological method*, the text must be interpreted with consideration for the context in which it was written. If the text is legislative, the interpreter will attempt to determine the spirit in which it was adopted, taking into consideration the social context in which it was enacted, as well as contemporaneous historical events. Lastly, according to the *pragmatic method* of interpretation, the text's meaning should be determined in the light of the consequences of each potential interpretation. The interpretation to be retained is the one that produces a fair and reasonable result.

In practice, an interpreter will often combine several methods to interpret a given text. The choice of interpretation methods depends on the nature of the text to be interpreted and the interpreter's perception of his role. In the end, the meaning of a text will vary depending on the interpreter and the relative importance he gives to the linguistic configuration of the text, his purpose, the context in which it was written, and the context in which it is interpreted.

REFERENCES

Beaulac, Stéphane, Pierre-André Côté, and Mathieu Devinat. 2011. *The Interpretation of Legislation in Canada*, 4th edition. Toronto, Thomson Carswell.

Dilthey, Wilhelm. 1988. *Introduction to the Human Sciences: An Attempt to Lay a Foundation for the Study of Society and History*. Detroit, Wayne State University Press.

Gadamer, Hans Georg. 1989. *Truth and Method*, 2nd edition. New York, Crossroad.

Heidegger, Martin. 1978. *Being and Time*. Oxford: Basil Blackwell.

Schleiermacher, Friedrich. 1998. *Schleiermacher: Hermeneutics and Criticism and Other Writings*. Cambridge, Cambridge University Press.

Taylor, Charles. 1985a. 'Self-interpreting Animals', in *Philosophical Papers*, Volume 1, *Human Agency and Language*, 45-76. Cambridge, Cambridge University Press.

Taylor, Charles. 1985b. 'Interpretation and the Sciences of Man', in *Philosophical Papers*, Volume 2, *Philosophy and the Human Sciences*, 15-57. Cambridge, Cambridge University Press.

HYPOTHESES

State of the Art and 'Best Practice'

Onna Malou van den Broek & Adam William Chalmers, King's College London

Empirical social scientific research often entails an interaction between observations and theory (a logical and precise speculation about an answer to a RESEARCH QUESTION) (King, Keohane, and Verba 1994: 19). In the application of DEDUCTIVE REASONING, a specific theory will inform a set of hypotheses that are then tested through empirical observations. Accordingly, hypotheses can be defined as 'testable propositions entailed by the logic of the theory' (Toshkov 2016: 64). A hypothesis articulates a statement, not a question. Though this 'reasoned, clearly specified hunch or expectation' can guide various types of research—qualitative and quantitative, confirmative and explanatory (Halperin and Heath 2012: 130)—this contribution explicitly focuses on causal hypotheses. CAUSATION assumes a directional relationship with an independent VARIABLE causing an effect on a dependent variable; hence, the hypothesis takes the form of, for example, 'if X, then Y' or 'the more of X, the more of Y'. In their seminal work, King, Keohane, and Verba (1994) propose five basic principles to build a theory. Although critics have pointed out that these principles are unsuitable for the investigation of a small number of cases due to the reliance on random selection and generalization (Laitin et al. 1995), it remains an important work in developing procedures for avoiding BIAS and making reliable inferences.

PRINCIPLE 1: MAKE IT FALSIFIABLE

The first principle is informed by Popper's FALSIFICATION criteria (created in 1968; Popper 2005, initially published in 1959), and requires that a hypothesis can potentially be proven false. Since it is impossible to test all potential observable implications and verify a theory, the core of scientific inquiry is falsification, i.e. to falsify a hypothesis (Halperin and Heath 2012: 32–33). Nevertheless, if the hypothesis is rejected, it is not to say the theory is rejected. Rather, the theory simply does not hold under these specific conditions (King, Keohane, and Verba 1994: 100). To be falsifiable, a hypothesis must be empirically testable and have the potential to be rejected based on a large amount of observable implications. Often-used examples of unfalsifiable theories are theological assumptions (Lakatos 1976) or speculative assumptions; for example, the hypothesis 'The EU will collapse before 2050' is unfalsifiable since it is impossible to prove it untrue through observation.

PRINCIPLE 2: CAREFULLY SELECT YOUR VARIABLES

A (causal) hypothesis consists of three elements: an independent VARIABLE (X), a dependent variable (Y), and a statement about the relationship between the two variables. Sometimes the relationship between two variables can be intervened by a third variable, an intervening variable (Z) (Halperin and Heath 2012: 144–148, 65), producing a hypothesis such as: X leads to Y, if Z. A hypothesis aims to explain variation in the dependent variable, therefore the dependent variable should not cause any variation in the independent variable. In other words, the dependent variable should vary (taking different outcomes) and it should reflect what you aim to measure in the RESEARCH QUESTION (King, Keohane, and Verba 1994: 107–109). To illustrate this principle, let us look at a hypothesis formulated by Anthony Downs. He states that: 'Political parties in a democracy formulate policy strictly as a means of gaining votes' (Downs 1957: 137). In this case the independent variable is expectations about voters' behaviour, the dependent variable is the policy formation, and the intervening variable is the system of government, namely democratic regimes.

PRINCIPLE 3: ENSURE THE HYPOTHESIS
HAS INTERNAL CONSISTENCY

Hypotheses need to be simple, one-dimensional, and one-directional so that they do not result in competing outcomes (see King, Keohane, and Verba 1994: 105–107 on internally consistent theories). Recall our example from Downs (1957); the hypothesis is straightforward and there are no internal contradictions. Now imagine the hypothesis was formulated as follows: political parties in democracies *and* authoritarian states formulate their policies to gain voters *or* to attract campaign contributions. The general rule is that a hypothesis reflects one dependent and one independent VARIABLE (and sometimes an intervening variable). Our example of a poorly formulated hypothesis, however, consists of two dependent and two independent variables. Therefore, if rejected, it remains unclear whether it is rejected for both democracies and authoritarian states, and both policy to gain voters and to attract campaign contributions. The hypothesis is therefore not one-dimensional. Hence, in this case it would be better to separate the hypothesis into four individual hypotheses. Additional to the four main hypotheses, and informed by theory, it is possible to subsequently choose to include an interaction effect. In an interaction effect you combine two hypotheses. For example, you could hypothesize that if X1 and X2, then Y1, or, if X1, then Y1 and Y2.

PRINCIPLE 4: MAXIMIZE THE CONCRETENESS

The fourth principle builds further on the FALSIFICATION principle: the concepts/VARIABLES that make up the hypothesis must be observable (see OPERATIONALIZATION). In the social sciences this is often a challenge. When studying concepts such as identity, culture, and national interest, the variables are not directly observable. To overcome this problem, we need to think about specific indicators or how to observe consequences of the concepts (King, Keohane, and Verba 1994: 109–112). In Downs's hypothesis on policy formulation, he argues that policy is used to gain votes assuming an underlying motivational mechanism. Motivation cannot be observed directly. When operationalizing this variable, we could potentially ask decision makers, through a survey or interview, about which factors they take into account when formulating policy. Democracy, on the other hand, can potentially be measured through indicators such as the degree of representation in formal government institutions. Hence, in formulating a hypothesis it is important to think ahead about how to measure the dependent and independent VARIABLES. Furthermore, think ahead about how to measure the assumed relationship between the two.

PRINCIPLE 5: BE SPECIFIC (BUT GENERIC)

The fifth principle marks a fundamental difference with the work of King, Keohane, and Verba (1994). Though theories need to be generally applicable, hypotheses need to be more specific. This is due to the function of hypotheses, which is to state part of the answer to a more generic RESEARCH QUESTION. By specifying the causal mechanisms that underlie a theory, the hypothesis becomes more relevant (Toshkov 2016: 65). By being specific, you state the direction of the relationship and the outcomes as well. A hypothesis is not an open-ended statement. In Downs's hypothesis, he indicates political parties as actors, a democratic mode of governance as the context, and the formulation of policy as an action that aims to gain votes as the specific outcome. At the same time, however, do not overuse specifications. Since CAUSALITY often relies on inference, make sure the hypothesis is generalizable (see SCOPE CONDITIONS). That is, results need to be relevant in your academic field. In the case of Downs, for example, it would be too specific to hypothesize that left-wing political parties with less than 10 per cent of the total amount of votes formulate their policies on economic advantages for migrants as a means to gain votes from middle-aged women with a medical background. This kind of specification would only be desirable and useful if it served a particular theoretical or practical purpose.

ILLUSTRATION: INGLEHART'S BASIC VALUE PRIORITY ASSUMPTION

Formulating a good hypothesis can be a challenging task. Let us therefore look at the hypotheses formulated by Ronald Inglehart in relation to his well-known work on the shifting values of the Western public. His main argument is that people have a hierarchical set of priorities. Over time this set of priorities has shifted for people in the West from materialist priorities towards 'post-materialist' priorities, which emphasize belonging, self-expression, and life quality (Inglehart 1981). To test the theory of hierarchical sets of priorities coupled with an empirical change, Inglehart formulates two hypotheses: the scarcity hypothesis and the socialization hypothesis. Let us look a bit more in depth at the first one, which states that: 'An individual's priorities reflect the socioeconomic environment: one places the greatest subjective value on those things that are in relatively short supply' (Inglehart 1981: 881). Does this hypothesis meet all the principles discussed earlier?

First, the hypothesis is clearly falsifiable. If we observe that a person places subjective value on things that are not in relatively short supply, we can reject the hypothesis. Furthermore, we can distinguish between the dependent VARIABLE, the independent variable, and the nature of their relationship: the supply of things (X) affects one's subjective value (Y), or in other words, the socio-economic environment affects an individual's priorities. In terms of internal coherence, there are no apparent internal contradictions. Though the hypothesis is formed in two parts, the latter clarifies the first. The evaluation of the fourth principle, concreteness, requires a bit more information. An individual's priorities are not directly observable and, as a consequence, the dependent variable is measured via indicators. Inglehart asked a sample of Western citizens what they personally considered to be the most important goal of the state, choosing from a list of twelve options ranging from maintaining order to making cities more beautiful. We could be critical and ask whether this operationalization reliably captures post-materialism, however this is beyond the scope of this chapter. The independent variable, on the other hand, is operationalized as a binary indicator capturing differences between the post-war generation and the pre-war generation, under the assumption that economic resources were scarce for the pre-war generation. Lastly, the hypothesis is rather generic. However, in the overall theory Inglehart does specify the 'actors' as the Western public and he addresses purely democratic states. Moreover, the second part of the hypothesis specifies and clarifies the more generic concepts of the first part.

Next steps:

After formulating the hypothesis (or hypotheses) based on your main theory, it is important to include an alternative or rival hypothesis (King, Keohane, and Verba 1994: 33). For example, what else could explain the variation in your dependent VARIABLE? Acknowledging and anticipating competing explanations increases the strength and trustworthiness of your research (see COUNTERFACTUAL ANALYSIS). Just as with your central hypothesis, an alternative hypothesis should be grounded in existing studies. The number of hypotheses varies per study, but in general a maximum of six hypotheses holds. If your study is explorative and/or conceptual in nature, your journey ends here. If you conduct an empirical study, you have to clearly operationalize the concepts (i.e. how can you measure the independent and dependent variables?) once all hypotheses are properly formulated. If you cannot directly observe the variables, look for indicators or observed consequences. Additionally, you have to make sure your methodology measures the expected relationship between the variables. Then the data collection can start, and you can empirically test your hypothesis.

One point of caution: you cannot change your hypotheses after the data collection process has commenced. Though in some cases it might be permitted to make your hypotheses less restrictive, it is bad practice to make them more restrictive under any circumstances (King, Keohane, and Verba 1994: 21).

REFERENCES

Downs, Anthony. 1957. 'An Economic Theory of Political Action in a Democracy'. *Journal of Political Economy* 65(2): 135-150.

Halperin, Sandra and Oliver Heath. 2012 *Political Research: Methods and Practical Skills.* Oxford, Oxford University Press.

Inglehart, Robert. 1981. 'Post-materialism in an Environment of Insecurity'. *American Political Science Review* 75(4): 880-900.

King, Gary, Robert Keohane, and Sidney Verba. 1994. *Designing Social Inquiry: Scientific Inference in Qualitative Research.* Princeton, NJ, Princeton University Press.

Laitin, David D., James A. Caporaso, David Collier, Ronald Rogowski, and Sidney Tarrow. 1995. 'Review Symposium: The Qualitative-Quantitative Disputation: Gary King, Robert O. Keohane, and Sidney Verba's *Designing Social Inquiry: Scientific Inference in Qualitative Research'. The American Political Science Review* 89(2): 454-481.

Lakatos, Imre. 1976. 'Falsification and the Methodology of Scientific Research Programmes', in *Can Theories be Refuted?: Essays on the Duhem-Quine Thesis*, ed. Sandra Harding, 205-259. Dordrecht, Springer.

Popper, Karl. 2005. *The Logic of Scientific Discovery.* New York, Routledge.

Toshkov, Dimiter. 2016. *Research Design in Political Science.* New York, Palgrave Macmillan.

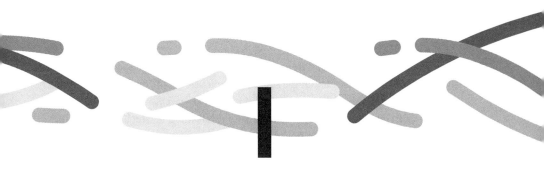

INTERDISCIPLINARITY

The Interaction of Different Disciplines for Understanding Common Problems

Roberto Carrillo & Lidia Núñez, Université libre de Bruxelles

The term interdisciplinary refers to a mode of conducting research that 'integrates information, data, techniques, tools, perspectives, concepts, and/or theories from two or more disciplines or bodies of specialized knowledge to advance fundamental understanding or to solve problems whose solutions are beyond the scope of a single discipline or area of research practice' (Committee on Facilitating Interdisciplinary Research, Committee on Science, Engineering, and Public Policy 2004: 2). Therefore, it is a way of conducting research that goes beyond the frontiers of traditional disciplines. This entry provides an overview of the main features of how interdisciplinarity is applied in the social sciences. It defines the concept and presents an overview of its origins and evolution, as well as the interrelationship between interdisciplinary studies, society, and the development of public policies. Following on from this, the measurement and analysis of interdisciplinarity is then discussed. Finally, the main criticisms of interdisciplinarity and its use in the social sciences are presented.

A BRIEF REVIEW OF THE CONCEPT

Interdisciplinary studies are characterized by a single approach that combines the onto-epistemological foundations of more than one discipline. Complex social phenomena, such as global warming or social conflicts, are often studied by interdisciplinary research teams. The knowledge produced by interdisciplinary research leads to the emergence of new **RESEARCH QUESTIONS**, new methodologies, new approaches to problems, and even to the development of new fields of research.

However, the combination of disciplines has important consequences. First, it raises the question of the cumulativeness of scientific knowledge (cf. **PARADIGMS AND RESEARCH PROGRAMMES**), which may jeopardize advances in knowledge. When different disciplinary foundations are applied, there is no consensus about how objects of study are problematized or about the standards for assessing the quality of the scientific findings. Second, the evolution of interdisciplinary research can lead to the emergence of new disciplines, through a process of autonomization, in which scholars share paradigms and standards. From this perspective, interdisciplinarity is merely a phase of the creative process to develop a new field of knowledge. Political science, for instance, emerged through a process of autonomization derived from political history, political philosophy, and law. Social psychology or gender, post-colonial, and peace research studies are other examples of new fields that emerged from interdisciplinary research.

ORIGINS AND EVOLUTION

Interdisciplinarity gained momentum in the 1950s and 1960s, when debates about social problems suggested that different disciplines might be able to solve them. This led to the creation of interdisciplinary research centres in both Europe and North America, where complex social and natural issues were studied with the aim of integrating different methods, data, and findings. The Tensions Project conducted by UNESCO in 1949 and the creation of the Centre for Interdisciplinary Research (ZIF) in Bielefeld, Germany in 1968 are two examples. It is important to note that interdisciplinary research is not only conducted by universities, but also non-profit organizations, private sector companies, as well as government organizations.

DISCIPLINARITY, MULTIDISCIPLINARITY, PLURIDISCIPLINARITY, INTERDISCIPLINARITY, AND TRANSDISCIPLINARITY

In 1972, Apostel edited a seminal work on interdisciplinarity, broaching the problems of teaching and research in universities. The work suggests that disciplines should be analysed in relation to the context and dynamics of social problems. One of the main contributions of the work constitutes a much quoted TYPOLOGY of interdisciplinarity. A distinction is made between three terms that are frequently used interchangeably: multidisciplinary, interdisciplinary, and transdisciplinary. However, before understanding the scope and limitations of these concepts, it is important to explain the concept of disciplinarity.

Disciplinarity refers to expertise in a specific domain or discipline. Since the creation of universities in the Middle Ages, the studies undertaken in the different disciplines have helped explain natural and social phenomena. In a disciplinary approach, each discipline evolves independently of other disciplines. Weingart and Stehr (2000: xi) define discipline as 'the intellectual structures in which the transfer of knowledge from one generation to the next is cast'. In their view, disciplines evolve over time and are characterized by their different size, structure, and goal orientation. In other words, disciplines have their own subject of study, ontological codes, and methods. For example, political science, psychology, and economics are disciplines.

The term multidisciplinarity refers to a 'variety of disciplines, offered simultaneously, but without making explicit possible relationships between them' (Apostel et al 1972: 106). In this case, the disciplines address a similar subject of study but speak as separate voices and there is no link between them. In multidisciplinary research, different disciplines cooperate and work on the same subject, but each discipline maintains its own specific perspective (Gibbons et al 1994). For instance, political science, economics, and psychology can address the same social issue without any interaction between the three disciplines.

Pluridisciplinarity is the juxtaposition of disciplines (Apostel et al 1972). Contrary to multidisciplinarity, the disciplines are more or less related. They cooperate when it comes to analysing a particular subject, however each discipline maintains its specific perspective. In other words, there is no exchange or methodological cooperation between the disciplines.

In the case of interdisciplinarity, the prefix *inter* indicates that a relationship exists between the disciplines. Interdisciplinarity combines the contributions of different disciplines to resolve a particular problem. Therefore, disciplines interact to produce a broader view of a given problem. It is important to note that interdisciplinarity is neither the sum of two or more disciplines, nor the synthesis of different approaches. Weingart and Stehr (2000) call for an interdisciplinarity of 'real' problems, in which different disciplines can contribute to the general understanding of the phenomenon under study. One example is to study electoral behaviour by integrating the perspectives used in psychology and political science (cf. BEHAVIOURISM).

Transdisciplinarity is a system of postulates that goes beyond disciplines, as the prefix *trans* suggests (Nicolescu 2002). The main feature of a transdisciplinary approach is to coordinate disciplines with the common purpose of producing knowledge (cf. Apostel et al 1972; Gibbons et al 1994). A recurrent example in this domain is Marxist theory. The postulates of Marxist theory have been applied to the analysis of different disciplines. Thus, Marxism has helped explain phenomena in fields such as economics, politics, and sociology as well as education. In each case, the Marxist perspective was maintained regarding social inequalities and the interests of those who control the means of production.

SOCIETY, INTERDISCIPLINARITY, AND POLICYMAKING

Some authors suggest that there is a link between interdisciplinary research and social protests. The reason for this is that interdisciplinary research gained importance in the 1960s and 1970s in a context of social protests about emerging social and environmental issues. Since then, interdisciplinary research has contributed to the design of policies that strive to address some of these issues (cf. Weingart and Stehr 2000). A frequently cited example is the anti-nuclear movement, which called for significant reforms in the use of nuclear technologies to protect nature and human life. In this context, the Öko Institut (an institute for applied ecology in Germany) was created in 1977. Its aim was to support the social movement, by providing scientific evidence and alerts about the potential impact of nuclear technology on a social and environmental level. The objectives of the Öko Institut were established jointly by different disciplines. The institute's research has broadened our understanding of nuclear issues, as well as issues relating to the environment and climate change.

Recently, the Öko Institut conducted an interdisciplinary study to measure the impact of palm oil production in Indonesia. Published in 2019, this study provided an interdisciplinary approach that was applied to understanding the environmental impact of this production. Focusing on specific areas such as the loss of biodiversity or greenhouse gas emissions, the report also concentrated on the economic impact (relating to a lack of regulations regarding working conditions), remunerations, social security; as well as the social impact (mainly from the perspective of human rights). This is an example of how interdisciplinary research can help governments design public policies to address these types of issues.

The field of gender studies provides a further example of the interaction between different disciplines. Gender, LGBT, or women's studies often focus on the social and cultural constructions of femininities and masculinities. In other words, theories, concepts, and methods from different disciplines such as sociology, political sciences, history, and psychology shed light on diverse elements and help explain these complex subjects. The results of research on gender studies have contributed to the development of policies related to equality and human rights in different countries.

So far, we have mentioned cases including disciplines that come from neighbouring disciplines. However, interdisciplinary research can go beyond this. For instance, artificial intelligence research connects computational sciences, social sciences, and humanities in order to better understand and develop interactions between machines and humans. Hence, interdisciplinary research often dictates that disciplines with a different ONTOLOGY and methodological approach communicate with each other to find a common answer to societal challenges and research questions.

A new field of research strives to measure and analyse the degree of interdisciplinarity across different sciences. For instance, quantitative measurements can generate indicators to measure the interdisciplinarity of scientific output, using a bibliometric approach (the statistical analysis of scientific publications). Wagner et al (2011) discusses different methods for measuring interdisciplinary research.

CRITICS

Academic rigour can be assessed by combining ontological and epistemological postulates from different disciplines. According to Frodeman (2010: xxix), 'conventions concerning the proper depth of inquiry or degree of academic rigour tend to marginalize unconventional claims or approaches, which are often hard to document or measure'. In interdisciplinary topics, the pertinence and quality of a contribution can be assessed by peers that have experience in different disciplines and different standards. Gibbons et al (1994) suggests that the broad-based quality control process does not necessarily mean that the quality of the research is poor (Gibbons et al 1994: 8). Frodeman (2010) also defends interdisciplinarity because it produces knowledge in an innovative way and makes knowledge more relevant, by drawing on expertise from different disciplines.

Other criticisms claim that interdisciplinarity is associated with the impossibility of unifying disciplines, which are based on apparently contradictory epistemological foundations (cf. **EPISTEMOLOGY**) and theoretical traditions. However, Gibbons notes that interdisciplinary research arises only if it 'is based upon a common theoretical understanding and must be accompanied by a mutual interpenetration of disciplinary epistemologies' (Gibbons et al 1994: 29). Paul Feyerabend proposes a more extreme approach, the concept of 'epistemological anarchism'. He argues that making a commitment to a specific method or discipline jeopardizes the advancement of knowledge and the process of discovery.

REFERENCES

Apostel, Léo, Guy Berger, Asa Briggs, and Guy Michaud. 1972. *Interdisciplinarity: Problems of Teaching and Research in Universities*. Paris, Organisation for Economic Co-operation and Development.

Committee on Facilitating Interdisciplinary Research, Committee on Science, Engineering, and Public Policy. 2004. *Facilitating Interdisciplinary Research*. Washington, DC, National Academy Press.

Frodeman, Robert. 2010. *The Oxford Handbook of Interdisciplinarity*. Oxford, Oxford University Press.

Gibbons Michael, Camille Limoges, Helga Nowotny, Simon Schwartzman, Peter Scott, and Martin Trow. 1994. *The New Production of Knowledge: The Dynamics of Science and Research in Contemporary Societies*. Thousand Oaks, CA, SAGE Publications.

Nicolescu, Basarab. 2002. *Manifesto of Transdisciplinarity*. Albany, NY, Suny Press.

Wagner, Caroline, David Roessner, Kamau Bobb, Julie Klein, Kevin Boyack, Joann Keyton, Ismael Rafols, and Katy Börner. 2011. 'Approaches to Understanding and Measuring Interdisciplinary Scientific Research (IDR): A Review of the Literature'. *Journal of Informetrics* 5(1): 14-26.

Weingart, Peter and Nico Stehr. 2000. *Practising Interdisciplinarity*. Toronto, University of Toronto Press.

I

INTERVIEW TECHNIQUES

Matrakova Marta, Université libre de Bruxelles and LUISS Guido Carli di Roma

INTRODUCTION: DEFINITION AND EPISTEMOLOGICAL COMMITMENTS

The use of interviews in social science expanded during the twentieth century. Research interviews with industrial, commercial, and market objectives have also contributed to their development as one of the main methods of social inquiry. The extensive use of interviews as a means of investigation and self-representation in modern society has contributed to their position as the 'characteristic format for personal narratives' (Gubrium and Holstein 2002: 92).

A comprehensive definition of an interview must consider the main possible variants and their constitutive elements. In broad terms 'an interview is a conversation that has a structure [. . . wherein the] purpose' is to obtain 'thoroughly tested knowledge' (Kvale and Brinkmann 2009: 3). Interviewer and interviewee have different roles, with the former controlling the situation by asking questions to the interviewee, who is expected to react within this framework (Gubrium and Holstein 2002). As a result of the diverse theoretical appreciation of interviewing, its conceptualization has evolved from 'a simple information-gathering operation' to 'a site of [. . .] producing knowledge' (Gubrium and Holstein 2003: 4).

From a POSITIVIST perspective, the main characteristics of interviews pose serious difficulties for their consideration as a scientific method. As positivists look for underlying and unchanging truths, they identify possible ambiguities and contradictions as the main source of error. In addition, the lack of uniform knowledge and experience between researcher and interviewee can make it impossible to correctly interpret the data communicated (Kvale and Brinkmann 2009). On the other hand, post-positivist and constructivist theorists are interested in the shared meaning constructed in a specific cultural context and in the lenses that individuals use to interpret social reality. In order to determine the shared views and meanings in any particular group, they analyse and synthesize the detailed reports of all the interviewees involved in the research (Rubin and Rubin 2005).

In addition, constructivists recognize the cultural assumptions of the interviewer. They claim that it is important to be cautious because these preconceptions may prevent the researcher from correctly *hearing* the perspective of his/her conversational counterpart (Rubin and Rubin 2005). It is also important to consider this to avoid BIAS caused by answers being inferred from the way in which questions are posed (Bourdieu 1972). Reflexive objectivity is a method introduced in response to these claims. Consequently, the interviewer should reflect on his/her unavoidable prejudices and consider how they might affect the research project (Kvale and Brinkmann 2009).

To summarize, while POSITIVISTS conceive interviewers as *miners* whose main objective is data collection, post-positivists view them as *travellers* who unravel the intersubjective process of knowledge construction. These different epistemological conceptions of interview research have led to the development of various techniques (Kvale and Brinkmann 2009), examined in turn in the next section.

TYPES OF INTERVIEWS

The *structured/directed interview* is characterized by the 'highly structured role of the interviewer', who asks predefined questions in a neutral way (Gubrium and Holstein 2003: 60). It is a highly standardized interview that aims to eliminate any errors stemming from the interviewer's intervention and to expose all the respondents to an identical experience. As a predefined set of optional answers is provided to the interviewee, this technique has been compared to a 'verbally administered questionnaire' or SURVEY (Gillham 2005: 80). This allows the researcher to administer many interviews in a relatively short period of time. The main strength of this technique is its capacity to accurately measure population characteristics. However, four types of error are still possible: sampling errors, coverage errors, non-response error, and measurement errors. In order to avoid these errors, the researchers structure the study in the following phases: formulation of objectives, identification of target population, design of the sample, translation of concepts into appropriate questions, selection of data collection method, pretesting, and interviewing (Gubrium and Holstein 2003). Research on EU institutional development has on occasions combined the use of surveys with semi-structured interviews (Henökl 2015).

The *semi-structured/semi-directive interview* provides the researcher with a good balance between structure and flexibility. It is comparatively less structured than the previous technique, due mainly to the use of open-ended questions, without predefined options for the respondent. In addition, the interviewer may use probes or follow-up questions when he/she considers that more information is required on a specific point. The questions are developed in a way that ensures their topic focus and the same questions are posed to all the respondents (Gillham 2005). The roles of investigator and respondent are more balanced and collaborative. This research technique is used mainly when the concepts and the relationship between VARIABLES are relatively well understood, as it facilitates discovery and allows analysis in terms of commonalities (Gillham 2005). In the preparation phase, it is important to ensure that 'one question leads into another', to achieve a satisfactory narrative (Gillham 2005: 74). The drawbacks of this technique include the length of the process and the importance of the skills of the researcher for adequate performance (Gillham 2005: 74). Specific examples of use of semi-structured interviews can be found in EU studies and international relations literature (Peetz 2018; Field 2019).

The *in-depth non-directive interview* does not follow a structure defined in advance by the researcher. Instead, the interviewer opens up the possibility for the respondent to lead the conversation, following the internal logic and narrative of the story. These types of interviews prioritize the need for narrative inquiry and their proponents are critical of conventional question-and-answer interviews (Gillham 2005). They tend to be longer in duration and so help the interviewer build confidence and establish rapport with the respondent. Thus, mutual self-disclosure between the participants provides deeper understanding and more detailed knowledge. The information gathered may include very personal matters, such as lived experience, value interpretation, or cultural knowledge (Gubrium and Holstein 2002).

In addition, as in-depth interviews facilitate discovery, they are considered as a useful initial technique that provides insight on topics that need to be 'investigated in a subsequent, more structured, stage' (Gillham 2005: 45). Thus, exploratory interviews constitute a specific use of in-depth interviews in which the researcher introduces the topic and follows on the information provided by the interviewee in order to uncover new points of view (Kvale and Brinkmann 2009).

In non-directive interviews the roles of the researcher and the interviewee shift, allowing greater initiative and leading capacity to the interviewee. In addition, the investigator enjoys more space for expression of the self and provides more personal commitment and reciprocity on the side of the interviewer, which enables access to more intimate or complete knowledge (Gubrium and Holstein 2002). Kvale and Brinkmann (2009) claim that successful in-depth interviewing does not depend on standard procedures or rules, as it relies on the high level of skill of the interviewer, his/her knowledge about the topic and understanding of the methodological options available, and the conceptual issues of producing knowledge. Consequently, they conceive research interviewing as a 'craft that, if well carried out, can become an art' (Kvale and Brinkmann 2009: 15).

In-depth interviewing has been compared with OBSERVATIONAL METHODS. While ethnography focuses on cultural and 'lived experience, set in the eternal present', the focus of the interview is verbal communication in a biographical past-future perspective (Gubrium and Holstein 2002: 85). Where these two perspectives might be complementary, researchers combine interviews and ethnographic data. ORAL HISTORY AND LIFE HISTORY can be considered as subtypes of non-directive interview (Denzin and Lincoln 2011).

In the framework of non-directive interviews, group interviews can be differentiated from individual interviews. The researcher adopts the role of a 'moderator' or 'facilitator' and defines the major topic that the participants discuss. It is argued that the group social interaction technique uncovers feeling, perceptions, and events that might be rationalized or suppressed in the context of a one-to-one interview. As with in-depth interviews, it can be successfully used as an introductory technique. FOCUS GROUPS are also used in qualitative research and differ from group interviews in their tightly defined topic for discussion and stricter group composition (Gillham 2005).

INTERVIEW ELEMENTS

The research process with interview techniques can follow a flexible, iterative design in which the study is continually adapted to new findings (Rubin and Rubin 2005). The interviewing process can also develop through the following stages, with specific issues to be addressed in each phase:

- Thematizing involves formulation of the purpose and the theme to be investigated.

- Designing entails planning the design of the study regarding the intended knowledge and its moral implications. The elaboration of an interview guide at this stage will depend on the type, the topic of the interview, and the general approach adopted. For instance, post-positivists and constructivists would prioritize questions on the general context and biography of the respondent.

- The use of appropriate SAMPLING TECHNIQUES is essential to guarantee the objectivity and representativity of the research. In in-depth interviewing, snowball sampling is a very common technique, when the interviewer turns to people who have already been interviewed for referral to other potential interviewees.

- The actual interviewing is conducted on the basis of the interview guide defined earlier. How strictly the researcher follows the sequence of questions will depend on the type of interview. In some contexts, the interviewer will count mainly on his/her own judgement for defining the questions and the order in which they are put forward. Active listening is essential for the art of asking second questions (Kvale and Brinkmann 2009). It is also important for the interviewer to consciously use different types of questions. For instance, probing questions might be used to make evident potential conflicts in the positions adopted by the interviewee. The researcher can also display deliberate naivety in order to show his/her 'openness to new and unexpected phenomena' (Kvale and Brinkmann 2009: 28). In addition, on certain occasions confrontational questions can encourage the respondent to challenge the interviewer's assumptions.

- Transcription consists in the translation of narrative discourse into written text. The main methods of recording information for transcription are audio/video recording, note taking, and remembering. The choice between these different options will depend on the epistemological approach of the research. For instance, the post-positivist interest in the 'linguistic constitution of reality [and] on the contextuality of meaning' implies greater focus on this stage of the research (Kvale and Brinkmann 2009: 186).

- The analysis implies a choice of the most appropriate mode of analysis based on the purpose and topic of the investigation, and on the interview material collected. The different modes of analysis may focus on the meaning of what is said or on choice of language.

- Verification satisfies the need to determine the validity, reliability, and generalizability of the data. The number of interviews conducted and the data that needs to be collected will depend on the specific RESEARCH QUESTION. A point of saturation will be reached when 'further interviews yield little new knowledge' (Kvale and Brinkmann 2009: 113). The new information and its interpretation by the researcher can be validated by the respondent, the general public, or scholars familiar with the topic.

- Reporting involves the communication of the findings and the methods of the study (Kvale and Brinkmann 2009).

Progress through these stages of the interviewing process is not always linear. For instance, very often specific initial findings might require a certain degree of analysis as part of the interviewing stage in order to make possible their confirmation. Therefore, a very good overview of the entire process and of the specific requirements of each stage is required in order to manage it successfully (Kvale and Brinkmann 2009).

The ETHICS of interviewing need to be considered throughout all stages of the research process. The main ethical issues include the identification of the researcher, the purposes of the study, and the expectations towards the participants. Confidentiality considerations may lead to different ways of quoting the information obtained— inclusion of full names, fictitious names, or anonymously (Kvale and Brinkmann

2009). More rigorous requirements for consent and protection of personal information are adopted when the research deals with vulnerable or dependent social groups (Gillham 2005).

REFERENCES

Bourdieu, Pierre. 1972. 'Public Opinion Does Not Exist', in *Communication and Class Struggle*, ed. Armand Mattelart and Seth Siegelaub. 124-130. New York, International General.

Denzin, Norman K. and Yvonna S. Lincoln. 2011. *The SAGE Handbook of Qualitative Research*. Thousand Oaks, CA, SAGE Publications.

Field, Mark. 2019. 'Conducting Elite Interviews to Explore Variations in Attitudes to Transparency Among Members of the European Parliament'. *SAGE Research Methods Cases in Political Science and International Relations*. Available at https://methods.sagepub.com/case/elite-interviews-attitudes-to-transparency-members-of-european-parliament (Accessed 6 August 2020).

Gillham, Bill. 2005. *Research Interviewing: The Range of Techniques*. Berkshire, Open University Press.

Gubrium, Jaber F. and James A. Holstein. 2002. *Handbook of Interview Research: Context & Method*. Thousand Oaks, CA, SAGE Publications.

Gubrium, Jaber F. and James A. Holstein. 2003. *Inside Interviewing: New Lenses, New Concerns*. Thousand Oaks, CA, SAGE Publications.

Henökl, Thomas E. 2015. 'How do EU Foreign Policy-Makers Decide? Institutional Orientations within the European External Action Service.' *West European Politics* 38(3): 679-708.

Kvale, Steinar and Svend Brinkmann. 2009. *Interviews: Learning the Craft of Qualitative Research Interviewing*. Thousand Oaks, CA, SAGE Publications.

Peetz, Julia. 2018. 'Semi-Structured Elite Interviews With U.S. Presidential Speechwriters in Interdisciplinary Research on Politics and Performance.' *SAGE Research Methods Cases in Political Science and International Relations*.

Rubin, Herbert J. and Irene S. Rubin. 2005. *Qualitative Interviewing: The Art of Hearing Data*. Thousand Oaks, CA, SAGE Publications.

LEVELS OF ANALYSIS

Mauro Caprioli & Claire Dupuy, University of Louvain

Research in the social sciences may be interested in subjects located at different levels of analysis. The level of analysis indicates the position at which social and political phenomena are analysed within a gradual order of abstraction or aggregation that is constructed analytically. Its definition and boundaries vary across social science disciplines. In general, the micro level refers to the individual level and focuses on citizens' attitudes or politicians' and diplomats' behaviours. Analyses at the meso level focus on groups and organizations, like political parties, social movements, and public administrations. The macro level corresponds to structures that are national, social, economic, cultural, or institutional—for example, countries and national or supranational political regimes.

The level of analysis of a given study depends on the **RESEARCH QUESTION**. For example, the rise of right-wing populism in Western democracies can be approached at different levels by political scientists. Scholars may examine what motivates individuals to vote for populist parties, such as their grievances about the current state of affairs, political elites, or the undeserving. In this case, their research question is located at the micro level. Alternatively, scholars may consider how the characteristics of populist parties influence electoral results. This could involve the examination of the political platform, the leadership, or the differences between them and other parties. Here, the focus is on the meso level. The populist parties' electoral success can also be approached from another perspective, by considering how major societal change, such as economic crises and globalization, can explain their resurgence (Mudde 2007). This type of research question is situated at the macro level. However, a research question can also be addressed at more than one level of analysis. Let us consider another important issue: the causes of war. Kenneth Waltz (1992) categorized the causes using three distinct images, corresponding to different levels of analysis. The first image pertains to theories that claim that war is caused by factors that operate at an individual level, such as human nature. The second image refers to theories that claim that wars are primarily caused by states. The third image accounts for wars at the systemic or international level, with specific emphasis on its anarchic nature.

Levels of analysis are also linked to the choice of theory. Some theories highlight explanations that are located at a specific level. Let us consider two strands of neo-institutionalism that are widely discussed across the social sciences: rational choice and historical neo-institutionalism (Hall and Taylor 1996). Rational choice neo-institutionalist scholars consider that self-interested individuals select institutions on the basis of exogenous preferences. For instance, research on democratization shows that rich rulers oppose democratization when income inequality is high because they fear redistribution by popular governments. Redistribution would run opposite to their interests (Acemoglu and Robinson 2001). Thus, their approach is actor-centred— in other words, geared to the micro level. By contrast, historical neo-institutionalists argue that existing institutions and their development over time shape actors' preferences and can alter power relations and coalitions. Works on how interest groups form their own interest are illustrative. It has been shown that firms' interests in global trade are partly shaped by existing regulations and governmental action, and thereby vary across institutional contexts (Woll 2008). Therefore, in these scholars' view, actors' preferences are ENDOGENOUSLY shaped. Hence, their approach focuses on organizations and institutions at the meso level in order to account for political preferences and outcomes. The seminal epistemological debate between METHODOLOGICAL INDIVIDUALISM AND HOLISM, as well as the problem of agency vs structure, provide additional illustrations of how theories are sometimes embedded at one level of analysis. As a general rule, the RESEARCH QUESTION and the theories should have the same level of analysis.

In research, the level of analysis has implications for the selection of UNITS OF ANALYSIS AND OBSERVATION. Broadly speaking, this constitutes the methods of data collection and data analysis. Certain research methods are better adapted to observations at a specific level of analysis. SURVEY RESEARCH, for instance, is strong when it involves collecting individual data. However, the level of data collection should not be mistaken for the level of data analysis. For example, INTERVIEW TECH-NIQUES can be used to collect data about the interviewee, but they can also be very informative about the institution where the interviewee works. In other words, the explanandum (what research aims to account for), the explanans (the explanations), the unit of analysis, and data collection can be located at different levels.

ECOLOGICAL AND ATOMISTIC FALLACIES

In practice, social scientists are often limited by practical or financial constraints when it comes to choosing the methods of data collection or use. Nevertheless, it is important to think carefully about data and the UNIT OF ANALYSIS in order to avoid two main errors commonly associated with aggregation and levels of analysis: ecological and atomistic fallacies. Both stem from wrongly assuming that because a relationship exists at one level of analysis, it is also present at a different level. The incorrect inference that a relationship or characteristic at an aggregated level is mirrored at a lower level is called the ecological fallacy. Its opposite, the atomistic fallacy (or the problem of related emergent properties) is the incorrect inference that a phenomenon that occurs at a low level of analysis, also occurs at higher levels of analysis.

First, let us imagine that research at the macro level reveals a strong positive relationship between supporting populism and being unemployed; and second, that an individual populist voter shares xenophobic content on social media. It would be an ecological fallacy—in this case stereotyping—to infer from their support for populism that the person on social media is unemployed. Similarly, it would be an atomistic fallacy to infer that all populist voters share xenophobic content online. The Condorcet paradox, also known as the voting paradox, offers another illustration of the emergent property problem. Let us consider three voters (1, 2, and 3) and three political parties (A, B, and C). Each voter has an ordered preference for the different parties: 1: A>B>C; 2: B>C>A; 3: C>A>B. Suppose that for each two-way combination of parties (A, B; B, C; C, A) the voters have to say which party they prefer above the other. If we then aggregate their preferences for one party over another, we will find that two of them prefer A to B, two of them B to C, and two C to A. Hence, A is preferred to B, B to C, but C to A, and therefore no winner can be declared. In this case then, the aggregation or grouping of preferences, although linear at the individual level, results in a cyclical and paradoxical situation at the aggregated level. The paradox is due to the intransitive nature of the grouped or aggregated preferences.

COMBINING LEVELS OF ANALYSIS

In the social sciences, single-level-of-analysis research is very common. Yet, research is not necessarily confined to just one level of analysis. Analytical traction may be gained by studying how processes, relationships, or effects theorized at one level of analysis could possibly influence (or originate from) what happens at a different level of analysis. The literature on policy feedback exemplifies the value-added of multilevel analysis. In her book on American pensioners, Andrea Campbell (2003) shows that they are über-citizens. Their level of political participation is far higher than can be explained by individual-level factors (income, age, or education). She demonstrates that macro-level explanations should be considered: namely, the public policies that benefit pensioners and trigger specific outcomes at the individual level. The aforementioned causes of war provide a further illustration of the insights to be gained from multilevel analysis. Levy and Thompson argue that if we are to fully understand the causes of war, we should acknowledge their multilevel nature. This way, the question shifts from what level is the most important to how factors at different levels of analysis interact (Levy and Thompson 2010). In this sense, multilevel analyses are designed to address the problem of incommensurability. Quantitative multilevel analyses, in particular, seek to resolve the problem not only by building explanatory models at one level, but also by modelling the effects and interactions between the different levels. Lastly, multilevel analyses are instrumental when it comes to avoiding the problem of scales, where the chosen level of analysis may be overemphasized, regardless of what occurs at other levels of analysis.

REFERENCES

Acemoglu, Daron and James A. Robinson. 2001. 'A Theory of Political Transitions'. *American Economic Review* 91(4): 938-963.

Campbell, Andrea Louise. 2003. *How Policies Make Citizens: Senior Political Activism and the American Welfare State*. Princeton, NJ, Princeton University Press.

Hall, Peter A. and Rosemary C. R. Taylor. 1996. 'Political Science and the Three New Institutionalisms'. *Political Studies* 44(5): 936-957.

Levy, Jack S. and William R. Thompson. 2010. *Causes of War*. Chichester, West Sussex, Wiley-Blackwell.

Mudde, Cas. 2007. *Populist Radical Right Parties in Europe*. Cambridge, Cambridge University Press.

Waltz, Kenneth N. 1992. *Man, the State and War: A Theoretical Analysis*. New York, Columbia University Press.

Woll, Cornelia. 2008. *Firm Interests: How Governments Shape Business Lobbying on Global Trade*. Ithaca, NY, Cornell University Press.

LITERATURE REVIEW

Mathieu Ouimet & Pierre-Olivier Bédard, Université Laval

Reviewing the published literature is one of the key activities of social science research, as a way to position one's academic contribution, but also to get a bird's eye view of what the relevant literature says on a given topic or RESEARCH QUESTION. Many guides have been created to assist academic researchers and students in conducting a literature review, but there is no consensus on the most appropriate method to do so (e.g., Galvan, 2017). One of the reasons for this lack of consensus is the plurality of epistemological attitudes that coexist in the social sciences. To some extent, researchers do not agree on the amount of objectivity or subjectivity a given researcher should be allowed to inject into her project. As such, one finds considerable variation in the methods adopted, the level of description and factual content, and the levels of personal interpretation in literature reviews.

TABLE 5 **Literature review approach**

Purpose	Traditional literature review	Systematic literature review
Inform and position a primary research study	Literature review embedded in a primary research study with few methodological details regarding literature search, selection, and synthesis	
Synthesize and assess research findings on a specific topic or question	Stand-alone literature review with few methodological details regarding literature search, selection, and synthesis (e.g. review articles)	Stand-alone literature review with explicit and accountable methods regarding literature search, selection, and synthesis (e.g. systematic reviews, scoping reviews)

The lack of consensus regarding the most appropriate methods for conducting literature reviews is partly due to the fact that literature reviews fit multiple purposes. In effect, a literature review can have two broad uses (see Table 5). First, traditional literature reviews are often produced to inform the design of primary research studies, as a way to assess and take advantage of previous relevant research, avoid duplication, and locate one's own contribution. By primary research, we refer to original empirical research findings, usually contained and presented in a single research paper or report. One would normally find a traditional literature review in an academic article. This section would point the reader to a number of past studies relevant to the current question, as determined by the author. In a way, the author informally curates the studies included. For instance, if the article is about citizen trust towards government, the author would weave in books and articles as a way to set up his argument, highlight past contributions, illustrate possible gaps, and generally position his study around this question. The literature review section is a way to set up the study and explore existing research and, as such, is distinct from the analytical/theoretical framework used to guide the study. By contrast, a research synthesis summarizes multiple primary studies, following a specific aggregation and analytical approach (this is distinct from the primary/secondary data terminology, which refers to the source of the data used).

Literature reviews that fulfil the first purpose carry several functions, such as presenting the findings of prior studies that relate to the primary study being reported, linking the study to the larger debates and dialogues about the topic that is being investigated, identifying gaps in prior studies, providing a framework for justifying the relevance of the primary study, and/or comparing the findings found in prior studies with those of the primary study (Creswell 2013). A master's thesis, doctoral dissertation, or academic article would be unlikely to be positively evaluated by a committee of reviewers if it did not include a section in which the authors report on the results of previous studies, identify strengths and weaknesses in those studies, and explain how their study adds to existing knowledge by overcoming one or more of the limitations they have identified. An example of a literature review integrated into a primary study would be a review of the literature present in a typical academic article. It would draw the reader's attention to a particular argument that the researcher is trying to make, help to highlight a theory and formulate hypotheses, and illustrate where the research fits into the larger picture, before the methodology and results of the new research are discussed. Thus, if you are writing a paper on what determines the influence of lobbyists on public policy, you will need to position your argument and hypotheses in relation to existing theories and empirical findings by addressing the different ways of defining and measuring influence, and by explaining and justifying the theoretical and methodological choices you have made in your study by comparing them to those of researchers who have examined this phenomenon before you.

The second broad purpose of a literature review is to summarize the state of the conceptual, theoretical, and/or empirical research on a given topic or question. Literature reviews that fulfil this purpose usually take the form of stand-alone review articles. A good example is the review article written by Starke (2006) who narratively reviewed a selected sample of theoretical approaches related to the politics of welfare state retrenchment. Such literature reviews are usually welcomed by academics working in a particular research field when they succeed in accurately identifying major advances, important gaps, current debates, and/or ideas for future research. Traditionally, review articles like Starke's (2006) article are based on a purposive selection of works that the author believes are the most important, and provide little detail regarding the methods used to find, select, synthesize, and interpret the studies included in the literature review. However, with more and more research articles and books being made available online via electronic bibliographic databases, the social sciences have entered into the new era of systematic literature reviews.

A systematic review is 'a review of the research literature using systematic and explicit accountable methods' (Gough, Oliver, and Thomas 2012: 5). Promoted by academic and non-governmental organizations such as the Campbell Collaboration, systematic reviews follow common stages including the formulation of the review question and the selection criteria, the search strategy, a description of the characteristics of the studies included in the review, an assessment of risk of BIAS in the studies included, and a synthesis of the findings. A systematic review can address different types of RESEARCH QUESTIONS answerable through quantitative (e.g. EXPERIMENTATION, CROSS-SECTIONAL AND LONGITUDINAL STUDIES), qualitative (e.g. OBSERVATIONAL METHODS), and MIXED METHODS. What distinguishes systematic reviews from traditional literature reviews is notably that each stage is performed systematically using specific tools and methods. For example, the population, intervention/issue, comparison, outcome, and context/time (PICOC/T) framework facilitates the formulation of a review question that is sufficiently precise to be amenable to a systematic review (Brunton, Stansfield, and Thomas 2012: 110).

When, rather than reviewing studies on a specific research question, the researcher is interested in examining studies on a broader topic, a systematic scoping review (Arksey and O'Malley 2005) can be performed, which is methodologically very similar to a systematic review. Methods exist to synthesize findings from both qualitative (e.g. meta-ethnography, thematic synthesis) and quantitative (e.g. thematic summary, meta-analysis) studies (Thomas, Harden, and Newman 2012). Researchers who wish to conduct systematic reviews (including scoping reviews) can use the quality assurance criteria included in *A Measurement Tool to Assess Systematic Reviews* (AMSTAR—https://amstar.ca) to improve the quality of their work. For example, following AMSTAR's second criterion, there should be at least two independent reviewers, and a consensus procedure for disagreements should be in place for study selection and information extraction. Systematic reviews are thus more resource-intensive than traditional literature reviews, which makes them difficult to conduct as part of research projects such as doctoral dissertations (Daigneault, Jacob, and Ouimet 2014).

A good illustrative example of a systematic review on a social sciences topic is the review entitled 'Preventive Interventions to Reduce Youth Involvement in Gangs and Gang Crime in Low- and Middle-income Countries' (Higginson et al. 2016). The objectives of this systematic review were to summarize and examine the variability in effectiveness of interventions to prevent youth involvement in gangs and gang crime in low- and middle-income countries and explain why these interventions either failed or succeeded. Six people authored the publication, which indicates the magnitude of the work that was undertaken. Diverse inclusion and exclusion criteria guided the search and selection process, notably on the research design, which had to be of the experimental or quasi-experimental type. Thirty-five sources of information including bibliographic databases, journals, and websites of key organizations were searched. The search strategy generated 2,901 unique references that were screened on title and abstract, 2,135 of which were excluded based on the inclusion and exclusion criteria. From the 766 potentially eligible documents to be retrieved for full-text screening, 52 could not be located. From the remaining 714 documents screened on full-text, only five were finally included in the review. The main findings of this systematic review were the lack of research evidence about which interventions are most effective in reducing youth involvement in gangs, and the need for rigorous evaluation of the effectiveness of preventive gang programmes in the field. Such conclusions are commonplace when conducting systematic literature reviews, and are meant to signal an important gap in the evidence base on a specific question.

In conclusion, before initiating a literature review, the researcher should start by clarifying the need for and the purpose of the review. As highlighted in this entry, there are multiple approaches available and the selection of the literature review approach should be guided by such considerations. Once this has been clarified, the actual review procotol, tools, and databases to be used will need to be determined to strike a balance between the scope of the study (i.e. how wide/narrow is the driving question) and the depth of the review (i.e. how superficial or exhaustive the literature search and analysis is to be).

REFERENCES

Arksey, Hilary and Lisa O'Malley. 2005. 'Scoping Studies: Towards a Methodological Framework'. *International Journal of Social Research Methodology* 8(1): 19–32.

Brunton, Ginny, Claire Stansfield, and James Thomas. 2012. 'Finding Relevant Studies', in *An Introduction to Systematic Reviews*, ed. David Gough, Sandy Oliver, and James Thomas, 107–134. Thousand Oaks, CA, SAGE Publications.

Creswell, J. W. 2013. *Research design: Qualitative, quantitative, and mixed methods approaches*. London: Thousand Oaks, New Delhi: Sage Publications, Inc, 2013.

Daigneault, Pierre-Marc, Steve Jacob, and Mathieu Ouimet. 2014. 'Using Systematic Review Methods within a PhD Dissertation in Political Science: Challenges and Lessons Learned from Practice'. *International Journal of Social Research Methodology* 17(3): 267–283.

Galvan, Jose L. 2017. *Writing Literature Reviews: A Guide for Students of the Social and Behavioral Sciences*, 6th edition. New York, Routledge.

Gough, David, Sandy Oliver, and James Thomas. 2012. 'Introducing Systematic Reviews', in *An Introduction to Systematic Reviews*, ed. David Gough, Sandy Oliver, and James Thomas, 1–16. Thousand Oaks, CA, SAGE Publications.

Higginson, Angela, Kathryn Benier, Yulia Shenderovich, Laura Bedford, Lorraine Mazerolle, and Joseph Murray. 2016. 'Preventive Interventions to Reduce Youth Involvement in Gangs and Gang Crime in Low- and Middle-income Countries: A Systematic Review'. *Campbell Systematic Reviews* 11(1): 1–176.

Starke, Peter. 2006. 'The Politics of Welfare State Retrenchment: A Literature Review'. *Social Policy and Administration* 40(1): 104–120.

Thomas, James, Angela Harden, and Mark Newman. 2012. 'Synthesis: Combining Results Systematically and Appropriately', in *An Introduction to Systematic Reviews*, ed. David Gough, Sandy Oliver, and James Thomas, 179–226. Thousand Oaks, CA, SAGE Publications.

M

META-ANALYSIS

A Solution to Deal with Scientific Information Overload when Conducting Research Syntheses

Noémie Laurens, Université Laval

In the last decades, the production of social science research has increased exponentially, to the point that it has become almost impossible for researchers to keep up to date with every new study published in their field of expertise. At the same time, any research study is required to include a synthesis of the existing literature on the same topic (see LITERATURE REVIEW). Therefore, in many areas, organization of the extant social science research may arguably be more desirable than further research (Card 2012).

As such, meta-analysis, defined as the 'statistical analysis of a large collection of analysis results from individual studies for the purpose of integrating the findings' (Glass 1976),[1] is a powerful methodological tool. An early classic example is the meta-analysis conducted by Smith and Glass (1977), which assessed the efficacy of psychotherapy by combining the results of nearly 400 studies. Beyond clinical psychology, the practice of meta-analysis has then diffused, inter alia, to medicine, economics, political science, and educational research. The examples provided in this chapter draw on the widely cited meta-analysis of Durlak et al. (2011) about the influence of social and emotional learning (SEL) programmes on student outcomes, such as emotional skills and academic performance.

[1] Gene V. Glass coined the term 'meta-analysis' in 1976 and his work with Mary Lee Smith (Smith and Glass 1977) marked the beginning of the modern era of meta-analysis, even though the practice existed before then.

META-ANALYSIS: WHAT IT IS, WHAT IT
IS NOT, AND HOW IT WORKS

A meta-analysis is a specific type of LITERATURE REVIEW, and more precisely a type of research synthesis, alongside traditional narrative reviews. Unlike in primary research, the UNIT OF ANALYSIS of a meta-analysis is the results of individual studies. And unlike traditional reviews, meta-analysis only applies to: (1) empirical research studies (2) with quantitative findings (3) that are conceptually comparable and (4) configured in similar statistical forms (Lipsey and Wilson 2001).

What further distinguishes meta-analysis from other research syntheses is the method of synthesizing the results of studies—i.e. the use of statistics and, in particular, of effect sizes. Card (2012: 87) usefully describes an effect size as 'an index of the direction and magnitude of association between two variables'. Put differently, an effect size represents the degree to which the phenomenon under study exists (Cohen 1988). For example, in Durlak et al. (2011), the effect size of each study examined corresponds to the magnitude of social and emotional learning programmes' impact on student outcomes. This information is more useful than the p-value, which can only tell if the effect is different from zero (see STATISTICAL SIGNIFICANCE). Three metrics are commonly used to measure the strength of the relationship between two VARIABLES in a meta-analysis: the standardized mean difference (d- or g-index); the correlation coefficient (r) when effect sizes are based on two continuous variables; and the odds and risk ratios when effect sizes are based on two dichotomous variables (see in particular Borenstein et al. 2009; Card 2012; Cooper 2015).

An important aspect of meta-analysis is the variation between effect sizes across studies: in other words heterogeneity. Indeed, the implications are quite different if social and emotional learning programmes consistently increase students' academic performance, as compared with if these programmes have a high impact on student outcomes in some studies but no impact at all in others. The heterogeneity of effect sizes is usually assessed by calculating the Q statistic, and the I^2 statistic provides information on the magnitude of heterogeneity. Finally, the mean of all the effect sizes, called the summary effect, is computed, with more weight being assigned to the more precise studies.[2] This allows conclusions to be drawn about the specific set of studies analysed (if the meta-analysis uses a fixed-effects model), or to generalize the findings to a larger population of studies (if the meta-analysis uses a random-effects model).

ARE TRADITIONAL NARRATIVE REVIEWS PREFERABLE?

Meta-analysis is subject to recurrent criticisms. First and foremost, preparing a meta-analysis undeniably takes more time and expertise than a traditional narrative review (Lipsey and Wilson 2001). Furthermore, some critics argue that meta-analyses fail to make 'creative, nuanced conclusions about the literature' (Card 2012).

---

[2] In fixed-effects models, imprecision in study effect sizes is assumed to be due to the standard error of the effect size, whereas in random-effects models, imprecision is assumed to be due to population variance and sampling fluctuation (Card 2012).

Besides the criticisms on the method itself, the three most persistent criticisms of meta-analysis deal with its application. Meta-analysis is often dubbed as a 'mix of apples and oranges' since it consists in combining studies that can differ in various ways. The classic response of advocates of meta-analysis is that it actually answers questions about fruit, for which apples and oranges provide useful information (Borenstein et al. 2009; Card 2012). The file drawer problem, also known as publication bias, refers to the fact that studies that conclude to a non-significant impact are less likely to be published, and therefore tend to remain in researchers' drawers. For this reason, meta-analysis runs the risk of examining a **BIASED** sample of studies. However, this problem applies to any kind of literature review. Finally, the axiom 'garbage in, garbage out' implies that poor quality research studies inevitably result in poor quality meta-analyses. The assessment of studies' quality nevertheless features among the steps listed by Cooper (2015) for conducting a proper research synthesis.

In sum, even though meta-analysis displays some weaknesses of which the researcher must be cognizant, it allows research findings to be summarized in a more sophisticated and disciplined way than traditional literature reviews, and to unveil effects that other research syntheses leave in the shadows (Lipsey and Wilson 2001). As Glass rightly points out, the conventional literature review 'in which one cites a couple dozen studies from the obvious journals can't do justice to the voluminous literature [. . .] that we now confront' (Glass 1976: 4).

REFERENCES

Borenstein, Michael, Larry V. Hedges, Julian P. T. Higgins, and Hannah R. Rothstein. 2009. *Introduction to Meta-Analysis*. Hoboken, NJ, John Wiley & Sons.

Card, Noel A. 2012. *Applied Meta-analysis for Social Science Research*. New York, Guilford Publications.

Cohen, Jacob. 1988. *Statistical Power Analysis for the Behavioral Sciences*, 2nd edition. Hillsdale, NJ, Lawrence Erlbaum Associates.

Cooper, Harris. 2015. *Research Synthesis and Meta-analysis: A Step-by-step Approach*, 5th edition. Thousand Oaks, CA, SAGE Publications.

Durlak, Joseph A., Roger P. Weissberg, Allison B. Dymnicki, Rebecca D. Taylor, and Kriston B. Schellinger. 2011. 'The Impact of Enhancing Students' Social and Emotional Learning: A Meta analysis of School based Universal Interventions'. *Child Development* 82(1): 405–432.

Glass, Gene V. 1976. 'Primary, Secondary, and Meta-analysis of Research'. *Educational Researcher* 5(10): 3–8.

Lipsey, Mark W. and David B. Wilson. 2001. *Practical Meta-analysis*. Thousand Oaks, CA, SAGE Publications.

Smith, Mary L. and Gene V. Glass. 1977. 'Meta-analysis of Psychotherapy Outcome Studies'. *American Psychologist* 32(9): 752–760.

METHODOLOGICAL INDIVIDUALISM AND HOLISM

Suzan Gibril, Université libre de Bruxelles

Methodological individualism and holism are often the focus of ontological debate. The two perspectives adopt widely different ontologies in their explanation of social processes and realities. The discussion is centred on whether agents are chiefly constituted by structures or whether structures are the product of pre-existing agents (see LEVELS OF ANALYSIS and EPISTEMOLOGY). Agents are the actors in society, including individuals and collective entities, such as states and organizations, while structures refer to the patterned and stable relations, institutions and material arrangements through which the different actors in society interact. Structures might also refer to the norms and values that shape individuals within a given social system.

Methodological individualism (MI) is a paradigm in the social sciences that emerged from sociology and philosophy. The sociological definition was developed by Max Weber in *Economy and Society*. However, the specific term was coined by his disciple, Joseph Schumpeter, in 1909 (Udehn 2001). In Weber's view, 'collectivities must be treated as the resultants and modes of organization of the particular acts of individual persons, since these alone can be treated as agents in a course of subjectively understandable action' (Weber 1978: 13). Here, the 'individual' does not necessarily refer to a single human being. Indeed, Weber was the first to introduce the idea that organizations, states, and companies can be analysed as individuals. All that is required is an intentional state with an underlying motive (List and Spiekermann 2013). In this definition, the main purpose of MI is not to favour the individual over the collective, but to explain the occurrence of social phenomena by an action-driven rhetoric, which is motivated by intentional states. MI can be interpreted in many ways, and all its variations cannot be explained in depth here. In short, MI is primarily based on three postulates: the *individualistic postulate* (each societal phenomenon is the result of a combination of individual actions, beliefs, and attitudes); the *comprehension postulate* (understanding versus explanation: to understand an action, attitude, or belief, we must understand the meaning attributed to it by the individual) (see DESCRIPTIVE, EXPLANATORY, AND INTERPRETIVE APPROACHES); and the *rationality postulate* (the meaning given to the action by the individual is tied to his/her reasons for adopting it). Actors act the way they act and believe what they believe for different reasons, which may vary depending on the circumstances. Therefore, it is difficult to classify actors into simple types (Boudon and Bourricaud 2002).[1]

---

[1] Other defenders of MI have added more postulates, which make the definition more precise but more restrictive. For instance, the *egotistical postulate* and *CBC postulate* (cost–benefit calculation) state that the individual will only be interested in the actions that concern him/her personally (Zahle and Collin 2014). These postulates are specific to the field of economics and are generally known as rational choice theory (RCT). For further reading and examples on MI and its variations, see Zahle and Collin (2014).

The philosophical definition was developed by scholars such as Popper and Hayek around the 1950s. Popperian methodological rigour suggests that researchers should only consider individual social action, given that individuals represent the only perceivable and observable elements of society. Indeed, society would not exist without individuals (List and Spiekermann 2013). In Hayek's view, methodological individualists must refrain from analysing *pseudo-entities*[2] as 'facts and systematically start from the concepts which guide the individuals in their actions [instead of starting from] the results of the theorisation of their actions' (Hayek 1942: 286).

Contemporary applications of MI can be found in game theory (see **FORMAL MODELLING**), which is based on a 'mathematical model of conflict and cooperation between rational decision-makers' (Myerson 1991: xiii). Originally, it addressed zero-sum games[3] in which one person's gains resulted in losses for the others. Today, it is applied to the analysis and prediction of human behaviour in strategic situations, in order to determine how events will unfold, given that people and organizations act in what they perceive to be their best interests (Myerson 1991). Practically, numerical values are attributed to each player's goals, motivations, and influence (the players can be individuals, organizations, firms, etc.). The computer model then investigates the options available to the various players, determines the likely course of action, and evaluates the possible influence to predict the course of events (Camerer 2001).

Holism, in contrast, is based on the idea that society cannot be reduced solely to its constituent parts—i.e. individuals. Individuals are the product of societies, histories, economic inequalities, social status, and so on. Therefore, they should be treated as objects that can only be perceived and understood from within. They should be explained through causal mechanisms that go beyond the individuals themselves. This vision was advocated by Emile Durkheim (1981: 59) in his research on social facts, which in his view exert an external constraint on the individual. Following this holistic view, the best approach for studying social phenomena is by analysing processes, forces, cultures, and organizations; and society should be understood as autonomous regarding the individuals within it (Bhargava 1998). In other words, holists argue that social phenomena exist over and above individuals, and impose themselves on and are influenced by these individuals (Zahle 2016).

Other variations of social holism exist. For instance, the Marxian tradition essentially uses economic factors to account for the transformation of social phenomena: 'it is not the consciousness of men that determines their existence, it is on the contrary their social existence that determines their consciousness' (Marx 1859, cited in Bhargava 1998). The functionalist tradition, represented by Parsons or Merton, maintains that social facts can be reduced to their specific function in society. Finally, structuralism, as developed by Levi-Strauss, Foucault, and to some extent Bourdieu

---

[2] Here he is referring to abstractions such as 'society', 'culture', 'economic system', etc.

[3] Zero-sum games are a mathematical representation of a situation in which each participant's gain or loss of utility (consumer satisfaction) is exactly balanced by the gain or loss of other participants.

(whose work primarily focuses on the dynamics of power and social order), argues that social structures exercise autonomous causal properties on individuals and society. Structuralists strive to go beyond the individual meaning given to discourse and action in order to reveal the underlying latent structures that determine social functioning.[4]

There are various practical applications of these methods in modern sociology. For instance, SOCIAL NETWORK ANALYSIS focuses on relationships between social entities (Wasserman 1994). It investigates social structures using networks, for example friends and acquaintances, meme spreads, social media, patterns in disease transmission, economic transactions between corporations, trade and treaties between nations, or sexual relationships (e.g. Wasserman 1994; D'Andrea 2009). Once established, these networks can be visualized using sociograms,[5] where the nodes (individuals) are represented as dots and the ties as lines. Similarly, relational sociology (RS) argues for a conceptualization of social relations as a particular ontological object irreducible to any other (Powell and Depelteau 2013). Emirbayer, an eminent figure of this school of thought, argues that this relational approach avoids the conception of social relations and processes as either 'structures' or 'individuals', or both (see Emirbayer 1997). In other words, RS contends that the social world is a network of ties and interactions between actors who are, themselves, shaped and constituted in those interactions.

The debate surrounding methodological individualism and holism (see ONTOLOGY) focuses on whether the occurrence of social facts should be treated as configurations of individuals' actions, relations, and attitudes or as events at their own macroscopic LEVEL OF ANALYSIS.[6] For instance, when studying a specific topic such as organized crime, each school of thought will go about it differently: MI will narrow in on individual motivations for participating in organized crime, while holism will look into the societal structures that enabled the development of this phenomenon in the first place. Ultimately, the question is, do social structures exist over and above individuals? Advocates of MI highlight that social facts are constituted by the thoughts and behaviour of individuals, while social organizations are composed of individuals with specific beliefs and values (Bhargava 1998).

However, the next step is to encourage the different approaches to interact and coexist. Some social scientists now advocate a pluralistic approach, where society is considered inseparably as the product and matrix of individual action (see Zahle and Collin 2014). This largely echoes Elias's (1987) argument that we cannot take the individual out of society or society out of the individual. Instead, his starting point is the idea of a socialized individual, from which he builds more complex social processes and structures.

[4] For further examples of holism in the social sciences, see Zahle (2016).
[5] A graphic representation of a person's different social links.
[6] Researchers influenced by economic methodology, such as rational choice theorists, are most commonly methodological individualists, while researchers influenced by sociological and historical methodologies are more likely to be influenced by holism.

REFERENCES

d'Andrea, Alessia, Fernando Ferri, and Patricia Grifoni. 2010. An overview of methods for virtual social network analysis (3-25). In Abraham, Hassanien, Snasel (eds), *Computational Social Network Analysis: Trends, Tools and Research Advances*. London: Springer

Bhargava, Rajeev. 1998. 'Holism and Individualism in History and Social Science', in *Routledge Encyclopaedia of Philosophy*, ed. Edward Craig, 358-362. London, Routledge.

Boudon, Raymond and Bourricaud, François. 2002. Rationality. In: *A Critical Dictionary of Sociology*, 299-305. New York: Routledge.

Camerer, C.F. 2011. *Behavioral game theory: Experiments in strategic interaction*. Princeton, Princeton University Press.

Durkheim, Emile. 1981. The realm of sociology as a science. *Social Forces* 59(4): 1054-1070.

Elias, N. 1987. On human beings and their emotions: a process-sociological essay. *Theory, Culture and Society* 4(2-3): 339-361.

Emirbayer, Mustafa. 1997. 'Manifesto for a Relational Sociology'. *American Journal of Sociology* 103(2): 281-317.

Hayek, Friedrich A. 1942. 'Scientism and the Study of Society'. *Economica* 9(35): 267-291.

List, Christian and Kai Spiekermann. 2013. 'Methodological Individualism and Holism in Political Science: A Reconciliation'. *American Political Science Review* 107(4): 629-643.

Myerson, Roger B., 1991. On the value of game theory in social science. *Rationality and Society*, 4(1): 62-73.

Powell, Christopher J. and François Depelteau (eds). 2013. *Conceptualizing Relational Sociology: Ontological and Theoretical Issues*. New York, Palgrave Macmillan.

Udehn, Lars. 2001. *Methodological Individualism: Background, History and Meaning*. London: Routledge.

Wasserman, S. 1994. *Social network analysis: Methods and applications* (Vol. 8). Cambridge, Cambridge University Press.

Weber, Max. 1978. *Economy and Society*, vol. 1. Berkeley, CA, University of California Press.

Zahle, Julie. 2016. 'Methodological Holism in the Social Sciences', in *The Stanford Encyclopaedia of Philosophy* (Summer 2016 edition), ed. Edward N. Zalta. Available at: https://plato.stanford.edu/archives/sum2016/entries/holism-social/ (Accessed 12 August 2020).

Zahle, Julie and Finn Collin (eds). 2014. *Rethinking the Individualism-Holism Debate: Essays in the Philosophy of Social Science*. Cham, Springer.

M

MIXED METHODS

Combination of Quantitative and Qualitative Research Approaches

Manfredi Valeriani, University of Hamburg and LUISS Guido Carli di Roma
Vicki L. Plano Clark, University of Cincinnati

INTRODUCTION

Mixed methods research is an approach that involves the integration of quantitative and qualitative methods at one or more stages of a research study. The central idea behind mixed methods research is that the intentional combination of numeric-based methods with narrative-based methods can best provide answers to some research questions.

Although there are examples of researchers and evaluators combining both methods throughout the 1900s, it is relatively new as a recognized approach. Scholars initially discussed and formalized the idea of a mixed methods approach in the 1970s and 1980s. Originally this approach was also referred to as multi-method research, but today scholars largely distinguish mixed methods research from multi-method research. The difference between the two approaches lies in the fact that while mixed methods involves both qualitative and quantitative methods, multi-method research applies multiple qualitative (or quantitative) methods. Today mixed methods research is actively used across a wide range of disciplines, supported by a series of dedicated conferences, journals, and professional organizations.[1]

EARLY DEBATES ABOUT MIXING METHODS

To understand mixed methods research today, it is important to understand the early debates that helped to shape this approach. The early stages of the development of mixed methods were contentious as scholars attempted to find an EPISTEMO-LOGICAL ground for combining qualitative and quantitative methods. Mixed methods researchers were immediately criticized with regard to the logical coherence and utility of mixing different methodologies. This initial critique is often referred to as the 'incompatibility thesis'. The incompatibility thesis argues that quantitative and qualitative methodologies cannot be mixed due to insuperable ontological and epistemological differences.

Although this argument may sound odd for those active in other fields, in the social sciences it remains an important issue. ONTOLOGICAL and epistemological debates have dominated discussions of mixed methods research for years. Starting from POS-ITIVIST approaches that assume a knowable reality and which borrowed their methodology from hard sciences, the academic debate has evolved to recognize the higher complexity of the social world. This recognition has resulted in theories such as constructivism. Constructivists see the social world as malleable, unstable and complex. Therefore, they prefer more qualitative approaches that can allow for deeper understandings of individual experiences and meanings.

As far as the field of mixed methods is concerned, this debate about incompatibility now seems to be mostly overcome, with the discussion moving towards describing the different ontological foundations on which mixed methods can be based (Creswell and Plano Clark 2018; Tashakkori and Teddlie 2010). This leap forward has made been possible by new theories and stances that provide mixed methods with the foundations it needs to establish itself in the field of social sciences. For example, mixed methods is often linked to pragmatism (Bryman 2006; Johnson, Onwuegbuzie, and Turner 2007),

---

[1] For example: *Journal of Mixed Methods Research*, Mixed Methods International Research Association.

a philosophical stance that moves the focus from theoretical assumptions to real-world practices. As a matter of fact, the mixed methods approach proposes a dynamic practice that can be (and has to be) adapted to the different research approaches, which finds good support in the theoretical assumptions of pragmatism.

Another approach that shows how the scholarly debate has moved beyond the 'classical' traditions is analytical eclecticism. Analytical eclecticism is an intellectual stance that supports the use of multiple perspectives and methodologies in research. As with pragmatism, the eclectic approach focuses on the RESEARCH QUESTION, choosing methods and theories depending on a case-by-case analysis (Sil and Katzenstein 2010). Other possibilities of epistemological positions for mixed methods can also be found in CRITICAL REALISM, transformative-ideological perspectives, and dialectical perspectives that purposively combine POSITIVISM and constructivism in dialogue with each other (Creswell and Plano Clark 2018; Tashakkori and Teddlie 2010).

Building from these different perspectives about mixed methods research, debates have also revolved around the definition of mixed methods research. Due to the complexity of perspectives about and the variety of uses of mixed methods, the literature provides different definitions that vary depending on the moment, level, purpose, and nature of the integration of quantitative and qualitative methods. This heterogeneity is highlighted and addressed by Johnson, Onwuegbuzie, and Turner (2007). In their article, the authors surveyed a range of prominent definitions and proposed their own more overarching one that highlights the combination of viewpoints in addition to methods. The definition they arrive at conceives of mixed methods as: 'the type of research in which a researcher or team of researchers combines elements of qualitative and quantitative research approaches (e.g., use of qualitative and quantitative viewpoints, data collection, analysis, inference techniques) for the broad purposes of breadth and depth of understanding and corroboration' (Johnson, Onwuegbuzie, and Turner 2007: 123).

APPLYING A MIXED METHODS APPROACH: WHY AND HOW?

From the definition of mixed methods research, we can extract two essential considerations that need to be addressed: purpose of the mixing and combination of the methods. In short, why and how can one use a mixed methods approach? Greene, Caracelli, and Graham (1989) identify five core purposes for mixed methods research: TRIANGULATION (achieving higher validity), complementarity (obtaining more complete understandings), development (using results of one method to inform the use of the other), initiation (seeking paradox and contradictions), and expansion (increasing the breadth of the research). In short, mixed methods are used because the research aims to generate integrated results and conclusions that are more valid, complete, deep, thought-provoking, or broad-reaching than results achieved by using a single method.

How the methods are combined to accomplish these purposes is another important consideration in mixed methods research. Bryman (2006) has built on the work of

Greene, Caracelli, and Graham (1989) to examine five core aspects involved in doing mixed methods research. These five aspects are: the simultaneous or sequential use of the quantitative and qualitative data, the type of data that has the priority or emphasis, the function of the integration, the stage of the research where the methods are mixed, and the number of data strands. The key is for the researcher to effectively combine the methods while exploiting the strengths and avoiding the weaknesses of the qualitative and quantitative approaches.

MIXED METHODS IN PRACTICE: A FEW COMMON COMBINATIONS

Among various possible examples, de Visser and McDonnell's (2012) study provides an example of how researchers apply the mixed methods considerations of combination and purpose. Working from a CRITICAL REALIST perspective, the authors used mixed methods to examine how university students' alcohol use is shaped by gender role beliefs and gender identity. They employed a sequential approach, conducting a quantitative phase first and a follow-up qualitative phase second. Since the quantitative phase set the direction of the study, the quantitative data seemed to have priority in the study. The two data strands were integrated at two stages. First, the two strands were integrated when the researchers used the quantitative survey results to select the participants with the most and least egalitarian gender role beliefs for the qualitative INTERVIEWS (a mixing purpose of development). Second, the results of the two strands were integrated during the analysis and interpretation when the researchers used the qualitative interview findings to explain the quantitative SURVEY results (a mixing purpose of expansion). There are many ways in which researchers can apply the five aspects highlighted by Bryman in mixed methods study designs (Creswell and Plano Clark 2018). As found in the example of the study by de Visser and McDonnell, many mixed methods studies use an 'explanatory sequential' design by starting with a quantitative survey to obtain preliminary results and then proceeding with in-depth qualitative INTERVIEWS that help uncover and explain the issues in detail.

Of course, this is not the only possible pattern, and the two approaches can be integrated at different stages, or with different purposes. Using a mixing purpose of development, many other mixed methods studies use an 'exploratory sequential' design. This design starts with qualitative explorations of a topic and then uses the resulting findings to develop an instrument, which is subsequently administered to gather quantitative data about the topic. It is also common for the quantitative and qualitative data to be gathered simultaneously and then analysed and merged for purposes of TRIANGULATION or complementarity in a 'convergent concurrent' design. Furthermore, it is not rare to have the two methods, in the same research study, answering two slightly different RESEARCH QUESTIONS for the purpose of expansion. More complex mixed methods designs occur when researchers combine these basic designs with other frameworks, such as a 'mixed methods experiment' that involves the researcher mixing methods during the implementation of an experimental design.

MAKING ORDER FROM THE VARIOUS TYPES OF MIXED METHODS RESEARCH DESIGNS

With so many possibilities for why and how mixed methods researchers can combine the quantitative and qualitative approaches in a study, scholars have worked to simplify and homogenize the field by categorizing the possibilities into **TYPOLOGIES** of mixed methods designs, such as the designs named earlier from Creswell and Plano Clark (2018). In contrast, Guest (2013) argued in a commentary that it is more useful to focus on how to describe mixed methods designs than to focus on naming the different designs. Guest argued that there is value in reducing the basis for describing mixed methods designs to two main aspects: timing and purpose of integration. As mentioned before, the integration of the approaches may occur at different stages. For example, quantitative and qualitative data may be mixed during the data-gathering phase; or qualitative and quantitative approaches may be conducted in parallel without having any integration until the very last interpretation stage of the research. Furthermore, there are also different reasons for integration. Increased validity through **TRIANGULATION** seems to be the most popular. However, integration may also be chosen for development reasons. For example, quantitative analysis may provide information on how to structure the qualitative analysis. Guest notices that most mixed methods studies are uncomplicated and the existing **TYPOLOGIES** of mixed methods designs work well with them. However, the presence of more complicated research challenges the simplification he attempts to achieve.

M

CONCLUSION

In conclusion, the ongoing attempts to construct a simple and common conceptualization of mixed methods provide a good indicator of the status of mixed methods itself. Mixed methods research has emerged as a formalized methodology well suited to addressing complex problems, and is currently applied throughout the social sciences and beyond. Mixed methods research is a dynamic methodology that continues to evolve and become more sophisticated. Nowadays, researchers interested in combining quantitative and qualitative methods can benefit from the growing knowledge about the epistemological foundations, essential considerations, and rigorous designs that have been advanced for mixed methods research.

REFERENCES

Bryman, Alan. 2006. Integrating Quantitative and Qualitative Research: How Is It Done? *Qualitative Research* 6(1): 97–113.

Creswell, W. John and Vicki L. Plano Clark. 2018. *Designing and Conducting Mixed Methods Research*, 3rd edition. London, SAGE Publications.

De Visser, Richard O. and Elizabeth J. McDonnell. 2012. '"That's OK. He's a Guy": A Mixed methods Study of Gender Double-standards for Alcohol Use'. *Psychology and Health* 27(5): 618–639.

Greene, Jennifer C., Valerie J. Caracelli, and Wendy F. Graham. 1989. 'Toward a Conceptual Framework for Mixed-method Evaluation Designs'. *Educational Evaluation and Policy Analysis* 11(3): 255–274.

Guest, Greg. 2013. 'Describing Mixed Methods Research: An Alternative to Typologies'. *Journal of Mixed Methods Research* 7(2): 141–151.

Johnson, R. Burke, Anthony J. Onwuegbuzie, and Lisa Turner. 2007. 'Toward a Definition of Mixed Methods Research'. *Journal of Mixed Methods Research* 1(2): 112–133.

Sil, Rudra and Peter J. Katzenstein. 2010. 'Analytic Eclecticism in the Study of World Politics: Reconfiguring Problems and Mechanisms across Research Traditions'. *Perspectives on Politics* 8(2): 411–431.

Tashakkori, Abbas and Charles Teddlie. 2010. *Sage Handbook of Mixed Methods in Social & Behavioral Research*, 2nd edition. London, SAGE Publications.

MULTICAUSALITY AND EQUIFINALITY

Johann Wolfschwenger, Université libre de Bruxelles and Université de Genève
Kevin L. Young, University of Massachusetts Amherst

Multicausality and equifinality refer to a research situation whereby an outcome is explained by more than one causal factor. The term 'equifinality' stems from SYSTEMS ANALYSIS, and refers to a situation in which 'the same final state may be reached from different initial conditions and in different ways' (Bertalanffy 1968: 40). 'Equifinality' also appears in related disciplines such as psychology, archaeology, or environmental studies, while 'multicausality' is often used in literature on social science methodology. In this article we treat both concepts as one and the same EPISTEMOLOGICAL challenge.

While many approaches to the study of social phenomena privilege explanatory parsimony, situations of multicausality, which privilege explanatory comprehensiveness, are relatively ubiquitous in the social world we experience and observe, and stand in contrast to experimental settings in which singular causes are examined through a controlled environment (see EXPERIMENTATION). Thus, multicausality and equifinality are important reasons why social phenomena are particularly challenging to study.

How the relationship between the multiple causal pathways is approached depends on the research set-up and methodological orientation the researcher adopts. One view on multicausality contends that one outcome is determined by multiple independent causes, each of which alone would be sufficient to determine the outcome (overdetermination). However, King, Keohane, and Verba (1994: 87) argue that such a definition is misleading if we allow for the possibility that causes are probabilistic, since the distinction between necessity and sufficiency largely disappears. Another view understands multicausality in terms of 'conjunctural CAUSATION', which describes situations in which several conditions *combine* to induce an effect on an outcome of interest.[1] In this case it is possible for one conjuncture (e.g. A+B) to lead to an outcome (A+B → Y). Given the possibility of various combinations of factors, instances of intervening VARIABLES, retroactive feedback loops, cases of ultimate, proximate, or distal CAUSATION, etc. may also be approached as cases of multicausality. According to the latter view, multicausality may be contained by the quest to identify a set of multiple necessary or sufficient conditions that combine to a causal path that is sufficient to determine the outcome (e.g. QUALITATIVE COMPARATIVE ANALYSIS or PROCESS TRACING). Other methods, adopting the former view, measure the effect of one out of potentially multiple independent VARIABLES on the outcome (e.g. multivariate REGRESSION ANALYSIS).

Multicausality and equifinality are often explored by research traditions and methods of social inquiry that approach causal processes through a 'causes-of-effects' approach, rather than an 'effect-of-causes' approach (see Goertz and Mahoney 2012: 41–50). Confronting a RESEARCH QUESTION from a causes-of-effects approach is most often associated with qualitative research, where there is some outcome to be explained and the researcher focuses their attention on maximizing the full explanatory power of the (potentially multiple) causes that work to explain that outcome. For example, if you want to explain why child poverty occurs you must consider all the factors that contribute to child poverty. This is different from an effect-of-causes approach in which it is the *cause* itself—and usually a singular cause—that is of interest, and is more commonly deployed in quantitative analysis. This is, for example, the case in an experimental research design, in which it is the effects of a cause—or 'treatment'—on an outcome, and not the full variation in the outcome itself, that is of interest to the researcher. An example of this would be a randomly assigned school breakfast programme as a 'treatment' in school districts, to see its specific effects on child poverty. Confronting a research question in this latter way entails asking what the causal effect of a given VARIABLE is on an outcome, while the degree to which that variable explains overall variation in that outcome is of secondary importance. Scholarship in this vein often assesses multiple variables through a 'net effects' approach. The variables considered are multiple, but it is their independent force that is of greatest interpretive interest—i.e. their correlation with an outcome 'controlling for' all the other variables.

How to approach multicausality can be illuminated if we use the following example: consider a research situation in which we aim to understand the causes of democratic stability in East European countries. Based on literature in the field of EU studies and international relations, we argue that European integration (explanatory VARIABLE, X) has a positive impact on democratic stability (dependent VARIABLE, Y).

---

[1] An overview of possible combinatorics of multiple causal factors is provided by Braumoeller (2003: 210f).

However, further literature in the field of comparative politics suggests that the choice of constitutional set-up (i.e. parliamentary vs presidential system, Z) and the degree of economic development (D) may also have an impact on democratic stability. Thus, we assume that democratic stability in East European countries depends on multiple causal factors that may or may not interact with each other.

To confront such a puzzle, a statistical effect-of-causes approach (e.g. REGRES-SION ANALYSIS that is interpreted for the STATISTICAL SIGNIFICANCE of a set of VARIABLES) seeks to control third variables in which the assumed con-founding factors (in this case Z and D) are kept constant by holding them at their means. We observe the effect of the explanatory variable (European integration, X) on the dependent variable (democratic stability, Y) separately in countries with parliamentary and presidential systems. Only if the correlation between X and Y remains for both of Z's values, is a causal relationship plausible, subject to partic-ular statistical tests (e.g. p-values). Controlling for intervening variables in this way is thus the basic inferential framework in which one deals with multicausality. Such an approach handles multiple variables through 'net effects' thinking—that is, the assessment of the effect of only one VARIABLE conditioning on the effects from the others.[2]

A set of methods that researchers use to address multicausality explicitly is known as QUALITATIVE COMPARATIVE ANALYSIS (QCA). QCA proponents sometimes claim that it is a useful method to deploy precisely in situations where multicausality may be present. This is because QCA does not assess the 'net effect' of one VARIABLE's variation with an outcome, whereby a researcher 'controls for' or 'holds constant' all the independent variables in the regression when each one is being tested. Rather, in QCA one might ask in the example above which of the conditions X, Z, D are sufficient conditions for the presence of Y. Those relationships of sufficiency can be assessed one by one or through the combinations of X, Z, and D as they correspond with Y. It is for this reason that practitioners of QCA not only speak of multicausality but of *causal* complexity—an inference about a causal factor is not assessed through 'controlling' or 'conditioning' on other causal factors, but rather through exploring the causal path-ways that the data reveal are possible, relative to all those that could be possible. Equi-finality is thus explicitly entertained as an empirical possibility, because in QCA there can be multiple paths to the same outcome (sometimes referred to as multiple 'causal recipes').

Besides statistical methods and COMPARATIVE ANALYSIS, qualitative with-in-case methods have also systematized the handling of multicausality. One promi-nent strategy is PROCESS TRACING, which may be useful in that it seeks to 'identify the intervening causal processes—the causal chain and causal mechanisms—between an independent VARIABLE and the outcome of the dependent variable' (George and

---

[2] To be sure, some specific methods and techniques in quantitative analysis do entertain the specification of models where there are multiple causal paths to the same outcome (e.g. see Imai and Yamamoto 2013; Braumoeller 2003). Yet most techniques tend to model relationships through the simpler 'net effects' process described here.

Bennett 2005: 206). Process tracing entertains the possibility of equifinality and conjunctural CAUSATION by encouraging the researcher to take into account a wide array of intervening variables in the causal chain, or multiple causal pathways. Central to the idea of process tracing is that some pieces of evidence provide higher inferential power than others. Depending on the research design, process tracing entertains multicausality in different ways. When conducted deductively, it helps to identify the probative value of evidence relative to competing causal factors, similar to QCA (Bennett and Checkel 2015: 16). When conducted inductively, it aids the researcher in conceptualizing potential causal mechanisms or alternative explanatory pathways that have not been captured by other methods or existing scholarship.

REFERENCES

Bennett, Andrew and Jeffrey Checkel. 2015. *Process Tracing: From Metaphor to Analytic Tool.* Cambridge, Cambridge University Press.

Bertalanffy, Ludwig von. 1968. *General System Theory.* New York, George Braziller.

Braumoeller, Bear. 2003. 'Causal Complexity and the Study of Politics'. *Political Analysis* 11(3): 209–233.

George, Alexander and Andrew Bennett. 2005. *Case Studies and Theory Development in the Social Sciences.* Cambridge, MA, MIT Press.

Goertz, Gary and James Mahoney. 2012. *A Tale of Two Cultures: Qualitative and Quantitative Research in the Social Sciences.* Princeton, NJ, Princeton University Press.

Imai, Kosuke and Teppei Yamamoto. 2013. 'Identification and Sensitivity Analysis for Multiple Causal Mechanisms: Evidence from Framing Experiments'. *Political Analysis* 21(2): 141–171.

King, Gary, Robert Keohane, and Sidney Verba. 1994. *Designing Social Inquiry: Scientific Inference in Qualitative Research.* Princeton, NJ, Princeton University Press.

M

MULTIPLE CORRESPONDENCE ANALYSIS AND GEOMETRIC DATA ANALYSIS

Amal Tawfik, University of Lausanne and School of Health Sciences HESAV, HES-SO University of Applied Sciences and Arts Western Switzerland Stephan Davidshofer, University of Geneva (Global Studies Institute) and Geneva Center for Security Studies

Multiple correspondence analysis (MCA) is a FACTOR ANALYSIS statistical method used to analyse relations between a large set of categorical VARIABLES. Developed by Jean-Paul Benzécri in the early 1970s, MCA is one of the principal methods of geometric data analysis (GDA). It can be considered the poster child of the so-called *French school of data analysis*. MCA was further systematized by French mathematicians and applied in sociology with Pierre Bourdieu's work (1989). As a result, it gained some traction in other social sciences, such as political science and international relations (e.g. Pouliot 2016), and also reached out beyond French academia (e.g. Bennett 2009).

GDA is based on three principles that distinguish it clearly from REGRESSION ANALYSIS: geometric data modelling in the form of a table, representing individuals and VARIABLES (or categories) as two clouds of points; a formal approach drawing on linear algebra; and, above all, an inductive and descriptive approach based on the idea that the model follows the data, rather than the other way around (Le Roux and Rouanet 2010).

Three different statistical methods can be identified as GDA: correspondence analysis (CA), which enables the cross-tabulation of two categorical variables; MCA for the analysis of a matrix of individuals and categorical variables; and principal component analysis (PCA), which uses numerical variables. In GDA, data is represented as a cloud of points to allow statistical interpretations. A cloud of points is a geometric display 'like a geographic map with the same distance scale in all directions' (Le Roux and Rouanet 2010: 7). Like any other form of dimensional statistical method, GDA aims to reduce a wide array of information (the variables) into a few dimensions that are represented graphically.

Although MCA is a relational method, it differs from SOCIAL NETWORK ANAL- YSIS (SNA) as it focuses on the objective relations that characterize actors or groups, rather than the effective relations—i.e. social aspects (age, education, social class) in- stead of relational aspects (friendship, cross-referencing, common participation at events). Finally, MCA can be usefully combined with FOCUS GROUPS and quali- tative INTERVIEWS in a MIXED METHOD research design. These complementary qualitative methods can enhance the understanding of the patterns that emerge from MCA. The strength of a mixed design lies in its capacity to position the individuals (who participate in the FOCUS GROUPS and the individuals interviewed) in the space produced by the MCA.

MCA: FROM DATA MATRIX TO THE INTERPRETATION OF AXES

MCA is a method of geometric decomposition used to position individuals and VARI- ABLES on the same geometric plane. Based on a data matrix, it starts by defining two clouds of points (Le Roux and Rouanet 2010): the cloud of individuals and the cloud of categories (cf. Figure 4).

Individuals are positioned on a plane of x dimensions according to the similarities of their response categories. The distance between two individuals increases if they diverge on a high number of VARIABLES and only share a few of the chosen categories (e.g. male/female). In Figure 4, in the lower right-hand matrix, the cloud of individu- als, i_1 and i_3 are further apart than i_1 and i_2. This distance indicates that i_1 and i_3 diverge on a higher number of VARIABLES (almost all of them) than i_1 and i_2. Individuals who have the same responses share the same location. Thus, the more infrequent a response, the more it will create distance between individuals.

MCA also defines a cloud of categories. The distance between two categories diminishes when the same individuals chose them. In Figure 4, in the upper right-hand matrix, the cloud of categories, a closeness between two categories indicates that they characterize relatively similar individuals, whereas a large distance between categories, as can be seen between a_1 and a_4, signals that they have not been chosen by the same individuals. A category that is rare moves away from the centre of the cloud, creating distance. This geometric representation makes it possible to highlight proximities, oppositions, and distances between individuals based on **VARIABLES**.

The main axes of the cloud of individuals coincide with the main axes of the cloud of categories. The projection of cloud points onto the first axis provides the best one-dimensional adjustment of the cloud, i.e. the main structuring factor (Duval 2017). To evaluate the relative importance of the axes, we recommend using modified rates of inertia (Le Roux and Rouanet 2010: 39). Determining the number of selected axes is based on an examination of the eigenvalues and modified rates, as well as the ability to interpret the axes.

FIGURE 4 **Data matrix and clouds of categories and individuals**

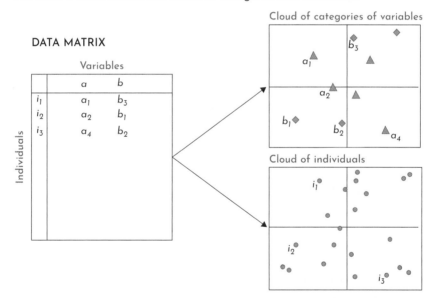

Only so-called *active variables* and individuals contribute to the construction of the factorial plane and to determining the axes. In contrast, *supplementary variables* and individuals do not participate in the construction of the axes or in defining the distance between the individuals. However, they have a certain explanatory power, when projected onto the factorial plan. The **RESEARCH QUESTIONS** and the construction of the object of research determine the distinction between an active and a supplementary variable. For example, in order to analyse the relationship between lifestyle and social position, Bourdieu (1989) used musical or interior design taste as active variables and projected social class indicators (education, profession, income) as supplementary variables.

The axes are interpreted from the cloud of categories by drawing on the active categories and VARIABLES. In order to interpret an axis, only categories with an above average contribution are considered. The two poles of the axis must be clearly designated.

The analysis of the cloud of individuals depends on the interpretation of the axes. It involves a series of operations, such as: studying the shape and structure of the cloud in relation to additional information provided by *supplementary variables*; analysing the variance of each subgroup of individuals; and interpreting the distances between individuals of the same group or between different groups.

MCA AND THE FIELD

MCA is a powerful visualization tool. Pierre Bourdieu and researchers influenced by his work have used it widely because it is compatible with the concept of field (Bourdieu 2005: 70), as a spatial representation of social spaces. Thus, MCA is a tool that can objectify 'theoretical spaces' (Duval 2017). In his studies of different social fields, Bourdieu often combines PROSOPOGRAPHY and MCA. The aim of prosopography is to produce and collect data on a set of individuals, groups, or institutions (social origin, education, position in the field, resources, etc.), which can then be used to identify the history of the field and build a social space using MCA.

Bourdieu uses indicators of efficient capital to identify the main factors that structure a given field. In other words, MCA can be used to determine the structure of a field (spatial representation of social space) to shed light on how power and capital are distributed among individuals and institutions.

THE EXAMPLE OF CENTRAL BANKERS IN THE CONTEMPORARY GLOBAL FIELD OF POWER

Frédéric Lebaron is one of the leading academics that uses and develops MCA. He analyses the importance of central bankers as a key component of the new global elites. He argues that 'their action and beliefs have become determinant for the reproduction of the economic and social order as a whole' (Lebaron 2008). In order to understand the social reality behind the emergence of the major agents of global governance, he constructed a space to represent the world's leading monetary policy councils. He identified eleven active VARIABLES corresponding to five categories: socio-demographic characteristics, education, professional trajectory, symbolic capital, position and seniority. The analysis concerns thirty-nine individuals, who have been voting members of the world's three leading monetary councils since 2003: the Federal Open Market Committee (Fed), the Governing Council of the European Central Bank (ECB), and the Policy Council of the Bank of Japan (BoJ).

Figure 5 shows the cloud of active categories corresponding to the main characteristics of the individuals in the sample (the central bankers). The first two axes (i.e. the most important for structuring the space under analysis) are interpreted as follows: the first axis (horizontal) has a political pole on the right with accumulated, established, and institutional capital. This contrasts with a more academic pole on the left, which characterizes newcomers with no symbolic capital. The second (vertical) axis contrasts an economic-practical (industrial) pole at the top with an intellectual-academic pole at the bottom. Lebaron likens this polarity to 'pragmatics' (or doves) and 'dogmatics' (or hawks), in which academics appear to be closer to economic dogmas than applied economists.

Figure 6 shows the cloud of individuals: each point represents a central banker. The mean-points of the supplementary **VARIABLE** 'central banks' (ECB/Fed/BoJ) have been projected into this cloud. The variable 'central bank' is considered as a structuring factor in the space of individuals. The subclouds and the category mean-points of the central banks occupy different positions within the space. The different point shapes indicate the individuals' affiliation to one of the three central banks. In addition, the names of some individuals are displayed. The first axis shows an opposition between ECB and the two other central banks, based on the endowment of symbolic capital. The Fed and BoJ appear on the side with lower levels of symbolic capital, while the ECB is associated with higher levels of symbolic capital. On the second axis, the Fed and ECB appear on the side of academic legitimacy, whereas BoJ is closer to 'practical' and industrial legitimacy. In this example, MCA is used to map the social structure of the space occupied by central bankers. Therefore, it sheds some light on the economic behaviour of central banks.

FIGURE 5 The space of monetary policy councils, cloud of categories in plane 1-2

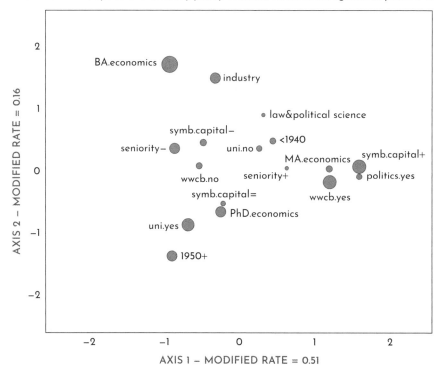

FIGURE 6 The space of monetary policy councils, cloud of individuals in plane 1-2 with mean-points of the central banks

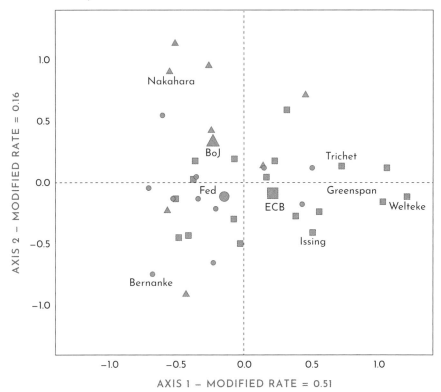

M

THE ARTICULATION OF MCA WITH OTHER STATISTICAL METHODS

The results of an MCA (the factorial axis) can be used to perform a cluster analysis or as **VARIABLES** for **REGRESSION ANALYSIS**. MCA can also be combined with **SOCIAL NETWORK ANALYSIS** (Grenfell and Lebaron 2014). In this case, SNA centrality indexes can be used as active variables in MCA to measure the symbolic capital, for example (e.g. Davidshofer, Tawfik, and Hagmann 2016). Finally, the outputs of a **SEQUENCE ANALYSIS** (i.e. clusters of a sequence analysis) can be integrated as active or supplementary variables in MCA.

SOFTWARE

The recent development of open source software epitomizes the growing popularity of MCA. Once closely tied to the expensive data-mining software SPAD, MCA can now be conducted cheaply thanks to numerous free R packages, such as GDAtools, FactoMineR, ade4, soc.ca, and the visualization tool explor.

REFERENCES

Bennett, Tony, Mike Savage, Elizabeth Bortolaia Silva, Alan Warde, Modesto Gayo-Cal and David Wright. 2009. *Culture, Class, Distinction*. London, Routledge.

Bourdieu, Pierre. 1989. *Distinction: A Social Critique of the Judgement of Taste*. London, Routledge.

Bourdieu Pierre. 2005. *The Social Structures of the Economy*. Cambridge, Polity.

Davidshofer, Stephan, Amal Tawfik, and Jonas Hagmann. 2016. 'Analyse du champ de la sécurité en Suisse: vers une hypertrophie de la sécurité intérieure et autres réflexions méthodologiques'. *Cultures & Conflits* 102(2): 59-93.

Duval, Julien. 2017. 'Multiple correspondence analysis'. *Politika*. Available at https://www.politika.io/en/notice/multiple-correspondence-analysis (Accessed 19 February 2020).

Grenfell, Michael and Frédéric Lebaron (eds). 2014. *Bourdieu and Data Analysis: Methodological Principles and Practice*. Oxford, Peter Lang.

Le Roux, Brigitte and Henry Rouanet. 2010. *Multiple Correspondence Analysis*. Thousand Oaks, CA, SAGE Publications.

Lebaron, Frédéric. 2008. 'Central Bankers in the Contemporary Global Field of Power: A "Social Space" Approach'. *The Sociological Review* 56(Suppl 1): 121-144.

Pouliot, Vincent. 2016. *International Pecking Orders: The Politics and Practice of Multilateral Diplomacy*. Cambridge, Cambridge University Press.

M

N

NOMOTHETIC AND IDIOGRAPHIC METHODS

Nicky Hayes, Canterbury Christ Church University

Research can serve many purposes: to evaluate innovation, to inform decision-making, to investigate a scientific HYPOTHESIS, to identify new areas for research, among many others. The purpose of our research determines how we go about it, so clarifying that is an essential first step.

Knowing the purpose helps us to define the SCOPE CONDITIONS of the research, and will also tell us whether our research should be nomothetic or idiographic. These terms were originally coined by the German philosopher Wilhelm Windelband in 1894 (Windelband 1998 [1894]), and became popular in psychology through Gordon Allport's (1937) influential text on personality theory. *Nomothetic research* aims to identify laws about human behaviour—the Greek word 'nomos' means 'law'. It assumes that it is possible to discover regularities of influence or behaviour, allowing experts to predict the likely outcomes of possible actions or innovations. So it looks for general principles, not special cases.

Idiographic research, by contrast, is all about exploring individuality or uniqueness. Idiographic research tends to focus on a single example, which might be a person, an event, a phenomenon, or an organization, and to analyse that example in depth. As a result, idiographic methods are often used in CASE STUDIES, and are characteristic of ETHNOGRAPHIC research. Idiographic studies are likely to adopt an INDUCTIVE rather than a DEDUCTIVE approach, working on the idea that we may discover general principles through a deeper understanding of one or two instances, rather than by looking for common factors.

As you might expect, then, the two approaches involve different research tools. Nomothetic research, for example, often involves the use of statistical analysis, which averages out or disregards variations and special cases. Its emphasis is on group characteristics, looking at the differences and similarities between groups; and it depends on statistical processes which are dealt with in other chapters, such as STATISTICAL SIGNIFICANCE, SAMPLING TECHNIQUES, and REPLICATION.

Idiographic research places less emphasis on statistical generalization, and more on ways of describing and analysing individuality. An idiographic project in marketing or psychology might use psychometric techniques allowing detailed exploration of how an individual sees their world; an idiographic study conducted by an anthropologist might analyse personal accounts from significant community members; an idiographic management project might apply thematic analysis of employee interviews to identify distinctive experiences of working in that particular organization; an idiographic organizational project might explore the economic growth and development of a single organization such as IBM or Costa Coffee; or an idiographic study of entrepreneurs might look in detail at the life of someone like Richard Branson, Steve Jobs, or Mark Zuckerberg. All of which means that idiographic analyses tend to go into a lot of detail, using individual-focused approaches such as CASE STUDIES and TRIANGULATION.

Deciding whether a study is idiographic or nomothetic does not depend on the method: it depends on the reason for the study. Experiments are often nomothetic, exploring the responses of groups of people. But if we were studying a brain injury, we might conduct experiments to identify its effects on that person's behaviour. Those experiments wouldn't involve large groups of people—such comparison would be meaningless. Instead, the comparison is with data from the same person, for example comparing their ability to recognize images of relatives' faces with their recognition of other faces.

The nomothetic/idiographic distinction means that 'classic' principles of research are only relevant in some cases and not others. Sampling, for example, is an important issue in nomothetic research. Deducing general laws or principles can only be done from a representative sample of the population we are studying. But it is of less concern in idiographic research, which seeks to understand the individual, person, or case by exploring their uniqueness.

In some cases, the same research technique can be used in either nomothetic or idiographic research. Reason (1979) used diary methods to study errors of memory, asking people to note down any memory lapses or other errors, as soon as they noticed that they had made them. This was an example of nomothetic research using a diary approach: the results from several research participants were combined to identify general trends and mechanisms. In a different study, Linton (1975) kept a diary in which she noted two significant events a day, over a five-year period. Every few months, she selected two items randomly, read the description, and tried to recall the date on which it had happened. If she had no recollection of the event, it was dropped from later samples. The pattern of forgetting and memory loss illustrated a number of well-established principles of memory, like primacy effects and the importance of rehearsal. But it also gave some surprising results—for example, that highly emotional events did not turn out to be particularly memorable. This idiographic study had only one research participant, but it made a significant contribution to knowledge, stimulating further research.

In epistemological terms, nomothetic research is often associated with POSITIVISTIC approaches, and the belief that universal laws governing human behaviour can be identified, while idiographic research is often associated with **POST-POSITIVIST** approaches, seeing knowledge as relative in its context but not necessarily universal. At the sociological/anthropological level, idiographic research is exemplified in the 'thick description' described by Geertz (1973), in which an interpretive approach to culture uses 'ethnographic miniatures' drawn from individual accounts to explore the symbolic input of things and events, allowing the researcher to distinguish different frames of interpretation.

Each type of research has its strengths: identifying common laws or principles has proved valuable in many areas of the social sciences, while studying uniqueness has brought useful insights and has often been the key to opening up new research areas. Which is why, to come back to where we started, clarifying the purpose of the research is such a vital first step.

REFERENCES

Allport, Gordon W. 1937. *Personality: A Psychological Interpretation*. New York, Holt.

Geertz, Clifford. 1973. *The Interpretation of Cultures*. New York, Basic Books.

Linton, M. 1975. 'Memory for Real-world Events', in *Explorations in Cognition*, ed. Donald A. Norman and David E. Rumelhart, 376–404. San Francisco, Freeman.

Reason, J. T. 1979. 'Actions not as Planned: The Price of Automatisation', in *Aspects of Consciousness*, volume I, ed. Geoffrey Underwood and Robin Stevens, 1–67. London, Academic Press.

Windelband, Wilhelm. 1998 [1894]. 'History and Natural Science'. *Theory & Psychology* 8(1): 5–22.

N

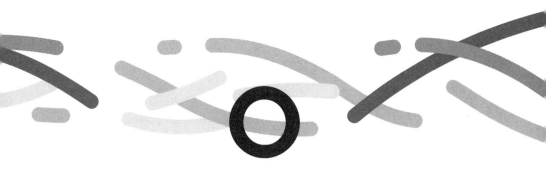

OBSERVATIONAL METHODS

Combining Critical Distance and Inside Knowledge?

Christian Olsson, Université libre de Bruxelles

Observation plays a crucial role in scientific research. The mental images through which we make sense of a concept or theory are linked to experiences acquired through observation. Many social scientists consider that if social mechanisms are to have epistemological relevance, they must be at least partially or indirectly observable. When scientific objects or phenomena are said to be observable, this might involve the mediation of instruments (indirect observation through microscope, telescope . . .) and often it is the traces left rather than the object itself that is being observed (partial observation, for example of photographic pictures showing a very limited visual manifestation of the object). It is, however, important to distinguish the epistemological question of the observable nature of that which can be known (Jackson 2016), and observation as method, as activity involving the direct experience and perception of one's research object in real-life situations.

In this context, what distinguishes observational methods, and particularly participant observation (PO), from other data-gathering methods is, among others, that it privileges direct observation over the use of instruments. This implies that the observation is likely to be holistic, in the sense of involving our five senses, rather than only one of our senses (typically our sight). PO also privileges observation in real time over the retrospective observation of traces left by past activities (texts, pictures, filmed sequences). It allows us to observe discourses, practices, interactions, and context together rather than separately. It focuses on first-hand observation, as opposed to observation based on secondary sources (involving a mediator or third person). PO is sometimes accused of harbouring a naive belief in the scientific virtue of 'gut feeling'. Its fundamental tenet is however to be as sceptical as Thomas, the apostle: to prefer seeing before believing.

A MULTIPLICITY OF APPROACHES

There are arguably two types of observational methods: structured and participant observation (PO). *Structured observation* is the factual description of a UNIT OF OBSERVATION, generally involving the production of ordinal data, such as: Who? How many? How often? For example, by directly observing cars at a crossing (observation may be automated), statistics can be established about traffic at this precise location. This type of observation is said to be structured because it focuses on frequencies, durations, or the number of strictly defined occurrences—in other words on circumscribed and quantifiable aspects of reality. This type of observation is sometimes also, perhaps misleadingly, called direct observation because in principle it only involves the perception of the research object and tries to avoid any interaction with it.

Participant observation (PO) is a much more flexible and challenging method, initially practised by anthropologists such as Malinowski, Mauss, or Mead. Unlike structured observation, PO foregrounds qualitative data and encourages the observer to 'blend in' to the social setting.

'Participant' does not mean that the researcher is necessarily engaged in all the activities under study. In fact, there are four alternative or concurrent meanings of participation. First, it refers to immersion in the observed social context, both to understand it 'from within' and to ensure that the outsider's presence does not provoke unusual reactions on the part of the insiders. Second, it describes the process of learning by doing: by taking part in the social game, the participant observer gains access to tacit background knowledge and the informal rules of the game. Third, it might refer to a transaction between the observer and the observed: for example, the researcher can accept work as a fundraiser for an NGO in exchange for the opportunity to gather data on the NGO in the context of the research. Fourth, it is about studying how people react to the researcher's actions, in which case observation will focus primarily on insider–outsider interactions and encounters. In this fourth case, one often talks of 'field experiments', an experiment in which the researcher tries to establish a causal relation between independent and dependent variables by manipulating the former one in real-life situations.

Hence, PO spans a continuum ranging from unobtrusive observation to 'full participation'. Some researchers who give priority to participation prefer to call it 'observant participation'. This is the case for Wacquant, who trained six times a week for three years at a boxing club in an African American ghetto in Chicago to get to know its (male) population, despite being white (Wacquant 2004). Here, the focus is typically on immersion, local acceptance, and complicity with the studied population, rather than on the outsider's critical distance. On the spectrum from distant to proximate, there is always a trade-off between critical distance and immersion (Bueger and Mireanu 2014).

PO is sometimes equated with ETHNOGRAPHY or fieldwork. However, ethnography describes a specific approach to PO that is long term, comprehensive, but also relatively unstructured. It is the approach preferred by most anthropologists. Other social and behavioural scientists tend to prefer less immersive, more structured and focused PO. Fieldwork refers to empirical research conducted on the site where the phenomena under consideration occur or leave observable traces. It can involve PO, as well as other methods, such as field experiments, FOCUS GROUPS, INTERVIEW TECHNIQUES, ORAL HISTORY, or SURVEY RESEARCH.

PARTICIPANT OBSERVATION: WHEN?

PO is the best way to acquire a fine-grained understanding of a specific social site, particularly in two types of settings. The first are societies or groups that the researcher knows little about because they are relatively closed or have not been documented (little available literature). These are typically the 'exotic' communities that early anthropologists were interested in. Of course, they could have been studied by testing deductively produced HYPOTHESES. However, in the absence of literature, there are inherent limits to abstract thinking when it comes to researching a 'social universe' that we are not familiar with. In this type of setting, in which the 'field' can resist the researcher's preconceptions, PO forces us to think 'outside the box', inductively. But PO is not suited exclusively to the study of social enclaves. In 'social universes' that communicate about themselves, PO sheds light on what happens behind the scenes. Just as the first anthropologists learned 'native' languages, PO allows the contemporary researcher to learn the insider's vernacular (the 'emic' categories). The researcher can then 'translate' this into his own 'etic' categories and concepts. It is by no means a coincidence that participant observers tend to foreground social meaning and privilege interpretive approaches.

The second setting is that of highly bureaucratized organizations, where there is generally a disjuncture between formal rules and informal practices. For example, even though bureaucracies have strict hierarchies, there is usually significant space for reinterpreting decisions at the lower echelons. Interviewing techniques can be useful in this regard, but they fail to reveal the differences between what people say they do and what they actually do. Moreover, interviews tend to revolve around past events, and recollection may alter perception. Bureaucratic organizations of course produce documents that can be analysed, but only PO can highlight how documents have been written, for what purpose (internal or external use), and whether they are internally contested (Neumann 2007). Typically, PO has established that many street-level bureaucrats not only implement, but actually define policies for which they are responsible, using margins of discretion that are absent from official documents and from their own accounts of their work (Lipsky 1980).

In fact, PO can be used to research any relatively small-scale group that shares practices and language, for example a laboratory, football club, parliament, summer camp, hairdresser, etc. However, the UNIT OF OBSERVATION does not have to be a group; it could be a practice or a place (the waiting area in an airport, a harbour, etc.). In the latter case, it is approached as a site interconnecting people or shaping their social trajectories rather than as a clearly delineated 'field'.

PO is particularly well suited for researchers who want to highlight CONTEXTUAL ANALYSIS, complexity, nuance, plurality of meanings, and contingency for epistemological or theoretical reasons. What constitutes background noise from the point of view of parsimonious models might often be of major interest to the participant observer. On the whole, adepts of PO consider that this type of approach allows them to avoid the errors associated with decontextualized or purely deductive approaches. They focus on the 'realism' of their interpretations, not on formal 'testability' (Brodkin 2017).

PARTICIPANT OBSERVATION: HOW?

There are few established rules pertaining to PO beyond the need to ensure access to the 'field' and make sure that one has the necessary time to build rapport with the studied group. Depending on the proximity–distance continuum, the participant observer might be either transparent or clandestine (the observer may or may not disclose that they are a researcher), internal or external (the observer may or may not be a member of the observed group), peripheral or complete (is he/she just talking the talk or also walking the walk?).

PO does not preclude other data-gathering methods (interviews, recordings, SURVEY RESEARCH), and data analysis can involve other methods (SOCIAL NETWORK ANALY-SIS, DISCOURSE ANALYSIS). Sometimes PO is used to fine-tune questionnaires prior to interviews or surveys. PO is also open to TRIANGULATION and MIXED METHODS.

During PO, it is advisable to take extensive notes of one's observations—field notes are useful as a repository for observations that might otherwise be forgotten. They also encourage the researcher to put his/her own perceptions into perspective (reflexivity). For example, the researcher can highlight how his/her assumptions are progressively challenged in and by the field. The researcher's observations always relate to his/her own social position and perspective. In order to give a reflexive account of the observed setting, it is important that the observations reported in the field notes include the researcher. Notes should be descriptive, as well as analytical, interpretive, and reflexive. If the participatory activity prevents the researcher from taking notes at the time, it is advisable to write them down as soon as possible afterwards to ensure that they are precise and detailed.

PO is a very flexible method. It can be exploratory or explanatory. When exploratory, it can be used to identify questions and formulate hypotheses to be tested by other methods. In fact, there is always an exploratory dimension to PO. With deductive approaches, HYPOTHESES can be tested without changing the initial research design, but PO inevitably challenges initial assumptions. Cultural anthropologists often emphasize the study of subjectivities, meanings, emotions, and lifeworlds in their PO. In comparison, some participant observers focus on material practices, bureaucratic routines, standard operating procedures, discourse, etc.

Although PO-based studies are usually idiographic and have limited nomothetic ambitions, observational fieldwork can be consistent with both NOMOTHETIC AND IDIOGRAPHIC approaches. However, ETHNOGRAPHIC observations are typically generalized inductively, rather than deductively. If the initial hypothesis to be tested is formulated in macro-sociological terms, there is a risk that when undertaking fieldwork the researcher will simply see the 'tree that hides the forest'—i.e. the micro-level realities that muddle the broader picture. Therefore, most ethnographers and anthropologists prefer not to generalize by concluding that there is a 'forest' until it has been established that all the entities populating the site are 'trees' (particulars).

ETHICS IN RESEARCH raises important questions for participant observers. Does informed consent apply? Must the researcher be transparent about his/her aims when involved in PO? In response to the first question, it is not always possible to apply standardized informed consent protocols. What if the people concerned cannot read or write? How do you apply informed consent when the 'field' is an online chat room where only nicknames are shown? What about research in authoritarian states, where the request to sign a document may appear suspicious or threatening? In many circumstances, the researcher must gauge when there is implied consent and when verbal consent is satisfactory. However, some rules are categorical. For example, recording the 'observed' is not considered permissible without consent, at least verbal consent. Any account of PO must make sure that the interlocutors remain anonymous, unless they have clearly given their permission to do otherwise.

There is no clear answer to the second question either. Most ethnographers consider that some deception—at least by omission—is permissible. For example, when participating in a carnival or a public funeral ceremony, a researcher need not explain his/her presence to all of the participants (he/she can inform a select few), and joining in the celebratory or grieving mood is not reprehensible. However, direct untruthfulness is not advisable because of ethical and safety concerns. This is especially the case when carrying out PO in deviant groups. Covert research in such groups exposes one to the accusation of seeking to infiltrate them. Although it might not be intentional on the part of the researcher, this accusation is not far-fetched as the publication of the research could undermine the confidentiality that the group might have enjoyed until then.

CRITIQUE AND WEAKNESSES

The debate on the strengths and weaknesses of PO is not dissimilar to the wider debate on large-N/small-N designs. On a practical level, one of the main problems is that PO is time-consuming, expensive, and requires in-depth cultural and linguistic knowledge of the 'field'. Conducting this type of research is difficult if you teach every other day.

At the methodological level, some researchers consider that PO is unsystematic, non-rigorous, non-parsimonious, potentially BIASED, and too much like investigative journalism. It is true that the 'results' drawn from PO typically raise questions of REPLICATION AND REPRODUCIBILITY. They are difficult to falsify and might even be contradicted by studies conducted by other participant observers. Indeed, the observer's social properties inevitably influence data collection. If you research neo-Nazis in the US, you will probably obtain different results depending on your skin colour, accent, etc. Limitations that are linked to the relational nature of PO are usually built into the participant observer's EPISTEMOLOGY, which typically focuses on context, reflexivity, and contingency. Moreover, most adepts of PO see knowledge as situated—i.e. there is a vantage point for any observation, a positionality.

At the epistemological level, PO is criticized for being too limited to 'understanding from inside' and being blind to social structures that might be unobservable yet real. However, this is arguably not linked to the methodology, but to the ethnomethodological epistemological tradition that is still very much alive among cultural anthropologists.

NEW PERSPECTIVES

Historically, the term 'field' in fieldwork was linked to the anthropological study of 'exotic societies', which were often thought to be small, relatively confined communities. While this is no longer the case, PO still conveys the idea that there must be an easily circumscribed location where all research can be conducted. This type of assumption is problematic in a world where people circulate globally and at increasing speed. Two types of approaches have been developed to overcome this limitation. First, in 'multi-situated ethnography' PO is conducted at multiple interconnected places (Marcus 1995). Second, in the 'extended case method' the 'field' is not necessarily bordered (Burawoj 1998). However, the researcher may establish a field boundary for heuristic reasons. When it comes to fieldwork, a transnational network can be just as interesting as a tribe in the Brazilian jungle.

REFERENCES

Brodkin, Evelyn Z. 2017. 'The Ethnographic Turn in Political Science: Reflections on the State of the Art'. *PS: Political Science & Politics* 50(1): 131-134.

Bueger, C. and M. Mireanu. 2014. 'Proximity in Critical Security Methods', in *Critical Security Methods: New Frameworks for Analysis*, ed. Claudia Aradau, Jef Huysmans, Andrew Neal, and Nadine Voelkner, 118-141. London, Routledge.

Burawoj, Michael. 1998. 'The Extended Case Method'. *Sociological Theory* 16(1): 4-33.

Jackson, Patrick Thaddeus. 2016. *The Conduct of Inquiry in International Relations: Philosophy of Science and Its Implications for the Study of World Politics*. London, Routledge.

Lipsky, Michael. 1980. *Street-level Bureaucracy: Dilemmas of the Individual in Public Services*. New York, Russell Sage Foundation.

Marcus, George E. 1995. 'Ethnography in/of the World System: The Emergence of Multi-sited Ethnography'. *Annual Review of Anthropology* 24(1): 95-117.

Neumann, Iver B. 2007. 'A Speech that the Entire Ministry May Stand For or: Why Diplomats Never Produce Anything New'. *International Political Sociology* 1(2): 183-200.

Wacquant, Loïc. 2004. *Body & Soul: Notebooks of an Apprentice Boxer*. Oxford, Oxford University Press.

ONTOLOGY

Eric Fabri, Université libre de Bruxelles and University of Oxford

The word ontology comes from the ancient Greek *ontos* ('*being*'—present participle of '*eimi*', to be) and *logos* (knowledge, rational discourse). It is the branch of philosophy concerned with the nature of being. The classical questions addressed in ontology since the Pre-Socratics (especially Parmenides), Plato, and Aristotle are: 'What is being?',

'Which categories of objects exist?', or 'Do social phenomena exist in the same way as physical objects?' Therefore, as a branch of metaphysics, ontology is mainly concerned with the modes of existence of different entities (tangible and intangible), such as material objects, social phenomena, concepts, mythological divinities, or numbers.

'Ontology' also has a second meaning. It refers to a coherent representation of the world, its fundamental elements, and the relations between them. *An* ontology is a simplified or abstract depiction of being, which provides a general framework for the analysis of the different elements that have been defined, how they interact and obey general laws. In this second definition, an ontology is partial and aims to explain a single dimension of being, whereas 'ontology', as the science of being, addresses the general question of being.

The reflection on ontology is intrinsically linked to epistemological questions (see EPISTEMOLOGY). A 'world of reference' or an ontology is a set of ontological statements that specify what is and what is not. A given statement (knowledge) can be considered true or false depending on the ontology used as a reference. All scientific discourse relates to an object that is presumed to exist in this or that form according to a given ontology, which defines being and indicates whether a particular statement about an object is true or false according to the axioms of that ontology.

This is particularly clear in the case of the social sciences. Every subdiscipline relies on an ontology that defines which elements really matter when it comes to explaining the phenomenon they set out to elucidate. Imagine, for instance, that John must go to the marketplace and choose where to buy his vegetables. He has different options: one shop is the cheapest, another has the nicest seller, a third is closer to his current location, while the last shop offers the best guarantee of quality. Once his choice has been made, it can be explained in various ways, depending on what is thought to be the determining causal factor—i.e. the ontological understanding of what the situation *is* and the factors that the researcher considers are crucial for explaining John's choice. A psychoanalyst might explain the choice on the basis of the unconscious pressure to buy vegetables in the shop that reminded him of when he went shopping with his mother. An economist could argue that he was maximizing his utility. A feminist researcher might claim that John went to the shop with the nicest seller because of sexist advertising and gender representations. The same phenomenon can be explained in various ways that each involve the existence of different ontological elements and of different relations between these elements that make sense in this ontology.

Each explanatory theory necessarily relies on an 'explicit' ontology, which explicitly defines the relevant units for this given theory (John's subconscious, his memories, the market, his utility, gender representations, etc.) and the laws governing their interactions at different levels (see LEVELS OF ANALYSIS). In each ontology, some units are fundamental because they have a causal role (they cause John's behaviour), while others are secondary. Note however that the ontology on which a theory relies is also partially 'implicit', in so far as it relies on an intuitive concept of being, in general, that is assumed to be uncontroversially shared by the members of a society. The underlying 'implicit ontology' also 'fills the gaps' of explicit ontologies by giving meaning to the elements and causal relations that aren't explicitly defined because it is assumed that every member of the society has the same uncontroversial opinion of what they are.

Different ontologies are not necessarily incompatible (some disciplines embrace different ontologies, like sociology or political science for instance). In the previous example, each discipline explained John's behaviour from a different perspective, using concepts that have ontological priority in terms of how they conceive being. But it is possible to combine various explanations drawn from economics, psychoanalysis, and feminism, etc. Some explicit ontologies can be combined to form richer ontologies. However, the original complexity of John's behaviour calls for simpler explanatory models that have more general scope (but explain only one aspect of John's behaviour). To do so, the researcher has to build an ontology, which defines the fundamental entities (see UNIT OF ANALYSIS) that are relevant in her view, and explain how they interact in specific circumstances. The ultimate goal of scientific research is of course to grasp a complete understanding of John's choice, but the incredible difficulty of combining all the different aspects of his choice (and their corresponding ontologies) explains why researchers try first to explain each of these aspects one by one.

As already suggested, this process is typical of scientific research. When seeking to explain a phenomenon (in either the social or natural sciences), the researcher's main aim is to develop an abstract representation of the phenomenon to help explain the causal mechanism involved (see CAUSATION). A process of abstraction is used to achieve this: the characteristics of the phenomenon considered irrelevant are discarded. This can be likened to ontological pruning, whereby the researcher intuitively isolates the crucial parameters. For example, imagine a researcher wants to explain how and why an apple falls from an apple tree at a specific moment, in order to develop a model that can explain the fall of 'any' apple. In a first abstract model, the researcher ontologically defines what the apple is and determines which VARIABLES are important (weight, wood resistance, or wind) and unimportant (the apple's colour or texture). While building the explanatory model, the researcher disregards many of the characteristics that define the unique apple he is studying. Thus, the abstract model will only include the characteristics considered relevant to explain its fall.

Therefore, when developing an explanatory model, general characteristics are abstracted from singular exemplars of the things observed (a definite conception of 'an apple' is abstracted from the observation of many specific apples). Selection is guided by the researcher's intention and her pre-reflexive understanding of what being is—i.e. her intuition about how causality operates in the case to be explained. Science sets out to establish general laws, but it is confronted with particular cases; therefore, abstraction is required. Thus, science necessarily builds an ontologically simplified model of being. Consequently, every scientific theory (in the natural or social sciences) is based on an explicit ontology, or a 'world of reference'. But this explicit ontology is inevitably deficient when being is considered in absolute terms. Therefore, it is crucial for the researcher to be aware of the fact that her inquiry is driven by a pre-reflexive (and often unclear) representation of being, that is, by what we called an 'implicit ontology'.

With these concepts at hand, we can illustrate as follows the relations between the researcher's implicit ontology, his explicit ontology, his epistemological commitments, and the explanatory theory he creates to explain a phenomenon.

FIGURE 7   A simplified representation of the different ontological elements and layers used to explain a phenomenon

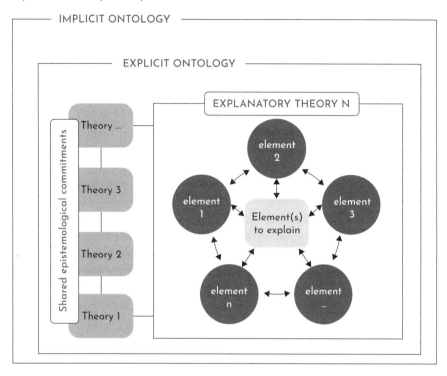

Figure 7 illustrates how the explanation of the central element implies the ontological position of other elements that make sense in this theory. The lines between these elements represent the relations existing between them (and the central element to be explained) that the researcher wants to clarify by using this specific explanatory theory. The other 'theories' outside the 'explanatory theory' (but inside the same 'explicit ontology') express the fact that, to be accepted, the explanatory theory must be relatable to other existing theories of the discipline (except in the case of a paradigm-changing theory—see later in this entry). The fact that these theories share the same epistemological commitments explains that they are part of the same explicit ontology. Note, however, that this illustration presents a highly simplified representation of what can be very complex relations. For instance, a discipline can rely on different ontologies, and elements belonging to different ontologies can coexist in the same explanatory theory. Moreover, contrary to what this representation suggests, ontologies don't tend to be 'closed'. They rather evolve permanently, they are the objects of theoretical disputes, and their borders are often blurred. Finally, recall that the 'elements' appearing in the centre of the explanatory theory have been 'pruned': they are abstract and 're-duced' versions of what they 'are' for the implicit ontology that encompasses the whole.

This illustration also underlines how important the implicit ontology is, for it precedes and conditions the validity of alternative explicit ontologies. As Thomas Kuhn has shown in *The Structure of Scientific Revolutions* (Kuhn 1962), the implicit ontology of a society sets the limits within which the researcher's theory will (usually) develop, by conditioning the possible explanatory models. Thomas Kuhn's most famous example is the paradigm shift from geocentrism to heliocentrism in astronomy. Here, a conjunction of technical progress and social factors triggered a change in the ontological framework. Until then, the prevailing ontological framework placed the earth at the centre of the universe. The new perception put the sun at the centre of the planetary system. Once researchers were able to conceive of 'reality' in a different way, they endorsed the new paradigm and its ontology. But before that could happen, a change in the implicit ontology was necessary: it must have been possible to think 'the earth is not the centre of the universe' and not immediately dismiss this idea as heretical or as pure nonsense.

In the social sciences, the ontological status of objects like 'nation', 'patriarchy', or 'crime' is less clear than in the case of the natural sciences. As a result, a specific branch of ontology is devoted to the modes of existence of social phenomena: social ontology. Two main positions emerge: realism and constructivism. SCIENTIFIC REALISM assumes that social phenomena have an objective existence, independent of the subject. In the view of realist philosophers like Bhaskar, social phenomena can be understood as the product of social structures that have an independent existence. The objective structures are 'structures producing social phenomena analogous to the causal mechanisms of nature' (Bhaskar 1986: 108). Realism in social ontology is similar to ontological realism in the natural sciences. It also shares some assumptions with pragmatism, as developed by philosophers like Charles Sanders Peirce, William James, and John Dewey. Pragmatism acknowledges the evanescent nature of social phenomena, but overcomes the difficulty by studying the real effects and actions they produce.

By contrast, *constructivism* claims that social phenomena have no objective existence and are a construction of the human mind. Its fundamental axiom is that, even if reality exists outside the subject's perception, the subject cannot reach it without perceiving it. This implies the mediation of imaginary structures, which are provided by social groups. There is no possible access to something like an objective and independent being. Social phenomena, in particular, have no objective existence, but they have meaning, interpretations, and social representations that are built coherently by a subject, in its own language. For constructivist philosophers like Peter Berger and Thomas Luckmann (Berger and Luckmann 1966), every individual builds her own world with the categories and ontological entities she learned during her education. Social phenomena are the results of how the individuals in a given society construct their own world and how they act within it according to socially acquired motivations. Therefore, the key epistemological question in constructivism is not 'what is the reality?' but 'how is it socially constructed?'

To conclude, it is important to note that many other positions exist apart from realism and constructivism. Empiricists adopt an empirical approach to human behaviour, while FALSIFICATIONISTS acknowledge the utility of abstract theories and request that their predictions can be empirically verified. Finally, it is worth mentioning Cornélius Castoriadis's theory of the imaginary institution of being (Castoriadis 1998).

It proposes an ontology that is based on imaginary creation, which reconciles social imagination and the constraints generated by the materiality of being. This provides key concepts to help the researcher in the social sciences to clarify how imaginary creation relates to his object and to the materiality of being.

REFERENCES

Berger, Peter and Thomas Luckmann. 1966. *The Social Construction of Reality: A Treatise in the Sociology of Knowledge*. Garden City, NY, Doubleday.

Bhaskar, Roy. 1986. *Scientific Realism and Human Emancipation*. London, Verso.

Castoriadis, Cornélius. 1998. *The Imaginary Institution of Society*. Cambridge, MA, MIT Press.

Kuhn, Thomas S. 1962. *The Structure of Scientific Revolutions*. Chicago, Chicago University Press.

OPERATIONALIZATION

From the Concepts to the Data

Anne-Laure Mahé, Institut de Recherche Stratégique de l'École Militaire
Theodore McLauchlin, Université de Montréal

DEFINITION

Operationalization refers to the intellectual operations the researcher undertakes to decide how to observe a concept in reality. This is a crucial step of the research process, as many concepts in the social sciences are too abstract to be immediately observed. How can we observe alienation, democracy, or social capital? Operationalizing these concepts means transforming them into empirically observable units (see UNIT OF ANALYSIS). The key issue is whether what you observe means what you think it does.

LINKING DATA AND CONCEPTS

Researchers should take operationalization into account when developing concepts (Gerring 2012: 116–117). Operationalization is not an afterthought, because concepts and theories must have some way of being observed, whether directly or indirectly. But the tasks involved in these two stages should not be confused. Operationalization is far from the only criterion for a useful concept; see CONCEPT CONSTRUCTION for a full treatment.

The task of operationalizing a concept is also not isolated from the *theoretical* context of a concept. An operationalization of a concept that is appropriate for one **RESEARCH QUESTION** might not be for another. For example, the well-known Polity index is an attempt to operationalize the concept of regime type, ranging from -10 (most authoritarian) to +10 (most democratic). One of the five components of this index is political competition, constructed such that factional political competition, characterized by hostility and violence and including civil wars in extreme cases, pushes the overall Polity index to the middle of the scale. This operationalization decision makes sense for many research purposes, since such violence suggests that a country is not under full authoritarian control, but is hardly democratic either. But it does not work well for all purposes. Many researchers in conflict studies have found that countries in the middle of the Polity scale are especially likely to experience civil wars. But this relationship seems due largely to factional political competition. This may be as much a consequence of a coming civil war as a cause; at worst, since the **VARIABLE** includes the words 'civil war' explicitly, it may be tautological (Vreeland 2008).

In order to operationalize a concept, the researcher needs to devise indicators. The relationship between the concept and its indicators can be causal, meaning indicators are either a cause or an effect of the concept they operationalize. A measure of the ideological positions of members of the United States Congress might be by their votes, which are presumed to be caused by such ideologies (Gerring 2012: 181–182). More commonly, the idea is simply that the indicator signals the presence of the concept directly: electoral democracy, which cannot be directly observed, is signalled by the presence of competitive elections, which can—at least more easily (Gerring 2012: 162–163).

VALIDITY

But what makes a 'good' indicator, and hence a successful operationalization? The central issue is validity, that is, the match between the concept and indicators (Gerring 2012: 82–83, 161). An indicator is valid in so far as it captures the concept it is claiming to capture. Validity does not exist on its own; it needs to be evaluated in relation to the concept it is operationalizing. Validity is the central aim of operationalization, and often its hardest challenge. Indicators do not exist outside of the researcher and are not to be found—they are constructed.

For many purposes, it is impossible to avoid some arbitrary decisions, and therefore some slippage between concept and indicator will necessarily occur. 'Civil war' seems to imply a severely violent conflict, so indicators of civil war often involve numerical thresholds of deaths in combat. But authors disagree on the required number. Why 1,000 (as is common)? This might exclude some cases that look a good deal like what we mean by civil wars and include others that seem to fit the concept poorly (Sambanis 2004).

Assessing validity involves both reasoning *and* empirical analysis. As Gerring (2012: 161) argues, validity (and hence operationalization) 'is never a purely empirical problem', because it concerns the relationship between something we can observe and something we cannot. Evaluating validity is therefore, first, an exercise involving reasoning about how well indicators match concepts. What phenomena, other than the concept of interest, might the indicator be picking up? For instance, if an indicator of civil wars has a threshold of 1,000 deaths, should the number be reached in one year for the events to be coded a civil war, or is it cumulative? If cumulative, it would be possible to 'code as a civil war any minor conflict or terrorist campaign that causes 25 deaths per year for more than 40 years' (Sambanis 2004: 819), which seems not to quite capture what the concept of 'civil war' generally means. Sambanis (2004: 830) therefore adds to the cumulative number of deaths an indicator for a sustained level of violence throughout the year.

This reasoning process also indicates that operationalization is not at all a linear process from concept to indicator. Instead, there are feedback loops between the levels of conceptualization and operationalization. An indicator can produce unexpected observations, leading the researcher to modify the systematized concepts—for instance, discovering that an indicator of civil conflict excludes some crucial cases and includes some dubious ones. Faced with such issues, the researcher needs to go back to the conceptualization stage to devise new and more appropriate indicators.

Researchers can also assess validity by appealing to other indicators that, according to a concept or to a theory about the relationships among concepts, should have a relationship with the indicator in question (this is the idea of *construct validity*, which is often taken to be the single overarching criterion of validity in general; e.g. Messick 1995). To take a classic example, one sign that a question on a maths test may need reconsidering is if there is little correspondence between how well students do on that question and how well they do on most others. Empirical procedures can help, because it is hard to be fully confident that one has thought of everything that might limit the validity of an indicator. Here, quantitative researchers often use correlations among multiple items, such as survey responses. Qualitative researchers, however, can make use of similar procedures, such as **TRIANGULATION** among data sources like archival documents, interviews, and participant observation (Creswell and Miller 2000: 126–127). In either case, the ultimate result is that an indicator does not stand on its own; instead, multiple indicators support each other in a conceptual argument.

ASSESSING RELIABILITY

In addition to validity, reliability is the indicator's consistency across multiple uses: if you use the same procedure multiple times, how close will you come to the same result each time? An indicator is *valid* to the extent that it is free from systematic error; it is *reliable* to the extent that it is free from random error. This means that the results of an inquiry can be valid and unreliable at the same time, and vice versa. Reliability means that repeated tests of inference present results that are close to each other, but that does not mean that they are close to the concept the researcher is trying to measure. If they are, then they are both valid and reliable (Gerring 2012: 82).

Consider how to measure someone's political ideology, taken as an ensemble of political attitudes that go together. Some ways of measuring this concept in SURVEY RE-SEARCH run into serious reliability problems. For example, it may not be especially easy to place oneself on a ten-point scale from most liberal to most conservative: the respondent may only have a vague idea of what the terms mean; the numeric scale may be too abstract and too fine-grained to elicit a meaningful answer (what does 'three' mean, and can it really be interpreted as different from two and four?); and the respondent is being asked to summarize many different attitudes at once (Alwin and Krosnick 1991; Treier and Hillygus 2009). But the respondent often feels under pressure to give *some* sort of answer; and so their answers will be to a certain extent random—that is, unreliable. Ask them on a different day and they may give a different response, without anything meaningful changing. In contrast, it may be easier to answer a more concrete question, such as whether you intend to vote for the Conservative Party, and answers to this are likely to be more reliable. But this is not necessarily a *valid* measure of political ideology; there are many reasons besides ideology to vote for a party, from inherited party identification to current economic conditions to opinion about the party leader. Finally, some work combines answers to questions about concrete issues to uncover latent ideologies among survey respondents (e.g. Treier and Hillygus 2009). This method seeks to balance the reliability of answers to concrete questions with the validity of a measure of ideology as broad orientations to politics.

OPERATIONALIZATION IN DIFFERENT CONTEXTS

Crucially, indicators are context-sensitive: what an indicator allows us to see in one context does not necessarily work in another, since what we observe is inscribed in broader social systems. For example, whether a gift to an official is a token of respect or an abuse of power is difficult, if not impossible, to say without an understanding of the social context in which the gift is given (Gerring 2012: 161).

This does not mean that one should only study one's own context, but parsing out these meanings accurately can require a considerable research effort by itself, and is the fundamental task that scholars using OBSERVATIONAL METHODS often set for themselves. Researchers in this tradition, based on a different EPISTEMOLOGY, may try to avoid operationalizing entirely before immersing themselves in a social setting, because operationalizing always involves the researcher deciding to link an observation with a concept, imposing a meaning that may not correspond to the meaning given in the social setting under study. Immersing oneself in a field site or in first-person texts for long periods of time in order to better access these meanings, and verifying the meaning of indicators with one's study participants, are among the tools that qualitative researchers have at their disposal to address this issue (Creswell and Miller 2000).

Indeed, some scholars build on this problem to propose *credibility* as an alternative criterion to validity, which they deem inappropriate for qualitative research (Lincoln and Guba 1986: 76). They argue that to assess qualitative study, the main question is not whether the indicators accurately capture the 'truth'—as reality does not exist outside of the observer and there are therefore multiple 'truths'—but whether there is a match between participants' constructed realities and how the researcher represents those realities (Lincoln and Guba 1986: 75). These researchers are also uncomfortable with the criterion of reliability, since it assumes REPLICATION AND REPRODUC-IBILITY, meaning that we can repeatedly test our inferences. This is difficult to do with qualitative methods, where the nature of the data collected is influenced by the specific context in which the research takes place as well as the researcher's identity. Depending on age, gender, ethnicity, or sexual orientation, different researchers will not have access to the same social spaces and individuals, and hence might not produce the same inferences or get to the same results. In sum, researchers must be aware of these debates when operationalizing, to be able to assess their own indicators in accordance with their epistemological and methodological choices.

CONCLUSION

The most important criteria of a successful operationalization are consequently the consistency between each step of the research design, from theory formation to data collection, and the degree to which the indicators effectively allow the researcher to gather observations that work well in the context under study. One way to synthesize these points is that operationalization should enable the researcher to respect the principle of double adequacy, as explained by Olivier de Sardan (2015). First, the researcher's conceptual argument and the operationalized data should correspond. Second, there is a need for adequacy between those data and the 'reference reality'. This implies that we should always be aware of the limits of our data, and transparent about them. Just as it is often difficult to find valid indicators of our concepts, these indicators can never perfectly reflect the reference reality, and we should question which of its aspects our operational definitions and indicators enable us to know and which ones they do not. This reflexivity is central to the operationalization stage. It sometimes means that we have to go back to the drawing board to improve the tools that enable us to observe and interpret.

REFERENCES

Alwin, Duane F. and Jon A. Krosnick. 1991. 'The Reliability of Survey Attitude Measurement: The Influence of Question and Respondent Attributes'. *Sociological Methods & Research* 20(1): 139–181.

Creswell, John W. and Dana L. Miller. 2000. 'Determining Validity in Qualitative Inquiry'. *Theory Into Practice* 39(3): 124–130.

Gerring, John. 2012. *Social Science Methodology: A Unified Framework*, 2nd edition. Cambridge and New York, Cambridge University Press.

Lincoln, Yvonna S. and Egon G. Guba. 1986. 'But Is It Rigorous? Trustworthiness and Authenticity in Naturalistic Evaluation'. *New Directions for Evaluation* 1986(30): 73–84.

Messick, Samuel. 1995. 'Validity of Psychological Assessment: Validation of Inferences from Persons' Responses and Performances as Scientific Inquiry into Score Meaning'. *American Psychologist* 50(9): 741–749.

Olivier de Sardan, Jean-Pierre. 2015. *Epistemology, Fieldwork, and Anthropology*. Translated by Antoinette Tidjani Alou. London: Palgrave Macmillan.

Sambanis, Nicholas. 2004. 'What Is Civil War? Conceptual and Empirical Complexities of an Operational Definition'. *Journal of Conflict Resolution* 48(6): 814-858.

Treier, Shawn and D. Sunshine Hillygus. 2009. 'The Nature of Political Ideology in the Contemporary Electorate'. *Public Opinion Quarterly* 73(4): 679-703.

Vreeland, James Raymond. 2008. 'The Effect of Political Regime on War'. *Journal of Conflict Resolution* 52(3): 401-425.

ORAL HISTORY AND LIFE HISTORY

Julien Pomarède, Université libre de Bruxelles

Oral history and life history can be defined as the methods used to analyse the way actors narrate their past experiences. In oral history, the material is collected by an external observer (biographies, INTERVIEWS) and is mainly used to focus on delimited past sequences. Life history involves an examination of self-written accounts, such as autobiographies (memoirs), letters, or diaries (see ARCHIVAL RESEARCH). It serves the biographical objective of reconstituting individual or collective trajectories. Oral and life history can, therefore, be useful for analysing typical trajectories (the story of a member of a larger group), extraordinary experiences (or 'deviant cases'), and actors' knowledge (relevant to their professional situation). This entry focuses on key epistemological issues regarding the challenges, opportunities, and limits of using oral and life history as a research method.

The subjective dimension of oral and life history has sparked a significant number of debates. The empirical material analysed in the framework of these methods is drawn from actors' backgrounds and subjectivities. An individual's social position plays a role in his/her storytelling, regardless of whether it is oral or written. How people recount their experiences and the language chosen reflects their present and/or past condition (social origins and position) (Gubrium and Holstein 1998). Sometimes, it is also the product of (un)conscious calculations (an interest in telling the story in a certain way). In other words, individuals reconstruct their trajectories. Hence, oral and life accounts are not objective stories, but reconstructions of the past (Bertaux and Kohli 1984). For instance, Bourdieu suggests that autobiographical truth is a 'biographical illusion' because it is a teleological reading of the past in the light of the present (life is reviewed as logical sequences of events and decisions) (Bourdieu 1986). It has been noticed that working-class people face some difficulties in openly recounting their past experiences, precisely because dominated groups tend to consider and reconstruct their trajectories in a coherent but pessimistic manner (with emphasis on what they perceive as an inevitable and logical succession of 'failures' or 'mistakes') (Bourdieu 1999: 608–611). Past events are reinterpreted, exaggerated, or omitted from accounts for various reasons, which may be linked to strategic interests, such as a need for recognition or to maintain a reputation. More basic factors can also influence the content of oral and life history, such as a low (or high) self-esteem, suffering, and memory lapse (Bruneteaux 2007).

In the political and social sciences, oral and life history are used for three main purposes: collecting information about past events or individuals' trajectories; understanding actors' subjective experiences; identifying the larger political and social context in which the histories are elaborated and that they reflect.

First, oral and life history serve to collect factual information. It is therefore useful in approaches like **PROSOPOGRAPHY**, which reconstructs the historical trajectory of (groups of) individuals. Given the biographical details accessible through oral and life history, it is indeed possible to proceed to a close investigation of people's past experiences. Then, it is necessary to 'control' and pay attention to the reconstructions in order to distinguish between misleading or false information (underestimations, exaggerations) and exploitable data (see **SOURCE CRITICISM**) (Linde 1993: 51–97). The reconstruction of the past is an intrinsic property of life and oral history. When information is gathered orally, spending time with the observed actors is important so they have confidence in the researcher and overcome the barrier of self-protection/promotion (see **OBSERVATIONAL METHODS**). Stories from different actors can be compared (see **TRIANGULATION**) to verify factual accuracy and identify the accuracy of the events narrated and the real importance of some dynamics. For instance, the accuracy of soldiers' published memoirs about military life in wartime varies depending on the narrator's objectives. For instance, some soldiers exaggerate the intensity of battles or tell their story in a spectacular way to ensure the commercial success of their book (Woodward and Jenkings 2018: 65–90). While those sources provide first-hand information about soldiers' life at war, the researcher nevertheless needs to be cautious in their use, by comparing the accounts and by eventually excluding the unreliable ones.

Second, oral and life history is useful for understanding the logic of individual and collective experience (Atkinson 2002: 129). In that sense, empirical control of oral and life accounts, though necessary, should not obscure their heuristic value (see **DISCOURSE ANALYSIS**). The use of oral and life accounts should not be seen exclusively as serving descriptive/factual approaches or as a means to collect objective information to reconstruct causal chains (the **POSITIVIST** explanation). The positivist distinction between 'fact' and 'interpretation' tends to discredit oral and written accounts because of their subjectivity. In contrast, the **POST-POSITIVIST** view assumes that 'anxiety over the anomalous nature of autobiography is largely beside the point, because, like all narrative, autobiography provides neither an "accurate" nor "inaccurate" description of pre-existing "real" experience but instead helps to give experience form' (Stivers 1993: 420).

Oral and life history is, importantly, used in interpretive sociology and phenomenology, where subjectivities are viewed as generative forces that are crucial for constructing social facts. As Robert Atkinson argues: 'Historical truth is not the main issue in narrative; telling a story implies a certain, maybe unique, point of view. It is more important that the life story be deemed "trustworthy" than that it be "true." We are seeking the subjective reality, after all' (Atkinson 2002: 134). The study of discursive codifications (or silences) through 'narrative analysis' gives an indication of how the actors make sense of their role, actions, and how they relate to the environment they belong to (Moen 2006). In military memoirs, the enthusiasm, exhaustiveness, fear, or hatred with which soldiers evoke their training and battles are indications for analysing war as a contingent process of coercive embodiment ('learning to kill'), identity constitution (the 'warrior ethos'), and gendered power relations ('military masculinity') (Dyvik 2016). Similarly, soldiers sometimes mention their reluctance to kill. The (emotional) complexity of soldiers' accounts of their experiences of combat is a key element when it comes to grasping the subtle social conditions in which human beings overcome the natural aversion to death and reach the point of killing (Bourke 2001: 321). As such, the soldiers' discursive reconstruction of their experience of combat does not have an exclusively factual interest. It also indicates how soldiers' agency is constituted. The subjective dimension in oral and life history brings nuances to the construction of theoretical generalities.

Subjectivity indeed matters in the study of experience, but it is important to differentiate between the discursive categories employed by actors in their accounts and scientific concepts. As already argued, the rationale of oral or written accounts is not to provide objective explanations but to communicate a socially and politically situated point of view. As such, the use of oral and life stories as a research method is in itself a (necessary) reconstruction, because it involves the transformation or translation of the data collected into scientifically exploitable indicators, variables, and factors (Rosenthal 1993: 59–91). While it is crucial to consider how actors describe their experiences, rigorous and general concepts are important when it comes to expressing with a certain level of accuracy and objectivity the reality evoked in actors' histories (Friedlander 2003: 315–316). Joan Sangster uses oral history to analyse the (non)engagement of women in workers' strikes. She questions the heuristic potential of the personal justifications given by the interviewees to explain their (non)participation (family situation, perception of the protest's violence, financial needs, etc.). Sangster gathers a variety of categories under the VARIABLES of 'class', 'age', and 'ethnicity'. With this conceptual reconstruction, the author suggests that the fragmented aspect of the collected stories reveals the weight of gender-related factors in the non(engagement) in strikes, as well as how they permeate other types of power relations (Sangster 1994). Nevertheless, this conceptual work should be a corollary of a reflexive approach to reduce the likelihood of the researcher projecting their own analytical intentions onto the actors' accounts (this could distort the meaning of the original accounts) (see ETHICS IN RESEARCH). This is especially the case with oral history. The interviewer can (un)consciously orient the answers of the interviewee, particularly when the researcher speaks with individuals from vulnerable or dominated populations: '[T]he dominant position of the researcher—who knows all the questions to ask and by implication all the answers—can subdue the narrator' (Yow 1997: 67).

Finally, oral and life histories can shed light on the political context that they relate to. Therefore, they should be analysed in the context of their historical framework. The military memoirs published during the recent wars in Iraq and Afghanistan illustrate the role of context. Their contents are part of a popular culture, which reproduces the dominant representations of these conflicts (Woodward and Jenkings 2012). A significant number of memoirs or biographies deal with special forces and lethal military practices (like 'snipers'). The public prominence of killing elites can be interpreted as a mirror of the political-military ONTOLOGY of the 'war on terror'. While violence is the key enemy (the so-called 'terror'), the 'warrior' is one of the political centres of gravity of the 'war on terror'. Throughout the numerous accounts of lethal actions conducted in Iraq or Afghanistan, the lethal and bloody 'warrior' figure, a prerequisite for the 'war on terror', is visible to society. In this way, military memoirs encourage the normalization of violence in the public sphere. They provide a platform where the 'war on terror', as a political-military project and as an everyday visual/sensorial reality, is played out (Dyvik 2016). Therefore, the utility of oral and life history is not circumscribed to the micro/mezzo-analysis of individual or group dynamics. It is also relevant to capture how specific stories reflect and reproduce macro tendencies that influence the very evolution of societies.

In brief, if oral and life accounts are used for scientific research, they should be accepted for what they are: subjectively created accounts. Oral and life histories are useful tools for investigating the intersection between individual trajectories and historical dynamics, as well as the contingency that social agents use to make sense of their experiences.

REFERENCES

Atkinson, Robert. 2002. 'The Life History Interview', in *Handbook and Interview Research: Context and Methods*, ed. Jaber F. Gubrium and James A. Holstein, 121–140. London, SAGE Publications.

Bertaux, Daniel and Martin Kohli. 1984. 'The Life Story Approach: A Continental View'. *Annual Review of Sociology* 10: 215–237.

Bourdieu, Pierre. 1986. 'L'illusion biographique'. *Actes de la recherche en sciences sociales* 62(1): 69–72.

Bourdieu, Pierre. 1999. 'Understanding', in *The Weight of the World: Social Suffering in Contemporary Society*, ed. Pierre Bourdieu et al., 607–626. Cambridge, Polity Press.

Bourke, Joanna. 2001. 'The Emotions in War: Fear and the British and American Military 1914–45.' *Historical Research* 74(185): 314–330.

Bruneteaux, Patrick. 2007. 'Les politiques de l'urgence à l'épreuve d'une ethnobiographie d'un SDF'. *Revue Française de Science Politique* 57(1): 47–67.

Dyvik, Synne. 2016. 'Valhalla Rising: Gender, Embodiment and Experience in Military Memoirs'. *Security Dialogue* 47(2): 133–150.

Friedlander, Peter. 2003. 'Theory, Method and Oral History', in *The Oral History Reader*, ed. Robert Perks and Alistair Thomson, 311–319. London, Routledge.

Gubrium, Jaber and James Holstein. 1998. 'Narrative Practice and the Coherence of Personal Stories'. *Sociological Quarterly* 39(1): 163–187.

Linde, Charlotte. 1993. 'Methods and Data for Studying the Life Story', in *Life Stories: The Creation of Coherence*, 51–97. Oxford, Oxford University Press.

Moen, Torill. 2006. 'Reflections on the Narrative Research Approach'. *International Journal of Qualitative Methods* 5(4): 56–69.

Rosenthal, Gabriele. 1993. 'Reconstruction of Life Stories: Principles of Selection in Generating Stories for Narrative Biographical Interviews', in *The Narrative Study of Lives*, Volume I, ed. Ruthellen Josselson and Amia Lieblich, 59–91. Newbury Park, SAGE Publications.

Sangster, Joan. 1994. 'Telling our Stories: Feminist Debates and the Use of Oral History'. *Women's History Review* 3(1): 5–28.

Stivers, Camilla. 1993. 'Reflections on the Role of Personal Narrative in Social Science'. *Signs* 18(2): 408–425.

Woodward, Rachel and Neil Jenkings. 2012. 'This Place Isn't Worth the Left Boot of One of our Boys: Geopolitics, Militarism and Memoirs of the Afghanistan War'. *Political Geography* 31(8): 495–508.

Woodward, Rachel and Neil Jenkings. 2018. 'Why Are Military Memoirs Written?', in *Bringing War to Book: Writing and Producing the Military Memoir*, ed. Rachel Woodward and K. Neil Jenkings, 65–90. London, Palgrave Macmillan.

Yow, Valerie. 1997. '"Do I like Them Too Much?": Effects of the Oral History Interview on the Interviewer and Vice-Versa'. *The Oral History Review* 24(1): 55–79.

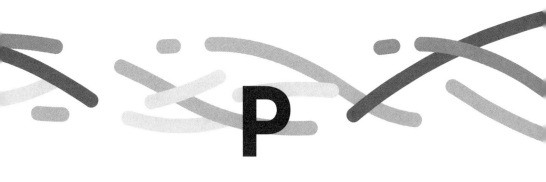

PARADIGMS AND RESEARCH PROGRAMMES

Andreas Dimmelmeier, University of Warwick and Copenhagen Business School
Sheila Dow, University of Stirling

The term paradigm was developed by the physicist-turned-philosopher-of-science Thomas Kuhn in his 1962 book *The Structure of Scientific Revolutions*. A paradigm consists of a set of understandings of a scientific community during a historical period. At the most fundamental level, paradigms employ ontological assumptions. This means that the scientific community agrees on which things and phenomena (e.g. institutions, systems, or causal relations) exist and are meaningful for scientific inquiry. These assumptions determine the type of scientific investigations that are deemed worth pursuing. Secondly, scientists inside a paradigm share a common methodological understanding of how to do science. They agree, for instance, on appraisal criteria like how to conduct an experiment without **BIAS** or how to develop and test a **HYPOTHESIS** with 'scientific rigour'. Whereas the language of experiments and hypotheses is related to positivist approaches, post-positivist researchers also formulate appraisal criteria. Here, examples would include common standards on how to conduct fieldwork or how to reflect on the role of the researcher. These criteria are then used to judge whether something can be thought of as reliable knowledge, as well as to determine suitable methods. Additionally, paradigms make assumptions about which (social) phenomena matter most and how they unfold. Frequently, paradigms single out general tendencies or laws regarding the behaviour of the **UNITS OF ANALYSIS** (e.g. humans or states).

Against the background of these broad and general understandings, scientists inside a paradigm formulate theories and carry out empirical research. While there might be different theories within a paradigm as well as disagreements between the advocates of these theories, the broad underlying assumptions regarding **ONTOLOGY** as well as the appropriate forms of scientific inquiry—to which scientists are often introduced via textbooks—are never questioned. This enables researchers in the paradigm to carry out 'normal science' (Kuhn 1996 [1962]: Chapters 2, 3)—i.e. to develop and test ever more sophisticated and esoteric theories and to systematically gather data. Normal science is, in this regard, different from pre-paradigmatic science, where scientists keep debating fundamental issues, since there is not yet an agreed framework for doing science.

Kuhn uses the metaphor of 'puzzle-solving' to describe normal science, because it is assumed that something can be explained inside the paradigm if only enough skill and resources are devoted to it. For Kuhn, this activity is necessary for science since, as opposed to discussion of the big questions, it leads to the generation of new knowledge (Kuhn 1996 [1962]: 36). Puzzle-solving, however, is not always successful. In some cases, observations are made that do not fit into the paradigm. Sometimes scientists will just ignore these observations, which Kuhn terms 'anomalies'. During scientific revolutions, however, much weight is given to them and a new rival paradigm provides novel explanations that are incompatible with the fundamentals of the old paradigm. Once the paradigm shift has occurred by persuasion—or by a generational shift—normal science is carried out again within the new paradigm. During the shift from the geocentric to the heliocentric view, for instance, both paradigms sought to provide explanations for planetary movements.

Kuhn was sceptical of extending the concept of paradigm to the social sciences since historically there has not been a dominant set of assumptions, as there is in Newtonian physics, that extends to all parts of the social sciences. Still, the concept of paradigm has been applied to disciplines such as political science, economics, sociology, and international relations, albeit with different—that is arguably non-Kuhnian—connotations. In these applications, the commonality of assumptions and understandings that holds together a community of scientists is emphasized. This stands in contrast to the view that stresses the all-encompassing nature of a paradigm during a historical period.

To give a few examples of this modified use of the term, in international relations, there are among others realist, liberal, and constructivist paradigms. Each of these is held together by different commonalities such as their UNIT OF ANALYSIS, their terminology, their fundamental assumptions, and the ways of conducting and evaluating research. Whereas realists' principal unit of analysis is the state, constructivists emphasize the centrality of discourse. As to the paradigms' fundamental assumptions, realism maintains that states will *always* maximize their power. Constructivists, on the other hand, would retort that the meaning of 'maximizing power' is a discursive construction in the first place.

While international relations provides a good illustration of the characteristics of paradigms, when it comes to the dominance of a single paradigm and to paradigm shifts, economics is arguably a better example. The discipline of economics has a rich history of schools of thought (paradigms) as well as of controversies between them. During the *Marginalist Revolution* in the late nineteenth century, the neoclassical paradigm, which emphasizes mathematical formalism and utility-maximizing individuals, replaced institutional economics, which understood political economy in broader terms and refrained mostly from abstract modelling (Milonakis and Fine 2009: 91ff.). While the neoclassical mainstream tightened its hold on the discipline after World War II, alternatives including classical economics, Marxist economics, institutionalist economics, post-Keynesian economics, complexity economics, and feminist economics emerged or continued to exist at the margins. The dominance of the neoclassical main-stream was, however, challenged in the aftermath of the global financial crisis of 2007–2008. Both mainstream macroeconomics, which had not paid much attention to the financial sector since it tends to see it as nothing but a neutral transmission mecha-nism, and financial theory, which stresses the efficiency of financial markets, struggled to explain the crisis. The significance of the crisis and the perceived inability of neo-classical economics to explain why it occurred meant that it constituted an anomaly for the dominant paradigm. As a consequence, competing paradigms that place stronger emphasis on financial dynamics, such as post-Keynesian economics, have received in-creased attention.

RESEARCH PROGRAMMES

Imre Lakatos developed the concept of 'research programmes' as an alternative to 'par-adigms'. While Lakatos also rejected 'naïve empiricism' based on objective facts, he was unhappy with the implication that the different assumptions and evaluative standards of paradigms would shield them from comparison with each other and would make common standards of all scientific inquiry like FALSIFICATION[1] obsolete. To solve this, Lakatos suggested that there is a hierarchy of assumptions. At the 'hard core' of a re-search programme there are ontological assumptions that are not falsifiable. Examples from a social science context might be 'individuals maximize utility' or 'societies consist of antagonistic classes'. Surrounding the hard core of the research programme is what Lakatos termed the 'protective belt', where lower-level HYPOTHESES are specified and tested against empirical observations. The evaluative standard that Lakatos introduced is novelty in empirical and theoretical content. This means that if a research programme T' can equally explain all the unfalsified content of research programme T and further-more predicts novel facts, i.e. facts improbable or forbidden in T, then T' should replace T. As opposed to the rejection of an individual theory by the observation of a count-er-instance, this test is concerned with whether the research programme as a whole is capable of delivering more cumulative knowledge than its competitors (Lakatos 1970).

Regarding the protective belt, it is possible for research programmes to expand their reach and reformulate their HYPOTHESES in such a way that they can integrate FAL-SIFICATIONS. If such a modified research programme leads to novel facts it can be considered as being 'progressive'. If, however, the reformulation of the protective belt is only a linguistic exercise to deflect criticism, the research programme is 'degenerative'. An instance of a modification of a research programme is that the utility-maximizing approach to economics, in the version that focused only on monetary value, was re-formulated to include notions of fairness and altruism once behavioural experiments

---

[1] Lakatos advocated for a methodological falsificationism that considers decisions and judge-ments from scientists rather than a 'dogmatic' falsificationism, in which objective facts disprove hypotheses (Lakatos 1970: 108ff.).

showed that the earlier conception was not consistent with observations.[2] The financial crisis posed an important research question for mainstream economics, apparently falsifying the core concept of equilibrating markets. Debate has ensued between research programmes as to whether the solution of incorporating impediments to market forces in the model is evidence of a progressive or a degenerating research programme.

Research programmes, furthermore, possess negative and positive heuristics. These are rules of thumb that tell scientists what to avoid and what to do. The negative heuristic is not to go against the hard core. This means that, for instance, a Marxist who does not mention social classes in his/her research would arguably no longer be inside the research programme of Marxism.[3] The positive heuristics tell the researcher what are 'best practices' in theory building, experiments, and methods. A possible positive heuristic for a neoclassical economist is to engage in FORMAL MODELLING and then test the model against econometric data, whereas a post-structuralist anthropologist would be advised to use HERMENEUTIC approaches. Additionally, the positive heuristic offers direction for future research by suggesting which aspects of a theory should be further elaborated.

ISSUES AND DEBATES

Kuhn's account of scientific revolutions suggests that there is no overarching framework or measure (with shared meanings and understandings) that allows scientists to judge between different paradigms. This impossibility, of comparing different paradigms according to common external standards, is also known as 'incommensurability'. For example, Newtonian mechanics can only be deemed to be 'wrong' from the perspective of its successor paradigm, Einsteinian mechanics, rather than in absolute terms. Thus, science does not advance linearly to an ever more complete understanding of the world by researchers building on the work of their predecessors. Instead, science appears to be a succession of incompatible belief systems, each of which seeks to expand its reach in explaining as many phenomena as possible until overthrown by another belief system. There are no universal guidelines on how to decide which paradigm is better; rather, paradigm change happens due to the (sociological) dynamics inside the scientific community.

Some philosophers of science have challenged this view. Lakatos tried to reintroduce a common standard by referring to novel predictions as a test for whether a paradigm is progressive or degenerative. Larry Laudan disputes Kuhn's claim that scientific debates are about fundamentally different ontological understandings (Laudan 1996: 95). Instead, he advocates common standards of problem-solving to which different research communities can subscribe. For example, the validity of a theory can be tested by its consistency, its ability to generate surprising results, and the passing of different tests (Laudan 1996: 46). Alan Chalmers (2009) only disputes the incommensurability thesis in its

---

[2] See Akerlof and Kranton (2000) for an attempt to incorporate non-monetary issues into a utility-maximizing framework.

[3] See Resnick and Wolff (2006: Chapter 13) on the importance of class as a unifying characteristic for Marxism.

strong version, and highlights the shared context against which 'paradigm shifts' occur in so far as there are common referents regarding observations and scientific practice to which the contenders in the debate refer. These might change gradually but still provide a common ground for discussions (Chalmers 2009: 170). Paul Feyerabend, by contrast, embraced the strong incommensurability thesis, arguing in favour of scientific relativism. Feyerabend thus advocated for an 'epistemological anarchism', where 'anything goes' and science is liberated from the straitjacket imposed by common scientific rules.

For Kuhn, the dominant-paradigmatic character of science is necessary to generate new knowledge. Advocates of intellectual pluralism or analytical eclecticism have, however, argued that competing paradigms (in the social science use of the term) can complement each other in producing knowledge. A common argument to defend this position is that social phenomena are complex and can be analysed from many different angles. This is because by necessity each perspective or paradigm focuses on certain things at the expense of others. Advocates of multiparadigmatic approaches, therefore, call for a problem-based analysis, where phenomena are researched starting from different assumptions (Katzenstein and Sil 2008). They want to generate knowledge that can be used to improve (political) decisions rather than generating an overarching social theory. Even though different schools of thought are incommensurable, some communication is still possible, since the common subject matter provides *some* shared focuses and understandings (Dow 2004: 278). Furthermore, allowing competing paradigms is a form of hedging, since a discipline relying only on one sort of explanations is more likely to be caught off guard by crisis relating to phenomena and dynamics not duly analysed in the paradigm. However, pluralists also recognize that there are substantial differences between paradigms and that even though there is a possibility for cross-fertilization, analyses based on different ontological assumptions do not fit neatly with each other. Thus, advocates of pluralism argue for fostering an atmosphere of mutual understanding and respect, which induces reflection among scientists and cautions them against becoming 'blinded' by their own paradigmatic outlook.

REFERENCES

Akerlof, George and Rachel Kranton. 2000. 'Economics and Identity'. *Quarterly Journal of Economics* 15(3): 715-753.

Chalmers, Alan. 2009 [2001]. *What is This Thing Called Science?*, 3rd edition. Buckingham, Open University Press.

Dow, Sheila. 2004. 'Structured Pluralism'. *Journal of Economic Methodology* 11(3): 275-290.

Katzenstein, Peter and Rudra Sil. 2008. *Rethinking Japanese Security: Internal and External Dimensions*. London, Routledge.

Kuhn, Thomas. 1996 [1962]. *The Structure of Scientific Revolutions*, 3rd edition. Chicago, University of Chicago Press.

Lakatos, Imre. 1970. 'Falsification and the Methodology of Scientific Research Programmes', in *Criticism and the Growth of Knowledge*, ed. Imre Lakatos and Alan Musgrave, 91-196. London, Cambridge University Press.

Laudan, Larry. 1996. *Beyond Positivism and Relativism: Theory, Method, and Evidence*. Boulder, CO, Westview Press.

Milonakis, Dimitris and Ben Fine. 2009. *From Political Economy to Economics: Method, the Social and the Historical in the Evolution of Economic Theory*. London, Routledge.

Resnick, Stephen and Richard Wolff. 2006. *New Departures in Marxian Theory*. London, Routledge.

POSITIVISM, POST-POSITIVISM, AND SOCIAL SCIENCE

Patrick Thaddeus Jackson & Lucas Dolan, American University

'Post-positivism', much like 'positivism', is a notoriously imprecise term that nonetheless does significantly effective work in shaping academic controversies. As a precise notion in the philosophy of science, the former refers to the Popperian critique of the Vienna Circle, and the replacement of the principle of verifiability with the principle of falsifiability as the appropriate demarcation criterion for scientific knowledge. But in contemporary social-scientific parlance, post-positivism refers to a disparate set of critiques of both several distinct kinds of positivism (including the logical positivism of the Vienna Circle) *and* Popperian FALSIFICATION. Contemporary 'neo-positivism' includes much of the mainstream in social science disciplines such as economics, political science, and to a lesser degree sociology. Approaches in this family are typically characterized by empiricist assumptions, favour quantitative methods, and view the experimental setting as an ideal to be approximated. By contrast, post-positivist approaches are loosely organized around a common rejection of the notion that the social sciences should take the natural sciences as their EPISTEMIC model. This rejection, which is a dissent from the naturalist position that all the sciences belong together and produce the same kind of knowledge in similar ways, often also includes a rejection of what are taken to be the central components of a natural-scientific approach: a dualist separation of knowing subjects from their objects of study, and a limitation of knowledge to the tangible and measurable.

To get a handle on 'post-positivism' we will discuss these three rejections in turn.

NATURALISM

The word 'naturalism' means different things in different subfields of philosophy. Here we are concerned with naturalism as a position regarding the relationship between the natural and social (also referred to as human or moral) sciences. In this context, naturalism is the position that asserts a fundamental ONTOLOGICAL and methodological continuity between these sciences. In practical terms, since the natural sciences are generally regarded as the more successful of the two, the normative implication of this position is that social scientists should directly imitate, or perhaps adapt, the methods and assumptions of natural scientists to produce more successes in their own disciplines. BEHAVIOURISM, which reduces social activity to the physical motion of individuals, is a striking example.

If naturalism is the position that a certain idealized vision of how the natural sciences function provides the best epistemic model for how valid knowledge should be generated in every domain, then most self-identified post-positivists are anti-naturalists. This holds even as there are disputes among post-positivists about what precisely constitutes the essence of the natural-scientific approach that they are rejecting. Historically, an important benchmark for these debates regarding naturalism is the thesis of unified science.

The most ambitious attempt to develop a rigorous vision of unified science came from the logical positivists of the Vienna Circle, particularly Rudolf Carnap and Otto Neurath. The Vienna Circle philosophers adopted a form of radical ontological agnosticism in which they only made assertions about statements and the relationships between statements, while refraining from any assertions about the status of 'things' or 'reality'. In doing so, the impetus for uniting science came from the structure of statements about entities in space and time, rather than any intrinsic properties of physical entities themselves: if all entities capable of scientific study could be described in physical language, then it followed that the objects social science investigated could ultimately be reduced to physical properties that could be studied in a fundamentally similar way, even if identical methods were not employed. The Vienna Circle philosophers thus extended the spirit, if not the specifics, of Auguste Comte's earlier 'positivist' project of setting all of human knowledge on a unified basis.

While opposition to a naturalist approach can manifest through a variety of positions (see DESCRIPTIVE, EXPLANATORY, AND INTERPRETIVE APPROACHES), here we consider two ideal-typical alternatives: the interpretivist and critical approaches to social science. Interpretivism receives perhaps its most sophisticated treatment in Peter Winch (1990). In contrast to naturalism, interpretivism holds that human beings are fundamentally different from physical objects and therefore cannot be satisfactorily studied using techniques appropriate to the natural sciences. Rather than searching for law-like correlations across cases and placing a premium on predictability, interpretivists reject CAUSALITY and assert that social science can only be about the investigation of meaning(s). This position leads them to diverge from another important pillar of positivist thought—namely that social science must involve the collection of data that could be replicated by another researcher (see REPLICATION AND REPRODUCIBILITY). With interpretivism, we move towards Clifford Geertz's (2000: 6–7) position that understanding the difference between a wink and a twitch in a particular social context is at the heart of social science.

The critical approach to social science shares many of the interpretivist critiques of naturalism, but adopts a more prescriptive stance. Jürgen Habermas's *Knowledge and Human Interests* (1971) provides a telling example of a critical approach that diverges from interpretivism in this way. For Habermas, the goal of social science is to differentiate the latent and manifest content of social consciousness and to assist in uncovering the latent content. Here the researcher has an active role, as uncovering this content has a liberating effect on the subjects of study.

There are also mixed positions that combine aspects of both naturalism and anti-naturalism. Emile Durkheim, an important figure for the establishment of the social sciences, offers what Andrew Abbott (1992: 432) calls a 'seductive blend of resolute social emergentism and quantitative empiricism'. In effect, Durkheim maintains that the subject matter of social science is distinct but that the social scientist need not disavow quantification and formal methods. From this perspective, the natural and social sciences are closer in methodology than they are in ONTOLOGY.

DUALISM

Both naturalists and anti-naturalists typically presume that mind–world dualism is essential to the natural sciences, differing on whether it is appropriate to the social sciences. In a dualist conception, the knowing subject is thought to stand in some sense outside of the world that she is studying, and the problem of knowledge is to cross that gap—to establish correspondence between subject and object in a valid way. Subject–object separation is sometimes thought to underpin the 'objectivity' of natural-scientific knowledge, ensuring that results are not due to the subject's interests or desires, but instead are based in passive sense-data and therefore correspond to how things actually stand. But dualism is not a consensus position in the philosophy of science, as there is an established 'monist' alternative that takes as its starting point not the separation of knowing subjects from objects, but the mutual implication of both subjects and objects in practical experience.

Rejections of dualism, and associated articulations of monism, have a long history. The first major philosophical challenge to dualism actually precedes positivism, stemming from Immanuel Kant's attempt to synthesize rationalist and empiricist theories of knowledge. Kant posited space and time as conditions of possible experience rather than objective qualities of external reality. Under this conception, the mind was not a receiver of raw information, but a subject that actively participated in the process of perception/experience. Along similar lines, John Dewey's pragmatist alternative to what he called the 'spectator theory of knowledge' posited an active and creative role for the mind in perception, and work in Gestalt psychology maintained that perceptions of form were not simple inductions from raw 'sense-data', but instead were active conceptual shapings of sensory consciousness. Although these monisms may have been intended to shore up the possibility of scientific objectivity, their reformulation of the traditional notions pointed in a different direction.

This direction was not immediately followed, because the philosophy of science in the early twentieth century became part of a broader project of shoring up the credibility of the natural sciences, rather than a critical examination of knowledge-production more broadly. With the arrival of German émigrés fleeing Nazi Germany, and with subsequent anti-communist persecution, these scholars and their colleagues adopted the seemingly 'apolitical' language of neutral and objective facts as a way of defusing the suspicion that they were radical social reformers (Reisch 2005). Particularly in American philosophy of science, a narrow and technical form of positivism became the dominant approach. The earlier critiques of dualism were therefore lost for some decades. Many of these themes did not re-emerge until internal critiques of positivism by Quine (1951), Kuhn (2012), and Rorty (1979), together with the rise of the 'post-modern' scepticism of grand narratives of all kinds, put alternatives to positivism back on the philosophical agenda (although Rorty's articulation of neo-pragmatism did make clear that the classical pragmatists were the original authors of many of the ostensibly novel ideas of the 1960s and 1970s).

EMPIRICISM

Anti-naturalists also tend to presume that an emphasis on tangible, measurable objects is fundamentally constitutive of the natural sciences. To this empiricism, anti-naturalists in the social sciences often juxtapose notions about the unobservable in principle—and hence non-empirical—aspects of social life: meaning, consciousness, intentionality, and so on. But while much work in the natural sciences takes an empiricist bent, it is unclear that observability and tangibility are fundamental to the scientific enterprise per se. Indeed, work in particle physics suggests that the fundamental constituents of reality are better thought of as fields and potentials than as discrete objects, and to even *detect* those fields requires specialized equipment and interpretive practices that strain the limits of 'empiricism'.

Regardless, the critique of empiricism is fundamental to many approaches in the social sciences. Beginning with structuralism in linguistics and anthropology, anti-naturalist scholars began to look at ordering principles and abductively inferred relations that were thought to underpin or underlie observed phenomena. The 'post-structuralist' critique of such structuralism did not reject the notion that unobservable relations were important; instead, at issue was the character of those relations and whether or not they could be seamlessly woven into a unified conception. Spurred on by Lyotard's (1984) rejection of 'grand narratives', post-structuralist work aims to reveal the holes and gaps in apparently unified accounts of social life—and how those holes and gaps are covered over by 'performances' that, if successful, make social life appear to be a seamless whole (Butler 1999).

The extreme lengths to which some anti-empiricists go in articulating their opposition to the notion that the only meaningful account of social life must be grounded on observable data has sometimes led to an equally caricatured backlash, in which the meaning of 'empiricism' is stretched to simply mean the position that things exist independently of observers (the position that we have called 'dualism' in the previous section), and critics of such empiricism are held to be subjective idealists or some other variant of the claim that mind makes the world. But the rejection of empiricism as a foundational principle for social science is not the same as a rejection of the tangible world per se; it is instead a rejection of the limitation of the field of the social to those things that are susceptible of precise and intersubjectively compelling measurement. No post-positivist believes that nothing exists outside of mind, or that reality is a function of subjective commitment, although most do maintain that existence cannot be reduced to the merely perceivable. Nor do all post-positivists reject the systematic collection of empirical data; instead, they disagree with the notion that all such systematic collection must take a quantitative form, and with the underlying philosophical proposition that only general empirical patterns constitute a valid basis for reliable knowledge.

CONCLUSION

Outside relatively specialized niches, direct engagement with philosophy of science is quite limited in the social sciences. Indeed, methodology proper, the logic of how our philosophical wagers about reality and our concrete research tools link up, is also rarely discussed. Too often textbooks and graduate training programmes jump directly to methods, taking for granted a particular methodology and philosophy of science. This entry takes two steps back, reflecting on the philosophical commitments that underlie both the logic of methodology and specific tools or methods employed in practical research.

Particularly when read in conjunction with other conceptual entries, we have attempted to give readers a sense of the rich diversity of social science, specifically the broad array of approaches that reject key elements of contemporary positivism. We identified these key elements as naturalism, dualism, and empiricism, and discussed what is at stake in their rejection. Post-positivist approaches may relax or reject one of these commitments and yet be committed to explanatory causal analysis, or they may depart in more thoroughgoing manner, posing an entirely different objective of the social sciences, as with the interpretivist and critical approaches discussed above.

Readers should be aware that much of the key vocabulary in this entry is often used pejoratively in disciplinary disputes over the right to wield the mantle of 'science', or whether such a mantle is even necessary to cling to in pursuit of valid social research. Critics paint post-positivism as relativistic and lacking in rigour, while 'positivism' may be deployed uncharitably by opponents as meaning little more than a preference for mathematical formalism and the collection and analysis of quantitative data.

Post-positivist research traditions are more unified by what they reject than by what they share. What post-positivists reject are the tenets of naturalism, particularly the dualism and empiricism that often underpin a claim that the social world can and should be studied in the same way that the natural world is. But they agree with naturalists and positivists that the social world can be studied systematically, and that such study generates knowledge that is something other than mere partisan opinion.

REFERENCES

Abbott, Andrew. 1992. 'From Causes to Events: Notes on Narrative Positivism'. *Sociological Methods & Research* 20(4): 428–455.

Butler, Judith. 1999. *Gender Trouble: Feminism and the Subversion of Identity*. New York, Routledge.

Geertz, Clifford. 2000. *The Interpretation of Cultures: Selected Essays*. New York, Basic Books.

Habermas, Jürgen. 1971. *Knowledge and Human Interests*. Boston, MA, Beacon Press.

Kuhn, Thomas S. 2012. *The Structure of Scientific Revolutions*, 4th edition. Chicago and London, University of Chicago Press.

Lyotard, Jean François. 1984. *The Postmodern Condition: A Report on Knowledge*. Minneapolis, University of Minnesota Press.

Quine, Willard Van Orman. 1951. 'Main Trends in Recent Philosophy: Two Dogmas of Empiricism'. *The Philosophical Review* 60(1): 20–43.

Reisch, George A. 2005. *How the Cold War Transformed Philosophy of Science: To the Icy Slopes of Logic*. New York, Cambridge University Press.

Rorty, Richard. 1979. *Philosophy and the Mirror of Nature*. Princeton, NJ, Princeton University Press.

Winch, Peter. 1990. *The Idea of a Social Science and Its Relation to Philosophy*, 2nd edition. London, Routledge.

PROCESS TRACING

Tracing the Causal Pathways between Independent and Dependent Variables

Jochem Rietveld, LUISS Guido Carli di Roma and University of Warwick
Seda Gürkan, Université libre de Bruxelles

DEFINING PROCESS TRACING

Process tracing (PT) is a qualitative within-case data analysis technique used to iden-tify causal relations. It is mostly used in single **CASE STUDY** research designs to make strong within-case inferences. Although there are several distinct definitions of the PT method (George and Bennett 2005; Hall 2013; Beach and Pedersen 2013), schol-ars largely agree that 'the process-tracing method attempts to identify the interven-ing causal process (or the causal chain or causal mechanism) between an independent **VARIABLE** and the dependent variable (George and Bennett 2005: 206). As clarified by this definition, the term 'causal mechanism', which links dependent (Y) and inde-pendent variables (X), is central. Therefore, in accordance with the scientific realist perspective, which uses mechanisms and processes to reveal the external social reality, ontologically, PT adopts a distinct approach to **CAUSATION** that goes beyond a mere correlation between variables (Beach and Pedersen 2013: 5). This understanding of causation suggests that it involves a mechanism that transfers causal 'energy' (similar to the movement of toothed wheels) from a given starting point, and which can explain the outcome (Kittel and Kuehn 2013: 4). Salmon defines causal mechanisms as causal interactions and processes that 'are capable of transmitting energy, information, and causal influence from one part of spacetime to another' (Salmon 1998: 71). In a simi-lar vein, Glennan (1996: 52) defines a causal mechanism as 'a complex system which produces an outcome by the interaction of a number of parts'. Consequently, in the PT method, the ultimate challenge for the researcher is to identify the causal mechanism.

By way of example, Skocpol's study of social revolutions is a clear and detailed illus-tration of how the tracing method is used to uncover causal processes linking different variables. The author considers two independent variables—international pressure on the state and peasant rebellion—in order to shed light on the causes and mechanisms of social revolution in France, Russia, and China. In the case of Russia, Skocpol (1979) shows how Tsarist Russia was under considerable military pressure from more eco-nomically developed countries. This factor, combined with the backward agrarian sec-tor (the Russian government had failed to reform the sector and increase agricultural productivity), led to peasant rebellion and, ultimately, to a social revolution (Skocpol 1979). Skocpol makes excellent use of the PT method. She identifies a complex se-quence of events to depict how each of the variables sets a complex causal chain in

P

motion. She then demonstrates how the two causal sequences (derived from two independent variables) come together to trigger a social revolution in each state.

TYPES OF PROCESS TRACING

The PT method can be used for theory testing and theory building. When it is applied to theory testing, a hypothetical causal mechanism is tested against empirical evidence. The research goal is to test whether a theorized mechanism is present in a given case, or whether the mechanism functions as expected in the selected case. When tracing is applied to theory building, the goal is to identify causal processes for which there is no available prior theoretical HYPOTHESIS in the literature (George and Bennett 2005: 217). Here, the aim of the research is to develop theory. In some instances, PT is used to explain the outcomes of particularly puzzling cases. Indeed, the method is useful for explaining deviant cases that are unpredictable or for which existing theories have failed to provide a satisfactory explanation (George and Bennett 2005: 215). In recent years, scholars developed interpretive process tracing (IPT), a variant of 'explaining outcome process-tracing'. IPT provides an analysis of causal mechanisms, by taking context and history into account. Hence, scholars claim that IPT offers 'more nuanced and accurate' explanations. It provides specific information about the setting and considers the importance of social identities when determining a particular outcome (Norman 2015; Guzzini 2012).

HOW TO USE THE PROCESS-TRACING METHOD

Identifying the parts of a causal mechanism, studying their dynamic interaction (causal forces), and, in particular, how the causal forces produce the outcome (Y) are essential to PT analysis. Therefore, the data collection strategy is important when it comes to constructing a causal pathway (mechanism) or proving whether it exists. First, the PT method requires a large amount of empirical material (observations) obtained from various sources, including primary and secondary sources, interviews, archives, official documents, and news reports. The key to compiling observations is to adopt a 'non-random selection strategy', using a theory-driven collection of data (Beach and Pederson 2013: 123). Therefore, the key is to collect the empirical data on the basis of empirical predictions (what type of evidence should we expect to find if the hypothesized causal mechanism holds?) Second, the researcher should critically assess each observation before submitting it as evidence. Here, two aspects of critical assessment are important. The researcher should triangulate the data across various sources to determine the accuracy of the evidence. For example, if a given meeting is of interest to the researcher, the testimony of participants should be complemented by the transcripts of that meeting. In addition, each observation should be evaluated within its specific 'historical, situational, and communication' contexts (Beach and Pederson 2013: 126). In other words, a researcher's contextual knowledge helps to determine the robustness of evidence collected (can we trust the evidence collected?)

On the basis of the data collected and/or well-founded empirical evidence, the analyst constructs a hypothetical causal mechanism, which is then tested empirically. As noted by Beach and Pederson (2013: 95), this involves 'formulating case-specific predictions' for 'the expected observable manifestations'. The empirical observations will confirm whether or not a causal mechanism exists. An excellent example of how process tracing can be used in practice is Beach and Pedersen's (2013: 107–119) case of the role of bureaucratic politics in interministerial coordination of national positions on the issue of the transfer of sovereignty to the EU. The authors provide a step-by-step approach and explicitly show what type of evidence one has to look for to check the presence of hypothesized bureaucratic politics causal mechanisms.

STRENGTHS AND LIMITATIONS OF THE PROCESS-TRACING METHOD

PT offers at least three advantages when it comes to studying causality in depth. First, its main strength is that it opens up the 'black box' of causality. While large-N studies define causal effects (based on association) and demonstrate relationships between VARIABLES, they do little to broaden our understanding of how variables are related (or which processes are involved). PT is essential for moving beyond a mere COVARIANCE, as it aspires to 'explain by giving accounts of how causal mechanisms and processes give rise to observed associations' (Salmon 1989 cited Waldner 2012, 72). Thus, the method provides a solid foundation for drawing causal inferences on the basis of one or more CASE STUDIES (George and Bennett 2005: 223–224). Second, PT is useful for generating and analysing data on causal mechanisms, as well as checking for spuriousness. Third, it can identify alternative causal paths to the same outcomes and alternative outcomes for the same causal factor, which makes it suitable for dealing with the problem of MULTICAUSALITY AND EQUIFINALITY (George and Bennett 2005: 223–224).

PT also has limitations. The first relates to the risks associated with establishing an uninterrupted causal pathway linking the putative causes to the observed effects (George and Bennett 2005). For example, in cases of temporal dependence, where the causal effect of a VARIABLE changes over time, or in instances where the dependent variable might have an impact on the independent variable (ENDOGENEITY), constructing causal mechanisms might pose methodological challenges. The second limitation is that most theories focus on widely defined social processes. Consequently, not all the steps in a causal process are detailed, which means that only provisional conclusions are generated (George and Bennett 2005: 222). Third, while the internal validity is very high, the external validity is limited because PT is usually used for single case studies (Panke 2012: 136–137). As finding an identical causal mechanism in two (or more) distinct cases might be highly unlikely, PT might not be appropriate for comparative (or even small-N) research designs, reducing the potential for generalization (external validity). (On the use of PT in small-N research designs see Panke 2012.) A fourth problem is related to multiple mechanisms. This arises when two distinct theoretical accounts lead to the same outcome or when two scholars working in the same theoretical tradition construct distinct causal mechanisms that are equally pertinent for explaining the outcome.

CONCLUSION

Process tracing is a qualitative research method that has gained prominence in the social sciences in the last few decades. It is best suited to small-N research with one or only a few cases. The goal of process tracing is to uncover the causal chain that runs from the independent VARIABLES to the dependent VARIABLE, linked by causal mechanisms. Although the method is criticized for its poor external validity, it has some significant advantages. It examines the 'black box' of causality and can draw causal inferences on the basis of very few cases with a high degree of certainty. In addition, the method is suitable for dealing with problems related to causality (e.g. equifinality) or for testing rival theories in a small-N research design. However, the ultimate challenge for analysts that apply process tracing is to establish an uninterrupted causal path based on multiple observations and empirical evidence collected from various sources. If the researcher can overcome this, the method is a promising tool for broadening our knowledge on causality in the social sciences.

REFERENCES

Beach, Derek and Rasmus Pedersen. 2013. *Process-tracing Methods: Foundations and Guidelines*. Ann Arbor, University of Michigan Press.

George, Alexander and Andrew Bennett. 2005. *Case Studies and Theory Development in the Social Sciences*. Cambridge, MA, MIT Press.

Glennan, Stuart. 1996. 'Mechanisms and the Nature of Causation'. *Erkenntnis* 44(1): 49-71.

Guzzini, Stefano. 2012. *The Return of Geopolitics in Europe?: Social Mechanisms and Foreign Policy Identity Crises*. Cambridge, Cambridge University Press.

Hall, Peter. 2013. 'Tracing the Progress of Process Tracing'. *European Political Science* 12(1): 1-9.

Kittel, Bernard and David Kuehn. 2013. 'Introduction: Reassessing the Methodology of Process Tracing'. *European Political Science* 12(1): 20-30.

Norman, Ludwig. 2015. 'Interpretive Process Tracing and Causal Explanations'. *Qualitative and Multi-method Research* 13(2): 4-10.

Panke, Diana. 2012. 'Process-Tracing: Testing Multiple Hypotheses with a Small Number of Cases', in *Research Design in European Studies: Establishing Causality in Europeanization*, ed. Theofanis Exadaktylos and Claudio M. Radaelli, 125-140. Basingstoke, Palgrave Macmillan.

Salmon, Wesley. 1998. *Causality and Explanation*. Oxford, Oxford University Press.

Skocpol, Theda. 1979. *States and Social Revolutions: A Comparative Analysis of France, Russia, and China*. Cambridge, Cambridge University Press.

Waldner, David. 2012. 'Process Tracing and Causal Mechanisms', in *The Oxford Handbook of Philosophy of Social Science*, ed. Harold Kincaid, 65-84. Oxford, Oxford University Press.

PROSOPOGRAPHY

Jacob A. Hasselbalch & Leonard Seabrooke, Copenhagen Business School

INTRODUCTION

Who is the power elite? How is power and wealth transferred between generations? How do professionals maintain control over their work? Some questions can be answered by studying traits of particular groups, the trajectories of individuals within them, and how they relate to society. In a seminal paper, historian Lawrence Stone (1971: 46) defined prosopography as 'the investigation of the common background characteristics of a group of actors in history by means of a collective study of their lives'. The etymology of the word suggests that prosopography is about describing or recording a person's appearance or life (from Ancient Greek, '*prosopon*' meaning 'face'), but prosopography differs from biography in that it analyses structured biographical data of groups of individuals that have something in common: 'prosopography is about what the analysis of the sum of data about many individuals can tell us about the different types of connection between them, and hence about how they operated within and upon the institutions—social, political, legal, economic, intellectual—of their time' (Keats-Rohan 2000).

Prosopography emerged primarily as a method for historical research. Outside of historical research, it is more commonly known as 'group biography' or 'career-path analysis' (MacLeod and Nuvolari 2006: 760). Prosopography has also been a key element of 'field-based' research on social groups (Bourdieu 1996) and the sociology of professions (Abbott and Hrycak 1990; Margadant 1990), and is more of an approach than a method *sui generis*: it implies the systematic organization of data in such a way that connections and patterns that influence historical processes are revealed. The approach generally involves 'asking' a large group of people from a predefined population a common set of questions. As such, prosopography can be a corrective to the risk of generalizing from individual, exemplar cases. For example, a prosopographical study of politicians under the regime of Napoleon III can tell us something about the career structures *in general* of average politicians during that time, as well as how they intersected with and differed from each other and with the institutional landscape (Margadant 1990: 36).

It is easier to understand what prosopography is when we understand what it is not. Prosopography is more than just a collection of biographies, or a different word for genealogical research (as practised by family historians): the goal is to uncover the connections between groups of people to answer broader questions about the world those people lived in. Whereas ORAL HISTORY AND LIFE HISTORIES emphasize the collection and recording of detailed first-hand, primary material, prosopography emphasizes the structured comparison and analysis of larger sets of biographical data—multiple biographies, oral histories, careers, or life histories can serve as inputs to the method, but the method is not reducible to them. A different way to put it is that while biographies and oral/life histories are interested in highlighting the unique, prosopography is interested in differentiation—that is, the ways in which a group of people both resemble and differ from each other. Prosopographic research highlights the importance of groups as well as points of differentiation, or modes of distinction, within the group (Bourdieu 1996). The approach emphasizes the relationality of social space in establishing group boundaries as well as 'in-group' distinctions made by individuals. The combination of boundary identification and internal differentiation permits an analysis that highlights tensions in political, social, economic, and cultural relationships.

FIVE STAGES OF PROSOPOGRAPHY

Prosopography establishes identity and draws out connections and patterns through five distinct stages (adapted from Verboven, Carlier, and Dumolyn 2007).

1. *Stage 1: Define the group or groups to be studied.* The population on which to base a prosopographical study should be thematically, geographically, and chronologically demarcated. Of these three, the thematic limitation is necessary, whereas the other two are merely helpful, but can be omitted. The thematic boundary should be common and observable, such as groups within an organized cadre (priests, city government, guilds, etc.). Points of internal differentiation, modes of distinction, and forms of connection should also be established among individuals in the group.

2. *Stage 2: Determine the sources to be used.* Several kinds of sources are useful for discovering biographical data for the analysis. It is best to use a range of sources to correct erroneous interpretations or one-sided views. Anything that provides economic, political, demographic, or other pertinent information on the population can be considered. ARCHIVAL RESEARCH and curricula vitae can be particularly helpful.

3. *Stage 3: Formulate the questions to ask of the data.* Prosopographers must determine a common set of questions to 'ask' of the data, in order to build a structured database that provides a basis for comparison and analysis. Frequently used data include: names, life dates, geographical data, family, education, career roles, material wealth, religious beliefs, and cultural attitudes.

4. *Stage 4: Build a systematic prosopographical database* (see ETHICS IN RESEARCH). Acquired data should be stored in a database. The structure of the database is given by the contents of the 'questionnaire', where cases are persons and VARIABLES are answers to the 'questionnaire'. It is best to include as much data as feasible, because analysis can only begin when the database is complete, and it is sometimes hard to guess which elements may generate the most interesting insights. Databases can contain both quantitative and qualitative data,

but depending on the type of analysis that follows, it may be more helpful to separate the two.

5. *Stage 5: Analyse the database and synthesize the results.* Once the database is complete, the final step of the prosopographical method is to analyse the data it contains to draw out connections and patterns that speak to the social world of the population under study. There are many ways to do this. The simplest approaches include statistical overviews of key characteristics, tabulation by outlining relevant criteria and calculating percentages, or using cross tables to find correlations. SEQUENCE ANALYSIS can be used to compare characteristics of groups and differentiate them into clusters based on their similarity (Blair-Loy 1999). SOCIAL NETWORK ANALYSIS can be used to analyse ties between persons in the data, while MULTIPLE CORRESPONDENCE ANALYSIS can be used to differentiate them by their characteristics (Lebaron 2009). These methods can also be fruitfully combined (Henriksen and Seabrooke 2017).

ADVANTAGES AND DISADVANTAGES OF PROSOPOGRAPHY

Because prosopography is more of a research approach rather than a distinct method with a strict set of rules, it has always changed and evolved to fit the needs of the researcher and field. This flexibility is certainly one advantage of prosopography. Perhaps its greatest advantage is to provide a check on those accounts that overinterpret or generalize from singular or exceptional cases of which we know a lot—prosopography can build on collections of scattered data to tell us what is average and typical instead of unique. Sometimes we want to know about one, sometimes about the other.

MacLeod and Nuvolari (2006) caution against the unreflective inclusion of sources on which prosopographies are based: it is hard to say whether the biographies presented in collections of sources constitute representative or random samples. There is also a BIAS in that collecting detailed information on elites and prominent figures is often easier than others, leading to sampling bias. Prosopographers also risk unquestioningly reproducing classes and categories of the past rather than interrogating them. It is important for the research to establish the context in which those studied are positioned, to attempt to assess them objectively. The value of prosopography lies in how the data is analysed and interpreted, which makes it an inductive method (see DEDUCTIVE, INDUCTIVE, AND RETRODUCTIVE REASONING). Here, the common pitfalls of CAUSATION versus correlation and circular reasoning apply (see ENDOGENEITY).

EXAMPLES FROM THE FIELD

Prosopography featured centrally in Bourdieu's (1996) classic study on *The State Nobility*. For Bourdieu, prosopography was a way to systematically gather data pertaining to actors he understood to be inhabiting a common 'field'. For example, to better understand the characteristics of the field of elite actors inhabiting key positions in the

French bureaucracy, he collected data from numerous biographies and directories on the following dimensions: place and date of birth, place of residence, father's occupation, seniority in class, education, career, and so on. This allowed him and his research team to construct a database with information on the French state nobility, on which structured and comparative analyses could be conducted. Specifically, Bourdieu employed the method of **MULTIPLE CORRESPONDENCE ANALYSIS** to visualize the hidden structure of the field, discovering how a public versus private distinction on one axis and an established versus newcomer distinction on a second axis provided a comprehensive and intuitive way to view the field as a two-dimensional space (Lebaron 2009).

In a different prosopographical study on French academia in the wake of the 1968 student protests, Bourdieu (1988) collected background data on social characteristics (as in the previous example), but combined it with qualitative data on 'position-takings' such as declared public support for certain key persons. This study is a good example of how prosopography may be combined with other methods, such as **CONTENT ANALYSIS** or qualitative data from **SURVEY RESEARCH** or **INTERVIEWS**.

Like Bourdieu, many researchers today are actively working with prosopography to better understand elite groups of actors in society. To give three recent examples of this, Kipping, Bühlmann, and David (2019) created a unique database on the professional careers of elite McKinsey consultants to study pathways to professionalization. Seabrooke and Tsingou (2020) conducted a **SEQUENCE ANALYSIS** of the career histories of international finance professionals to study the extent of 'revolving doors' between business and regulators. Similarly, Ellersgaard et al. (2019) used multichannel sequence analysis to distinguish the occupational and institutional pathways of the power elite in Denmark. Prosopography finds many uses and is easy to combine with other kinds of methods.

REFERENCES

Abbott, Andrew and Alexandra Hrycak. 1990. 'Measuring Resemblance in Sequence Data: An Optimal Matching Analysis of Musicians' Careers'. *American Journal of Sociology* 96(1): 144–185.

Blair-Loy, Mary. 1999. 'Career Patterns of Executive Women in Finance: An Optimal Matching Analysis'. *American Journal of Sociology* 104(5): 1346–1397.

Bourdieu, Pierre. 1988. *Homo Academicus*. Stanford, CA, University of Stanford Press.

Bourdieu, Pierre. 1996. *The State Nobility: Elite Schools in the Field of Power*. Stanford, CA, University of Stanford Press.

Ellersgaard, Christoph Houman, Jacob Aagaard Lunding, Lasse Folke Henriksen, and Anton Grau Larsen. 2019. 'Pathways to the Power Elite: The Organizational Landscape of Elite Careers'. *The Sociological Review* 67(5): 1170–1192.

Henriksen, Lasse F. and Leonard Seabrooke. 2017. 'Networks and Sequences in the Study of Professionals and Organizations', in *Professional Networks in Transnational Governance*, ed. Leonard Seabrooke and Lasse Folke Henriksen, 50–64. Cambridge, Cambridge University Press.

Keats-Rohan, Katharine S. B. 2000. 'Prosopography and Computing: A Marriage Made in Heaven?' *History and Computing* 12(1): 1–11.

Kipping, Matthias, Felix Bühlmann, and Thomas David. 2019. 'Professionalization through Symbolic and Social Capital: Evidence from the Careers of Elite Consultants'. *Journal of Professions and Organization* 6(3): 265–285.

Lebaron, Frédéric. 2009. 'How Bourdieu "Quantified" Bourdieu: The Geometric Modelling of Data', in *Quantifying Theory: Pierre Bourdieu*, ed. Kate Robson and Chris Sanders, 11-29. Dordrecht, Springer.

MacLeod, Christine and Alessandro Nuvolari. 2006. 'The Pitfalls of Prosopography: Inventors in the "Dictionary of National Biography"'. *Technology and Culture* 47(4): 757-776.

Margadant, Jo Burr. 1990. *Madame le professeur: Women Educators in the Third Republic*. Princeton, NJ, Princeton University Press.

Seabrooke, Leonard and Eleni Tsingou. 2020. 'Revolving Doors in International Financial Governance'. *Global Networks* 20. [Early view published online: https://doi.org/10.1111/glob.12286 (Accessed 14 August 2020).]

Stone, Lawrence. 1971. 'Prosopography'. *Daedalus* 100(1): 46-79.

Verboven, Koenraad, Myriam Carlier, and Jan Dumolyn. 2007. 'A Short Manual to the Art of Prosopography', in *Prosopography Approaches and Applications: A Handbook*, ed. Katharine S. B. Keats-Rohan, 35-69. Oxford, Linacre College and the University of Oxford.

P

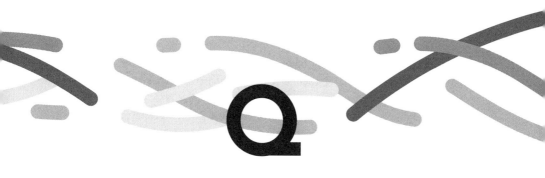

QUALITATIVE COMPARATIVE ANALYSIS

Kevin Kalomeni, LUISS Guido Carli di Roma and Université Laval,
Claudius Wagemann, University of Frankfurt

Qualitative comparative analysis (QCA) strives to bridge the methodological rift between case study-based research and quantitative studies. It combines some of the strengths of qualitative and quantitative research methods (Marx, Rihoux, and Ragin 2014: 114). QCA belongs to the broader family of configurational comparative methods (CCMs) (Rihoux and Ragin 2009). It attempts to bridge nomothetic and idiographic methods, which makes it a prime example of comparative methods. This is manifest in the title of Charles Ragin's book, which launched QCA: *The Comparative Method: Moving Beyond Qualitative and Quantitative Strategies* (Ragin 1987). Ragin reviews the legacy of John Stuart Mill's 'method of agreement', or most different systems design (MDSD) and 'method of difference' or most similar systems design (MSSD) (see CASE SELECTION). For the first time, he formally introduces case study comparative methods, based on Boolean algebra. His aim was to maintain the richness of small-N type studies and propose a caveat that allows the systematic study of cross-case patterns, typical of large-N research. The desire to combine the opposing features of qualitative and quantitative studies is also reflected in the number of cases analysed in a QCA (typically between ten and fifty, though sometimes more) (Rihoux and Ragin 2009: 4).

From an analytical perspective, QCA can be distinguished from quantitative approaches. The emphasis shifts from COVARIANCE to the analysis of set relations (see DESCRIPTIVE, EXPLANATORY, AND INTERPRETIVE APPROACHES). Being strongly tied to a profound theoretical and conceptual reasoning which is typical for comparison in general, the analysis of set relations is based on three steps: first, a score is attributed to a social phenomenon (representing either a dichotomous or a graded set membership), usually in relation to other phenomena. Second, necessary conditions are defined. Third, through the help of a truth table analysis, (combinations of) sufficient conditions are analysed. This enables the researcher to make a causal argument with reference to INUS and SUIN conditions, which are defined as 'insufficient but necessary parts of a condition which is itself unnecessary but sufficient for the result' (INUS) and 'sufficient, but unnecessary parts of a factor that is insufficient, but necessary for the result' (SUIN) (Schneider and Wagemann 2012: 3, 79) and are seen as typical for qualitative research (Mahoney and Goertz 2006: 229).

There are different ways to calibrate a social object's membership in a given set. Originally, crisp sets relied on binary values where 1 represents full membership and 0 non-membership (Schneider and Wagemann 2012: 31). A good illustration of this dichotomy is a state's ratification or non-ratification of an international treaty—it can either happen or not happen. This approach was widely criticized in the literature as being too simplistic (Rihoux and Ragin 2009: 147–148). This critique triggered the introduction of fuzzy sets, which offer greater variation and allow for values between 0 and 1 to qualify the degree of membership. Obviously, a key concept such as 'democracy' is better described in degrees, rather than in a dichotomy. Further developments led to multivalue QCA, for example, which allows for multiple non-hierarchical categories instead of exclusive graded values, and temporal QCA, which allows 'for specific ways of formally incorporating the temporal ordering of conditions as causally relevant information' (Schneider and Wagemann 2012: 16).

A 'truth table' is at the heart of all the available variants. A truth table 'might look a lot like a standard data matrix', with an important difference: 'In a standard data matrix, each row denotes a different case (or unit of observation). In a truth table, each row instead represents one of the logically possible [conditions] AND combinations … [of] conditions' (Schneider and Wagemann 2012: 92). Different software packages can be used to construct and analyse (or minimize, using Boolean algebra, respectively) a truth table. In particular, open-source R software is available for QCA analyses. Table 6 represents a schematic version of a truth table.

The functioning of QCA can be best illustrated with the help of an example: Grauvogel and von Soest (2014) investigated why sanctions fail to induce democratization in authoritarian regimes. Using a large data set of international sanctions implemented from 1990 to 2011, the authors organized their cases according to episodes of sanctions and not to countries. In this way, they accumulated a sample of 120 episodes of sanctions imposed by the EU, the UN, or the US (Grauvogel and von Soest 2014: 640). This illustrates the research opportunities offered by QCA beyond small and medium-sized numbers of cases. Three main hypotheses were put forward: sanctions may trigger a 'rally-around-the-flag' effect, reinforcing the regime's domestic claim for legitimacy; a regime with strong legitimacy that is nationally popular may be more inclined to use softer repression

TABLE 6 Schematic truth table

	Conditions			Outcome
	A	B	C	Y
1	0	1	0	0
2	1	1	1	1
3	0	0	1	1
4	1	0	0	0

techniques; finally, a weak linkage (economic, political, and cultural ties) between the country/body that imposes the sanction and its target may undermine the effectiveness of sanctions. The same effect is also observed in the case of a target country that is not particularly vulnerable to external pressure (Grauvogel and von Soest 2014: 637, 639–640). From these hypotheses, six dimensions were calibrated: persistence of authoritarian rule, sanction comprehensiveness, claims to legitimacy, repression, vulnerability, and linkage. Calibration relies on various qualitative and quantitative sources, such as the Political Terror Scale data to assess the degree of repression (Grauvogel and von Soest 2014: 642). In order to create a data matrix, all cases under investigation receive a score, according to the previously defined dimensions. As mentioned, for fuzzy values, the score is between 0 and 1. The persistence of *authoritarian rule* counts as the outcome, whereas the other five dimensions are considered as conditions. The authors subsequently identified thirty-two possible configurations of conditions, with four logical remainders. The latter constitute those configurations that are theoretically possible, but do not exist empirically (Grauvogel and von Soest 2014: 423).

When analysing necessary conditions, the result was that there were no necessary conditions. An analysis of sufficiency was then conducted. This produced different solution formulas, which are the combinations of conditions formalized under Boolean algebra minimization, such as: CLAIMS TO LEGITIMACY * repression → PERSISTENCE OF AUTHORITARIAN RULE (Grauvogel and von Soest 2014: 645). This is just one of the five different pathways which were identified. It counts as one combination of the conditions that are sufficient to imply the outcome (persistence of authoritarianism).

To assess this solution, QCA provides two parameters of fit: solution coverage and solution consistency. Consistency specifies the degree to which the empirical observations are in accordance with the proposed set relations (Schneider and Wagemann 2012: 324). Coverage considers the degree of overlap between the condition and the outcome. More precisely, this examines how much of the outcome is 'covered' by that specific condition, in the sense of how much of the outcome is explained (Schneider and Wagemann 2012: 130). In this particular example, the solution consistency is 0.78, implying that 78 per cent of the empirical information confirms the sufficiency relation. Coverage is 0.72; the solution accounts for 72 per cent of the outcome (Grauvogel and von Soest 2014: 626). It is important to note that, during the analysis, each of the solutions was discussed and illustrated using specific single cases in order to unpack the specificity of each context and to avoid creating a discrepancy between the general observations (obtained from the results) and specific local circumstances. This study confirmed that sanctions were used by authoritarian regimes to enhance their legitimacy under certain conditions, by triggering a 'rally-around-the-flag' effect which reinforced their domestic support (Grauvogel and von Soest 2014: 648). From a QCA perspective, the research illustrated how the method is able to provide the type of explanation—the linkage between specific conditions and cases—which is typical for qualitative approaches. It also showed how the method can be combined with the test of theoretical statements, which is usually considered to be the main objective of quantitative procedures.

In their article, Marx, Rihoux, and Ragin (2014) reviewed the application of QCA over a twenty-five-year period since 1987, in more than 750 publications. Recalling the criticisms levelled at QCA, they identified several methodological debates. The presumption that cases do not interrelate and influence each other still seems problematic. However, the authors argue that upcoming methodological improvements might solve this issue, for example by integrating other methods into the research design, such as process tracing, or using specific tools dedicated to interrelatedness, such as social network analysis (Marx, Rihoux, and Ragin 2014: 123). Other major challenges have also been raised, including limited diversity, which remains a recurring issue for QCA. It specifically addresses 'the problem of determining the outcome for unobserved combinations of independent variables' (Seawright 2014: 119). Given that limited diversity is not a methodological artefact, but present in real social life, QCA often seems to fail to grasp the full scope of the potential effect of other variables. Therefore, a degree of caution is required when interpreting results in terms of causality.

In conclusion, QCA has limitations, like any other methodological approach. Without any doubt, it should be in a good fit with the research question. Indeed, its prospects are promising, such as synergies with data collection techniques, e.g. **INTER-VIEWS**. Ultimately, it may even be possible to transcend the artificial division between qualitative and quantitative methods (see **MIXED METHODS** research design).

REFERENCES

Grauvogel, Julia and Christian von Soest. 2014. 'Claims to Legitimacy Count: Why Sanctions Fail to Instigate Democratisation in Authoritarian Regimes'. *European Journal of Political Research* 53(4): 635-653.

Mahoney, J. and Goertz, G. 2006. A Tale of Two Cultures: Contrasting Quantitative and Qualitative Research. *Political Analysis*, 14(3): 227-249.

Marx, Axel, Benoit Rihoux, and Charles Ragin. 2014. 'The Origins, Development, and Application of Qualitative Comparative Analysis: The First 25 Years'. *European Political Science Review* 6(1): 115-142.

Ragin, Charles. 1987. *The Comparative Methods: Moving Beyond Qualitative and Quantitative Strategies*. Berkeley, Los Angeles, and London, University of California Press.

Rihoux, Benoit and Charles Ragin. 2009. *Configurational Comparative Methods: Qualitative Comparative Analysis (QCA) and Related Techniques*. London, SAGE Publications.

Schneider, Carten Q. and Claudius Wagemann. 2012. *Set-theoretic Methods for the Social Sciences: A Guide to Qualitative Comparative Analysis*. Cambridge, Cambridge University Press.

Seawright, Jason. 2014. 'Comment: Limited Diversity and the Unreliability of QCA'. *Sociological Methodology* 44(1): 118-121.

For additional information and useful tools, please consult COMPASSS website:

COMPASSS. 2016. *Comparative Methods for Systematic Cross-case Analysis*. Available at http://www.compasss.org (Accessed 6 March 2017).

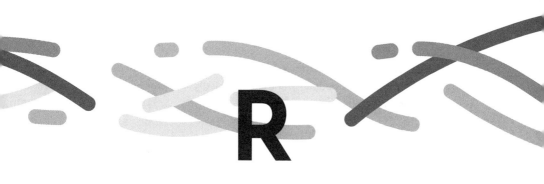

REGRESSION ANALYSIS

Kamil Marcinkiewicz & Kai-Uwe Schnapp, University of Hamburg

Regression analysis uses quantitative and sometimes also qualitative independent **VARIABLES** to explain or predict change in a quantitative dependent **VARIABLE**. To attain this goal, it relies on the principles of **COVARIANCE** and correlation. Its most basic form is linear regression, also known as ordinary least squares (OLS) regression. In addition, there are many other varieties of regression methods for different **RESEARCH QUESTIONS** and data characteristics, such as time-oriented questions or data with a limited range of values. Researchers use regression analysis especially to analyse complex patterns of correlation in situations with more than one explanatory variable. Often such patterns are interpreted in the context of causal theories (see **CAUSATION**).

The concept of regression goes back to Francis Galton's study on human height (Galton 1886). Galton found that taller parents in general have taller children, while shorter parents tend to have shorter ones. However, very tall parents tend to have children whose height is closer to the average height of the general population than their own. The equivalent is true for children of very small parents: they are on average slightly taller than their parents. Galton spoke of this tendency as regression to the mean (Gujarati 1995: 15). It was detected using the statistical method described in this chapter and gave it the name it still carries today: regression analysis.

THE CONCEPT OF REGRESSION ANALYSIS

Regression analysis uses independent or explanatory **VARIABLES**, usually denoted X, to explain or predict the values of a dependent variable, usually denoted Y. In the example in Figure 8 the independent variable is education, measured in years, and the dependent variable is annual income, measured in US dollars. Every data point represents one observation (here a person) with her respective years of education and income. Focusing on the solid line running through the data, the so-called regression line, we can easily observe that there is a systematic relationship between

FIGURE 8 Graphical representation of the relationship between education and income, including regression line (the idea for this figure comes from Lewis-Beck and Lewis-Beck 2016: 9)

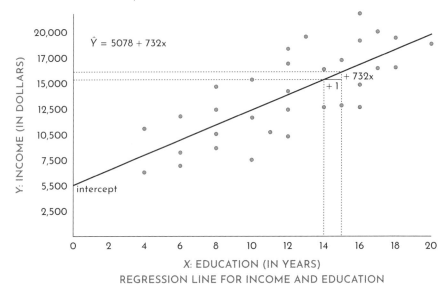

REGRESSION LINE FOR INCOME AND EDUCATION

X and Y with the following characteristic: the higher the individual X values, the higher the individual Y values. The equation depicted in Figure 8 provides a precise mathematical model of this relationship. The equation states that for an increase of one unit in the independent **VARIABLE** X (here educational years) there will be an increase of 732 units in the dependent **VARIABLE** Y (here monthly income in US dollars). This relationship is depicted by the small triangle in the right-hand part of Figure 8, where one can see how a change of 1 unit in X relates to a change of 732 units in Y.

Apparently, none of the data points is located directly on this regression line. This is to be expected for real-life data. To account for this 'disturbance', the equation necessary to completely describe data like those in Figure 8 looks like this:

$$Y_i = \beta_0 + \beta_1 X_i + e_i$$

Let us take a closer look at the elements of Equation 1: Y again is the dependent **VARIABLE**, and X is the independent **VARIABLE**. β_1 is the so-called regression coefficient or slope parameter. It explains how much Y changes when X increases by one unit, which is then similar to saying that it describes the slope or steepness of the regression line. β_1 is the central part in the substantive explanation of the behaviour of Y through X. In our example $\beta_1 = 732$ and represents the 732 additional dollars earned per additional year of education. β_0 is the intercept parameter, indicating the point at which the regression line cuts through the Y-axis. β_0 often does not have a meaningful substantive interpretation but is always needed for mathematical reasons. In order to be able to fully describe the data we also need e, the so-called error term or distur-bance. e takes into account the fact that the individual data points are not located on the regression line but stray from it. Y, X, and e are all indexed with i because each respondent has an income and education value as well as an individual disturbance ('error') describing the individual deviation from the regression line.

Equation 1 describes the whole regression model including the disturbance. The following equation only describes the regression line, i.e. the deterministic relation-ship between the explanatory variable X and the prediction of Y based on the re-gression model.

$$\hat{Y}_i = \beta_0 + \beta_1 X_i$$

The $\hat{Y}_i$ in Equation 2 represents the predicted values for the individual observations i. The individual differences between the predicted values $\hat{Y}_i$ and the observed values Y are called residuals. The sum of the residuals can be used to compute the explanatory power of the regression model, the so-called explained variance or R^2. R^2 is computed by subtracting the sum of the squared residuals (denoted E2) from the variance of Y (denoted E1). This difference is then divided by the variance of Y (E1):

$$R^2 = \frac{E_1 - E_2}{E_1}$$

The method by which we determine $\beta1$ and $\beta0$ in this example is the method of least squares, often referred to as ordinary least squares (OLS). This term derives from the fact that the regression line is computed such that the sum of the squared residuals is minimized (for more details see Lewis-Beck and Lewis-Beck 2016: Chapter 1). If data are drawn from a representative sample, a number of tests can be used to examine whether the relationship expressed through the regression coefficients reaches conven-tional levels of STATISTICAL SIGNIFICANCE.

EXTENSIONS OF THE BASIC MODEL: MULTIPLE INDEPENDENT VARIABLES, CATEGORICAL VARIABLES, AND INTERACTIONS

Models are rarely based on just one VARIABLE in the social realm (see MULTICAU-SALITY). So instead of only one explanatory variable there could be two or more. For each of the explanatory variables ($X1$, $X2$, $X3$, etc.) we now have one regression coef-ficient ($\beta1$, $\beta2$, $\beta3$, etc.). The regression is now called a multiple regression. However, the interpretation of the regression coefficients is the same as explained in the previous section.

In addition to metric variables, in practice it is often necessary to include categorical variables in a regression model. Categorical variables such as country or the electoral choice of a person contain qualitative rather than metric information. This information can only be used in a regression when we set up so-called dummy variables. These variables are coded 1 or 0, where 1 means the respective category is present for this observation and 0 means it is not. The number of dummy variables necessary to include all information from a categorical variable with k categories amounts to k-1. One category will not be transformed into a dummy variable. This is the so-called reference category. The regression coefficient of a dummy variable represents the difference in the dependent variable Y when the respective category is present instead of the reference category being present.

Interactions are used in a regression model when a HYPOTHESIS assumes that VARIABLES not only have independent effects but that their interactions also have an effect on each other—e.g. when medications cause different effects depending on whether they are applied individually or in tandem. Putting it more technically, a conditional hypothesis assumes that a certain effect is observable only for a subsample of a population. This subsample is defined by specific values of a second explanatory variable, e.g. a dummy variable indicating the specific condition or treatment. Interaction terms are created by multiplying the values of the individual variables with each other. When using interactions in a regression model, it is necessary to pay attention to all terms involved in the interaction. That means the constituent variables as well as the interaction need to be part of the estimated regression equation (Brambor, Clark, and Golder 2006).

THE ASSUMPTIONS OF THE LINEAR REGRESSION MODEL

For linear regressions to be applicable, the data needs to be characterized by a number of particular features. We usually call these characteristics regression assumptions (for more details see Lewis-Beck and Lewis-Beck 2016: 23 ff.). (1) Linearity: for a linear regression to be applicable, the relationship between X and Y must obviously follow a linear pattern. (2) Zero mean variance of disturbance: the mean value of the errors (the residuals) is zero. (3) Homoscedasticity: the variance of the errors is constant across the whole range of the dependent VARIABLE Y. (4) No auto-correlation: the error terms for any two neighbouring values of X are not correlated. (Note: neighbourhood must be a substantive characteristic of the data, like neighbourhood in time or space. Just being 'neighbours' in a data set is not sufficient.) (5) Zero COVARIANCE between e and X: the error term and the explanatory variable X are uncorrelated. (6) Multicollinearity: in multiple regressions, no two explanatory variables should be (perfectly) correlated. (7) There should be no influential cases that individually impact the regression result. Suppose there is an additional data point in Figure 8 at twenty years of education but with only 1,000 dollars of income. This case would change the regression coefficient $\beta1$ from \$732 to \$478. That is, instead of earning 732 additional dollars per additional educational year, the additional earning would only amount to an extra 478 dollars—indeed, a quite different a result. Therefore, such influential cases need to be given special care to avoid inappropriate data interpretations (for more detail see Wooldridge 2003: 312–317).

In addition to those assumptions, the number of observations i needs to be larger than the number of explanatory VARIABLES: as a rule of thumb there should be at least ten observations per explanatory variable. And, finally, there should be no specification errors. That means first that all relevant explanatory variables are part of the model. Second, if the mathematical function linking the dependent and independent variable(s) is not linear, appropriate measures need to be taken to mathematically linearize this relationship. The so-called log-transformation is a frequently used function in these cases. Instead of the original variable values, the regression model is then based on the logarithms of those values. Further types of transformation include the quadratic or cubic form of a variable, exponentiation, and other algebraic functions (Taagepera 2011). After linearization, the straightforward interpretation of the regression coefficients as presented in the example earlier in this chapter is no longer applicable. All results will have to be transformed back to the original scale for substantive interpretations.

MORE ADVANCED REGRESSION MODELS

Besides linear regression based on OLS logic, there are numerous alternative regression models that are used to account for different characteristics of the data. Examples of such characteristics include a dichotomous dependent VARIABLE, a dependent variable that is a fraction, data including different levels of analysis like pupils nested in classes, or data that has a time or spatial component.

An often used model for binary dependent variables is the (binary) logistic regression model. It is particularly well suited for estimating the relationship between a dichotomous dependent variable and one or several independent variables that may be either metric or categorical (see the discussion on dummy variables in the section 'Extensions of the basic model'). Extensions of binary logistic regression include, among others, multinomial logistic regression, ordered (ordinal) logistic regression, or conditional logistic regression models, which account for different characteristics of the dependent VARIABLE. Fractional logit and beta regression are often used when the dependent variable is a fraction (share) and its values are bound between 0 and 1. Poisson regression appropriately models count data. Multilevel regression models are used when observations are clustered in groups; a classic example would be pupils in classes, where individual- as well as class-level characteristics explain a certain outcome—e.g. learning success. TIME SERIES models are appropriate when data that is ordered in time is analysed. Spatial regression models have been developed in order to properly deal with spatial neighbourhood of data points. As this is a very selective overview, the interested reader is referred to the literature listed in the References to explore these topics in greater detail.

R

In summary, regression analysis is the workhorse method for the analysis of quantitative data. It allows for a rather precise estimation of the relationship between a dependent VARIABLE and the independent VARIABLES. However, and despite its many varieties, it cannot be applied to all data, because the data need to fulfil certain criteria for regression to be applicable. In addition, regression is not well suited for research problems with small numbers of observations. Finally, interpretation needs to be handled with care, for regression offers only a simplified model of reality and relies on data which is never perfect.

REFERENCES

Brambor, Thomas, William R. Clark, and Matt Golder. 2006. 'Understanding Interaction Models: Improving Empirical Analyses'. *Political Analysis* 14(1): 63-82.

Galton, Francis. 1886. 'Regression Towards Mediocrity in Hereditary Stature'. *The Journal of the Anthropological Institute of Great Britain and Ireland* 15: 246-263.

Gelman, Andrew and Jennifer Hill. 2007. *Data Analysis Using Regression and Multilevel/ Hierarchical Models.* Cambridge, Cambridge University Press.

Gujarati, Damodar N. 1995. *Basic Econometrics.* New York, McGraw-Hill.

King, Gary. 2000. 'How not to Lie with Statistics. Improving Interpretation and Presentation'. *American Journal of Political Science* 30(3): 666-687.

King, Gary, Michael Tomz, and Jason Wittenberg. 2000. 'Making the Most of Statistical Analyses: Improving Interpretation and Presentation'. *American Journal of Political Science* 44(2): 341-355.

Lewis-Beck, Colin and Michael S. Lewis-Beck. 2016. *Applied Regression: An Introduction.* Newbury Park, SAGE Publications.

Taagepera, Rein. 2011. 'Adding Meaning to Regression'. *European Political Science* 10(1): 73-85.

Wooldridge, Jeffrey M. 2003. *Introductory Econometrics: A Modern Approach.* Mason, OH, Thomson South-Western.

REPLICATION AND REPRODUCIBILITY

Stefan Schmidt, University of Freiburg

R

A single observation cannot be trusted. Similarly, findings from a single experimental investigation may reflect some regularity but they may also be due to chance (see STATISTICAL SIGNIFICANCE), artefacts, or misinterpretations. Therefore, it is necessary to repeat the respective research procedure in order to validate the observations from the first study. Such a repetition is called *replication*. It is a very basic methodological tool that serves to transform an observation into a piece of validated knowledge. An observation or relationship that is found repeatedly and is also found under various SCOPE CONDITIONS fulfils the important scientific criteria of *reproducibility*.

An example illustrates the importance and the difficulties of this process. In 1988 Strack, Martin, and Stepper published a study that reported that participants holding a pen between their teeth, and thus smiling, rate cartoons as funnier compared to when holding the pen between their lips, which results in frowning. For the replication of this study a thorough protocol was developed and registered. Seventeen independent replications were conducted according to this protocol and analysed meta-analytically (Wagenmakers et al. 2016). The original finding could not be replicated. However, there was one difference between the original study and the replications. Unlike in the original study, participants were monitored by a video camera in the replications. Another study replicated the experiment in conditions with and without camera. Here the effect could only be replicated in the absence of the camera (Noah, Schul, and Mayo 2018).

There are different types of replications. The most basic distinction is between a narrow-bounded notion of replication termed *direct replication* and a wider notion of replication termed *conceptual replication*. In a direct replication the experimental procedures of the original study are repeated. A conceptual replication aims to test either a certain HYPOTHESIS or the result of a prior study by using a *different* experimental set-up or a *different* methodological approach.

A FUNCTIONAL APPROACH FOR EXPERIMENTAL STUDIES

For a replication study to have some confirmatory power, it needs a mixture of procedures that are repeated from the original study and others that need to be changed. Also, some of the original procedures cannot be repeated at all. One cannot repeat the same study with the same 3-year-old child one year later—the child will then be aged 4. In order to find out which procedures should be maintained and which need to be changed, a systematic functional approach to replication studies was suggested (Schmidt 2009). It starts by determining the function of a planned replication study in the first place. Possible functions are: (a) to control for sampling error (chance result), (b) to control for artefacts (lack of internal validity), (c) to control for the impact of questionable research practices (QRPs) as well as fraud, (d) to generalize results to a larger or to a different population, and (e) to verify the underlying HYPOTHESIS of the earlier study (Schmidt 2017: 239). Furthermore, all aspects of an empirical study can be grouped into one of four classes: (1) primary information focus, (2) contextual background, (3) selection of participants, and (4) constitution of dependent VARIABLES (for more details see Schmidt 2009). Table 7 displays a grid of the various functions and classes of experimental aspects and identifies the respective demands for changes and constants. In the lower part of the table one can see the respective type of replication, the respective scientific benefit, and the risk that is associated with the different functions. Conceptual replications have a higher risk if they fail than direct replications. If a conceptual replication fails, one cannot make a conclusion as to whether this is due to a failure of the new study or whether the hypothesis or result of the original study is not replicable.

R

TABLE 7 Schematic description of the various functions of replications and the associated demands for changes and constants in the four classes of variables describing a research situation. Changes = classes of VARIABLES which should be at least partially changed in order to run this type of replication; constant = these variables should be kept constant; QRPs = questionable research practices.

		Function of the replication				
class		to control for sampling error	to control for artefact	to control for QRPs/ fraud	to generalize results	to verify a hypothesis
1	Primary informa-tion focus (immaterial)	constant	constant	constant	constant	constant
	Primary informa-tion focus (material realization)	constant	constant	constant	constant	changes
2	Contextual background	constant	changes§	changes‡	constant	changes
3	Selection of participants	constant*	constant	constant	change	constant&
4	constitu-tion of dependent variable	constant	changes§	changes‡	constant	changes

type of replication	direct replication		conceptual replication
scientific gain	fact confirmation	knowledge extension	under-standing
risk	low risk		high risk

* This means to apply the same procedures to select participants from the population, which will result in a *different* sample.

§ Changes here refer to building up the same set-up with different material and equip-ment. If there is a specific hypothesis regarding the alleged artefact available, then this hypothesis will make clear which aspects of class 2 and/or 4 must be changed.

† Changes here refer to the personnel involved in the study, and it depends on the new ex-perimental realization whether the participants can be drawn from the same population.

‡ Changes here refer to establishing a study protocol beforehand that specifies all relevant procedures in order to control for known QRPs.

& It depends on the new experimental realization whether the participants can be drawn from the same population.

(Adapted from Schmidt 2009)

REPLICATION IN THE SOCIAL SCIENCES

Although replicating studies is one of the most important scientific procedures to confirm and secure knowledge, this procedure was—until recently—very unpopular in the social sciences. The reason for this is that academic norms in this field did not encourage doing the same thing again. Replication studies were difficult to publish; scientific careers are built on genuineness and novelty but not on repeating existing work; funding agencies demand originality in proposals and are reluctant to fund work that has already been published in a similar fashion. Based on these sociological conditions, a culture arose which emphasized the importance of replication on the theoretical side but ignored this procedure entirely when it came to conducting practical science. A study from 2012 in the field of psychology identified an overall replication rate of 1.07 per cent (Makel, Plucker, and Hegarty 2012).

The absence of replications raises the chance of false-positive results (see BIAS). In the same climate that led to neglecting replications in favour of novelty and innovation, several questionable research practices (QRPs) also evolved. QRPs describe procedures of data handling that favour the HYPOTHESIS under investigation. Examples are incomplete reporting in publications (selection of positive VARIABLES or experimental conditions with positive outcomes) or decisions on data inclusion/exclusion based on the knowledge of the results (for more details see John, Loewenstein, and Prelec 2012). The application of QRPs—which are according to surveys ubiquitous—in the absence of replication raises the likelihood of false-positive results even more, but until recently nobody raised any critique on these practices.

THE REPRODUCIBILITY PROJECT

A debate on the likely rate of false-positive results (Ioannidis 2005; Pashler and Wagenmakers 2012) finally led, among other things, to the realization of the *Reproducibility Project* by Brian Nosek and the Open Science Collaboration. This group empirically assessed the reliability of published findings by the direct replication of 100 studies that were published by three major psychology journals in 2008. Out of ninety-seven original studies reporting significant findings, only thirty-five did so in their replications (Open Science Collaboration 2015). This demonstrates—at least for the field of psychology—that the neglect of replication procedures, especially in combination with QRPs, leads to considerable damage to the validity and credibility of published findings.

R

THE NEW ROLE OF REPLICATION

Starting from this debate, many recommendations were made in order to give replications the status they deserve (see ETHICS IN RESEARCH). The stakeholders of science have mostly understood that they need to change their policies, and also to give incentives for conducting and publishing replications. One such possibility is to submit study protocols of replication studies to certain journals for review in order to achieve a status of 'in principle acceptance' even before the data are collected. This gives the authors the guarantee of publication regardless of the results. Other procedures to raise the transparency of research practices are for example the preregistration of study protocols before the start of data collection. By doing this, BIASES like not reporting all VARIABLES or not publishing negative studies or negative experimental conditions can be reduced. Another instrument is the request to make the raw data of a study publicly available once the study is published. Such transparency can reduce the likelihood of QRP applications and may also serve to reflect on the current scientific culture and to increase the focus on the validation and reproducibility of findings.

REFERENCES

Ioannidis, John P. A. 2005. 'Why Most Published Research Findings Are False'. *PLoS Med* 2(8): e124.

John, Leslie K., George Loewenstein, and Drazen Prelec. 2012. 'Measuring the Prevalence of Questionable Research Practices with Incentives for Truth Telling'. *Psychological Science* 23(5): 524-532.

Makel, Matthew C., Jonathan A. Plucker, and Boyd Hegarty. 2012. 'Replications in Psychology Research: How Often Do They Really Occur?' *Perspectives on Psychological Science* 7(6): 537-542.

Noah, Tom, Yaacov Schul, and Ruth Mayo. 2018. 'When Both the Original Study and and Its Failed Replication Are Correct: Feeling Observed Eliminates the Facial-Feedback Effect'. *Journal of Personality and Social Psychology* 114(5): 657-664.

Open Science Collaboration. 2015. 'Estimating the Reproducibility of Psychological Science'. *Science* 349(6251): 1-8.

Pashler, Harold and Eric-Jan Wagenmakers. 2012. 'Editors' Introduction to the Special Section on Replicability in Psychological Science: A Crisis of Confidence?' *Perspectives on Psychological Science* 7(6): 528-530.

Schmidt, Stefan. 2009. 'Shall We Really Do It Again? The Powerful Concept of Replication Is Neglected in the Social Sciences'. *Review of General Psychology* 13(2): 90-100.

Schmidt, Stefan. 2017. 'Replication', in *Toward a More Perfect Psychology: Improving Trust, Accuracy, and Transparency in Research*, ed. Matthew C. Maker and Jonathan A. Plucker, 233 253. Washington, DC, American Psychological Association.

Strack, Fritz, Leonard L. Martin, and Sabine Stepper 1998. 'Inhibiting and Facilitating Conditions of the Human Smile: A Nonobtrusive Test of the Facial Feedback Hypothesis'. *Journal of Personality and Social Psychology* 54(5): 768-777.

Wagenmakers, Eric-Jan et al. 2016. 'Registered Replication Report: Strack, Martin, and Stepper (1988)'. *Perspectives on Psychological Science* 11(6): 917-928.

R

RESEARCH QUESTION

Irene Wieczorek, University of Durham, Piergiuseppe Parisi, University of York

Research questions identify what the researcher wants to find out or understand. They are a crucial component of any study and are connected to all parts of the research. Depending on the type of study, the research question may either serve as the starting point of the entire research or change in response to the research design. For example, empirical research designs not only seek to answer the specific research question(s) that prompts them, but also contribute to the reformulation of the research question itself as the limitations to the inquiry become clear.

Research questions should be distinguished from research objectives, which are what a researcher aims to deliver at the end of the research process. The latter can be, for instance, policy recommendations. Research questions should also be distinguished from research HYPOTHESES. A research question should naturally be formulated in an interrogative manner and should be a query to which the answer is not known at the outset of the research process.

Research questions have a twofold *purpose*. They define the boundaries of a research project, thus guiding the investigation (Watts 2001; Maxwell 2009: 229; George and Bennett 2005: 74), and they are meant to spark the reader's interest.

Michael Watts (2001) has identified four key desirable *characteristics* of research questions in the field of social sciences (although these may be broadly applicable to legal research as well): they should be evocative, relevant, clear, and researchable.

Evocative questions should capture the reader's interest by posing 'innovative approaches to the exploration of problems'. More concretely, evocative questions are those that aim to fill a gap in the knowledge of a specific problem. A question which is formulated in terms of 'What is the state of the discussion/literature on the principle of proportionality in EU law?' is not evocative, as it only envisages an exercise of knowledge gathering, rather than knowledge seeking. This gap-filling exercise can be achieved either by addressing puzzling and new dilemmas, or by seeking to untangle old problems in new, unexplored ways. However, gap-filling per se is not sufficient. The problem which has not yet been explored—the gap the research intends to fill—must have some relevance. In other words, there need to be specific reasons supporting the need to carry out the planned exercise.

Relevant questions are those, for instance, which spark the interest of society in general or of a targeted community, by addressing a specific topic and making a connection with broader trends or contexts. Thus, it is commonly argued that answering a sound research question should entail broader implications for the researcher's field of expertise (Turabian et al 2013: 13). For example, in the field of human rights leadership studies, a relevant research question may be: 'What characteristics make for a good leader in the human rights movement?' The relevance of this question can be understood in connection with the specific constituency it is concerned with (that is, the human rights movement), and in light of the broader issue that it addresses (that is, leadership in a non-business context), given the lack of research on the issue. In order to be relevant, a research question must also be consequential. That is to say, its relevance must not depend on the nature of the results. For instance, a good research question which postulates a positive or a negative answer must lead to relevant research regardless of the nature, positive or negative, of the answer itself. If, for either a positive or negative answer to the research question, the findings would not add anything to existing knowledge, then the research question cannot be considered relevant. An example could be: 'Has the increase of fees for higher education led to a decrease

R

in low-income background students' applications to university?' Finally, one should note that research questions may also arise from the researcher's genuine curiosity to investigate a seemingly trivial phenomenon or puzzle (Turabianet al 2013: 13). In this case, the relevance of such a question may only become apparent once it has been investigated.

Clear research questions are easily understandable and straightforward. Too abstract or obscure questions should be avoided and so should questions that combine too many **VARIABLES**. For example, it may be argued that a question such as 'What is the relation between offenders and deterrence?' is unclear, because the reader cannot fully understand what the researcher intends to investigate. Conversely, 'What are the factors that contribute to deterring offenders from reoffending?' may be more straightforward in that it makes clear that the focus of the study, for instance in the field of criminology, is deterrence rather than its variables.

Finally, research questions should be clearly '*researchable*' (Salter and Mason 2007: 12). Watts frames this last attribute in terms of resources and constraints. While formulating a research question, one should be aware of how much time and resources will be needed to carry out the research. A less ambitious research question that can be answered thoroughly is certainly more valuable than a question that cannot be answered comprehensively within the available time frame and resource constraints. A question such as 'How do UN Resolutions influence the behaviour of multinational companies?' may be too broad in scope and require time and resources that the researcher may not have. Thus, they may want to narrow down the scope of the investigation, for example, to the question: 'Have UN Resolutions on human rights led to the inclusion of human rights clauses in multinational companies' contracts?'

There exist different types of research questions, which are summarized in Table 8.

A tight relation exists between research questions and *research methodology*. Differently framed research questions warrant different methods of inquiry (Yin 2009: 8; Van Hoecke 2011: viii). This is not to say that a research question can *only* be answered by recourse to one method, but in some cases a specific method of inquiry may be *more suited* to answering a certain question. For instance, variance questions (such as '*Is there a relationship* between income inequality and political preferences?' or, '*Is there a relationship* between income level and political preferences?') may be better answered by using quantitative approaches (Maxwell 2009: 232). On the other hand, questions that require an in-depth analysis of a specific phenomenon (such as 'Why do African Americans vote less often than other minorities?') may be better investigated with a qualitative approach (Yin 2009: 8).

Specific issues concerning the interaction between research question and research methodology may arise about the type of research being conducted. Qualitative research requires, at least in its initial phase, a continuous interaction between the research design and the research question, the latter being subject to a meticulous process of redefinition and refinement (Maxwell 2009: 229–233). For instance, the redefinition of a research project may be dependent on the clarification of preliminary assumptions hidden in the research question or on the **OPERATIONALIZATION** of a question formulated in general and abstract terms. If, for example, the researcher,

TABLE 8   Different types of research questions

Type of question	What it seeks to investigate	How to recognize them
Descriptive questions	They generally aim to describe, i.e. quantify the variables that the researcher is using	They are normally formulated as: 'how much?', 'how often?', 'what percentage?', 'what proportion?'
Comparative questions	They seek to identify the differences between two or more groups in relation to one or more dependent variables	They are normally formulated as: 'what is the difference in Z between Y and X?'
Relational questions	They seek to establish whether variables are linked by a causal relationship or one of association or correlation, as well as whether such variables interact or there is a trend amongst them	They are normally formulated as: 'what is the relationship between X and Y?'
Exploratory questions	They seek to understand qualitatively something that is under-studied	They may be formulated as: 'what is the role of X in relation to Y?'
Predictive questions	They seek to understand the intention around a certain issue or topic, or prospective outcome	They are normally formulated as: 'why does X happen, given Y?' or 'how would X react, given Y?'
Interpretive questions	They seek to generate an understanding of how realities are constructed intersubjectively	They may be formulated as: 'how is X understood by individual/group Y?'

at some point during the research process, decides to answer the question 'How do concluding observations of UN human rights monitoring bodies influence state practice?' with a comparative CASE STUDY, they will probably want to revisit the initial formulation of the question, and specify the case studies selected and the time frame considered. A similar study was in fact conducted by Krommendijk (2014), who considered the impact and effectiveness of UN reporting mechanisms at the domestic level in three states.

Finally, there can be different *kinds* of research questions depending on the nature of the project. One can distinguish between monodisciplinary and INTERDISCIPLIN-ARY research questions. For instance, one can distinguish between monodisciplinary *law projects*—which inquire on the state of the law on a certain subject—and *projects about the law*—which aim to provide analysis and comment on existing law and which can have an interdisciplinary dimension. In the first case, the questions concern the state of the law. An example could be: 'Does the crime definition of money laundering also apply to self-laundering?' Specific law projects are doctrinal positive law projects,

R

which include a normative dimension, asking how the law can be applied. Questions can be something like: 'Can the norms on the use of force in international law be used to regulate cyber-attacks?' In the second case, projects about the law which include an interdisciplinary dimension, questions concern the qualities of the law. They would be questions such as: 'Are blacklisting and asset-freezing administrative sanctions *effective* in preventing terrorist financing?' (law and economics), 'Do European norms on the ban of the full veil show a *gender* BIAS?' (law and gender studies), or 'What does the current definition of human trafficking tell us about the weight of patriarchal values in Western democracies?' (law and cultural studies).

REFERENCES

George, Alexander L. and Andrew Bennett. 2005. *Case Studies and Theory Development in the Social Sciences.* Cambridge, MA, MIT Press.

Krommendijk, Jasper. 2014. *The Domestic Impact and Effectiveness of the Process of State Reporting under UN Human Rights Treaties in the Netherlands, New Zealand and Finland: Paper-pushing or Policy Prompting?* Cambridge, Intersentia.

Maxwell, Joseph A. 2009. 'Designing a Qualitative Study', in *The SAGE Handbook of Applied Social Research Methods,* 2nd edition, ed. Leonard Bickman and Debra J. Rog, 214–253. Thousand Oaks, CA, SAGE Publications.

Salter, Michael and Julie Mason. 2007. *Writing Law Dissertations: An Introduction and Guide to the Conduct of Legal Research.* Upper Saddle River, NJ, Pearson Education.

Turabian, Kate, Wayne C. Booth, Gregory G. Colomb, Joseph M. Williams, and the University of Chicago Press editorial staff. 2013. *A Manual for Writers of Research Papers, Theses, and Dissertations,* 8th edition. Chicago and London, University of Chicago Press.

Van Hoecke, Mark (ed.). 2011. *Methodologies of Legal Research: Which Kind of Method for What Kind of Discipline?* Oxford and Portland, Hart Publishing.

Watts, Michael. 2001. *The Holy Grail: In Pursuit of the Dissertation Proposal.* Regents of the University of California. Available at http://iis.berkeley.edu/node/424 (Accessed 14 August 2020).

Yin, Robert K. 2009. *Case Study Research: Design and Methods,* 4th edition. Thousand Oaks, CA, SAGE Publications.

R

S

SAMPLING TECHNIQUES

Sample Types and Sample Size

Emilie van Haute, Université libre de Bruxelles

In research, the term population refers to a well-defined set of UNITS OF ANALYSIS that are the focus of the study. The number of units that make up the population is symbolized by an upper-case *N*. These units of analysis can correspond to a set of individuals, countries, organizations, agencies, events, news items, years, scores, books, decisions, reforms, laws, etc. Let us consider a researcher interested in the study of how members of parliaments (MPs) conceive their roles as citizens' representatives. The population of the study (*N*) includes all members of parliaments in the world (46,552 according to the Global Parliamentary Report).[1]

However, researchers may restrict their data collection to a sample of that population for convenience or necessity if they lack the time and resources to collect data for the entire population. Therefore, a sample is 'any subset of units collected from a population' (Johnson and Reynolds 2012: 224). Its size is denoted by a lowercase *n*. The units that make up the sample are also referred to as 'elements' or 'individuals'. In our example, the researcher may lack the time, resources, or the willingness to collect data on all MPs in the world, and will proceed to select a number of MPs (*n*) from this population.

Research sampling techniques refer to CASE SELECTION strategy—the process and methods used to select a subset of units from a population (in our example, selecting MPs). While sampling techniques reduce the costs of data collection, they induce a loss in terms of comprehensiveness and accuracy, compared to working on the entire population. The data collected are subject to errors or BIAS. Two main decisions determine the size or margin of error and whether the results of a sample study can be generalized and applied to the entire population with accuracy: the choice of sample type and the sample size.

---

[1] http://archive.ipu.org/ (accessed 2 November 2017).

TYPES OF SAMPLES

In order to apply the findings derived from the sample to the general population (with a known sampling error), samples must be drawn using probability sampling methods.

A probability sample is a sample for which the probability of selecting each UNIT OF ANALYSIS (in the population) is known. In our example, probability sampling indicates the known probability that each MP in the world will be chosen for the subset of selected MPs. This allows the researcher to calculate how accurately the sample reflects the population and to infer or generalize the results to the population with a known margin of error. The four main probability sampling methods are: simple random sampling, systematic sampling, stratified sampling, and cluster sampling.

In a *simple random sample*, each UNIT OF ANALYSIS has an equal chance of being included in the sample. Units are randomly selected, preferably using a computerized system to reduce human interference, which may subconsciously introduce patterns, and therefore BIAS (Hibberts, Johnson, and Hudson 2012: 55–56). In our example, the researcher could use a random computerized technique to select MPs (from the world list) to include in the sample. (For additional examples of simple random techniques, see Johnson et al (2016).)

In a *systematic sample*, an interval k is determined by dividing the population size by the sample size (N/n). Then, a random starting point is selected from where the researcher selects every kth unit from the list of the population. This technique is sometimes easier to implement than computerized techniques. However, to avoid BIAS, it should not be used if the UNITS OF ANALYSIS are ranked in a list based on certain characteristics, or if they follow a certain pattern. In our example, the interval (k) would be determined by dividing the population size (46,552 MPs in the world) by the desired sample size (n), the number of MPs to include in the sample (for instance, 4,900). In this example, $k = 9.5$ (46,552/4,900). From the list of all MPs in the world, the researcher would randomly select a starting point (e.g. MP number 145) as the first unit in the sample. Then, the researcher selects every 9th MP on the list until they reach the necessary sample size or the required number of MPs to include in the sample (n). In this case, it is crucial to make sure that the list of MPs is not ordered according to specific characteristics, such as country or party of origin, gender, etc.

In a *stratified sample*, UNITS OF ANALYSIS are divided into groups based on one or more characteristics. If a sample is composed of individuals, these are usually socio-demographic characteristics. Then, units are selected within each group, using a simple random or systematic sample technique. Commonly, stratified samples are proportional—the sample size of each group is relative to their size and distribution in the population. Thus, the sample resembles the population as far as possible in terms of these characteristics. This is a way of avoiding BIAS when generalizing about the entire population, if we know from prior studies that these characteristics affect the object under study. Stratified samples can also be disproportional, so the sample size of each group differs from its proportion in the population. Here, certain groups may be over- or under-represented to compensate for small groups, which would generate a small n in the sample. It is used if the researcher intends to conduct analyses on the subgroups. In this case, the researcher uses weights to generalize about the population to compensate for these choices. In our example, all of the world's MPs could be grouped by country, and MPs to include in the sample could be randomly selected in each country. The number of MPs per country to include in the sample could be proportionate to the size of that country in relation to the total population of MPs in the world (proportionate stratified sample). However, the researcher could decide to over-represent MPs from smaller countries (e.g. Micronesia, which has just fourteen MPs) and under-represent MPs from larger countries (e.g. China, where the congress has 2,924 members) to ensure that there are enough MPs from each country (disproportionate stratified sample). In this case, when analysing the results, the researcher will have to use weights to correct the over- or under-representation of certain groups in the sample.

In a *cluster sample*, units that share one or more characteristics are put into groups. Then, only certain groups are randomly selected. Within each selected group, units are selected using random sampling. In our example, the researcher could randomly select a certain number of countries and then randomly select MPs in those countries. Cluster samples increase error, but can be useful to reduce the costs of data collection (e.g. when the UNITS OF ANALYSIS are geographically spread out). In our example, only selecting MPs from certain countries would reduce the costs of data collection. Cluster samples can also be used if information about the full population is not available.

Non-probability sampling

Probability samples are generally preferred because they increase accuracy and allow inference or generalization about the population. However, they are more expensive and not always an option because they require a list of all the units of analysis included in the population (and their characteristics, for stratified and cluster samples). In contrast, non-probability samples are samples in which each element in the population has an unknown probability of being included in the sample. In this case, inference or generalization cannot be conducted with a known margin of error or STATISTICAL SIGNIFICANCE. Therefore, they are generally not recommended in SURVEY RESEARCH. However, they may be useful for EXPERIMENTS, INTERVIEW TECHNIQUES, exploratory and qualitative research, or if the target population is impossible to identify. The four main non-probability sampling methods are: convenience sampling, purposive sampling, quota sampling, and snowball sampling.

In a *convenience sample*, UNITS OF ANALYSIS are included in the sample because they are available, as well as easy and convenient to select in the study. In our example, the researcher could include in the sample MPs from their country of origin and from neighbouring countries.

In a *purposive sample*, the researcher determines the characteristics of the target population and identifies units that match these characteristics to include in the sample. In our example, this would mean identifying all MPs from European parliamentary democracies and targeting them for the sample.

In a *quota sample*, units of analysis are divided into groups based on one or more characteristics. Then, units are selected within each group, using a purposive or convenience technique, which may or may not be in proportion to their distribution in the population. This technique is similar to a (dis)proportionate stratified sample, except that units are not randomly selected within the groups, but selected by purposive or convenience methods. In our example, this would mean dividing MPs into subgroups based on their country or party of origin, and then conveniently selecting MPs in these groups (the sample may or may not be proportional to their size in the population).

Lastly, in a *snowball sample*, the UNITS OF ANALYSIS (which must be individual respondents) identify potential additional respondents to include in the sample. In our example, this would mean targeting one MP and then asking them (in an interview) to identify colleagues to add to the sample. This is particularly useful for populations or worlds that are not easy to penetrate.

SAMPLE SIZE

When building a sample, a key decision relates to sample size. The larger the sample, the smaller the errors. At full sample size (i.e. when the entire population is included in the study), there is no error.

Contrary to common belief, sample size is not usually determined by population size, unless the population is rather small. In fact, the relationship between sample and population size is exponential (see Table 9). The factors that do determine sample size, however, are: the degree of heterogeneity of the population (more heterogeneity requires a larger sample); the expected differences between groups in the population (smaller expected differences require a larger sample); the sampling technique used (more complex sampling techniques require a larger sample); the type of analyses to be conducted (subgroup analyses require a larger sample); the margin of error the researcher is prepared to tolerate (lower margin of error requires a larger sample); and the expected response rate (in the case of a survey, a low response rate calls for a large sample).

Overall, thus sample type and sample size are two crucial pieces of information that researchers should have in mind when selecting a sample or using existing samples in their studies.

TABLE 9 Relationship between population size and sample size, based on margin of error (simple random sampling)

Population	Size of the sample needed based on a margin of error of ... (based on simple random sample)		
	10%	5%	1%
100	50	80	99
500	81	218	476
1,000	88	278	906
10,000	96	370	4,900
100,000	96	383	8,763
1,000,000 and more	97	384	9,513

REFERENCES

Chambers, Ray L. and Robert G. Clark. 2012. *An Introduction to Model-Based Survey Sampling with Applications*. Oxford, Oxford University Press.

Govindarajulu, Zakkula. 1999. *Elements of Sampling Theory and Methods*. Upper Saddle River, NJ, Prentice Hall.

Hibberts, Mary, R. Burke Johnson, and Kenneth Hudson. 2012. 'Common Survey Sampling Techniques', in *Handbook of Survey Methodology for the Social Sciences*, ed. Lior Gideon, 53–74. New York, Springer.

Johnson, Janet B. and H. T. Reynolds. 2012. *Political Science Research Methods*. New York, SAGE Publications.

Johnson, Janet B., H. T. Reynolds, and Jason D. Mycoff. 2016. *Political Science Research Methods*, 8th edition. Los Angeles, CQ Press.

Lohr, Sharon J. 2009. *Sampling: Design and Analysis*. Pacific Grove, CA, Duxbury Press.

Noy, Chaim. 2006. 'Sampling Knowledge: The Hermeneutics of Snowball Sampling in Qualitative Research'. *International Journal of Social Research Methodology* 11(4): 327–344.

Teddlie, Charles and Fen Yu. 2007. 'Mixed Methods Sampling. A Typology with Examples'. *Journal of Mixed Methods Research* 1(1): 77–100.

SCIENTIFIC REALISM

Heikki Patomäki, University of Helsinki

Metaphysical realists have long maintained that the world is real, and while reality may be independent of concepts, our concepts can make references to it and its essences. Medieval nominalists denied this and maintained instead that abstract concepts or universals are names only. For a nominalist, only particular or concrete beings exist. Thus to name a particular four-legged creature a 'dog' is just a human convention.

The debate between realism and nominalism assumed new meanings after pragmatically successful breakthroughs in physics, chemistry, biology, and medicine from Newton to Maxwell and from Jenner to Darwin. Especially since the nineteenth century, nominalists have been allied with modern-day empiricists, who tend to treat scientific theories instrumentally (theories are just tools indicating means to achieve ends), while realists have fixed their eyes on the realisticness of scientific theories (the task of theories is to depict reality). Both parties agree that modern scientific theories work better than earlier forms of human understanding. The question is: is this because they capture real essences and properties of the world? Or is it because we can formulate theories that may work and accord with observations, but have no necessary bearing on any deeper understanding of reality? Is the success of our theories just a miracle?

After the heyday of empiricism in the interwar period and its immediate aftermath (see **POSITIVISM AND POST-POSITIVISM**), many critical reactions to empiricism seemed to suggest scientific realism. For instance, Quine (1951) contested the idea of atomistic facts and Bunge (1959) the idea that **CAUSATION** is only or mainly about empirically regular connections between two events or observables. It was, moreover, widely agreed that scientific theories make references to things that cannot be directly observed (or at least seen), and thus emerged the issue of the status of non-observables.

As scientific realism became increasingly dominant, new philosophical stances such as van Fraassen's constructive empiricism were often defined in opposition to it. Van Fraassen (1980: 8) understands scientific realism as a claim that 'science aims to give us, in its theories, a literally true story of what the world is like; and acceptance of a scientific theory involves the belief that it is true'. Many scientific realists have defended weaker versions, however. For instance, Putnam (1981) introduces the concept of 'internal realism', involving the idea that it is impossible to compare conceptual frameworks directly with the world. More in line with established forms of scientific realism, Niiniluoto (2000) talks about *verisimilitude*, or truth-likeness. This concept is supposed to avoid the consequences of claiming to have access to the truth itself (if we know the truth itself, no further scientific progress seems possible).

The social sciences seem to pose difficulties for scientific realism. Can meaning, history, and the social world really exist independently of us humans and our meanings and conventions? Moreover, in the late twentieth century many fields of social science were commonly conceived in terms of interparadigm debates (see **PARADIGMS AND RESEARCH PROGRAMMES**). What could concepts such as *verisimilitude* mean in scholarly contexts where there appear to be several drastically different competing scientific theories and approaches? Which one of them is approaching the truth? Many varieties of **POST-POSITIVISM** have adopted a strong anti-realist stand. According to Bunge (1993) this has been a regressive move. Bunge stresses not only the reality of social systems and macrosocial phenomena, but also of subjective experiences. 'A realist should be willing, nay eager, to admit the relevance of feeling, belief and interest to social action, but he will insist that they be studied objectively' (Bunge 1993: 211).

If realist objectivism is possible also in the social sciences, what then explains the drastically different opinions of say John K. Galbraith and Milton Friedman in economics? Bunge maintains that while it is true that any given body of empirical data can be 'covered' by several different **HYPOTHESES**, for a realist an approximate empirical fit is only an indicator of truth. A realist also requires compatibility with a comprehensive theory. A theory that has the greatest explanatory power is likely to be complex and refer to deep mechanisms. Although the empirical underdetermination of theory can explain some of the differences between Galbraith and Friedman, Bunge accuses Friedman of philosophical 'fictionalism', of licensing assumptions that do not correspond to anything outside theorists' imagination. This kind of fictionalism is often freely admitted by rational choice theorists and any theorist thinking in 'as if' terms and under '*ceteris paribus*' conditions. Bunge's point is that assumptions can be false and appearances misleading, thus fictionalism is false.

Scientific realism has at times been criticized from the point of view of social constructivism, though many forms of social constructivism are realist. For instance, Searle (1995) distinguishes between 'brute facts' and 'institutional facts'. A piece of paper in my hand is a physical fact, but it is a social agreement that it is also a 20 euro note. We impose aesthetic, practical, and social functions on objects in terms of collective intentionality (i.e. shared beliefs, desires, and intentions) and constitutive rules:

X counts as Y in context C. We can refer to institutional facts as objectively as to brute facts; and the correspondence theory of truth is valid for both.

Of the founders of social sciences, at least Karl Marx and Emile Durkheim can plausibly be argued to have been scientific realists—and there are realist readings of Max Weber too. In modern social scientific contexts, the issue of non-observables concerns the existential status of beliefs, desires, and intentions; background competences; collective intentionality; social structures and systems; and macrosocial and macrohistorical phenomena. As scientific realists tend to defend the real existence of (at least some of) these, it seems clear that a scientific realist can be a methodological but not an ontological individualist (see METHODOLOGICAL INDIVIDUALISM AND HOLISM). From a realist viewpoint, however, the meaning of the former is unclear because realism is opposed to fictionalist as-if thinking (see ONTOLOGY).

Epistemologically, the main issue concerns the problems of correspondence and *verisimilitude*. How can we compare a claim or theory to the truth if we do not know the truth? Is there a confusion between the meaning and criteria of truth? A possible solution is to distinguish clearly between ONTOLOGY, EPISTEMOLOGY, and judgemental rationality (see CRITICAL REALISM). Finally, while scientific realism avoids the dead ends of anti-realism, it remains focused on science, and has so far paid too little attention to the questions specific to human sciences.

REFERENCES

Bunge, Mario. 1959. *Causality: The Place of the Causal Principle in Modern Science.* Cambridge, MA, Harvard University Press.
Bunge, Mario. 1993. 'Realism and Antirealism in Social Science'. *Theory and Decision* 35(3): 207–235.
Niiniluoto, Ilkka. 2000. *Critical Scientific Realism.* Oxford, Oxford University Press.
Putnam, Hilary. 1981. *Reason, Truth and History.* Cambridge, Cambridge University Press.
Quine, Willard. 1951. 'Two Dogmas of Empiricism'. *The Philosophical Review* 60(1): 20–43.
Searle, John. 1995. *The Construction of Social Reality.* New York, Free Press.
Van Fraassen, Bas C. 1980. *The Scientific Image.* Oxford, Clarendon Press.

SCOPE CONDITIONS

A Potential Escape from Systematic Theory Falsification

Mathilde Gauquelin, Laval University and Ghent University

S

The idea of scope conditions is rooted in Hempel's 'true–false' paradox of theoretical formulations: one can always find data to support a general theoretical proposition, but conversely, every proposition will also always be subject to contradicting evidence (Hempel 1965: 14–16). This realization led scholars to reflect on possible ways to evaluate theories: how can they ever be proven to be valid, if they can never escape FALSIFICATION? The concept of scope conditions suggests that when formulating general theoretical propositions, scholars may also identify the specific conditions under which they expect these propositions to apply. By doing so, the risk of systematic falsification decreases, and the development of cumulative knowledge becomes possible. This entry explains the role of scope conditions in theory development and provides guidance on their identification.

SCOPE CONDITIONS AND THEORY DEVELOPMENT

Generally, scope conditions suggest that any theoretical proposition should be accompanied by an explicit and constant set of conditions or parameters under which one expects the proposition to always be valid. A simple example illustrates this idea. Several researchers have suggested that states ratify environmental treaties because of domestic pressures from civil society (see for instance Roberts, Parks, and Vasquez 2004: 28). This proposition is a telling example of Hempel's paradox: it is so general that it is certainly possible to find evidence to support it, but also evidence against it. As a result, an additional condition has often been added to limit the scope of the statement: the proposition could apply only to democracies, where civil society is expected to be more organized, more informed, and have greater influence on government representatives (Neumayer 2002: 139).

In other words, scope conditions transform a universal proposition into a conditional one, by restricting its scope of application. Walker and Cohen thus clarify that scope statements do not make direct assertions about the relationship between certain theoretical concepts or VARIABLES. Rather, they are constants that affect the class of individuals or units to which the proposition applies, regardless of the proposed relationships between the variables (Walker and Cohen 1985: 291–293).

As such, scope conditions define the conditions under which empirical evidence that does not support a proposition—or negative evidence—can be used as a basis to actually reject a theoretical proposition. In this sense, scope conditions and empirical evidence can interact in three ways to contribute to theory development:

1   If scope limitations are satisfied, negative empirical evidence should falsify the proposition, because the latter should have been true under the stated limitations. That is to say, an instance where a democratic state that has been subject to domestic pressures chooses not to ratify a given treaty would falsify our original proposition.

2   However, if scope limitations are not satisfied, the evidence can only be irrelevant, because the proposition was not meant to apply outside the stated limitations and thus cannot be verified or falsified. For example, a study of autocracies' treaty ratification cannot directly prove or disprove an argument that solely applies to democracies.

3   Finally, if a theoretical formulation is in fact true, findings of negative evidence will imply that one of the scope limitations is unsatisfied, because the data should otherwise have supported the formulation (Walker and Cohen 1985: 291–293).

In the hypothetical (and very unlikely!) event that all democracies subject to domestic pressures indeed ratify environmental treaties, a state found *not* to ratify
an environmental treaty under domestic pressure could not be a democracy.

It follows logically that scope conditions also provide a framework to indicate where
evidence can be generalized, based on the idea that if a proposition is true within its
defined scope, there are always 'additional but unknown circumstances to which [it]
applies' (Walker and Cohen 1985: 295). The scientist's task then becomes to generalize the theory by expanding its scope of applicability to cover these circumstances.
This process is similar to fixing *ceteris paribus* parameters in economic theory: once
relative certainty about a causal relationship under given parameters is achieved, the
relationship can subsequently be tested under new parameters. Conversely, this also
implies that if a proposition is proven false under less restrictive scope conditions, it
has reached its potential for generalization and cannot see its scope further expanded
(Walker and Cohen 1985: 295–296).

IDENTIFYING SCOPE CONDITIONS

There is a push among scholars to encourage the explicit statement of scope conditions to
formulate clearer and more precise theoretical statements. Goertz remarks that many scientists implicitly assume conditions that directly limit the scope of their research in practice, but do not always explicitly discuss them (Goertz 2005: 196). This section explains
the forms that scope conditions can take, and how they can be identified.

Concretely, scope conditions can be spatial, temporal, substantive, or institutional,
among others (Rohlfing 2012: 206). For instance, the proposition that states ratify environmental treaties when they are subject to domestic pressure from civil society could be
limited to certain geographic regions, where civil society is expected to be more organized
or share a specific culture that makes it more apt to influence governments (*spatial condition*). Similarly, it could be limited to a certain time period, when global events increased
civil society's interest in environmental matters (*temporal condition*). It could further
be limited to specific environmental issues, such as climate change or biodiversity, with
which civil society is particularly preoccupied (*substantive condition*). Finally, treaty ratification could be limited based on the type of ratification procedure involved (*institutional
condition*). It is possible that a proposition may be associated with several scope conditions
in a single category, or with none at all in another one. The identification of relevant scope
conditions need not be dictated by a specific number, but rather by theoretical expectations and previous empirical knowledge.

Indeed, the identification of scope conditions can arise either from theory-driven
hypotheses, empirical observations, or both. In all cases, it is essential that scope conditions be defined prior to CASE SELECTION, as opposed to being inserted into the
research following empirical testing. Indeed, one must be careful to avoid adding conditions to an existing set of empirical observations, for instance by subsetting a data set,
to fit a previously formulated hypothesis (Walker and Cohen 1985: 291). For instance,

scholars have used the lens of scope conditions to discuss the conditions under which revolutions can be expected to take place in different countries. Scope statements suggest that regime type and colonial past are possible factors that could limit the application of a general theoretical proposition on revolutions (Goertz 2005: 204–207; see also Soifer 2012: 1582–1584). Within a single study, it would not be acceptable to apply such a scope statement retroactively with a view to limiting the cases studied, in order to increase their coherence or their fit with the original hypothesis. Nevertheless, scope conditions suggested by empirical evidence can subsequently become part of new theory-driven hypotheses, to be tested on a separate data set.

In short, when used correctly, scope conditions encourage increased transparency in research: both in the scientist's own mind, by encouraging reflection about one's proposed hypotheses and the conditions under which they can be verified, and vis-à-vis peers, by being clear about the scope of the research, its potential for generalization or lack thereof, and possible avenues for subsequent research, thus favouring **REPLICATION AND REPRODUCIBILITY**.

REFERENCES

Goertz, Gary. 2005. *Social Science Concepts: A User's Guide*. Princeton, NJ, Princeton University Press.

Hempel, Carl Gustav. 1965. *Aspects of Scientific Explanation: And Other Essays in the Philosophy of Science*. New York, Free Press.

Neumayer, Eric. 2002. 'Do Democracies Exhibit Stronger International Environmental Commitment? A Cross-Country Analysis'. *Journal of Peace Research* 39(2): 139-164.

Roberts, J. Timmons, Bradley C. Parks, and Alexis A. Vasquez. 2004. 'Who Ratifies Environmental Treaties and Why? Institutionalism, Structuralism and Participation by 192 Nations in 22 Treaties'. *Global Environmental Politics* 4(3): 22-64.

Rohlfing, Ingo. 2012. *Case Studies and Causal Inference: An Integrative Framework*. London, Palgrave Macmillan.

Soifer, Hillel David. 2012. 'The Causal Logic of Critical Junctures'. *Comparative Political Studies* 45(12): 1572-1597.

Walker, Henry A. and Bernard P. Cohen. 1985. 'Scope Statements: Imperatives for Evaluating Theory'. *American Sociological Review* 50(3): 288-301.

SEQUENCE ANALYSIS

Being Earnest with Time

Thomas Collas, University of Strasbourg, Philippe Blanchard, University of Warwick

Sequence analysis (SA) conceives the social world as happening in processes, in series of events experienced by social entities (e.g. groups, individuals, nations, etc.). SA refers to a set of tools used to summarize, represent, and compare sequences—

i.e. ordered lists of items. Job careers (succession of job positions) are typical examples of sequences. Various other topics have been studied through SA, such as steps in traditional English dances, country-level adoption of welfare policies over one century, or individual and family time-diaries (about recent developments, see Blanchard, Bühlmann, and Gauthier 2014; Ritschard and Studer 2018).

Temporal structures have been investigated by social and political theory for a long time, but their systematic empirical operationalization on samples of sequences was still missing until the diffusion of SA since the 1980s. In particular, previously available longitudinal methods would summarize a sequence by means of the total time spent in each state (thereby neglecting the order of events or experiences), or by means of a small number of time points, such as before and after a major event (thereby missing the possibly multiple and complex movements between the two time points) (Blanchard 2019).

Andrew Abbott played a pioneering role in the diffusion of SA. With colleagues, Abbott introduced optimal matching analysis (OMA) in the social sciences, a tool to compare sequences borrowed from computer science and previously adapted to DNA sequences. Abbott's work on SA was part of a wider methodological thinking on social processes (Abbott 1995).

COMPOSITION OF SEQUENCES

A sequence is a series of items. We focus here on the most common type of sequences in social science: categorical time series—i.e. successions of states with a duration defined on a more or less refined chronological scale (a year, a minute, a moment, etc.). Each state is a value from an 'alphabet' (or 'universe') of all distinct states observed in a set of sequences.

For example, Katherine Stovel (2001) uses data built from archival materials to compare 395 counties' histories of white-on-black violence in the US Deep South between 1882 and 1930. Stovel assumes that each lynching event is embedded in local sequential patterns. The author conceives each county's lynching history as a sequence of fourteen time periods each defined by a state which is the number of lynching events that occurred during the period. '10000000001100' is such a sequence made of a first period with one event, nine periods without any lynching event, two periods with one event and two periods without any event.

As a second and graphical example, Figure 9 renders the post-educational cross-field job careers of twenty recruits as special advisers in French ministerial offices between May 2012 and March 2014. Each column is a six-month period; the right end of the x-axis is the recruitment in a ministerial office. Each line is a sequence made of states drawn from a four-state alphabet (see legend) indicating positions in the public administration, in semi-public organizations (mainly state-owned companies and public agencies), in private-owned companies, and as a political aide. Time units preceding the first job position are blank on the figure. Data were collected from a detailed and time-stamped online source in the framework of an ongoing collective

FIGURE 9   Post-educational cross-sectoral job careers of a set of recruits as ministerial advisers in France

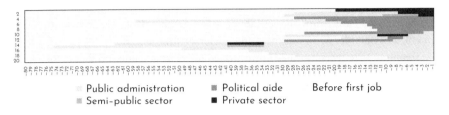

<table>
</table>

■ Public administration   ■ Political aide   Before first job
■ Semi-public sector   ■ Private sector

project Thomas Collas is part of. We were not only interested in the different types of job positions each adviser held, but also in the time spent in each field and in the order in which each adviser moved from one field to the other.

The detailed temporal data used by SA requires meticulous collection, whether using archives, ad hoc surveys (especially life-history calendars), web-cropped CVs, or web logs (see **PROSOPOGRAPHY**).

TOOLS TO DESCRIBE SEQUENTIAL PATTERNS

By contrast with other longitudinal methods that isolate antecedents to a given event (such as event history analysis), or estimate transition odds between states (such as Markov models), SA focuses on sequential patterns—i.e. the temporal structures drawn by the successions of states.

A wide collection of metric and graphical tools help to describe the features of a set of sequences. Several features are usually analysed. First, sequences are defined by the states they contain and the distribution of each state within each sequence. For instance, sequences 1 and 2 in Figure 9 both include positions in the private sector. The whole post-educational career is spent in this field for the former, 26 per cent for the latter. Composite metrics, such as the complexity index, assess the internal variety of sequences. Second, sequences are defined by the order in which states appear. The notion of subsequence captures this aspect (for instance, ABA and AAB both include subsequences AA and AB). Third, sequences differ regarding the duration of 'spells' (i.e. the number of successive time units with identical states). Fourth, they differ regarding the time at which each state appears, what is also called 'timing'. Tools help to capture the 'entropy' or synchrony of sequences—i.e. the fact that they contain the same state at the same time. Fifth, sequences are characterized by their overall length, since sequences can be of uneven length—as illustrated in Figure 9 which plots post-educational careers ranging from four and a half years (i.e. nine semesters, sequence 20) to thirty-seven years (sequence 15).

More details on these tools are available in the introduction to the R package TraMineR (Gabadinho et al. 2011), which has contributed to the spread and to routinizing the use of sequence analysis in the last decade.

FINDING TEMPORAL STRUCTURES
IN GROUPS OF SEQUENCES

Most research projects that rest on SA aim at identifying temporal structures that are shared within a set of sequences in three steps: first, measuring dissimilarities between sequences; second, grouping resembling ones with a clustering procedure (a vast and autonomous methodological territory); third, associating the groups with common typical patterns using sequential (see above) and non-sequential covariates.

For example, Laurent Lesnard and Man Yee Kan (2011) rely on data based on UK time-use surveys in 2000–2001 to study the scheduling of work. In this data, days are divided into 15-minute periods, each defined either by 'working' or 'not-working' (a two-state alphabet). They identify five types of workdays (standard days from 9 a.m. to 5 p.m., morning/night shift, etc.) by measuring pairwise dissimilarities between work-days and by using a clustering algorithm to group similar sequences.

The first step (measuring dissimilarities between sequences) is a central issue in SA (Studer and Ritschard 2016). The most popular family of metrics, to which belongs OMA, consists in editing a sequence into another through basic, state-by-state operations: inserting states, deleting states, and substituting one state for another. The term 'indels' is commonly used to designate both insertion and deletion, since deleting a state from one sequence to edit it into another is equivalent to inserting one state into the latter to edit it into the former. Some metrics use both indels and substitutions; some use one type only. As a toy example, take two sequences of four states: PART and SPAR. PART can be edited into SPAR by using four operations of substitution (P -> S, A -> P, R -> A, T ->R) or by inserting state S at the beginning of the sequence (PART becomes SPART) and by deleting the final T (SPART is edited into SPAR).

The more substitutions are used, the more the editing process alters the sequences' content; conversely, the more indels are used, the more it distorts their timing. This arbitration is managed by setting different costs (or weights) to each operation in the editing process. In the toy example, if each substitution costs 1 and each indel 2.5, then the first solution will be preferred over the second one. In the example of ministerial advisers, if the purpose is to pinpoint identical successive positions, but with switches between fields happening at different moments, then indels will be preferred over sub-stitutions. This is done by setting higher costs for substitutions. Reversely, if the focus is on groups of individuals experiencing simultaneously similar but not identical job positions and transitions, then substitutions are preferred over indels.

Substitutions between states are often attributed variable costs (for instance, substi-tuting T to S has a lower cost than substituting S to A) relying on theoretical assump-tions, empirical knowledge about the relative closeness between states, or data-driven parameters (such as transition rates between states observed in the sequences).

The variety of possible options (the relative costs of operations and of substitutions) has been criticized as a shortcoming of dissimilarity metrics by edition, yet it does not impinge much on how operational and fruitful they are. Controlling the parameters of the method by introducing relevant external empirical or theoretical knowledge is

S

actually common to many statistical methods. The analysis is only flawed where these controls are not duly reported and justified.

Alternative methods do not rely at all on editing operations, such as measures based on common elements (e.g. longest common subsequences) or tools based on geometric data analysis MULTIPLE CORRESPONDENCE ANALYSIS AND GEOMETRIC DATA ANALYSIS.

MULTICHANNEL SEQUENCES

SA users agree that histories of social entities unfold in multiple and linked areas. For instance, job careers are probably better understood when linked to residential and family histories. These constitute different 'dimensions' or 'channels' of a same sequence. Various ways to analyse these multiple dimensions have been introduced (for a seminal proposition, see Pollock 2007; for a summary of recent developments, see Blanchard 2019). However, such captivating perspectives demand quality multidimensional temporal data that are often unavailable (see CROSS-SECTIONAL AND LONGITUDINAL STUDIES).

SEQUENCES AND EVENTS

Many RESEARCH QUESTIONS deal with the relationship between isolated events and specific sequential patterns: exploring the antecedents and aftermath of a political, economic, or technological event (e.g. a crash, a putsch); questioning how a major life event modifies a life course (e.g. getting a tenure); investigating how a trajectory affects present outcomes, etc. Tools combining SA and different kinds of REGRESSION ANALYSIS (including event history analysis) offer means to address such questions by identifying sequential patterns and analysing their relationships to isolated events.

SEQUENCES AND NETWORKS

Scholars combining SA with SOCIAL NETWORK ANALYSIS see sequences as structures of relations between events, as means for historicizing relations, as successive positions within networks, or as bases for connections with other sequences through shared events (for a synthesis, see Cornwell 2015). The development of this latter perspective could notably bring new light to the study of interlinkages and synchrony between social processes.

To sum up:

- Sequence analysis refers to a set of quantitative tools used to analyse ordered lists of items, especially categorical time series.
- Describing sequential patterns, identifying temporal structures in a set of sequences, and analysing their relationships with other variables are typical operations of sequence analysis.

· The development of SA tools and their combination with other techniques enrich the study of time and processes in the social sciences.

REFERENCES

Abbott, Andrew. 1995. 'Sequence Analysis: New Methods for Old Ideas'. *Annual Review of Sociology* 21: 93–113.

Blanchard, Philippe. 2019. 'Sequence Analysis'. *Sage Research Methods–Foundation* [online], ed. Paul Atkinson, Sara Delamont, Alexandru Cernat, Joseph W. Sakshaug, and Richard A. Williams. Available at https://methods.sagepub.com/foundations/sequence-analysis (Accessed 13 August 2020).

Blanchard, Philippe, Felix Bühlmann, and Jacques-Antoine Gauthier (eds). 2014. *Advances in Sequence Analysis: Theory, Method, Applications.* London, Springer.

Cornwell, Benjamin. 2015. *Social Sequence Analysis: Methods and Applications.* Cambridge, Cambridge University Press.

Gabadinho, Alexis, Gilbert Ritschard, Matthias Studer, and Nicolas S. Müller. 2011. *Mining Sequence Data in R with the TraMineR Package: A User's Guide.* Geneva, University of Geneva.

Lesnard, Laurent and Man Yee Kan. 2011. 'Investigating Scheduling of Work: A Two-stage Optimal Matching Analysis of Workdays and Workweeks'. *Journal of the Royal Statistical Society Series A* 174(2): 349–368.

Pollock, Gary. 2007. 'Holistic Trajectories: A Study of Combined Employment, Housing and Family Careers by Using Multiple-sequence Analysis'. *Journal of the Royal Statistical Society Series A* 170(1): 167–183.

Ritschard, Gilbert and Matthias Studer. 2018. *Sequence Analysis and Related Approaches: Innovative Methods and Applications.* Cham, Springer.

Stovel, Katherine. 2001. 'Local Sequential Patterns: The Structure of Lynching in the Deep South, 1882–1930'. *Social Forces* 79(3): 843–880.

Studer, Matthias and Gilbert Ritschard. 2016. 'What Matters in Differences between Life Trajectories: A Comparative Review of Sequence Dissimilarity Measures'. *Journal of the Royal Statistical Society Series A* 179(2): 481–511.

SOCIAL NETWORK ANALYSIS

The Significance of Relations

Nicholas Haagensen, Copenhagen Business School and Université libre de Bruxelles,
Lasse Folke Henriksen, Copenhagen Business School

S

Social Network Analysis (SNA) is a methods toolbox for analysing the patterning of social ties and explaining how and why those patterns emerge and what consequences they have for social actors. For example, research on US high-school friendship networks found schools that successfully mix students by race for afterschool activities have lower racial friendship segregation (Moody 2001). A social network is a set of nodes (e.g. actors) and a set of edges (or ties) that interconnect to form paths between the nodes. Nodes can represent individuals, objects, organizations, events, or texts (Borgatti et al. 2009). Edges can represent relations—e.g. similarities, social relations, interactions, or flows. Edges can be codified in binary terms as present or absent, or can be assigned weights denoting their strength.

Social networks are ubiquitous in the social world, either unfolding in face-to-face interactions or digitally. In recent decades SNA has grown in popularity, appealing broadly to students interested in complex social structures. The recent availability of data based on digital traces of social relations (e.g. emails or social media profiles) has further prompted students to study these network structures.

The edges in a network indicate some form of relation between the nodes and the paths indicate how all the nodes are interconnected and can be reached from a distance. Analysing how actors are connected through other actors via paths may indicate how e.g. information or resources flow through the network via these ties. In his seminal article on 'The Strength of Weak Ties', Granovetter (1973) argues that weak ties such as acquaintanceships have strong benefits for individuals searching for novel opportunities such as jobs. Bridging to more distant regions of one's personal network, weak ties tend to carry non-redundant information, as opposed to our closer relationships which often reinforce our existing beliefs and information. Also, referring a job opportunity offered by a family member or a close friend to a significant other may carry certain risks—e.g. if one's significant other turns out to be an unreliable employee. Social network analysts often strive to look at how broader network structures matter, and not just pairwise (dyadic) relations between actors. Granovetter's study exemplifies how finding a job is shaped by the complex structure of paths across groups.

We can use various SNA techniques to tease out structural characteristics pertaining to the network as a whole and its individual nodes. The SNA idiom places nodes in positions within networks—positions that both enable and constrain action. Also, SNA allows for temporal fluidity, where, when the actors change positions (by changing ties), the network also changes, and vice versa. The network as analytical construct enables students to consider both aspects. Increasingly, SNA has been applied to a wide variety of empirical areas in the social sciences—e.g. policymaking, criminal/terrorist groups, interlocking boards of directors, citation patterns in scholarship, transnational professionals, the diffusion of innovations and ideas, etc.

The visualization of social networks enables students to interpret the meaning of network characteristics spatially and are a key component in SNA. We will thus introduce selected terms and measures using graphical representations. In Figure 10, a *path* is indicated passing from node *f* to *b* via *e*, *d* and *c*. When two nodes are connected by an edge, they are *adjacent*. Furthermore, when there is a sequence of edges and nodes connecting a pair of nodes, it is called a *path* and indicates that the pair is *reachable* (Wasserman and Faust 1994). The distance between two nodes is conventionally measured through the *shortest path distance*—i.e. the number of steps it requires for one node to reach the other. The distance between adjacent nodes is one.

Social networks can take various shapes. Figures 10 to 13 are stylized and simple networks with fundamentally different structural characteristics. For example, star-shaped networks are highly centralized around a centre (e.g. one central node) connecting peripheral 'satellites' (Figure 10). In contrast, cliques—maximally connected subgroups of three or more nodes—have a more dispersed structure (Figure 11). Networks can become highly complex, comprising hundreds of nodes and edges, in which case the analysis of their structure will require statistical measures. Next, we discuss various measures used in the analysis of both node-level and network-level characteristics of social networks.

At the node-level (see LEVELS OF ANALYSIS), a common approach for measuring the prominence of nodes is by looking at their *centrality*. There are multiple conceptions of network centrality and different measures have been developed to account for these conceptual differences. For example, *degree* centrality is simply the number of edges that are adjacent to a node (Freeman 1978). Thus, if a node has two edges it has a degree of two. Node *a* in Figure 10 has a high degree centrality as it is connected to all the nodes in the network, whereas node *b* has a low degree centrality being connected to only one node. Conceptually, degree centrality is a robust indication of the level of embeddedness of an actor in e.g. a criminal group (Sarnecki 2001), but does not necessarily capture well the network-wide influence of a node.

Node *d* in Figure 12 has a low degree centrality, being only connected to two nodes. However, it is positioned *between* two groups of nodes along a *path* and can thus exert some form of influence—e.g. control the flow of information. Thus, node *d* has a high *betweenness centrality*. This measure calculates the number of times a node is a unique connection point on the *shortest path* between two other nodes. Conceptually, an actor that is not central based on degree but on *betweenness* could wield influence by controlling the flow of information between e.g. two groups of criminals. Similarly, studies of epidemiology illustrate the utility of SNA in tracking the possible spread of a disease by determining an infected actor's unique position between different groups in a given network (Moody 2002). In that way, centrality measures offer different insights into how an actor's unique position, whether it is characterized by e.g. high degree centrality or betweenness centrality, may affect the overall structure of the network. In terms of epidemiology, the spread of coronavirus in 2020 offers an illustration of how infected actors can spread a disease via their interaction and movement between different groups across national borders.

At the network-level, a range of measures is available to account for different aspects of cohesion of the network. The level of cohesion in a network matters for information diffusion, the monitoring and enforcement of norms, and for the formation of tight group identities. For example, corporate elite scholars have shown that a densely-connected network of board members among the largest and most powerful corporations emerged in the US and the UK throughout the twentieth century and produced politically united corporate elites which developed class-based identities and spoke with one voice vis-à-vis the state (Useem 1984). More recently, this network has fractured, becoming less cohesive, leading to a corporate elite characterized by political fragmentation (Mizruchi 2013). Scholars have also examined how short-term strategies and performance of corporations, or short-termism, stems from the fragmentation of the American corporate elite network (Benton and Cobb 2019).

Network cohesion can be measured in different ways. The first is *average path distance*, which measures the average of the shortest path distances of all the pairs of nodes in the network. In Figure 11, the average path distance is 1 because every node is connected to every other, resulting in a high cohesion. By contrast, Figure 12 is more fragmented with an average path distance of approx. 2.2, and therefore has less cohesion. To measure other aspects of a network's cohesion, we use two complementary concepts: *centralization* and *density*. Density expresses the cohesion of the network based on the number of edges compared to the total number of possible edges, while centralization expresses to what degree 'cohesion is organised around particular focal points [nodes]' (Scott 2017: 102). In Figure 11, we can see that all nodes are connected to each other and therefore the network has the maximum number of edges, making it maximally dense with a density of 1. A network of *isolates*, none of which are connected to each other, is 0. While Figure 11 is highly cohesive, its centralization is low given that the edges are dispersed across the entire network, with all nodes connecting to all others. In contrast, Figure 10 is highly centralized around node *a*, but is less dense as there are fewer edges in terms of the total number of possible edges.

For SNA, the relevant data expresses connections between entities, thus it is considered *relational*. As such, sampling and measurement error are particularly problematic. Imagine that Figure 12 is a friendship network of a work team, where an edge is present if two nodes socialize outside of the work setting more than twice a year. Imagine again that node *b* failed to respond to a survey asking about the frequency of socializing among colleagues. Even if nodes *a* and *c* reported that they interact privately with *b*, which is a likely valid response, the lack of report from *b* means that the observed structure of the network is likely to be invalid. Given that all nodes are connected to at least two other nodes, the likelihood of *b* being connected to *c*, *f*, or *g* is non-negligible. If *b* is connected to the leftmost triad of nodes, any network- or node-level measure that relies on shortest path distances in the entire network are significantly altered. This also means that sampling network data involves pitfalls. Knowledge of whether some significant respondents are part of a network may be based on a specific respondent, whose concealment would lead to significant measurement error. Some measures however are relatively robust to sampling and measurement error—e.g. degree centrality.

A related problem is that of 'hidden populations' when we aim to uncover e.g. a policy network. Depending on our criteria of belonging to the network, we do not know who belongs to the network beforehand, thus there is no population. To overcome this, we can deploy snowball sampling (see **SAMPLING TECHNIQUES**) where a start population of known key policymakers is asked to report on collaborations with other policymakers. This survey is likely to yield hitherto unobserved policymakers that would again have to be surveyed about their collaborators in a second wave of the snowball. When no new names appear in the *n*th snowball iteration—indicating a saturated sample—the boundary of the network is identified. This is obviously not a random strategy, but it is considered viable if one wants to avoid the paucity of relations that often appear in random sampling in SNA (Scott 2017).

SNA has been criticized for being more descriptive than inferential—i.e. it entails mapping the nodes and edges and describing the characteristics of the network

FIGURES 10, 11, 12, 13 Social networks can take various shapes. Figures 10 to 13 represent stylized and simple networks

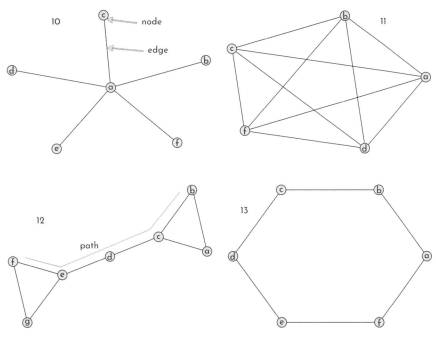

(Scott 2017). However, more recent methodological developments, and the collection and availability of temporal network data, has enabled significant advances in inferential network analytic techniques, such as random graph models, which are better able to explain the emergence of social networks, as opposed to only mapping them (Robins et al. 2007). For example, Lazega, Lemercier, and Mouniea (2006) developed a model based on longitudinal 'advice' network data of 240 court judges based on the patterns of advice seeking that occurs between them. The model suggests that, even though the pattern of advice seeking among the judges changes over time because of systematic job rotation, there is still a 'cognitive' elite—i.e. a few highly sought-after advisers—who maintain accumulated knowledge. Thus, this pattern of advice seeking centralizes the network.

Various software packages enable students to perform SNA. A high-quality entry-level software package is UCINET, which has an accessible graphical user interface and an associated visualization device (NetDraw). UCINET, as well as Pajek, offers a multitude of algorithms to calculate structural measures at both node, group, and network level, as well as statistical techniques to draw inferences on network structure. Gephi is also an accessible software package particularly well-suited for visualization. All of these packages enable the researcher to measure, manipulate, and visualize network data. More advanced software packages are developed within the R statistical programming environment as well as Python. This requires students to acquire programming skills.

SNA is a versatile method and can be used in conjunction with other methods, allowing for **TRIANGULATION**. For example, SNA can be used in conjunction with **PROSO-POGRAPHY**—the reconstruction of the collective biography of a group—to see whether certain attributes of the group members are associated with certain network positions. Finally, SNA somewhat resembles **SYSTEMS ANALYSIS**, which looks at the interdependent parts of a system, its emergent properties, and its evolution over time.

REFERENCES

Benton, Richard A. and J. Adam Cobb. 2019. 'Eyes on the Horizon? Fragmented Elites and the Short-term Focus of the American Corporation'. *American Journal of Sociology* 124(6): 1631-1684.

Borgatti, Stephan, Ajay Mehra, Daniel J. Brass, and Giuseppe Labianca. 2009. 'Network Analysis in the Social Sciences'. *Science* 323(5916): 892-895.

Freeman, Linton C. 1978. 'Centrality in Social Networks: Conceptual Clarification'. *Social Networks* 1(3): 215-239.

Granovetter, Mark. 1973. 'The Strength of Weak Ties'. *American Journal of Sociology* 78(6): 1360-1380.

Lazega, Emmanuel, Claire Lemercier, and Lise Mouniea. 2006. 'A Spinning Top Model of Formal Organization and Informal Behaviour: Dynamics of Advice Networks Among Judges in a Commercial Court'. *European Management Review* 3(2): 113-122.

Mizruchi, James. 2013. *The Fracturing of the American Corporate Elite*. Boston, MA, Harvard University Press.

Moody, James. 2001. 'Race, School Integration, and Friendship Segregation in America'. *American Journal of Sociology* 107(3): 679-716.

Moody, James. 2002. 'The Importance of Relationship Timing for Diffusion'. *Social Forces* 81(1): 25-56.

Robins, Garry L., Philippa E. Pattison, Yuval Kalish, and Dean Lusher. 2007. 'An Introduction to Exponential Random Graph (p*) Models for Social Networks'. *Social Networks* 29(2): 173-191.

Sarnecki, Jerzy. 2001. *Delinquent Networks: Youth Co-offending in Stockholm*. Cambridge, Cambridge University Press.

Scott, John. 2017. *Social Network Analysis*. Thousand Oaks, CA, SAGE Publications.

Useem, Michael. 1984. *The Inner Circle: Large Corporations and the Rise of Business Political Activity in the US and UK*. New York, Oxford University Press.

Wasserman, Stanley and Katherine Faust. 1994. *Social Network Analysis: Methods and Applications*. Cambridge, Cambridge University Press.

SOURCE CRITICISM

Kenneth Bertrams & Anne Weyembergh, Université libre de Bruxelles

Source criticism is a technical and intellectual method used to track down the itinerary of a source of information. It aims to identify the producer, determine its initial meaning and establish its conformity as an authentic unaltered source that yields truthful information. This provisional definition, which owes a great deal to the positivist legacy of nineteenth-century scholarship, applies especially to the document-based disciplines of the humanities (see **ARCHIVAL RESEARCH**), as well as to the early academic fields of law and theology. However, the notion of source has developed beyond the strictly defined printed document. Consequently, the general aims of source criticism are now widely shared by all social science disciplines. Though interdisciplinary in nature, its treatment and implementation vary according to the fields and sources concerned. The use and application of criticism can differ considerably depending on whether a study relies directly on people, documents, or other potential evidence. Different approaches often have common features, even when the objectives differ. For example, though their methods are very different, judges and historians show some convergence: they both collect evidence, sources, and clues to seek and establish a truth.

The principle is undisputed: source criticism provides scientific legitimacy and rigour in the social science disciplines, where the nature and diversity of levels of intermediation and interpretation in the observational and empirical process can often prove misleading. Hence, we could suggest (with exaggeration) that source criticism has become the backbone of modern scientific method in social science research and/or practice, much like **EXPERIMENTATION** in natural science. Source criticism has become an indispensable methodological tool for most social science researchers and scholars. It pertains to other types of textual methods (**CONTENT ANALYSIS, DISCOURSE ANALYSIS**) insofar as it corresponds to a qualitative methodology of analysis. However, source criticism does not share the social concerns and purposes of **CONTENT ANALYSIS**, conversation analysis, and **DISCOURSE ANALYSIS**. As a text-based documentary analysis, source criticism chiefly aims at examining the authenticity—and potential alteration—of original sources, as well as their successive reproduction leading to divergent levels of interpretation (**HERMENEUTICS**). As a method, it may have inspired the techniques that are used today to prevent plagiarism, though its initial scope in the early nineteenth century was limited to the small world of scholars.

It is widely accepted that the German historian Leopold von Ranke (1795–1886) was the first to provide a systematic set of critical questions that the scholar should ask when analysing (written) sources. These are usually broken down into two categories: external and internal criticism. It is important to note that the two methods are like both sides of the same coin: each type of criticism should be conducted individually, but only the synthesis of both operations indicates the validity of the sources examined. External criticism, which comes first, considers the source as an object. As such, it tends to determine the authenticity and origin of a document through the writing, the forms of language, etc. The questions pertaining to external criticism are: Where, when and who produced the source? Is the document an original or a copy? How did it travel through time? A practical technique used to flush out a potential counterfeit involves carefully cross-checking the various stages of production and diffusion of a source and comparing their successive versions. This protocol can reveal voluntary or unforced formal mistakes in a document, regardless of its content, in which case internal criticism is required. Internal criticism is a necessary complement to external criticism. It deals with the content and the meaning of the source. It is primarily concerned with the quality and reliability of the information contained in the source. It examines the author's precision, competence, sincerity, etc.

What did the author mean? Did the author believe in what he/she said? Internal criticism encompasses four different critical approaches to the source of information: interpretation, authority, exactitude, and sincerity. All of these subtypes may vary as a function of the nature of the source examined. For instance, a picture-based source may be loaded with different levels of meaning and be assigned contradictory interpretations. It is essential for the researcher to try to orient his criticism in reference to the author's original intention. Another example concerns the status of testimonies based on the observation provided by witnesses. To what extent are these documents a faithful expression of their authors' intention? Were the authors competent in the matter described? These questions, which also apply to the status of reports drafted by experts, belong to the (internal) criticism of authority. A combined analysis of the external and internal criticisms should then be conducted for each source. All sources should be analysed in relation to each other.

In the nineteenth century, Ranke's programme was rooted in the tenets of POSI-TIVISM. It was infused with the wider project of making history a full-fledged objective science despite its methodological concern with contingent, unique, and factual knowledge (see NOMOTHETIC AND IDIOGRAPHIC METHODS). Above all, source criticism was initially developed in (and designed for) all forms of scholarship with a strong philological or textual tradition.

Debunking falsehood became a central intellectual mission for scholars. This led the German philologist Karl Lachmann to develop a sophisticated method of textual criticism that revolved around the notion of 'archetype'. This was defined as an authentic copy of the (missing) original source, which could in turn produce several derivatives. The fundamentals of Lachmann's 'common error-method' were to track down all mistakes between the various copies, discard those with too many apparent errors, and organize the remaining manuscripts in chronological order until the most authentic copy—the archetype—has been established (Boone 2015: 105–109). Philip Graves, journalist at *The Times*, pursued a similar goal to distinguish truth from falsehood in written sources. In 1921, he exposed *The Protocols of the Elders of Zion* (which came to be known as one of the most virulent anti-Semitic pamphlets of the early twentieth century) as a hoax, the result of plagiarism and historical forgery (Jacobs and Weitzman 2003). Graves had first applied the method of external criticism before turning to internal criticism. Both techniques were instrumental to demonstrating the fraudulent origins and the fabricated nature of the document, as well as to rebut its status as historically accurate factual evidence.

The erudite legacy of critical scholarship is still very present in social science education. However, it is important to note that the basic principles of source criticism cannot be reduced to the traditional written or printed document. For example, in law, especially criminal law, establishing judicial truth—which is not necessarily identical to factual truth—involves source criticism, both with written and oral sources (testimonies). As mentioned previously, principles of source criticism apply to a wide array of disciplines, particularly in domains where manipulation, fraud, and falsification (in the sense of producing a forgery) can pervert the chain of information. Undoubtedly, text and image manipulation has never been simpler than in the digital age. As far as digital images are concerned, they 'have much less standardized production processes than photographs. These processes are less subject to institutional policing of uniformity, offer more opportunities for human intervention' (Mitchell 1994: 223). However, technological innovation is also beneficial to source criticism, since it makes it easier for scholars and other professionals to track down falsehood. The Vinland map is a useful illustration. It was publicly introduced at a scientific conference in 1965 and received wide academic acclaim. The document was presented as one of the oldest pre-Columbian world maps available. Shortly after the conference, several geographers questioned its authenticity by pointing out a strange similarity with more modern cartographic efforts. This sparked major controversy. Chemical analysis of the ink, x-ray experiments, and radiocarbon dating were conducted. All the techniques identified the use of modern pigments in a map that allegedly dated back to the fifteenth century. Significant portions of the Vinland map were simply not medieval (Seaver 2004). Since the Vinland map case, scientific techniques/methods to identify counterfeited or forged documents or objects have developed further. Here again, both sides of source criticism— internal and external—were applied, together with the use of technological equipment, to evaluate the claim of historical authenticity of a document.

Source criticism has a long history and, given its importance, it probably has an even longer future.

REFERENCES

Bloch, Marc. 1974 [1941]. *Apologie pour l'histoire ou Métier d'historien*. Paris, Armand Colin.

Boone, Marc. 2015. *Historicienhun métier: Een inleiding tot de historische kritiek*. Ghent, Academia Press.

De Broux, Pierre-Olivier. 2017-2018. *Critique des sources d'information*. Bruxelles, Université Saint-Louis.

Grafton, Anthony. 1997. *The Footnote: A Curious History*. London, Faber and Faber.

Jacobs, Steven L. and Mark Weitzman. 2003. *Dismantling the Big Lie: The Protocols of the Elders of Zion*. New York, Ktav Publishing.

Marquis, Nicolas, Emmanuelle Lenel, and Luc Van Campenhoudt. 2018. *Pratique de la lecture critique en sciences humaines et sociales*. Malakoff, Dunod.

Mitchell, William J. 1994. *The Reconfigured Eye: Visual Truth in the Post-Photographic Era*. Cambridge, MA, MIT Press.

Roth, Robert. 2004. 'Le juge et l'histoire', in *Crimes de l'histoire et réparations: les réponses du droit et de la justice*, ed. Laurence Boisson de Chazournes, Jean-François Quéguiner- and, Santiago Villalpando, 3-11. Brussels, Bruylant.

Seaver, Kirsten A. 2004. *Maps, Myths, and Men: The Story of the Vinland Map*. Stanford, Stanford University Press.

STATISTICAL SIGNIFICANCE

S

Olesya Tkacheva, Vesalius College, VUB

The key question in quantitative analysis is whether a pattern observed in a sample also holds for the population from which the sample was drawn. A positive answer to this question implies that the result is 'statistically significant'—i.e. it was not produced by a random variation from sample to sample, but, instead, reflects the pattern that exists in the population.[1] Suppose you asked a random sample of 100 students at your university to report their level of happiness on a scale from 0 to 100, and found that the average level of happiness in your sample is 76 and the standard deviation is 45. Does this value accurately capture the average happiness score for the entire university (i.e. the population for your study)? Since you do not have the time and resources to ask every student enrolled, you have to make an informed guess about how well the values you computed, based on your sample, approximate the values for the entire university.

The null hypothesis statistical test (NHST) has been a widely used approach for test-ing whether inference from a sample to the population is valid. To set up the NHST you should formulate a **HYPOTHESIS** about the value of your population parameter (i.e. the null hypothesis H_0). The NHST provides information about how likely you are to observe estimated values if your H_0 was true. For example, suppose based on prior studies you believe that the average happiness score for your school should be 66 (which is 10 points lower than your sample mean). The NHST is a decision-making rule that helps determine whether the sample came from the distribution with the mean 66 (H_0: $\mu = 66$) or some other distribution (HA: $\mu \neq 66$). One way to think about the values computed using NHST is as a distance (measured in standard errors (SE)) between the hypothesized under H_0 and observed parameters: $(T = \frac{\mu_{estimated} - \mu_0}{SE(\mu)})$. High values of T correspond to a low probability of observing a specific sample if H_0 was true. These probabilities are referred to as p-values. What constitutes a 'low' probability is in the eyes of the beholder. Some disci-plines consider p-values lower than 0.05 as sufficient evidence against H_0, whereas others require p to be lower than 0.01. It is a convention to call the results 'statistically significant' at 5 per cent level when $p < 0.05$ and at 1 per cent level when $p < 0.01$.

In the context of our example, the standard error $SE(\mu) = \frac{sample\ standard\ deviation}{\sqrt{sample\ size}}$ $= \frac{45}{10} = 4.5$, $T = \frac{76 - 66}{4.5} = 2.22 (df = 99)$, and a corresponding p-value (reported by a statistical software package) is 0.0287. This means that if the population mean is 66, the probability of observing the sample average of 76 is 2.87 per cent. If we believe this prob-ability is high, we do not reject H_0; if we believe that this probability is low, we reject H_0.

The NHST is applicable to a wide range of parameters, including *correlation* coef-ficient and *regression* coefficient. In the case of regression analysis, H_0 is usually for-mulated as 'regression coefficient(s) are equal to zero', and it is tested by computing a test-statistic $(T = \frac{\theta_{estimated} - \theta_0}{SE(\theta)})$ while assuming that H_0 is true (i.e. H_0: $\theta_0 = 0$).

The NHST blends together approaches proposed, respectively, by R. D. Fisher (1935) and by Neyman and Pearson (1933). The key difference between the two ap-proaches consists in the role of the decision rule. The Neyman–Pearson test calls for decision-making based on a critical threshold for rejecting H_0 in favour of the alterna-tive hypothesis. This threshold is frequently referred to a 'significance level' (denoted

---

[1] The question about statistical significance is not relevant to qualitative inquiry because the goal of most qualitative studies is to capture the processes and meanings particular to the specific context. Qualitative inquiry usually does not aspire to make statements generalizable to the pop-ulation outside of the context in which the study was conducted.

by α). We reject H_0 if $p < \alpha$, and fail to reject H_0 otherwise. In our example, we set $\alpha = 0.01$ and failed to reject H_0 at 1 per cent level, but we rejected H_0 at 5 per cent level. The Fisher version of the NHST does not impose any a priori threshold for rejecting H_0.

Statistical software packages report p-values along with parameter estimates. When interpreting them we need to keep in mind that the NHST is asymmetric—i.e. low p-value provides evidence against H_0, but high p-value is inconclusive and cannot be interpreted as favouring H_0. This has to do with the fact that the probability of observing the sample if H_0 is true is not the same as the probability that H_0 is true given the sample. Widespread misinterpretations of the NHST prompted the American Statistical Association to publish the following guidelines about the NHST:

1 P-value measures the probability of observing specific results (data) if H_0 is true. As such, it provides information only about the extent to which sample and corresponding test-statistic are consistent with the description of the population provided by H_0.

2 P-value does not provide any information about whether H_0 is true. Reversing the definition of p-value provided in (1) is incorrect because, in most cases, the probability of observing the specific sample if H_0 is true (definition of p-value) does not equal the probability of H_0 being true if a specific sample is observed. Neither does p-value provide information about the probability that the alternative hypothesis is true.

3 P-value does not provide any information about the magnitude of the effect because statistical significance is not the same as substantive significance of finding. One of the implications of this is that failure to reject H_0 should not be interpreted as meaning the true size of the effect is zero. Making this substantive conclusion is equivalent to accepting H_0. The reason why the language of accepting H_0 should be avoided is because NHST is asymmetric. It is useful for invalidation of H_0, but not for its confirmation.

4 The decision about statistical significance should not be based on p-value alone. Instead a holistic approach that takes into account the sample size, a research design, and other factors should be used.

5 P-value does not equal the probability of rejecting H_0 in the next replication of the study.

In the Neyman–Pearson version of the NHST, the selection of significance level α requires making a trade-off between Type I (rejecting H_0 when it is true) and Type II (failing to reject H_0 when it is false) errors. Lower α guards against Type I but increases the probability of Type II, and vice versa. Since Type II errors could be reduced by increasing sample size, the researcher can determine a priori the minimum required sample to lower the probability of Type II error to the acceptable level. In the context of our example, Type I error would mean concluding that the average level of happiness at your university is not 66, whereas in fact it is 66. Type II error means that you failed to reject that the average level of happiness is 66 when in fact it is not 66.

Increasingly, more scholars (Gill 1999; Krueger 2001; Nickerson 2000; Wasserstein, Schirm, and Lazar 2019) perceive the estimation approach, **BAYESIAN INFERENCE**, and meta-analysis as viable alternatives to the NHST. The estimation approach entails constructing confidence intervals around estimates to provide information about their sample-to-sample variability. When using the estimation approach with **REGRESSION ANALYSIS**, it is useful to report how sensitive confidence intervals are to alternative specifications of the regression equation (Leamer 1983). Bayesian analysis enables comparisons between H_0 and multiple alternative **HYPOTHESES** by computing likelihood ratios for each alternative model. Meta-analysis enables results to be compared systematically across multiple studies to determine whether the variance in a set of studies is attributable to the specific sample and the research design or whether it was produced by some real effect. Overall, seeking to test whether valid inferences about the population could be made based on the results from a single sample, a researcher should consider a wide variety of approaches and take into the account not only p-values, but also sampling process, sample size, the quality of measurement, and other factors that may influence the reliability of estimates.

REFERENCES

Gill, Jeff. 1999. 'The Insignificance of Null Hypothesis Significance Testing'. *Political Research Quarterly* 52(3): 647–674.

Krueger, Joachim. 2001. 'Null Hypothesis Significance Testing: On the Survival of a Flawed Method'. *American Psychologist* 56(1): 16–26.

Leamer, Edward E. 1983. 'Let's Take the Con Out of Econometrics'. *American Economic Review* 73(1): 31–43.

Nickerson, Raymond S. 2000. 'Null Hypothesis Significance Testing: A Review of an Old and Continuing Controversy'. *Psychological Methods* 5(2): 241–301.

Wasserstein, Ronald L., Allen L. Schirm, and Nicole A. Lazar. 2019. 'Moving to a World Beyond "p < 0.05"'. *The American Statistician* 73(1): 1–19.

SURVEY RESEARCH

Lior Gideon, John Jay College of Criminal Justice,
Kevin Barnes-Ceeney, University of New Haven

Surveys are a very common method of data collection used by many social researchers. As such, they are used in public opinion polls to gauge political trends and trait, but also in marketing research examining consumer behaviour and feedback. Surveys are also a common data collection method in many social research projects (e.g. examining punitive attitudes, and support of social policies). They are further used to evaluate needs, processes, and outcomes. Importantly, surveys are a unidirectional communication approach to collect data, which is very different from **OBSERVATIONAL METHODS**, semi-structured and structured **INTERVIEWS**, or other types of data collection where the researcher takes an active role. Specifically, using surveys, participants are presented with a set of instructions and predetermined questions. The researcher is not expected to engage in any participatory interaction or in-depth conversation with participants.

Surveys are commonly used by practitioners who seek to gain information about the services they render and ways to improve their connections with clients. While the term 'survey' may be used by researchers in various fields, in this entry surveys will be referred to as a basic data collection method in which the researcher collects data by asking questions to a sample (see SAMPLING TECHNIQUES) of respondents, to describe and generalize the results to the overall population/UNIT OF ANALYSIS of interest. Questions that are asked are an attempt, by the researcher, to gain accurate knowledge of the phenomena. Not only do surveys provide description, they also help measure, explain, and predict (e.g. election outcomes, consumer demand and consumer decision-making when buying products, support of policies based on evaluation research, etc.). Description, explanation, or prediction abilities will vary by the researcher's ability to design the survey and its components with high levels of sensitivity and accuracy. Such sensitivity and accuracy will be achieved by carefully designing survey items to be valid—does the survey measure the trait we want to measure?—and reliable—does the survey provide consistent observations over repeated measurements?

The information obtained by the survey leans on reports received at different points in time by multiple respondents. As such, surveys rely on unidirectional communication—one person asks the questions (e.g. open-ended questions, multiple-choice questions, or scale/ranked questions), and another is expected to provide the answers. Accordingly, a basic definition of a survey is:

> A method that relies on verbal reports about past, present, and future experiences, in such a way that will later allow the researcher to use statistical procedures to analyse the data gathered, using such methods as basic descriptive statistics, correlational analysis, and multivariate analysis models that will enable the researcher to conduct inferences from sample to population.

It is important to acknowledge that surveys are not free from error. Specifically, surveys lean on different methodologies, such as SAMPLING, question design, and mode of communication—face-to-face, telephone, mail, or web-based—and actual research design. Overwhelmingly research shows that paper-based surveys have higher response rates than emailed surveys (Yimeng et al 2016). It is within this context that surveys are vulnerable to potential errors and BIAS that may affect the survey reliability and validity. Accordingly, it is important to address issues of potential response errors, as well as non-response and sampling errors in surveys. Surveys using random sampling-based techniques to achieve a representative sample with high external validity, usually account for a margin of error of about 4.5 to 5 per cent. Such a margin of error provides a confidence interval of up to 95 per cent when inferring results from sample to population (see STATISTICAL SIGNIFICANCE). However, such a margin of error is almost negligent in scope compared to non-sampling errors that are often neglected or ignored during the design and execution of the survey.

It is estimated that non-sampling errors in surveys account for about 95 per cent of total survey errors (Fowler 2014; Gideon 2012; Weisberg 2005). These non-sampling errors are

S

usually located in the design of the survey, and how **VARIABLES** are conceptualized and constructed. Non-sampling errors are also a by-product of bad survey design that negatively affects the flow and rationale of the survey and may also jeopardize the researcher's ability to accurately examine research question/s and related variables of interests. Such errors affect the reliability and validity of the data collected (for a more in-depth discussion on non-sampling errors refer to Kott 1993; Lessler and Kalsbeek 1992). Specifically, non-sampling errors are divided into response errors and non-response errors.

Response errors may occur due to the following reasons:

1 Social desirability—In its most basic form, social desirability occurs when respondents tend to present themselves in a favourable manner. People usually do not like to be viewed negatively and, as a result, will change their responses in a way they believe will present themselves favourably to the interviewer. Topics that are commonly subject to social desirability **BIAS** include unfavourable political opinions, alcohol use, and aggressive, deviant, and criminal behaviours. Accordingly, issues of social desirability are particularly relevant when surveys are administered by an interviewer in a face-to-face interaction.

2 Visibility—Many times respondents will answer questions without proper consideration. In today's world people seem to be overwhelmed by many activities and thus tend to 'multitask'. Visibility manifests itself when respondents provide answers to survey questions when they are not fully focused on the actual survey and the questions asked. For example, many telephone surveys are conducted in the late afternoon/early evening when most people are preoccupied with different domestic chores, such as preparing dinner, and watching television. While respondents may be willing to respond to questions, they may not be fully committed to the survey, may not think thoroughly about the questions, and their responses may therefore be of low quality. Some strategies to minimize visibility issues may include short and simple questions, and an overall focused survey questionnaire with fewer questions. Building validity checks into the survey can also be useful. When asking about young people's drug use, Maguire, Wells, and Katz (2011) ask whether the non-existent drug phenoxydine had ever been used. The authors were then able to exclude from their analysis the surveys completed by the ninety-one young people who claimed they had used the made-up drug.

3 Sensitivity—Questions about income, political affiliation, sexual orientation, sexual partners, illegal activity, drug and alcohol consumption, extreme-right political preferences or racist beliefs are just few examples of sensitive topics examined by surveys. While surveys tend to be an appropriate method to collect primary source information, sensitive questions may receive response errors that are related to social desirability. Here, respondents may mask the truth by providing low-quality responses that will present themselves in a favourable light. Because surveys are self-reports, sensitive question items may be subject to questionable data that may result in systematic error. To overcome this problem, researchers tend to use a number of items that examine the exact same trait, thus promoting equivalent measurement reliability. For example, one question seeks to find out if the respondent

smokes, and a few questions later another question will ask what brand of cigarettes the respondent prefers. Obviously if a respondent answers 'no' to the first question the other question will have to receive a value of 'not applicable'.

4 Question BIAS—Researchers often fail to pay attention to the balance provided in response options to closed-ended questions. For example, researchers may provide names of leading candidates while ignoring the names of other candidates. Such bias leads to false perceptions of who the leading candidate may be and how truly popular she or he is. Question bias may also be introduced in the form of induced expected answers—answers that lead respondents to particular answers. A potential solution to this issue may be achieved by providing an 'other' category.

5 Unclear/cumbersome question phrasing—Related to question BIAS, but more broad, are poorly designed survey items. Designing survey questions is an art of creating a precise measurement tool. However, researchers often forget that the task of creating a survey item is not a conversational enquiry. Good survey questions maximize the relationship between the answers recorded and the trait the researcher is seeking to measure. Unfortunately, researchers are often careless when planning survey items and, as a result, craft badly phrased and structured questions. Poor phrasing of questions includes using unfamiliar or grammatically incorrect terminology, ambiguous terms and concepts, being overly wordy, and assuming respondent's knowledge that may not exist—all of which contribute to low-quality responses and systematic response errors. To overcome this problem, it is important to pilot-test survey items on a sample of people before the full launch of the survey.

Non-response errors may occur due to the following reasons:

1 Refusals—Potential respondents may refuse to participate or answer some of the survey questions. Refusal can be a result of various reasons such as lack of time or interest, embarrassment caused by sensitive topics, lack of trust in the organization conducting the survey, and even bad chemistry with the interviewer. If not monitored, refusals can result in selection BIAS and, as a result, affect survey outcomes.

2 Missing—Missing refers to two types of missing responses: selected respondents are difficult to locate and thus fail to participate in the survey, hence creating missing data; the other is missing responses for specific survey items. Missing responses for specific survey items can be either random or systematic. If the reason for non-response is missing participants, then it is important to understand why these potential participants are missing to control for selection BIAS within the sample. For example, researchers surveying school children about their experience of truancy may miss the views of those who truant frequently if the survey is only given to pupils during regular class periods in school. If, on the other hand, there are survey items that are missing responses, then it is essential to examine the items that are missing responses in terms of their phrasing, sensitivity, clarity, and visual appearance and location on the survey page. Visual appearance and location can account for random missing responses, while phrasing, clarity, and sensitivity can account for systematic missing responses, which may BIAS results.

3   Do not understand—A direct result of bad phrasing. Many times, researchers tend to phrase questions that seem clear to them but are not clear to participants. They do so by using professional language, high-level terminology, and convoluted sentences. Confused respondents may provide non-responses, or low-quality responses, as previously discussed in the response errors list. For example Agnew (1991), when examining peer delinquency, asks young people how many of their close friends have destroyed property. Using the term 'close' could be problematic for respondents, as closeness is not specifically defined. Agnew acknowledges that peer associations may be formed out of necessity rather than choice, and therefore the term 'close friends' may be poorly operationalized.

4   Literacy issues—These depend on the survey mode, and are particularly important when surveys are self-administered, and people are not fluent in the language used in the survey, so may not participate. This problem can be solved by identifying the target population ahead of time and ensuring that surveys are translated into the languages spoken within the target population. In addition, trained interviewers may be needed to assist during data collection.

Non-sampling error can be mitigated by the mode and administration of the survey. In face-to-face surveys, where interviewers are used to administer the survey and collect the data, great emphasis should be given to interviewer training. Interviewers can be considered as being on a continuum, from 'cold' to 'warm' personalities (see Hornik 1988). Both continuum ends may engender the systematic errors of low response rates, high levels of social desirability, and low-quality responses. 'Warm' interviewers tend to be overly talkative, providing information unrelated to the research. A 'warm personality' may be liked by the respondent and, while this may increase overall response rates, it may prompt social desirability BIAS, and negatively impact responses. On the other hand, 'cold personalities' are mechanical/robotic, following survey instructions and questions precisely in a monotonic fashion. As a result, respondents may feel that the interviewer is uninterested in their responses and may provide low-quality responses, or even refuse to respond. The desired personality takes the middle ground. This will be a person trained in the survey, with a mellow demeanour, speaking fluently and without any distinct accent, providing adequate feedback, and positively encouraging respondents to think about difficult questions and continue the survey to its conclusion. Accordingly, training of interviewers is important (see Gideon and Moskos 2019). Other traits such as social status, ethnicity, gender, and age of the interviewer, may also affect the quality of responses provided, and in particular when these are similar/different to the interviewee (see Hox, de Leeuw, and Kreft 1991). Pilot-testing the survey is critical to ensure that questions are easy to interpret and that the quality of responses received are adequate to the measures examined.

Careful and considered survey design is critical to overcome response and non-response errors (see Gideon 2012; Payne 2014). Although many people think that designing a survey is an easy task of identifying suitable questions, a good survey requires planning and careful examination of every item, the order in which item is presented, and the scales (i.e. levels of measurements) used. This is important as survey items should be treated as a measurement that aims to answer specific RESEARCH QUESTION/S, and thus survey items should correspond and relate to the big research question and the **VARIABLES** it aims to examine. Accordingly, each survey item is an independent construct of the main variables of the study and as such must enjoy face validity, construct validity, and internal reliability (see **CONCEPT CONSTRUCTION** and **OPERATIONALIZATION**).

REFERENCES

Agnew, Robert. 1991. 'The Interactive Effects of Peer Variables on Delinquency'. *Criminology* 29(1): 47–72.

Fowler, Floyd J. Jr. 2014. *Survey Research Methods*. Thousand Oaks, CA, SAGE Publications.

Gideon, Lior. 2012. *Handbook of Survey Methodology for the Social Sciences*. New York, Springer.

Gideon, Lior and Peter C. Moskos. 2019. 'Interviewing', in *Handbook of Survey Methodology for the Social Sciences*, 3rd edition, ed. Lior Gideon, 319–334. New York, Springer.

Hornik, Jacob. 1988. 'The Essence of Surveys', in *Surveys and Public Opinion Polls*, ed. Jacob Hornik, 17–29. Tel-Aviv, Open University Press.

Hox, Joop J., Edith D. de Leeuw, and Ita G. G. Kreft. 1991. 'The Effect of Interviewer and Respondent Characteristics on the Quality of Survey Data: A Multilevel Model', in *Measurement Errors in Surveys*, ed. Paul P. Biemer, Robert M. Groves, Lars E. Lyberg, Nancy A. Mathiowetz, and Seymour Sudman, 439–461. Hoboken, NJ, Wiley Publishing.

Kott, Phillip S. 1993. 'Non-sampling Error in Surveys'. *Journal of the American Statistical Association* 88(424): 1470–1472.

Lesser, Virginia M. and William D. Kalsbeek. 1992. *Non-sampling Error in Surveys*. New York, John Wiley.

Maguire, Edward R., William Wells, and Charles Katz. 2011. 'Measuring Community Risk and Protective Factors for Adolescent Problem Behaviors: Evidence from a Developing Nation'. *Journal of Research in Crime and Delinquency* 48(4): 594–620.

Payne, Stanley Le Baron. 2014. *The Art of Asking Questions: Studies in Public Opinion*, 3rd edition. Princeton, NJ, Princeton University Press.

Weisberg, Herbert F. 2005. *The Total Survey Error Approach: A Guide to the New Science of Survey Research*. Chicago, University of Chicago Press.

Yimeng, Guo, Jacek A. Kopec, Yolanda Cibere, Linda C. Li, and Charles H. Goldsmith. 2016. 'Population Survey Features and Response Rates: A Randomized Experiment'. *American Journal of Public Health* 106(8): 1422–1426.

SYSTEMS ANALYSIS

Guillaume Beaumier, University of Warwick and Université Laval,
Didier Wernli, University of Geneva

Systems analysis broadly refers to the theories and methods used in the study of interdependent elements forming a complex whole (i.e. a system). The field has developed in many areas of science since the middle of the twentieth century (Capra and Luisi 2014). At its heart, it departs from methodological reductionism or the idea that we can understand the whole by knowing the parts. In other words, *the whole is more than the sum of its parts*. In the wake of the work of Descartes and Newton, modern science has focused on explaining our world by splitting it into ever smaller components and mechanisms. Proponents of systems analysis hold that interacting systems exhibit properties that we cannot understand by only looking at their individual parts. Complexity science notably aims to explain the properties that govern complex systems such as non-linearity, emergence, self-regulation, and adaptation.

In both natural and social sciences, the systems view of life has gained traction in recent years. The number of studies adopting a systemic lens is increasing. Yet, systems analysis remains relatively marginal. This is particularly the case in the social sciences where, despite pioneer works by David Easton in political science, and Talcott Parsons and Niklas Luhmann in sociology, systems analysis has not been adopted by a broad set of scholars. Complex social systems are however ubiquitous. The market or the international system are two prominent examples. In both cases, the behaviour of the system emerges from the everyday interactions of multiple actors (i.e. economic agents or states) with limited central control. As these two examples suggest, the concept of system closely relates to the structure–agent debate. In the work of the political scientist Kenneth Waltz (1979), the international system is effectively perceived as a structure which constrains and influences states' actions. In other words, he uses the system as a VARIABLE to mechanically explain states' behaviour in the international realm. However, in recent years, complexity scholars have become increasingly interested in unpacking the processes emerging from the interactions between multiple units or agents. As such, they do not see the system as a VARIABLE, but as an outcome. They moreover consider that the different elements of a system are co-constituted and hence embrace a relational ONTOLOGY. The goal of systems analysis is then to understand how interactions between individual parts give rise to properties that cannot be explained by looking at them separately.

The first step in any systems analysis is to define its boundary. In effect, natural or social systems are always part of a broader environment. Biological cells are part of broader living organisms. Similarly, national states are constitutive elements of the international system. While boundaries are often obvious, some systems (e.g. ecosystem) have fuzzier boundaries. Contrary to closed systems, which function in isolation and remain in equilibrium, complex adaptive systems are notably open and dissipative. They require constant flows of energy from their environment to maintain and develop their complexity (Prigogine 1978. Those systems are thus both defined by a constant tension between closure and openness, which reflect the relative density and sparsity of the interactions between their constitutive elements and their environment. As a result, when analysing complex systems, it is crucial to state the rules behind the inclusion or exclusion of elements from the system under study. As Cilliers (2001: 141) points out, those rules will normally be both 'a function of the activity of the system itself, and a product of the strategy of description involved'. In the end, it is also important to remember that boundaries can be tools to describe interactions within and between systems.

Having defined a system's boundary, multiple methods are available to scholars wishing to perform systems analysis. In practice, systems analysis will often require the use of MIXED METHODS that combine the collection and analysis of quantitative and qualitative data. Data collection will importantly have to be adjusted on a case-by-case basis depending on the precise set of methods being used. That being said, the types and strength of relationships between the parts of a given system will often be relevant data as systems analysis primarily studies these very interactions. Measurements of diffusion of information, economic links between firms or countries, or friendships between individuals are just a few examples. In addition, as systems analysis transcends the boundaries of academic disciplines, it often requires an INTERDISCIPLINARY collaboration. Moreover, the fact that all elements of a system are interrelated and co-constituted limits the usefulness of REGRESSION ANALYSIS and other reductionist methodologies. Maintaining that all other things can stay equal (i.e. *ceteris paribus*) runs against the core idea of systems characterized by complex interrelationships, feedback loops, and emergent non-linear properties.

Causal loop diagrams are a first simple method used to establish mental models and conceptualize feedback loops in complex systems (see Figure 14). Feedback loops means that the effect of a cause can become the cause of another outcome (Jervis 1997: Chapter 4). As such, causal loop diagrams sustain a nonlinear view of CAUSATION. Feedbacks can, moreover, be positive or negative. Positive feedbacks reinforce an outcome, while negative feedbacks counteract it. An arms race is an unfortunate example of a positive feedback loop whereby the decision to build more weapons by one state pushes another to do the same ad infinitum. Negative feedbacks are, in contrast, supposed to keep a system in equilibrium. They are crucial for the tenets of self-regulated markets, in which a rise in a good's production will make its price drop and, in turn, its production drop. Another popular method for systems analysis is SOCIAL NETWORK ANALYSIS.

Recent advances in computational capacity have also progressively allowed the development of new techniques and methods, many of which rely on computation, simulation, and FORMAL MODELLING. Agent-based modelling (ABM) is, in that respect, one important formal method used to study the evolution and dynamics of complex systems. In ABM, researchers simulate the interactions between hypothetical agents based on a number of predetermined characteristics and preferences and aim to uncover what systemic patterns will emerge based on repeated computer simulations. ABM thus importantly does not rely on empirical data, but on a formal model devised by the researcher. Thomas Schelling is often mentioned as a pioneer of this method in social sciences. In his paper, 'Dynamic Models of Segregation' (Schelling 1971), he explained how some individual preferences for similar neighbours (i.e. black or white) can lead to a systemic segregation under some simple rules (i.e. agents will move to the closer location fitting their preferences). In political science, Axelrod (1997: 19) also famously used ABM to explain the evolution of cooperation in international relations. He more precisely tested how cooperation between heterogeneous agents embedded in a prisoner's dilemma would evolve in an iterative game. The software NetLogo is an easy tool that can be used to learn more about ABM and replicate Axelrod and Schelling's studies.

ABM is particularly valuable for understanding how interaction between numerous agents influence the performance of systems as a whole. It more precisely allows researchers to easily highlight how systemic effects emerge from micro-behaviours. It is also flexible enough to include agents with different preferences and thus model heterogeneous systems. Yet, ABM remains a heuristic simplification and has received its share of criticism for this. Some authors have argued that ABM merely acts as a black box. As such, it does not really explain how macro properties emerge from the interactions between individual agents. Others have also criticized ABM for not allowing agents to show creativity. In effect, all agents' actions are determined by the simple rules stated *ex ante* by the researcher. This predetermination of the agent's behaviour also means that ABM can hardly explain changes in agents' values or social representations. Finally, ABM traditionally does not account for exogenous influences, which can be very important in open systems. Nonetheless, ABM remains a useful tool for systems analysts. ABM can most notably produce useful data from a set of deduced assumptions, which can then be analysed inductively. As Axelrod (1997) put it, ABM should both be seen as a deductive and inductive approach.

There are several other methods associated with systems analysis, including visual methodologies and modelling/statistical approaches for data mining and analysis such as sensitivity analysis and TIME SERIES analysis. In the past, fractal geometry and system dynamics modelling (SDM) have notably been used to perform systems analysis (Mitleton-Kelly, Paraskevas, and Day 2018). In the first case, scholars investigated how patterns repeat themselves at different scales. It has been used to analyse the evolution of urban structures. In a recent book, Geoffrey West (2017) brilliantly discussed how the growth of urban structures and many other systems were actually following the same laws of scaling. In the second case, SDM is used to investigate how structural properties of systems interact in a nonlinear fashion. It was notably applied to study how the US political system affected the ecological environment.

In conclusion, systems analysis is not one single method but a vast and growing set of theories, methods, and approaches to study the properties arising from interactions between the parts of an interconnected whole. Importantly, the types of relevant data and tools will vary according to the precise set of methods used by researchers. While empirical information about the relationships between actors will be essential in social network analysis, ABM will, for example, rely on the use of hypothetical formal models. As modern information and communication technologies provide us with

Figure 14   Positive and negative feedback loops

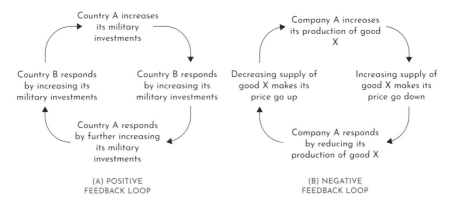

Country A increases its military investments

Country B responds by increasing its military investments

Country B responds by increasing its military investments

Country A responds by further increasing its military investments

(A) POSITIVE FEEDBACK LOOP

Company A increases its production of good X

Decreasing supply of good X makes its price go up

Increasing supply of good X makes its price go down

Company A responds by reducing its production of good X

(B) NEGATIVE FEEDBACK LOOP

increasingly large data sets and more computing power, new systems analysis methods are finally bound to allow more complex system modelization and to allow researchers to gain important insights into the design of various institutions, policies, and programs to tackle complex challenges.

REFERENCES

Axelrod, Robert. 1997. *The Complexity of Cooperation: Agent-Based Models of Competition and Collaboration*. Princeton, NJ, Princeton University Press.

Capra, Fritjof and Pier Luigi Luisi. 2014. *The Systems View of Life: A Unifying Vision*. Cambridge, Cambridge University Press.

Cilliers, Paul. 2001. 'Boundaries, Hierarchies and Networks in Complex Systems'. *International Journal of Innovation Management* 5(2): 135–147.

Jervis, Robert. 1997. *System Effects: Complexity in Political and Social Life*. Princeton, NJ, Princeton University Press.

Mitleton-Kelly, Eve, Alexandros Paraskevas, and Christopher Day (eds). 2018. *Handbook of Research Methods in Complexity Science: Theory and Applications*. Cheltenham, Edward Edgar Publishing.

Prigogine, Ilya. 1978. 'Time, Structure, and Fluctuations'. *Science* 201(4358): 777–785.

Schelling, Thomas C. 1971. 'Dynamic Models of Segregation'. *Journal of Mathematical Sociology* 1(2): 143–186.

Waltz, Kenneth. 1979. *Theory of International Politics*. Reading, MA, Addison-Wesley.

West, Geoffrey. 2017. *Scale: The Universal Laws of Growth, Innovation, Sustainability, and the Pace of Life in Organisms, Cities, Economies, and Companies*. New York, Penguin Press.

S

THEMATIC ANALYSIS

An Accessible and Flexible Approach for Qualitative Analysis

Virginia Braun, The University of Auckland,
Victoria Clarke, The University of the West of England

Qualitative researchers collect words as data—lots and lots of words. How do they distil what is important, exciting, interesting, and relevant about those words and produce some kind of report? They will be guided by a research question (although this can change and be refined through engaging with their data); they will be equipped with a toolkit of experiences, skills, disciplinary knowledge, and so forth (which they deploy from their subjective standpoint); and, typically, they will use one of the *many* qualitative analytic approaches that treat and analyse word-based data as words, rather than transforming them into numbers for statistical analysis.

One of the oldest and most widely used qualitative analytic method across the social sciences is thematic analysis (TA). TA is a flexible method for identifying and analysing patterns of meaning—'themes'—in qualitative data, with wide-ranging applications. The method has a long, if indeterminate, history in the social sciences, but seems likely to have evolved from early forms of (qualitative) CONTENT ANALYSIS. TA has always been widely used, but until recently it was often 'poorly demarcated, [and] rarely acknowledged' (Braun and Clarke 2006: 77), with typical reference to 'themes emerging' from data as description of the analytic process. TA is now more likely to be demarcated and acknowledged as a distinct method; however, confusion remains about what TA is, as we discuss further below. The popularity of TA as a distinct method received a considerable boost from the publication of 'Using Thematic Analysis in Psychology' by social psychologists Virginia Braun and Victoria Clarke in 2006, which has become one of the most cited academic papers of recent decades.

WHAT DOES THEMATIC ANALYSIS OFFER
SOCIAL SCIENCE RESEARCHERS?

TA offers social science researchers a flexible research tool—with few restrictions with regard to types of RESEARCH QUESTION that can be addressed, data collection methods used, sample size and constitution, and, indeed, overall theoretical orientation. TA has been used in everything from phenomenological research concerned with lived experience and subjective meaning making to critical interrogations of representational practice. One US study, for example, aimed to explore the intersectionality of gender and race through the lived experiences of African American women as they developed as leaders (Davis and Maldonado 2015); one New Zealand study used post-structuralist-informed TA to interrogate the textual representation of female and male (hetero)sexuality in popular women's magazines (Farvid and Braun 2006). Although mostly a method for analysing a wide range of talk- and text-based data, TA has recently started to be applied to creative, visual, and new and emerging forms of qualitative data.

As a theoretically flexible analytic *method* (rather than a theoretically embedded methodology), TA starts with fewer inbuilt restrictions than many other qualitative analytic approaches (e.g. DISCOURSE ANALYSIS). This means the social science researcher has considerable scope to shape their use of TA to suit their purpose and commitments—combining it with a variety of middle-range theories, such as feminism or queer theory, 'mashing' it up with other analytic methods or methodologies, such as CASE STUDIES, narrative analysis, and discourse analysis, or using it in pluralist or MIXED METHODS designs.

VARIATIONS IN APPROACHES TO THEMATIC ANALYSIS

Although TA is frequently (mis)understood as a singular method, many researchers in different (sub)disciplines within the social sciences have developed versions of it: for example, there is framework analysis from social policy (Ritchie and Spencer 1994), applied thematic analysis from public health (Guest, MacQueen, and Namey 2012), and both template analysis (King and Brooks 2017) and reflexive TA (Braun and Clarke 2019) from psychology. There are numerous (more or less widely used) versions of TA, often with significant procedural and philosophical differences, aligned with different PARADIGMS. So although TA in general can be described as a theoretically flexible method, specific iterations of TA encode particular ONTOLOGICAL and EPISTEMOLOGICAL assumptions that constrain this theoretical flexibility to a greater or lesser extent.

To map variation in TA, Braun et al. (2019) distinguished between three main approaches—which they called coding reliability, reflexive, and codebook approaches. TA can be more or less deductive or inductive (but the understanding of these is somewhat different from in quantitative research—see DEDUCTIVE, INDUCTIVE, AND RETRODUCTIVE REASONING). All forms of TA combine processes of coding and theme development or identification, and have as their aim the reporting of themes from the dataset. However, the purpose and practice of coding, and the conceptualization of a theme, does vary across forms of TA. Coding, in general, is a technique for systematically identifying small segments of the dataset that (might) meaningfully contribute to the broader patterns of meanings that are themes (we discuss how themes are conceptualized at the end of this section).

Coding reliability TA has the longest history and overlaps considerably with qualitative CONTENT ANALYSIS (see Boyatzis 1998). In these approaches, the analytic process starts with theme development (themes often map closely onto data collection questions, and offer summaries of a topic) and coding is understood as a process of searching for 'evidence' for themes, or organizing the data into predetermined themes. Typically, coding centres on the use of a structured codebook—including coding labels, definitions, and inclusion criteria—and ideally more than one coder applies the codebook to the data. To ensure the reliability or accuracy of coding, the level of 'agreement' between coders is calculated using a standardized statistical measure. Critics argue that, in coding reliability approaches, coding is inevitably limited to superficial or surface meaning to facilitate high levels of coding agreement. Coding reliability TA is underpinned by POSITIVIST notions of reliability typically associated with quantitative research, and therefore can be described as 'small q' qualitative—the use of qualitative techniques underpinned by positivist values and assumptions (Kidder and Fine 1987).

By contrast, reflexive TA represents a 'Big Q' fully qualitative approach; the use of qualitative techniques underpinned by a qualitative philosophy or paradigm (see Braun and Clarke 2006, 2019; Braun et al. 2019). Reflexive TA, like the concept of reflexivity more broadly, acknowledges that research is inevitably and inescapably shaped by the processes and practices of knowledge production, including the thoughts and actions of the researcher, the methods they have used, and the disciplinary location of the research. Reflexivity is integral to a qualitative paradigm, alongside an emphasis on subjective and situated meaning (Kidder and Fine 1987). In a qualitative paradigm, and in reflexive TA, the researcher's subjectivity is viewed as a resource rather than a potential threat to 'reliable' coding. The researcher is *active* in the analytic process in reflexive TA—themes are not in the data, waiting to passively *emerge*. Furthermore, the notion that coding can and should be accurate or reliable is rejected; instead, coding is conceptualized as an organic and evolving process. Good coding requires rigour and depth of engagement, not agreement between multiple coders. Good codes provide a rich, nuanced, and multifaceted account of the data. There is no one 'right' way to code data; coding is always a situated and subjective interpretation of data. Another important procedural difference between coding reliability and reflexive TA is that, in the latter, themes are the *output* of analysis rather than the input. They are developed later in the analytic process *from* the meanings identified through coding; ideally they go beyond superficial or surface meaning. The theoretical flexibility of reflexive TA is arguably less constrained than coding reliability TA, but reflexive TA is intended for use within a qualitative paradigm, and is it not compatible with positivism or SCIENTIFIC REALISM.

The third type of TA—codebook TA—sits somewhere between coding reliability and reflexive TA, sharing a structured coding approach and early theme development with coding reliability approaches, and the qualitative philosophy of reflexive TA. Codebook forms of TA are exemplified by approaches like template analysis (see King and Brooks 2017) that are often developed for use in applied research. The use of (some) predetermined themes and a structured codebook is argued to facilitate both meeting the predetermined and fixed information needs common in applied research, and the involvement of qualitative novices, such as practitioners, as co-researchers.

An important area of contestation within TA is around the definition of a theme. You might expect *this* to be something TA researchers agree on, but they do not. Braun et al. (2019) distinguished between two main conceptualizations of a theme—themes as shared topic or 'domain summaries' and themes as shared meaning, or patterns of meaning, united by a core concept. Topic summary themes, as the name suggests, typically summarize what was said by participants in relation to a particular topic or data collection question—the responses all relate to the same topic, rather than presenting a unified or coherent 'take' on the topic. Topic summary themes are common in coding reliability and codebook approaches; the focus on shared topics, rather than shared meaning, means they are readily identifiable early in the analytic process. Themes that capture shared meaning underpinned by a central organizing concept are associated with reflexive TA. Shared meaning is unlikely to be easily identified *before* data analysis—so coding cannot 'search for' themes—but are developed through analytic engagement. However, TA researchers often confuse these two types of themes, and there are numerous published examples of reflexive TA reporting topic summary-type themes. There are also numerous examples of researchers seemingly unknowingly 'mashing-up' different types of TA—the end result of which is often a theoretically incoherent research design and output.

A QUICK INTRODUCTION TO THE PROCESS OF REFLEXIVE THEMATIC ANALYSIS

Although some argue that TA is just a technique for data summary, rather than an *interpretative analytic method*, we understand TA as a method that produces—at its best—a rich interpretative account of patterned meanings across a dataset, and the implications of those. To understand why this is, you need to know a bit more about coding and theme development processes in reflexive TA, and some of the challenges these can throw up.

Reflexive TA provides a six-phase process moving from data familiarization into coding, and then initial theme development, theme revision, and refinement, and final 'writing up' of the project (the most detailed and accessible guidelines are in Braun and Clarke 2013). Data familiarization involves reading and rereading data (and listening or viewing if audio or visual) and becoming intimately familiar with the contents. Coding involves systematically working through the dataset, tagging excerpts of data with specific labels (the code or coding label) that identify particular segments that seem to be of analytic interest. Coding is a dual process of reducing the number of words in play (data reduction) and beginning to unpick what is interesting and important about the words in relation to the guiding research question (data interpretation). The phases of theme development centre on organizing the codes into clusters that evidence broader patterns of (shared) meaning. Initial clusters are revised, refined, and interpreted in light of the dataset, research questions, theoretical positioning, and wider scholarly (and real-world) contexts. In reporting TA, themes are typically discussed theme by theme, with a final wider consideration of the broader implications of the whole analysis. The analytic process is not strictly linear—it is better characterized as iterative and recursive, and requires a researcher who is reflexive and questioning of their developing analysis. The aim is a nuanced, situated, interpretative account of patterned meaning related to the research question.

An analogy we find useful for explaining codes and themes, and how they relate to each other, in reflexive TA, and the researcher's role in the process, is of building a mudbrick house from scratch—where you have an idea of what you want to do, but no blueprint to follow. The data are like the raw materials you gather to start with—the sand, the clay, the straw, etc. From these raw materials, you form bricks. Codes in reflexive TA are like these bricks—they are shaped and developed by the researcher, from the tools and materials at hand, and reflect the skill and perspectives of the researcher. Like the bricks, codes are a *product* of human activity that starts with the 'raw' materials (the data); codes are the 'outcome' of the coding process, just as bricks are the outcome of brickmaking. Once you have produced your mudbricks, you need to combine these into the walls of your house. Themes in reflexive TA are like the walls of this mudbrick house, each made up of lots of individual bricks. There is no obvious or singular way to combine the bricks into walls—for instance, you might wish to combine bricks of a particular size, or texture, or shape, or colour. You have to play around to find the best combinations and build a house with walls that are both robust and coherent. Your knowledge, experience, and skills provide the *tools* for creating bricks, and then combining these to make the walls; your preferences and world views help you determine when a house 'works' and when it does not, what it looks like, and ultimately whether it fulfils your purpose. Similarly, in reflexive TA, the researcher's skills, knowledge, paradigmatic orientations, and values all shape the final analysis. These are a resource in reflexive TA—in contrast to coding reliability, where researcher subjectivity is a threat to the quality of the analysis.

Conceptualizing subjectivity as a resource does not mean the subjective nature of reflexive TA coding and theme development is absent of challenges, especially for those with prior schooling in positivism. Those new to reflexive TA can experience considerable 'coding anxiety'—am I coding the 'right' things? Do I have enough codes or too many codes? etc. One of the coding challenges, then, is not trusting one's own subjective judgement. Another is moving from seeing very surface and descriptive patterns in the data, to identifying less obvious, more interpretative, or more latent patterns that can unite seemingly disparate content.

USING THEMATIC ANALYSIS—THE KEY TAKEAWAY

TA offers an accessible, widely used, but still evolving method for qualitative data analysis. However, the diversity of approaches creates a key limitation—misuse, where conceptual and practical aspects do not align. Therefore, it is crucial social science researchers understand that TA is not a singular approach and grasp the substantial divergences in philosophy and procedure between different types of TA.

REFERENCES

Boyatzis, Richard E. 1998. *Transforming Qualitative Information: Thematic Analysis and Code Development*. Thousand Oaks, CA, SAGE Publications.

Braun, Virginia and Victoria Clarke. 2006. 'Using Thematic Analysis in Psychology'. *Qualitative Research in Psychology* 3(2): 77-101.

Braun, Virginia and Victoria Clarke. 2013. *Successful Qualitative Research: A Practical Guide for Beginners*. London, SAGE Publications.

Braun, Virginia and Victoria Clarke. 2019. 'Reflecting on Reflexive Thematic Analysis'. *Qualitative Research in Sport, Exercise & Health* 11(4): 589-597.

Braun, Virginia, Victoria Clarke, Gareth Terry, and Nikki Hayfield. 2019. 'Thematic Analysis', in *Handbook of Research Methods in Health and Social Sciences*, ed. Pranee Liamputtong, 843-860. Singapore, Springer.

Davis, Deanna R. and Cecilia Maldonado. 2015. 'Shattering the Glass Ceiling: The Leadership Development of African American Women in Higher Education'. *Advancing Women in Leadership* 35: 48-64.

Farvid, Panteá and Virginia Braun. 2006. 'Most of Us Guys Are Raring to Go Anytime, Anyplace, Anywhere': Male and Female Sexuality in Cleo and Cosmo'. *Sex Roles: A Journal of Research* 55(5-6): 295-310.

Guest, Greg, Kathleen MacQueen, and Emily Namey. 2012. *Applied Thematic Analysis*. Thousand Oaks, CA, SAGE Publications.

Kidder, Louise H. and Michelle Fine. 1987. 'Qualitative and Quantitative Methods: When Stories Converge', in *New Directions in Program Evaluation*, ed. Melvin M. Mark and R. Lance Shotland, 57-75. San Francisco, Jossey-Bass.

King, Nigel and Joanna M. Brooks. 2017. *Template Analysis for Business and Management Students*. London, SAGE Publications.

Ritchie, Jane and Liz Spencer. 1994. 'Qualitative Data Analysis for Applied Policy Research', in *Analysing Qualitative Data*, ed. Alan Bryman and Robert G. Burgess, 173-194. London, Taylor & Francis.

TIME SERIES

A Statistical Method for Longitudinal Analysis

Nina Baur & Jannis Hergesell, Technische Universität Berlin

DATA REQUIREMENTS

Time series analysis is a statistical method of longitudinal analysis which is suitable if researchers are interested in the temporality of social phenomena and want to analyse social change and patterns of recurrence over time. In contrast to other statistical methods of longitudinal analysis (see CROSS-SECTIONAL AND LONGITUDINAL STUDIES), time series analysis can be applied even if researchers have only a few cases (maybe even only one) and only a few (maybe even only one) VARIABLES.

Time series can be built for any LEVEL OF ANALYSIS, as cases (see also UNIT OF ANALYSIS) can be persons, but are usually organizations or countries. For example, in Cruz, Bender, and Ombao's (2017) analysis of health care interventions, the cases are hospital units and the variables are patient satisfaction scores reported as aggregate scores per month. In Askitas's (2015) study on the Greek referendum on negotiations with the European Union in 2015, the case is Greece and the variables are the numbers of searches for the Greek referendum in Google. In Braudel and Spooner's (1967) classical economic analysis on price development, the cases are different European towns and the variables are the prices for various goods such as grain and metal. In Rufrancos et al.'s (2013) review on the effects of social inequality research on crime, the cases vary (neighbourhood, regions, countries) and the variables are various crimes.

In order to build a time series, the VARIABLES need to have been measured several times over a given period, and for each measurement one needs to know the measurement date. The temporal UNIT OF ANALYSIS can vary: Askitas (2015) measures the variable every hour, but Rufrancos et al. (2013) every year. The time span covered by the time series can vary too: Askitas's (2015) time series covers seven days, but it is also possible to analyse very long-term social processes. Braudel and Spooner (1967) even cover three centuries (1450–1750). However, the most important requirement for a time series is that there are as many measurement points as possible: Rufrancos et al.'s (2013) time series have something between nine and forty, and Askitas's (2015) time series has as many as 171 measurement points. More details on how a time series data set must be built can be found in Rahlf (2016).

There are different goals when doing time series analysis (Zeger, Irizarry, and Peng 2006; Box-Steffensmeier et al. 2015) which can be used in DESCRIPTIVE, EXPLANATORY, AND INTERPRETIVE APPROACHES.

DESCRIPTIVE APPROACHES: MODELLING SOCIAL PROCESSES

Very often, researchers simply want to model social processes—i.e. describe the development of social processes over time—and often this simply means plotting a time series and describing it verbally. If this first step is not sufficient, a second step in such a description is decomposing the time series into different components by using either REGRESSION ANALYSIS or the method of moving averages. In this way, cause–effect relationships between the different components can be recognized, regardless of short-term fluctuations in the time series. Usually, (at least) three components are distinguished:

1   The trend measures the long-term development of the social process—e.g. Braudel and Spooner (1967) show that prices rise over time. In most industrialized countries, birth rates have declined over the last decades. But patterns can also be more complex—e.g. in Askitas's (2015) study on the Greek referendum, the agreement to the referendum seems to first decline and then rise again, so there is a turning point in the pattern. This trend can be statistically modelled using non-linear REGRESSION ANALYSIS.

2   Very often, time series contain cyclical patterns, meaning that there is a system-
    atic fluctuation around the trend. For example, in agriculture, a seasonal cycle
    in Europe lasts one year with different production levels over the different sea-
    sons (spring, summer, autumn, winter). Often, several cycles of different dura-
    tion overlay each other. For example, in economic processes, there are very often
    seasonal cycles (1 year), Kitchin cycles (3.5 years), Juglar cycles (7–10 years),
    Kuznets cycles (18–25 years), Kondratieff cycles (45–60 years), and hegemonial
    cycles (> 100 years). These cycles can be statistically modelled using e.g. peri-
    odograms or spectral analysis, which make it possible to decompose complex
    data sets and thus to identify repetitive and cyclical patterns as well as periods of
    relative stability in the time series.

3   There is a rest component (also: error component)—i.e. there are always parts of
    the time series that cannot be explained by the statistical model.

Furthermore, time series analysis can detect breaks in all of these patterns. Abrupt
breaks are already apparent when looking at the graphical representation of the time
series. For example, the trend shifts from one point to the next up or down in a jerky
manner, or a cyclical pattern that was still there at one time is no longer there at another. But researchers may also observe smooth transitions—e.g. the slow dissolution
of a cyclical pattern.

EXPLANATORY APPROACHES: PREDICTIONS AND EXPLANATIONS

Once one has identified and modelled the trend and cyclical components, these models can be used for predictions and forecasts. For example, Askitas (2015) uses the
above time series for predicting the development of public opinion on the referendum.

If one has more than one VARIABLE, one can also aim at explaining one time series
with other time series by using time-sensitive REGRESSION ANALYSIS. For example, Rufrancos et al. (2013) analyse how various variables (such as income inequality,
other economic and socio-demographic factors, law enforcement, and social context)
influence various crimes rates. In contrast to cross-sectional regression analysis, time
series analysis has the advantage that one can also take temporality into account and
ask questions like: What is the order of events—i.e. what is actually cause and what is
effect? Is there a lag between cause and effect? Does maybe not the level of a variable,
but the overall pattern in time influence the outcome?

Another option is statistically modelling the turning point by methods of so-called
interrupted time series (ITS). For example, Cruz, Bender, and Ombao (2017) explain
changes in patient satisfaction by health interventions.

Note that, as time series usually use aggregated data, there is the danger of so-called
ecological fallacy: a prerequisite for causality are correlations on the individual level.
When using aggregated data, one only has data on the group level. Therefore, one
can logically only compute correlations on the group level but not on the individual

level—one can only assume that what correlates on the group level also correlates on the individual level. However, this assumption may be false: just because there are correlations on the group level, there need not be correlations on the individual level—e.g. Rufrancos et al. (2013) show that, usually, when income inequality increases, property-related crime such as burglaries increase. However, this does not mean that poor people or people with decreasing income actually become burglars—it could also be rich or middle-class people whose income is stable but who for example are afraid of their income decreasing.

INTERPRETATIVE APPROACHES: EXPLANATIONS AND CASE SELECTION

Qualitative and MIXED METHODS data can be also used for explaining turning points and the rest component, which is especially often done in CASE STUDY research. In this case, researchers interpret various data in order to explain how a turning point or unusual pattern came about.

In addition, time series can be used both for periodization and CASE SELECTION in qualitative research: if one wants to focus on social change, one would select a turning point and analyse the period before and after in order to explain the causes and results of the change. If one rather wants to focus on typical patterns, one would instead select a period of stability. Therefore, time series is a suitable method for researchers who want to describe the development of a phenomenon over a period of time and/or are interested in causal relations. For example, researchers can use time series to identify cause-and-effect relationships between previous and following events. Similarly, contemporary phenomena can be studied in terms of their underlying causes in the past to understand the course of their historical development.

REFERENCES

Askitas, Nikolaos. 2015. *Calling the Greek Referendum on the nose with Google Trends.* RatSWD Working Paper Series 249.

Box-Steffensmeier, Janet M., John R. Freeman, Matthew P. Hitt, and Jon C. W. Pevehouse. 2015. *Time Series Analysis for the Social Sciences.* Cambridge, Cambridge University Press.

Braudel, Fernand and Frank Spooner. 1967. *Prices in Europe from 1450 to 1750.* Reprinted in: E. E. Rich and C. H. Wilson. 2008. *The Cambridge Economic History of Europe from the Decline of the Roman Empire,* Volume 4, 374–486. Cambridge, Cambridge University Press.

Cruz, Maricela, Miriam Bender, and Hernando Ombao. 2017. 'A Robust Interrupted Time Series Model for Analysing Complex Health Care Intervention Data'. *Statistics in Medicine* 36(29): 4660–4676.

Rahlf, Thomas. 2016. 'The German Time Series Dataset 1834–2012'. *Jahrbücher für Nationalökonomie und Statistik* 236(1): 129–143.

Rufrancos, Hector Gutierrez, Madeleine Power, Kate E. Pickett, and Richard Wilkinson. 2013. 'Income Inequality and Crime: A Review and Explanation of the Time-Series Evidence'. *Sociology and Criminology—Open Access* 1(1), DOI: 10.4172/2375-4435.1000103.

Zeger, Scott L., Rafael Irizarry, and Roger D. Peng. 2006. 'On Time Series Analysis of Public Health and Biomedical Data'. *Annual Review of Public Health* 27: 57–79.

TRIANGULATION

Sabine Caillaud, Université Lumière Lyon 2, Uwe Flick, Freie Universität of Berlin

Triangulation is classically defined as looking at one research object from different per-spectives. However, this large and consensual definition masks different approaches to triangulation and ignores its historical evolution since its emergence in social sciences literature. To gain a better insight into its current definitions, we will first propose a brief historical overview and highlight its different meanings. Then, we will illustrate how triangulation can be used in a research design in order to gain *extra knowledge*. Finally, we will talk about MIXED METHODS research and its relationship with triangulation.

A BRIEF HISTORICAL OVERVIEW

In 1959, Campbell and Fiske proposed a multitrait-multimethod matrix to enhance the validity of the measurement of traits (e.g. personality traits). The basic idea was to increase the validity of a measurement by using different methods and by measur-ing different traits simultaneously. Webb et al. (1966) labelled this new technique *tri-angulation*, in reference to the navigation and military term describing the practice of locating the exact position of an object on the basis of two known points. Denzin (1978) introduced the concept in the discussion on qualitative research and further developed the concept. He distinguishes different kinds of triangulation: triangulation of data (comparing data at different times, in different spaces or for different persons); triangulation of researchers (to correct the BIAS from the individual); triangulation of theoretical perspectives (approaching a phenomenon with different theoretical points of view); and triangulation of methods. This latter strategy was defined as a process of playing 'each method off against the other so as to maximize the validity of field effort' (Denzin 1978: 304).

   Also, triangulation, in its first meaning, echoed some of the main concerns about data validity (see EPISTEMOLOGY). However, in the context of qualitative research, the ongoing debate on validity issues highlighted that this question cannot be treated as in quantitative methods. Indeed, most criteria commonly adopted in quantitative methodology (e.g.: REPLICATION, standardization, representative SAMPLING) are not relevant, and other strategies should be pursued (Barbour 2001). Triangulation, defined by Denzin (1978), supposes that there is *one* reality which can be analysed more *objectively* with multiple methods: if data obtained with different methods are similar, they are right. Thus, this definition ignores some of the main principles of qualitative research—e.g. different actors have different context-dependent points of view and each method constitutes the subject under study in a specific way. Also, some authors heavily criticized Denzin's definition and proposed that triangulation aims for broader and deeper understanding of what is studied. In this perspective, each method is considered to shed light on a specific aspect of the phenomenon under study (Flick 2017). Different metaphors were proposed to illustrate this perspective, such as for example:

> I propose that the central imaginary for validity for postmodernist texts is not the triangle—a rigid, fixed, two-dimensional object. Rather, the central imaginary is the crystal, which combines symmetry and substances, transmutations, multidimensionalities, and angles of approach … What we see depends upon our angle of repose. (Richardson 2000: 934)

Moreover, a rather pragmatic combination of methods developed too—i.e. different RESEARCH QUESTIONS call for different methods and each method answers a specific question.

Flick (2018) introduced a distinction between a weak programme of triangulation (used as a criterion of validity, pursuing convergence between results, or as a pragmatic combination of methods) and a strong programme of triangulation (or triangulation 3.0). The latter refers to the idea that triangulation is used as a source of extra knowledge—i.e. different methods can provide convergent, but also contradictory and complementary, results. In a weak programme of triangulation, contradictory results are considered doubtful and not valid; they are explained by referring to BIAS in the method. On the contrary, in a strong programme of triangulation, the researcher plans the design of the study by referring to the theoretical frames of each method in order to understand, at a later stage of the study, why some results are contradictory and/or complementary. Thus a strong programme of triangulation extends the research programme in a *comprehensive* manner: the combination of the results will hence allow for a deeper understanding of the phenomenon under study. Also, the aim should not be to confirm results from one method by comparing them to results from another. Rather, the aim is to include complementary and/or contradictory results.

ILLUSTRATIONS

Discussing the use of FOCUS GROUPS in a strong programme of triangulation, we proposed two illustrations of this approach. The study (Caillaud and Flick 2017) is about social representations of climate change and ecological practices in France and in Germany. The methodological design of the study includes focus groups and episodic (or semi-structured) INTERVIEWS. Adopting a strong programme of triangulation, we consider that interviews focus on the reconstruction of subjective knowledge, whereas focus groups refer to social interactions underpinning the social construction of representations. Interestingly, results obtained from focus groups and from interviews sometimes complement or even contradict each other. Indeed, many German and French interviewees in individual interviews acknowledge their poor understanding of climate change. In France, participants in focus groups do the same. However, in focus groups, German participants present themselves as knowing about climate change. This discourse contradicts the statements from interviews. In a weak programme of triangulation, the researcher will not be able to determine what the objective truth is: do they know or not know about climate change? However, as strong triangulation suggests, each method reveals different facets of the same phenomenon: subjective meaning and social construction of reality. Also, it becomes possible to give meaning to the apparent contradicting results: in Germany, climate change is a theme you have to know and speak about, even if you are not able to precisely explain the causes and consequences of it. In France, on the contrary, it is socially accepted to not know about climate change; it is something scientific experts know about, not citizens. Thus, the apparent contradiction between methods enables us to outline the normative dimensions of climate change in Germany (you have to talk about it in society) and its categorization as a scientific object in France. It provides a deeper understanding of the results (even in France, where results converge).

Concerning ecological practices and the way participants cope with the paradox that ecological practices are not effective if not all people act the same way (see also Caillaud and Flick 2013), results from interviews and **FOCUS GROUPS** are complementary (and not in contradiction). Indeed, when talking about their ecological practices during interviews, French and Germans refer to past habits to justify their daily practices (e.g. recycling household waste like in the past, in their family, organic waste was fed to chickens). During focus groups, the discussion about ecological practices and their effectiveness are anchored in a projection into a better future for humanity. Interpreting these different results by linking them to the theoretical perspectives of each method (social interactions and reconstruction of subjective knowledge), we obtain a deeper understanding of the meaning of ecological practices. Facing the paradox that ecological practices are only effective if everybody acts the same way, participants give different meanings to their habits by referring to the past during interviews (a method in which subjective knowledge is reconstructed) and by referring to the ideal future when group support is present.

The second illustration refers to a study about sleeping disorders and their management in long-term care facilities (Flick et al. 2012). The authors wanted to understand the prevalence of sleep disorders in the institutions, the different proposed treatments (drugs, other), and the related health consequences for residents. At the same time, the study seeks to understand the professional (physicians' and nurses') constructions of managing sleep disorders (awareness of the problem, their motivation to act, their attitudes toward treatment of sleeping problems and toward medication) and the residents' representation of their own disturbed sleep and the treatment received. Also, this study proposed a triangulation design starting from a quantitative epidemiological approach (health indicators from 7,505 nursing homes residents and longitudinal data from 1,375 residents), a qualitative comprehensive approach (episodic interviews with physicians (N = 20), nurses (N = 32), and residents (N = 30)). Finally, the routine practice (amount of drugs supplied, duration, etc.) was analysed on the basis of prescription data (N = 2,109). The epidemiological data show the high relevance of sleeping disorders and help contextualize the qualitative results. The interviews outlined the ambivalence toward medication of sleeping disorders for all actors. More specifically, for physicians and nurses, the use of hypnotics may be seen acceptable if there is medical indication; but residents' attitudes both varied from a strict rejection to seeing medication as indispensable for their own sleep. The interviews did not reveal treatment practices which became apparent through the quantitative analysis of prescriptions: only 16.7 per cent of the sample received hypnotic drugs at least once in the year, and only 1 per cent of the residents were exposed to the risk of addiction. Thus, in light of the quantitative analysis of prescriptions, the ambivalence outlined in interviews on all sides indicates that decisions for or against medication is dealt with a case-by-case analysis resulting in low prescriptions. Finally, the assessment data provide evidence that other forms of treatment are applied (e.g. activation during the day to reduce daily somnolence). Also, the triangulation of different methods complement each other and allow for a deeper understanding of the phenomenon under study.

TRIANGULATION AND/OR MIXED METHODS

Triangulation is often evoked in the context of MIXED METHODS RESEARCH (MMR) as well. In fact, in the context of the tensions opposing qualitative and quantitative research, triangulation (defined as corroboration through multiple methods) is used by MMR to justify that qualitative *and* quantitative methods should systematically be articulated. Thus, contrary to triangulation, the use of multiple qualitative methods is not evoked, and mixing is always considered between quantitative and qualitative. MMR focuses on technical issues in order to bring the qualitative and quantitative together to the detriment of conceptual and epistemological issues. Thus, if the reference to Denzin (1978) is a common point of departure for triangulation and MMR, the latter calls for eliminating it from their terminology and ignores the changes the concept of triangulation has undergone (Fetters and Molina-Azorin 2017). Behind the quarrel over the concept, Flick (2017) identifies a number of limits encountered by MMR and highlights that triangulation allows for the simultaneous use of qualitative and quantitative methods without, as in MMR, considering it necessary.

REFERENCES

Barbour, Rosaline. 2001. 'Checklists for Improving Rigour in Qualitative Research: A Case of the Tail Wagging the Dog?' *British Medical Journal* 322(7294): 1115–1117.

Caillaud, Sabine and Uwe Flick. 2013. 'New Meanings for Old Habits? Representations of Climate Change in France and Germany'. *International Review of Social Psychology* 26(3): 39–72.

Caillaud, Sabine and Uwe Flick. 2017. 'Focus Groups in Triangulation Contexts', in *A new Era in Focus Groups Research: Challenges, Innovation, and Practice*, ed. Rosaline Barbour and David Morgan, 155–177. Hampshire, Palgrave MacMillan.

Denzin, Norman. 1978. *The Research Act*, 2nd edition. Chicago, Aldine.

Fetters, Michael and José Molina-Azorin. 2017. 'The Journal of Mixed Methods Research Starts a New Decade: Principles for Bringing in the New and Divesting of the Old Language of the Field'. *Journal of Mixed Methods Research* 11(1): 3–10.

Flick, Uwe. 2017. 'Mantras and Myths: The Disenchantment of Mixed-methods Research and Revisiting Triangulation as a Perspective'. *Qualitative Inquiry* 23(1): 46–57.

Flick, Uwe. 2018. *Doing Triangulation and Mixed Methods*. London, SAGE Publications.

T

Flick, Uwe, Vjenka Garms-Homolová, Wolfram J. Herrmann, Joachim Kuck, and Röhnsch Gundula. 2012. "'I Can't Prescribe Something Just Because Someone Asks for it ...'" Using Mixed Methods in the Framework of Triangulation'. *Journal of Mixed Methods Research* 6(2): 97-110.

Richardson, Laurel. 2000. 'Writing: A Method of Inquiry', in *Handbook of Qualitative Research*, 2nd edition, ed. Norman Denzin and Yvonna Lincoln, 923-948. Thousand Oaks, CA, SAGE Publications.

Webb, Eugene J., Donald T. Campbell, Richard D. Schwartz, and Lee Sechrest. 1966. *Unobtrusive Measures: Nonreactive Research in the Social Sciences*. Chicago, Rand McNally.

TYPOLOGY

A Multidimensional Classification

Juraj Halas, Comenius University in Bratislava

The importance of typologies is contested. Some scholars view them as fundamental to **CONCEPT CONSTRUCTION** (Collier, LaPorte, and Seawright 2012: 222), while others consider that they are temporary devices at best and actually discourage their use (King, Keohane, and Verba 1994: 48). We shall focus here on the less problematic, heuristic roles of typologies. In this respect, typologies are a proven and widely used instrument for organizing knowledge and ideas at various stages of research, and especially for jump starting the process of generating hypotheses. Moreover, theories are often presented, e.g. for didactic purposes, by means of typologies. However, before turning to the uses of typologies, we need to introduce some measure of conceptual order, since the term 'typology' is equivocal.[1]

CLASSIFICATION, TYPOLOGY, TAXONOMY

In the literature, 'typology', 'classification', and 'taxonomy' are defined in a diverse range of ways, but the terms themselves are usually viewed as closely related. As far as terminology is concerned, we shall loosely follow Bailey (1994) and view typology as a kind of classification.

A *classification* is a system of classes (sets) that group objects, based on the values of a single nominal or ordinal **VARIABLE**. A simple classification divides states into 'democracies' and 'non-democracies'. Hence, classifications are unidimensional. However, the variable ('dimension') underlying a classification may be a compound

[1] This work was supported by the Slovak Research and Development Agency under contract No. APVV-0149-12.

VARIABLE. In our example, a particular state could be classified as a 'democracy' based on a checklist of criteria (e.g. free elections, freedom of the press, etc.). Each criterion is a necessary condition for membership in the class and together they form a sufficient condition. The set of all objects designated by the classification (e.g. all states) is the domain or universe of discourse. The range of values covered by the variable (e.g. 'democracy', 'non-democracy') form the *property space* of a classification.

All classification follows two general rules. First, classes must be mutually exclusive: an object from the domain can only be a member of a single class. Second, classes (taken together) must be exhaustive in relation to the domain: each object from the domain must be classifiable. The second rule may involve the creation of a *residual* class for objects that are dissimilar, but do not fit into any other class.

The basic function of a classification is to introduce order and reduce complexity (Bailey 1994: 12ff.). In this sense, classificatory procedures are related to the fundamental dimension of all knowledge, in as much as they impose order on (and, to some extent, *are derived from*) a diverse multifaceted reality. In addition, a classification should be systematically fruitful: values of the classifying VARIABLE should be known to highly correlate with other relevant characteristics, which are logically independent of that variable (Hempel 1965: 156). In our example, these could be economic growth or involvement in war. A productive classification allows for some rudimentary prediction and should lead to the formulation of a new HYPOTHESIS (Bailey 1994: 14).

These considerations also apply to typologies and taxonomies. However, unlike a classification, a *typology* is multidimensional. An object from the domain is assigned to one of the classes ('types') based on the values of two or more VARIABLES. Typologies are usually presented in the form of a matrix, which cross-tabulates the two (or more) variables, and each cell represents a distinct type (Collier, LaPorte, and Seawright 2012: 218). Consider the classic example in Table 10 (Lijphart 1968: 38).

Here, four types of democracies are distinguished on the basis of two dimensions that are conceptualized as dichotomous VARIABLES: 'elite behaviour' (rows) and 'political culture' (columns). Lijphart (1968: 38) states that the types should be associated with a decreasing measure of political stability (from the top left to the bottom right cell). To understand why, we would need to look at the underlying theory and the mechanisms it postulates. However, even with no knowledge of the details, this typology clearly lends itself to the formulation of at least one kind of predictions and HYPOTHESES.

TABLE 10 Lijphart's (1968) typology of democratic systems

| | | Political culture | |
		Homogenous	Fragmented
Elite behaviour	Coalescent	Depoliticized democracy	Consociational democracy
	Competitive	Centripetal democracy	Centrifugal democracy

Three different aspects of a type need to be distinguished: its *name, concept* (or *intension*), and *extension*. A type name is simply the conventional label for a cell in a typology (e.g. 'Depoliticized democracy'). A type concept is the meaning associated with a given type name. The concept corresponding to the top left type is *a democratic regime characterized by a homogeneous political culture and a coalescent elite* (i.e., an elite that 'sticks together' and prefers cooperation to competition). Lastly, the type extension is the set of all objects from the domain, which belong to a given type—in other words, all objects in the domain that satisfy the criteria postulated by the type concept. In this case, the objects would be the democratic systems of particular countries satisfying the respective variables. If there are none, the given type is 'empty'.

A typology may be presented in various ways. Above, type names expressing type concepts appear in the cells. Alternatively, we could list the names of (some or all) objects, which belong to each type's extension. In this case, the top left cell would then contain a list of countries. Another mode of presentation might include information on the relative proportion of the objects of a type in the whole domain. The different modes of presenting a typology are equally valid, but serve different purposes (see 'Building and using typologies').

Taxonomies differ from classifications in that they involve hierarchy: their classes have subclasses, which may contain sub-subclasses, etc. Classes of a taxonomy are called taxa. Objects assigned to a given taxon have all the properties required for membership in the superordinate taxon, but differ (in other properties) from objects in the other taxa in the same superordinate taxon. Due to their hierarchical nature, taxonomies are often presented in a tree-like diagram, where lines represent relations between subordinate and superordinate taxa.

BUILDING AND USING TYPOLOGIES

There are two basic approaches to constructing a typology: *top-down* and *bottom-up*. The first is often described as 'deductive', while the resulting types are termed 'conceptual' or 'ideal types'.[2] The second is usually called 'inductive' and the types it yields are sometimes characterized as 'extracted types' (Lehnert 2007: 63). From a logical point of view, both approaches result in the same kind of structure, but their uses can be different (see DEDUCTIVE, INDUCTIVE, AND RETRODUCTIVE REASONING).

The top-down approach can be illustrated by Lijphart's typology. It is formulated on the basis of pre-existing knowledge (an established theory or a set of conjectures). This knowledge is used to determine the relevant dimensions (as well as the ranges of the corresponding VARIABLES), which are cross-tabulated to yield a number of types. Subsequently, the typology is applied to the given domain: objects are sorted into types. However, the last step is not always desirable.

---

[2] Note that in its original usage (according to Max Weber), 'ideal type' refers to an idealized model quite independent of a typology, as defined here (Hempel 1965: 162).

The top-down approach can be used to *illustrate* the implications of a theory—e.g. to list the particular kinds of phenomena that the theory recognizes. This has a didactic purpose and may also be useful when contrasting competing theories. Similarly, the top-down approach can be used to explicate concepts and introduce new compound VARIABLES in order to measure or formulate HYPOTHESES. In this case, our primarily interest is the type concepts (or number of types), as opposed the extension of types (i.e. the particular objects per type, their number or distribution among types). This approach can lead to new RESEARCH QUESTIONS, such as:

1 Are all of the types postulated by the theory possible?
2 Do any of the types seem less probable than others and, if so, should they be under-represented in the domain?
3 Does the theory imply types without explicitly discussing them in order to widen its scope?

Here, typologies function as 'tools for thinking', which help identify problems and orient further research.

The heuristic import of typologies emerges when objects in a domain are sorted into types. For example, a typology could be used for CASE SELECTION to identify particular cases of interest for further examination (e.g. one or all objects in a type that is/ are suitable for a CASE STUDY). This approach raises the following questions:

1. Why is a given type empty or only sparsely populated?
2. What mechanisms could explain the correlation between the typology's dimensions and the characteristics associated with a particular type?
3. What mechanisms could explain differences in the associated characteristics of objects of the same type?

A particular case of the top-down approach is an 'explanatory typology'. Here, the dimensions (rows and columns) represent independent VARIABLES—i.e. causes— while types (cells) represent combinations of dependent variables—i.e. effects (Elman 2005: 296–297). It is important to note that all the explanatory work is based on the underlying theory. The typology is used to present predictions drawn from the theory—e.g. for purposes of COMPARATIVE ANALYSIS, to investigate interaction effects generated by multiple variables, to identify kinds of cases for further scrutiny or to help COUNTER-FACTUAL ANALYSIS.

In the bottom-up approach, we use the data about objects in the domain to identify similarities. This provides the basis for sorting the objects into types or 'clusters' (Bailey 1994: 34). When the domain is large (and requires immediate processing), the bottom-up approach may use complex quantitative methods and can be automated. However, the classic example of a bottom-up typology (more precisely, a taxonomy), that of biological species, emerged incrementally and without the use of quantitative methods. The resulting typology provides a quick overview of the (usually very large) domain. Similarly to a top-down typology, a bottom-up typology can be used for heuristic purposes to identify recurrent patterns or outliers.

With regard to the distinction between NOMOTHETIC AND IDIOGRAPHIC METHODS, typologies are usually related to the former, since types are seen as 'generalizations' of the common features of a number of diverse phenomena. However, as noted above, typologies can also be instruments of CASE SELECTION, by facilitating research designs associated with the idiographic approach.

MANAGING TYPOLOGIES

The number of types in a typology depends on the number of VARIABLES and the number of values within the range of variables. If all variables are dichotomous, the number of cells is twice the number of variables or '2n' for short. A greater number of types allows for finer distinctions between objects in the domain. However, the greater the number of types, the harder it is to manage the typology. Generally, a useful typology strikes a balance between *parsimony* and *discriminatory capacity* (Lehnert 2007: 64). This is often the result of a lengthy process of fine-tuning.

New types can be introduced by adding new VARIABLES or, if the existing variables are continuous, by redefining the intervals over which they range. Conversely, existing types can be eliminated to increase the parsimony (and generality) of the typology. Obviously, this can be achieved by removing variables or collapsing several types into one or by disregarding empty types. Alternatively, equal weights may be assigned to different combinations of variable values, whereby different types are treated as equal (Bailey 1994: 24–32).

REFERENCES

Bailey, Kenneth D. 1994. *Typologies and Taxonomies: An Introduction to Classification Techniques*. Thousand Oaks, CA, SAGE Publications.

Collier, David, Jody LaPorte, and Jason Seawright. 2012. 'Putting Typologies to Work: Concept Formation, Measurement, and Analytic Rigor'. *Political Research Quarterly* 65(1): 217–232.

Elman, Colin. 2005. 'Explanatory Typologies in Qualitative Studies of International Politics'. *International Organization* 59(2): 293-326.

Hempel, Carl Gustav. 1965. *Aspects of Scientific Explanation*, Chapters 6 and 7. New York, Free Press.

King, Gary, Robert O. Keohane, and Sidney Verba. 1994. *Designing Social Inquiry: Scientific Inference in Qualitative Research*. Princeton, NJ, Princeton University Press.

Lehnert, Matthias. 2007. 'Typologies in Social Inquiry', in *Research Design in Political Science: How to Practice what they Preach*, ed. Thomas Gschwend and Frank Schimmelfennig, 62-79. London, Palgrave Macmillan.

Lijphart, Abend. 1968. 'Typologies of Democratic Systems'. *Comparative Political Studies* 1(3): 3-44.

T

UNIT OF ANALYSIS AND OBSERVATION

Kimberly A. Neuendorf, Cleveland State University

DEFINITIONS

Each empirical social or behavioural science study typically includes the identification of one or more units of analysis. The unit is the entity, element, or grouping that constitutes the focus of the study's analyses, and multiple cases of this unit are analysed. A study's unit of analysis is quite often the person—the individual subject or participant.

However, the unit of analysis is not always a person. Units take a wide variety of forms. As Babbie (2013: 97) notes, 'In social research, there is virtually no limit to what or whom can be studied, or the units of analysis.' Possible units include the individual, the dyad, the friendship group, the classroom, the organization, the neighbourhood, the voting ward, the nation, and the society. A unit may be a message or message component, such as the word, the verbal clause, the utterance, the conversational turn, the theme (e.g. within a monologue), the tweet, the news article, the book, the television character, the act of alcohol consumption within a film, or the full film. Units may be discrete behavioural elements such as an act of physical aggression. Units may also be set time periods, such as the five-minute interval, the month, or the year. Research taking a qualitative approach may also utilize units such as the cultural practice, the episode (e.g. of crowd behaviour), the encounter, the social role, or the habitat (Lofland et al. 2006).

The unit of analysis is of primary importance, as this is the unit that is referred to in hypotheses or research questions and therefore the unit that is the focus of data analyses that address these hypotheses or research questions. But, there are two other types of units that need to be considered. In sum, the three types of units in any empirical study are (a) the unit of sampling, (b) the unit of observation or measurement (sometimes called the unit of inquiry or unit of data collection), and (c) the unit of analysis. These three types of units are defined in Table 11 (see also Neuendorf 2017: 70).

TABLE 11 Types of units used in empirical studies

Type of unit	Definition
Unit of sampling	The element that serves as the basis for identifying a study's population and the sampling frame, and for drawing a sample (see also SAMPLING TECHNIQUES)
Unit of observation/data collection	The element on which VARIABLES are measured–i.e. on which data are collected
Unit of analysis	The element that serves as the basis for conducting and reporting analyses; the element to which results apply and to which findings may be generalized in a larger population

In many studies, the units of sampling, observation, and analysis are one in the same—e.g. the individual person in an online survey of 450 respondents. In other cases, the units differ. For example, a study of discussion groups in a college course might have the group as the unit of sampling, the individual student as the unit of observation (via a survey instrument, for example), and the group as the unit of analysis. Note that while the group is the unit of analysis, characteristics are actually measured on components (members) of each group. Typically, a study's hypotheses or research questions are phrased as relating to the unit of analysis—for example, in this instance, 'Do racially homogenous groups experience greater cohesiveness than do racially heterogenous groups?' And, the element to which measurements are applied is the unit of observation, in this instance the individual group member who is queried in a survey.

As may be seen, it can be advantageous for the three types of units to differ within a single study. For example, in a CONTENT ANALYSIS studying images of women in television advertising, the unit of sampling might be the TV ad or a specified time period during which all ads are collected; the unit of observation may be each individual female character within the collected ads; the unit of analysis may be the character, or may be the ad. In fact, both units of analysis—the character and the ad—may be reported on in separate analyses within the research results, illustrating that one study may utilize more than one unit of analysis. Further, it is possible that all three types of units may be different within a single study, as in a survey that uses the neighbourhood as the unit of sampling, the individual person as the unit of observation, and the family as the unit of analysis.

Units are likely to be linked somewhat to the LEVEL OF ANALYSIS of a study. At a more microscopic, individual level, units are likely to be the individual person or the family or other small social grouping. At a more macroscopic or societal level, units may include institutions such as the hospital or the school, or even the nation. The level of analysis may be seen as comparable to the notion of geographic scale in political geography, moving from local to global.

UNITS AND DIMENSIONALITY

Units of sampling, observation, and analysis may be differentiated along one or more dimensions; primarily, these include spatial, temporal, and social lines. Spatial delineation may include geographical units such as the house, the city block, or the neighbourhood. For a CONTENT ANALYSIS of media, spatially defined units may include the column inch or the page. Units delineated by time may include the minute (e.g. of video content), the month (e.g. of Twitter activity), or the year. Social delineation of different units might be exemplified by the individual, the family, or the religious congregation.

UNITS AND PRECISION

The researcher may find it advantageous to sample and collect data/observations on smaller or more precise units (sometimes called 'basic units'), and then combine or aggregate these units for subsequent analyses. Greater precision in the unit of observation allows collapsing or combining into larger units of analysis; but large, less precise units of observation do not allow later decomposition at the analysis stage. For example, Weisburd, Groff, and Yang (2012) have identified the city 'street block' (both sides of the street between two intersections) as a meaningful geographic unit for the measurement of crime-related variables (e.g. frequency of various crimes, resident reactions to crime). They have found that 'larger geographical units [of observation] can lead the researcher to miss variability within those larger units that is important to understanding the development of crime' (p. 23).

In the realm of personality measurement, Little (2015) has for decades developed and modified the notion of 'personal projects' as units of observation and analysis that are more precise than the individual person. Following the work of Gordon Allport and others, Little has proposed that personality is situational, and therefore the measurement of aspects of personality is best accomplished through measures applied to self-selected personal projects, as opposed to the common method of self-report personality scales such as the Big 5 Inventory. Personal projects are defined as 'extended sets of personally salient action in context' (p. 94), and may include such wide-ranging things as 'walk the dog', 'attempt to lose weight', and 'try to be less anxious'. Thus, the unit of sampling may be the individual person, the unit of observation may be the personal project, and units of analysis may be the personal project and, ultimately, the individual person.

On the other hand, a broader unit of observation or analysis may be desirable. In work that explores the role of nonverbal behaviours in children's early acquisition of language, Kelly (2001: 345) notes that ecological validity can be enhanced '[b]y expanding the linguistic unit of analysis to include information conveyed through a communicator's hands, face, or tone of voice—that along with speech are likely to actively co-determine the meaning of an utterance'.

U

ISSUES REGARDING UNIT SELECTION

The selection of units of sampling, observation, and analysis is clearly dependent on the particular assumptions made by the researcher. For example, the level or scale of the study (from microscopic to macroscopic) will help determine the range of units feasible. That the level or scale may be socially constructed (Delaney and Leitner 1997) introduces an element of relativism. Other assumptions stemming from particular theoretic approaches to the research will introduce additional demands for the identification of appropriate units.

Failure to identify and utilize the units most appropriate to the chosen research task can result in threats to the validity of the study. For example, educational research has identified the so-called 'unit of analysis problem', whereby data collected on individuals in intact groups, such as classrooms, are problematic in that the individual-level data are nested within groupings that may be related to variables that are critical to the investigation.

Units of analysis that differ between studies of a common phenomenon may cause difficulties and confusion. Early in the era of research on Internet content, December (1996) noted the problem of integrating results from different studies of computer-mediated communication (CMC) because different, non-comparable units had been studied. And Altman and Bland (1997: 1874) have cautioned that varying units of analysis may lead to problems with interpretation. They present the example of a medical research project that included two data collections on the same sample of people, with each study using a different unit of observation and analysis. One study examined the individual patient as the unit, and the other focused on the individual human leg as the unit; after a one-year period, the rather confusing conclusion was that 22 per cent of the patients had expired, but only 16 per cent of the legs had failed to survive.

Two types of faulty reasoning related to the unit of analysis have been identified (e.g. Babbie 2013). First, the *ecological fallacy* is when a conclusion is made about smaller units from data analyses of a larger unit made up of those smaller units. In the social sciences, it may occur when conclusions are made that individuals have the characteristics of groups to which they belong, even though the individuals may not possess such characteristics, and 'thinking that relationships observed for groups necessarily hold for individuals' (Freedman 2001: 4028). For example, using the US state as the unit of analysis, Freedman found a positive correlation between the fraction of residents who were foreign-born and the fraction of residents with high incomes. The fallacy would be to conclude that foreign-born residents have higher incomes than US-born. In fact, when data were collected and analysed with the individual person as the unit, the opposite was found—foreign-born individuals were less likely to have high incomes. The explanation offered is that immigrants tend to settle in richer states.

The second type of faulty reasoning is in some ways the logical opposite—attempting to make a conclusion about a larger unit by pooling characteristics from smaller components of that unit. Based on the philosophical notion of *reductionism*, a fallacy arises when attempting such inference to a broader unit from characteristics of smaller units. For example, attempting to predict winning teams in professional sports by focusing on characteristics of individual players might be partially successful, but would ignore important team-level variables such as coaching, game strategies, and the contributions of the particular fan base. 'In philosophy of science, the term reductionism is used in a general sense to indicate the view that complex explanations can or should be reduced to simpler ones—for example, that biological phenomena can be explained by their chemical constituents' (Williams 2004: 933). In the social sciences, reductionism may be found in the controversial viewpoint that our genes are partly or wholly responsible for our psychological characteristics and certain behaviours, and that this genetic makeup is an outcome of natural selection (see also the methodological debate over holism vs individualism, which generally parallels these two types of reasoning: List and Spiekermann 2013).

THE PROCESS OF UNITIZING

In most cases, the process of unitizing—identifying individual units, usually for the observation process—is straightforward. A study of elementary schoolchildren will likely have the individual child as the unit of sampling, observation, and analysis, for example. But when studying some stream of behaviour or communication, the researcher will have the task of unitizing the stream into discrete, useful units. For example, a study of the distracting impact of smartphones might involve the video recording of participants' behaviours with their phones, and then the identification of each use of the phone (unitizing) and the coding of each unit for such variables as length and type of use could be conducted. Note that the unit of sampling would be the individual person, the unit of observation would be each separate use of the smartphone, and the unit of analysis would most likely be the individual person. A stream of information may require unitizing prior to actual coding. For example, in identifying instances of cigarette smoking in motion pictures, each instance of a character smoking needs to be identified before measures such as age of smoker, sex/gender of smoker, context of smoking, etc., can be applied.

This unitizing process is typically spelled out. In a classic example from CONTENT ANALYSIS research on television violence, George Gerbner and colleagues (The Cultural Indicators Research Team 1977) used coding instructions specifying how each unit of observation (in this case each instance of violent behaviour) would be identified: 'A violent act is "a scene of some violence confined to the same agents. Even if the scene is interrupted by a flashback, etc., as long as it continues in 'real time' it is the same act. However, if new agent(s) enter the scene it becomes another act" ' (p. 283).

For empirical studies, there is an emerging recommendation that the intercoder reliability of the unitizing process be assessed, especially when such unitizing is emic (i.e., units are discovered during the research process) (Neuendorf 2017). That is, more than one coder or rater will follow the unitizing process, and their independent outcomes will be compared; high agreement is a desired indicator that the process is not unduly subjective.

U

CONCLUSION

The selection of a unit of analysis for a study should be driven by the research hypotheses or questions. For example, the hypothesis, 'Individuals who report greater use of Twitter will report higher political engagement', could be tested in a study in which all units—sampling, observation/data collection, and analysis—consist of the individual person responding to an online survey that measures Twitter use and political engagement. As has been noted, the three types of units may not always be the same. For example, the hypothesis, 'Incarcerated women with minor children at home will report greater anxiety than those without minor children', could be tested via a study in which the unit of sampling is the prison housing 'pod' (or cell block), and the unit of observation and the unit of analysis are each the individual incarcerated woman. Ultimately, the unit of *analysis* needs to correspond to a hypothesis or question that has driven the research and to the conclusions that are made based on the findings.

REFERENCES

Altman, Douglas G. and J. Martin Bland. 1997. 'Statistics Notes: Units of Analysis'. *BMJ* 314(7098): 1874.

Babbie, Earl. 2013. *The Practice of Social Research*, 13th edition. Belmont, CA, Wadsworth.

December, John. 1996. 'Units of Analysis for Internet Communication'. *Journal of Communication* 46(1): 14-38.

Delaney, David and Helga Leitner. 1997. 'The Political Construction of Scale'. *Political Geography* 16(2): 93-97.

Freedman, D. A. 2001. 'Ecological Inference', in *International Encyclopedia of the Social and Behavioral Sciences*, Volume 6, ed. Neil J. Smelser and Paul B. Baltes, 4027-4030. Oxford, Elsevier.

Kelly, Spencer D. 2001. 'Broadening the Units of Analysis in Communication: Speech and Nonverbal Behaviours in Pragmatic Comprehension'. *Journal of Child Language* 28(2): 325-349.

List, Christian and Kai Spiekermann. 2013. 'Methodological Individualism and Holism in Political Science: A Reconciliation'. *American Political Science Review* 107(4): 629-643.

Little, Brian R. 2015. 'The Integrative Challenge in Personality Science: Personal Projects as Units of Analysis'. *Journal of Research in Personality* 56: 93-101.

Lofland, John, David A. Snow, Leon Anderson, and Lyn H. Lofland. 2006. *Analyzing Social Settings: A Guide to Qualitative Observation and Analysis*, 4th edition. Belmont, CA, Wadsworth.

Neuendorf, Kimberly. 2017. *The Content Analysis Guidebook*, 2nd edition. Thousand Oaks, CA, SAGE Publications.

The Cultural Indicators Research Team. 1977. '"The Gerbner Violence Profile"—An Analysis of the CBS Report'. *Journal of Broadcasting* 21(3): 280-286.

Weisburd, David, Elizabeth R. Groff, and Sue-Ming Yang. 2012. *The Criminology of Place: Street Segments and Our Understanding of the Crime Problem*. New York, Oxford University Press.

Williams, Malcolm. 2004. 'Reductionism', in *The Sage Encyclopedia of Social Science Research Methods*, Volume 3, ed. Michael S. Lewis-Beck, Alan E. Bryman, and Tim Futing Liao, 933. Thousand Oaks, CA, SAGE Publications.

VARIABLES

A Matter of Kind and Degree

Jean-Frédéric Morin & Alessandra Bonci, Université Laval

Variables are measurable representations. As such, they are located at the interface between theoretical constructs and empirical observations. For example, the concept of 'social capital' is a theoretical construct (see **CONCEPT CONSTRUCTION**) which can be **OPERATIONALIZED** using the variable 'social club membership'. The variable 'social club membership' is easier to measure than the abstract notion of 'social capital'. It also has more conceptual meaning than the observation that person A is a member of a book society.

Deductive research identifies variables by operationalizing abstract concepts. Inductive research typically constructs variables from the observation of units (see **DEDUCTIVE, INDUCTIVE, AND RETRODUCTIVE REASONING**). However, irrespective of whether the research is deductive and theory-driven or inductive and empirically driven, variables occupy a central position in research methodology. They lie halfway between the theoretical and empirical realms.

One of the key features of variables is that they vary across **UNITS**. Any variable can have at least two distinct values (also called attributes). As Gary King, Robert Keohane, and Sidney Verba argue, 'a variable can represent anything whose values change over a set of units' (King, Keohane, and Verba 1994: 51). For example, the national economy is not a well-defined variable as it is unclear on which dimension it varies. Variables for a given economy include the main factor of production (with qualitative values, such as labour, capital, and land) and the annual growth rate (with numerical values, ranging from 0 to an infinite number).

This contribution is divided into three parts. The first part distinguishes dependent and independent variables, the second part introduces other types of variables, and the third part presents different types of values. The conclusion discusses the **EPISTEMOLOGICAL** assumptions underlying the notion of variables. The variables of 'social club membership' and 'economic growth' are used throughout for illustrative purposes.

DEPENDENT AND INDEPENDENT VARIABLES

In positivism, research aims to identify a causal relationship between two different types of variables (see POSITIVISM, POST-POSITIVISM, AND SOCIAL SCIENCE). The first type is the independent variable (IV), otherwise known as the explanatory variable, predictor variable, treatment variable, input variable, explanans, or X variable. The second type is the dependent variable (DV), also known as the explained variable, predicted variable, response variable, output variable, explanandum, or Y variable. The independent variable is a potential cause of the dependent variable. For example, we could argue that the more people are members of social clubs, the higher their life expectancy. In this case, 'social club membership' is the independent variable because it does not depend on life expectancy, and 'life expectancy' is the dependent variable because it depends on social club membership.

RESEARCH QUESTIONS typically focus on a dependent variable, rather than an independent variable. For this reason, research projects often examine only one dependent variable, although they may consider several different independent variables. In fact, entire research programmes, research communities and, by extension, LITERATURE REVIEWS, are often organized around a single dependent variable. For example, most researchers working on economic growth focus on the causes of economic growth, rather than its consequences. Therefore, the causal relationship between economic growth and economic inequality is more likely to be explored by researchers interested in understanding the causes of inequality, than by experts on economic growth.

HYPOTHESES connect independent variables to dependent variables. It is easier to test a causal relationship when the independent variable is genuinely independent (from the dependent variable)—i.e. when the variation of the dependent variable has no impact on the independent variable. For this reason, the independent variable should be logically prior to the dependent variable. In the HYPOTHESIS that social club membership increases life expectancy, the independent variable seems to be sufficiently independent from the dependent variable. Indeed, it is unlikely that longevity has a causal effect on social club membership at a given age.

It can be difficult to establish whether the independent variable is truly independent, even when it precedes the dependent variable on a temporal level. For example, we can assume that social club membership increases the likelihood of being a candidate in a future election. Social club membership may affect people's perception and encourage them to start a political career (Putnam 2001). However, someone with political ambitions may join different social clubs for strategic reasons, as a way of building useful connections. In this case, social club membership would be the dependent variable, rather than the independent variable. Both variables may actually reinforce each other in a positive feedback loop. This can create an ENDOGENEITY problem, making it difficult to measure the effect that one variable has on the other.

OTHER TYPES OF VARIABLES

The interference of other types of variables can further complicate the identification of a causal relation between a dependent and independent variable. In social sciences, most phenomena are multicausal (see MULTICAUSALITY AND EQUIFINALITY). For example, economic growth is not caused by a single variable, but by several variables, including demographic growth, technological progress, rule of law, and trade openness. Measuring the impact of technological development on economic growth may be complicated by these other variables. Indeed, other variables may cause a high degree of variation on the dependent variable and, thus, conceal the significant relation between technological progress and economic growth.

This interference can be reduced by including control variables in the analysis. Control variables—also called extraneous variables—are not the primary focus of research. The researcher controls them in order to isolate the relationship between a dependent and independent variable. When a researcher claims that technological development leads to economic growth 'other things being equal', the control variables are these 'other things' that remain constant. For a methodological perspective, a variable can be controlled in numerous ways, including carefully selecting participants in SURVEY RESEARCH and EXPERIMENTATION (see SAMPLING TECHNIQUES), adding variables to the model in REGRESSION ANALYSIS, and comparing most similar cases in a CASE STUDY (see CASE SELECTION). Irrespective of the method used, a researcher should try to control all the variables that affect the dependent variables. Failure to include control variables may result in an omitted variable BIAS, which can lead to the overestimation or underestimation of the relation between the dependent and independent variables.

However, a perfectly controlled enquiry is extremely difficult to achieve in social sciences for at least three reasons. First, it is difficult to distinguish between relevant and irrelevant explanatory variables and make sure that all relevant control variables are considered. (Brady and Collier 2004: 59). Second, the number of UNITS OF ANALYSIS limits the number of variables that a researcher can control. Third, a researcher may find it challenging to document certain variables. In some cases, she or he might substitute a given variable for a proxy variable, which is strongly correlated with the missing variable. For example, gross domestic product (GDP) is frequently used as a proxy for population well-being. However, when no satisfactory proxy is available, the researcher may have to leave this variable latent, as illustrated in Figure 15.

One type of variable, which is important to control, is the confounding variable. This variable influences both dependent and independent variables. For example, economic downturns might lead to a political turnover, as well as to an increase in loans from the International Monetary Fund (IMF). If a researcher fails to account for the confounding variable of an economic downturn, he or she might find a spurious correlation between IMF loans and political turnovers—i.e. a covariation between two variables that have no causal link. If confounding variables are ignored, the null HYPOTHESIS may be rejected incorrectly and a correlation may be mistaken for CAUSATION.

V

FIGURE 15   Different types of variables

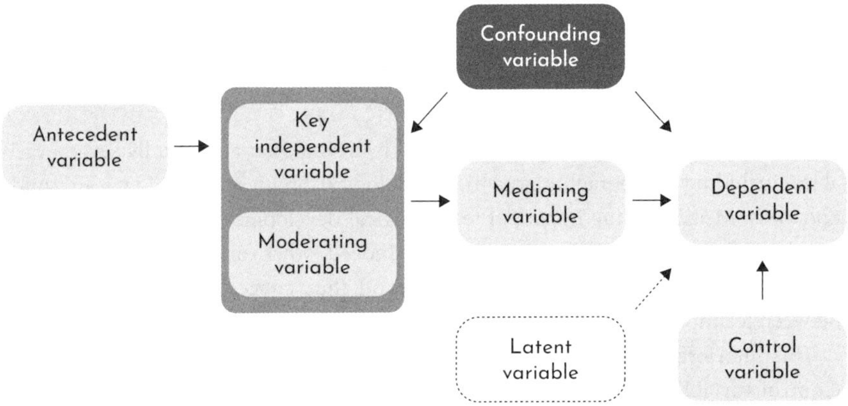

A moderating variable is another important type of variable. It can accentuate or diminish the relation between dependent and independent variables. For example, social club membership might increase annual income, but only for individuals who belong to the elite. On the contrary, an individual with a working-class background may not be able to use their social capital to generate additional income. In this case, social class is a moderating variable, which should be examined when studying the relation between social club membership and income.

Researchers can ignore other types of variables. For example, they may not consider antecedent variables (which precede the independent variables) and mediating variables, also known as intermediary variables (which transmit the effect of the independent variable to the dependent variable). Social club membership alone does not directly generate an increase in revenue. If we assume that there is a positive relation between the two variables, it is important to recognize that mediating variables also operate between the two. For example, the number of connections to potential clients is a mediating variable. However, it may be more difficult to determine the number of connections to potential clients than the number of social club memberships. A research design based on PROCESS TRACING can reveal the mediating variables. However, REGRESSION ANALYSIS often ignores variables, which are difficult to document or to substitute with a satisfactory proxy variable.

VALUES

When defining a variable, it is important to identify all of its possible values. The range of values should be exhaustive, in the sense that each observation should fit with at least one value, including 'unknown' and 'zero'.

There are different types of values. Categorical variables assign a nominal value to each observation, which is based on a given qualitative and non-hierarchical property. For example, the variable type of 'social clubs' can have the nominal values 'art clubs', 'sports clubs', and 'charity clubs'. Some analytical methods require that values be mutually exclusive, so that one observation corresponds to a single value only (see REGRESSION ANALYSIS). Since one individual can belong to several different types of clubs, a researcher can dichotomize a categorical variable into a set of binary variables, known as dummy variables. Membership of an art club, a sports club, and a charity club are then considered to be three distinct variables, instead of three values of the same variable. There are only two possible values for each these dummy variable: yes (1) or no (0).

Other categorical variables have ordinal values. Unlike nominal values, ordinal values can be ranked in a specific order. For example, the prestige of a social club can be ranked into three values: low, intermediary, and high status. Increasing the number of ordinal values for a given variable may improve its precision, but often at the expense of reliability. Classifying the prestige of a social club in a ten-point scale can be difficult. In addition, the encoded value may not be consistent if the measure is repeated.

Variables can also have numerical values. The number of social club memberships is associated with a finite quantity of cardinal numbers, including a true zero point, which indicates the absence of social club membership. The variable 'average number of social club memberships per 1,000 inhabitants' is a ratio value: it has an infinite number of continuous values.

The types of value condition the type of analysis. Importantly, it is impossible to measure the arithmetic mean of categorical variables because the distance between different points of the scale is not necessarily equivalent. For example, although we could assess the prestige of thousands of social clubs on a scale from 1 to 10, their mean prestige score cannot be measured. The mode (the most common value) is the only central tendency measure that can be applied to nominal variables. The median (the value of the middle-ranked observation) can also be used for ordinal variables. Ratio scale is the most malleable type of value because it allows for several types of central tendency measures, such as arithmetic mean (Stevens 1946).

CONCLUSION

The language of variable and values is used primarily in the positivist tradition (see POSITIVISM, POST-POSITIVISM, AND SOCIAL SCIENCE). Several researchers from this tradition argue that the rules guiding quantitative analysis should equally apply to qualitative research (King, Keohane and Verba 1994). For example, they claim that the proscription of selecting cases based on the dependent variable (see CASE SELECTION) also applies to qualitative analysis.

However, some qualitative researchers reject the quantitative template and the variable terminology (Brady and Collier 2004). They argue that focusing on variables restricts their analysis unnecessarily. It forces researchers to explain phenomena, rather than describe or understand them. The variable terminology also suggests that relations between variables are mechanical and linear, despite the fact that they are often intertwined in complex unstable ways. Most critics of variable terminology prefer a more in-depth holistic approach, especially when the number of cases is small and EPISTEMOLOGICAL ambitions are idiographic.

V

REFERENCES

Brady, Henry and David Collier. 2004. *Rethinking Social Inquiry: Diverse Tools, Shared Standards*. Lanham, MD, Rowman and Littlefield.

Hartmut, Esser. 1996. 'What is Wrong with "Variable Sociology"?' *European Sociological Review* 12(2): 159–166.

King, Gary, Robert Keohane, and Sidney Verba. 1994. *Designing Social Inquiry: Scientific Inference in Qualitative Research*. Princeton, NJ, Princeton University Press.

Putnam, Robert D. 2001. *Bowling Alone: The Collapse and Revival of American Community*. New York, Simon & Schuster.

Stevens, Stanley Smith. 1946. 'On the Theory of Scales of Measurement'. *Science* 103(2684): 677–680.

INDEX

Tables and figures are indicated by an italic *t* and *f* following the page number.